Taxation and Regulation of the Financial Sector

Taxation and Regulation of the Financial Sector

edited by Ruud de Mooij and Gaëtan Nicodème

CESifo Seminar Series

The MIT Press
Cambridge, Massachusetts
London, England

MIT Press books may be purchased at special quantity discounts for business or sales promotional use. For information, please email special_sales@mitpress.mit.edu.

This book was set in Palatino LT Std by Toppan Best-set Premedia Limited, Hong Kong. Printed and bound in the United States of America.

Library of Congress Cataloging-in-Publication Data

Taxation and regulation of the financial sector / edited by Ruud de Mooij and Gaëtan Nicodème.
    pages cm. – (CESifo seminar series)
  Includes bibliographical references and index.
  ISBN 978-0-262-02797-7 (hardcover : alk. paper)
  1. Banks and banking–Taxation. 2. Financial services industry–Taxation. 3. Financial institutions–Government policy. I. Mooij, Ruud A. de II. Nicodeme, Gaetan.
  HG1766.T39 2014
  336.2'783321–dc23
                                                  2014013209

10 9 8 7 6 5 4 3 2 1

Contents

Series Foreword

This book is part of the CESifo Seminar Series. The series aims to cover topical policy issues in economics from a largely European perspective. The books in this series are the products of the papers and intensive debates that took place during the seminars hosted by CESifo, an international research network of renowned economists organized jointly by the Center for Economic Studies at Ludwig-Maximilians-Universität, Munich, and the Ifo Institute for Economic Research. All publications in this series have been carefully selected and refereed by members of the CESifo research network.

1   Taxation and Regulation of the Financial Sector

Ruud de Mooij and Gaëtan Nicodème

1.1   Background

After one year of a rampant subprime crisis, the financial sector experienced a near-collapse of its entire system in September 2008 when, after the nationalization of Fannie Mae and Freddie Mac,[1] three major US financial actors ran into deep troubles within three days. Confronted with unsolvable liquidity problems, Merrill Lynch had to be sold to Bank of America, Lehman Brothers filed for bankruptcy, and the insurer and credit default swap provider American International Group avoided a similar fate only thanks to a large loan from the Federal Reserve. Faced with uncertainties about the liquidity and solvency of other financial companies, the interbank market came to a halt, thereby aggravating the situation for the whole economy. The subsequent credit crunch rapidly spread to the real economy, provoking the worst economic crisis since the Great Depression of the 1930s. The recession and the subsequent stimulus packages launched by governments bore on their public finances, aggravating deficits, increasing debt and washing away for many countries several decades of fiscal consolidation. In Europe the crisis revealed important macroeconomic imbalances that had built up over time, in particular among those member states of the European Union sharing the euro. The difficult situation of public finance of several euro area members led in turn to a sovereign debt crisis. The economic effects of the crisis now materialize on the labor markets and the situation on financial markets remains uncertain despite the recent relative calm. Notwithstanding a slow improvement in macroeconomic imbalances, the economic forecasts predict a slow growth for the years to come.

The financial crisis has revealed many problems in the transparency and functioning of the financial sector. The subprime crisis partly originated from a real estate housing bubble in the United States with too much lending to overindebted borrowers relying on overly priced collaterals. The creation of complex derivative products whose opacity in terms of the underlying assets and the development of tradable insurance products to cover their buyers led to an underestimation of risks. Also the role of rating agencies in assessing the inherent risks of companies was questioned. Thus the financial crisis highlighted problems of asymmetry of information and adverse selection problems as lenders had difficulties to distinguish between liquidity and solvency problems of the borrowers. Externalities between financial actors were aggravated by the procyclicality of capital and collaterals requirements due to mark-to-market evaluation that led to interdependent write-downs of cross-owned assets. Last, the sector was plagued by moral hazard problems in the misaligned remuneration incentives of managers to seek short-term profit and by the concentration of the sector leading to systemically important financial institutions that were too big to fail (when they did not prove too big to save).

The occurrence of events and the problems that arose have triggered intense debates in economic and policy circles as to the role of regulation and taxation of the financial sector. Economists and policy makers were challenged to understand the sequence of events and the complex interactions between financial markets and the real economy—often not captured by economic models. Many countries have started to rethink and to reform the taxation and regulation of the financial sector. In his Richard Musgrave Lecture 2010, Michael Keen notes nevertheless that "The underlying analytical issues, however, have received almost no attention in the public finance literature"(Keen 2011, p. 1). At the same time the literature on banking and finance has generally paid almost no attention to policy design, such as taxation and regulation issues. Recently a new field of research has emerged to bring together insights from public finance and banking, with the aim of better understanding what had happened and how policy could prevent a similar occurrence in the future. This volume contains a number of pioneering contributions in this new field on the critical issues for policy design.

1.2   Recent Developments in Taxation

The financial crisis has triggered new debates on regulation and taxation of the financial sector. In terms of taxation, the sector had not enjoyed specific advantages in the personal income or corporate income tax systems, besides a different treatment under thin capitalization rules or provisions for loans and/or doubtful debtors, which can be justified by the nature of the banking activities. Instead, a key difference in the tax treatment of the financial sector—and specifically for Europe—is its compulsory exemption, including insurances and investment funds, to value-added taxation under article 135(1) of the VAT Directive (PWC 2011). This exemption has been found to lower the VAT collection on the sector by about 0.15 percent of GDP and is seen as one of the rationales for imposing additional taxes on the sector (IMF 2010; EC 2011).

The deepness of the crisis, the perception that the financial sector bears responsibilities in its occurrence, the public support received by the sector and—in Europe—the finding that the sector may be undertaxed due to its exemption to VAT led to discussions on possible additional taxes. In response to the request of the G20 leaders to "prepare a report ... with regards to the range of options countries have adopted or are considering as to how the financial sector could make a fair and substantial contribution toward paying for any burden associated with government interventions to repair the banking system," the International Monetary Fund issued a report in September 2010 (IMF 2010).[2] After analyzing various options, it proposed two forms of contribution from the financial sector, serving distinct purposes: (1) a financial stability contribution (or bank levy) linked to a resolution mechanism and which would be levied at a flat rate on all financial institutions on a base reflecting their inherent riskiness and contribution to systemic risk, and (2) a financial activities tax (FAT) on the sum of profit and remuneration of individual institutions and paid to the general budget. About fifteen European countries—including France, Germany, and the United Kingdom and representing about 75 percent of the European banking sector (measured by assets)—and Korea have adopted bank taxes that resemble the bank levy as a way to support financial stability. Iceland, Israel, and Quebec have taxes of the FAT type, and France and Denmark have imperfect variants.

In the European Union, the European Commission (EC) has adopted in September 2011 a proposal for a Council directive on a common system of financial transaction tax (FTT) at rates of 0.1 percent for shares and bonds and 0.01 percent for derivatives. Given the absence of unanimity among the 27 member states, 11 of them wrote to the EC officially requesting enhanced cooperation on the FTT to be authorized, on the basis of the Commission's 2011 proposal. The EC set out such a proposal in February 2013, following the agreement of the European Finance Ministers in January.[3] Several member states have, however, already introduced FTTs on a unilateral basis.

In the United States, the Obama administration proposed in January 2010 a financial crisis responsibility fee in the form of an annual levy of 0.15 percent on noninsured liabilities of financial institutions with more than $50 billion in consolidated assets for a period of (minimum) ten years. This bank levy aimed at paying back the cost of the Troubled Asset Relief Program (TARP) which was implemented in October 2010 and consisted in the US Treasury buying illiquid and difficult-to-value assets of financial institutions and to discourage excessive risk-taking. Although factored in the US budget for 2013, the fee remains so far a proposal. Finally, US representative DeFazio (D-OR) and Senator Harkin (D-IA) have introduced a draft legislation to set up an FTT in the United States.

There is now also increased recognition of the distortions corporate tax systems impose on debt. In particular, interest paid is usually allowed as a deduction in calculating taxable profits, but the return to equity is not. This favorable tax treatment of debt at the corporate level is for most part not offset by taxes at personal level, and corporate taxes therefore create a "debt bias." Greater tax bias also raises bank leverage ratios, which in turn is associated with less financial stability and a greater chance of a financial crisis. Several countries have started to address this bias in two ways. First, many have introduced restrictions to the interest deductibility. These, however, do not fully address debt bias. Others have introduced allowances for corporate equity to neutralize the tax treatment of debt and equity, such as Belgium and Italy. The latter system has several attractive neutrality properties, not only with respect to the debt-equity choice but also to investment and depreciation rules.

1.3   Recent Developments in Regulation

When it comes to regulation, financial institutions on both sides of the Atlantic were operating under the Basel II rules issued in June 2004 by the Basel Committee on Banking Supervision and which replaced the 1988 Basel I rules. Those latter aimed at unifying capital standards of banks in the main developed economies (today 27 countries) based on the risk of their assets. They distinguished tier 1 capital (common stock and disclosed reserves) from tier 2 capital (revaluation reserves, undisclosed reserves, hybrid instruments and subordinated term debt) and imposed three capital requirements: (1) a minimum common equity to risk-weighted assets (RWA) of 2 percent, (2) a minimum tier 1 to RWA ratio of 4 percent, and (3) a minimum capital (tier 1 and tier 2) to RWA ratio of 8 percent. The Basel I rules became effective in the United States in 1992 and were part of the consolidated "One Single Banking" EU Directive of 2000. Basel II was an attempt to have a more risk-sensitive framework. One identified problem of Basel I was that financial innovation (in particular, securitization and credit derivatives) allowed for a repackaging of risk to artificially increase the capital ratios of financial institutions (Herring 2007). Basel II aimed at correcting this with three pillars: (1) to better distinguish across types of risks—credit risk, operational risk, and market risk—and to invest in risk measurement tools, (2) to improve supervisory review, and (3) to renew disclosure requirements about risk and risk assessment techniques. Basel II was implemented in the European Union in July 2006 by the entry into force of the recast Banking Directive (2006/48/EC) and the recast Capital Adequacy Directive (2006/49/EC), so that the Basel II framework was implemented on January 1, 2008. The United States adopted the regulation applying Basel II in late 2007, effective on April 1, 2008.

Much has been done in terms of regulatory changes since the crisis. The 2009 revisions of Basel II (also known as Basel II.5) and the 2010–2011 Basel III agreement guided most of those changes. Basel II.5 aims at a better identification of credit risk in the trading book of banks and requires improved disclosures of securitization (Getter 2012). These regulatory changes were implemented in the United States in June 2012 and effective from January 1, 2013. In immediate response to the crisis, the European Union had issued in November 2008 its so-called Capital Requirements Directive II (CRD II) package (2009/111/EC), which was adopted in September 2009. The package contained main amendments to the capital directive that aimed at improving the management of large exposures by restricting lending beyond a certain limit to any one party, enhancing the quality of banks' capital by tackling hybrid products, the liquidity risk management and the risk management for securitized products by requiring banks to retain some risk exposure on balance sheet when securitizing a loan. In addition it established a "colleges of supervisors" for cross-border supervision and crisis management. The implementation of Basel II.5 in the European Union is part of the CRD III package proposed in July 2009 and adopted in November 2010, which besides the Basel II.5 guidelines also contains higher capital requirements for re-securitizations and requirements for sound remuneration policies that do not encourage or reward excessive risk-taking.[4]

Basel III aims at strengthening even further capital requirements for financial institutions and introduces additional requirements for liquidity and leverage. Specifically, Basel III requests an increase in the common equity to RWA and tier 1 to RWA ratios to respectively 4.5 and 6 percent. On top of this, it introduces two top-up buffers in the form of a mandatory 2.5 percent capital conservation buffer and a countercyclical buffer up to 2.5 percent at the discretion of regulators. Additional buffers in the form of a systemic risk buffer and a Global-Systemically Important Financial Institutions (G-SIFI) surcharge will also be part of the regulatory framework under Basel III. Banks are further required to maintain a minimum 3 percent tier 1 capital to average total consolidated assets (leverage ratio), to cover over 30 days the total net cash outflows with high-quality liquid assets and stable funding (a weighted sum of equity, long-term wholesale funding and customer deposits) that exceeds (weighted) long-term assets. Those regulatory changes are to be gradually implemented between 2013 and 2018.

In the United States, planned regulatory changes are almost exhaustively included in the Dodd–Frank Wall Street Reform and Consumer Protection Act signed into law by President Obama on July 21, 2010. As made explicit in its full title, the Dodd–Frank Act is "an Act to promote the financial stability of the United States by improving accountability and transparency in the financial system, to end the 'too big to fail,' to protect the American taxpayer by ending bailouts, to protect consumers from abusive financial services practices, and for other purposes." In the European Union, comparable regulatory changes are foreseen or imposed through four initiatives: (1) the CRD IV package proposed by the EC in July 2011, (2) the Regulation (648/2012) on over-the-counter (OTC) derivatives, (3) central counterparties and trade repositories adopted in July 2012 and the subsequent technical standards, and (4) the proposed EU framework for bank recovery and resolution of June 2012 as well as the two proposals on respectively establishing a Single Supervisory Mechanism (SSM) run by the European Central Bank (17812/12) and new ECB powers for banking supervision as part of a banking union (17813/12), both adopted in October 2013.

The new capital, liquidity and leverage requirements (including the additional buffers) are included in the CRD IV package, which has been adopted in July 2013 and also adds a '"single rule book" to provide a single set of harmonized prudential rules (and definitions) throughout the European Union. In the United States, the Dodd–Frank Act provides the guidelines to be implemented by the regulators. Notably, it contains guidelines for a countercyclical capital requirement and section 171 (the Collins Amendment) establishes minimum leverage and risk-based capital requirements on a consolidated basis. In June 2012 the US federal banking agencies issued three proposed rules with the aim to apply them as of January 1, 2013, but the implementation has been delayed.

The financial crisis has highlighted the need for macroprudential supervision and the setup of a crisis management framework. The role of macroprudential supervision can be broadly defined as the identification of systemic risk, systemically important financial institutions and the links between the financial and macroeconomic sectors (Kern and Lantz 2012; IMF 2013). Prior to the crisis, those functions were either unfilled or part of the stability goals of national supervisors. The international interlinks between banks and the too-big-to-fail problem call for the setup of separate institutions for these tasks. In the European Union, following a recommendation by the *de Larosière* report,[5] a new European System of Financial Supervision was designed in 2010 and the macroprudential supervision is now in the hands of the new European Systemic Risk Board (ESRB).[6] In the United States, the Dodd–Frank Act has created the Financial Stability Oversight Council. Microprudential supervision remains organized at the level of market- or issue-specific bodies (Kern and Lantz 2012).

One important element of prudential supervision is the possibility of resolution and liquidation of financial institutions. In the United States this task is given to the Federal Deposit Insurance Corporation for banks. Previously the liquidation of non-bank financial institutions was done via the bankruptcy code or, for broker-dealers, via the Securities Investor Protection Act. However, the failure of several large complex institutions in 2008 showed that this was difficult to work in practice and the Dodd–Frank Act sets up the Orderly Liquidation Authority for the liquidation of non-bank financial institutions. It also foresees an orderly liquidation fund, separate from the deposit insurance fund, which will be capitalized by risk-based fees of large financial institutions (i.e., bank levy). In parallel, the deposit insurance guarantee experienced an increase in the amount of covered deposits from USD 100,000 to USD 250,000 per depositor and insured bank.[7] In the European Union, the EC adopted in July 2010 a legislative proposal (2009/14/EC) for a thorough revision of the Directive on Deposit Guarantee Schemes. In 2009, in a move to keep confidence of depositors, the minimum coverage was already increased from EUR 20,000 to EUR 100,000 per depositor and insured bank. With regard to resolution and liquidation, the EC issued a Communication in June 2010 calling for an EU network of bank resolution funds, funded ex ante from the banks. In June 2012, it issued a proposal for a Directive for a framework for the recovery and resolution of credit institutions and investment firms (COM (2012)0280) that sets a framework for resolution and enhances cooperation between national authorities and the European Banking Authority, the principle of which was eventually agreed by the Council of Finance Ministers (ECOFIN) in September 2013. The EC also published a Communication in September 2012 on a roadmap toward a Banking Union that would rest on four principles: "(i) a single EU deposit guarantee scheme covering all EU banks; (ii) a common resolution authority and a common resolution fund for the resolution of, at least, systemic and cross-border banks; (iii) a single EU supervisor with ultimate decision-making powers, in relation to systemic and cross border banks; and (iv) a uniform single rule book for the prudential supervision of all banks." Finally, the Commission proposed in July 2013 a Single Resolution Mechanism (SRM) for the Banking Union. This mechanism will complement the Single Supervisory Mechanism (SSM) and ensure that if a bank subject to the SSM faced serious difficulties, its resolution will be managed efficiently. On top of detailed rules for this mechanism, the proposal includes a Single Bank Resolution Fund to be underwritten by contributions from the banking sector, replacing the national resolution funds of the euro area member states and of member states participating in the Banking Union. This SRM proposal was subject to a provisional agreement between the European Parliament and the Council in March 2014 and adopted in April 2014. The resolution fund foreseen will be incrementally funded to reach EUR 55 billion after 8 years.

A famous element of the Dodd–Frank Act is the "Volcker Rule," effective April 1, 2014, which bans proprietary trading and limits the level of investment of banks in hedge or private equity fund to 3 percent of the bank's tier 1 capital. Other proposals have been made.

Liikanen (2012) proposes a mandatory separation of proprietary trading and other high-risk trading (market-making) activities from retail activities while Vickers[8] proposes to separate retail banking work from proprietary trading, market making and underwriting activities. Both Liikanen and Vickers do not propose to limit or ban those activities but rather to separate those via a compartmentalization or "ring-fencing." In January 2014 the EC proposed a regulation containing structural measures that would apply to the largest and most complex EU banks with significant trading activities. Those banks would be prohibited from engaging in proprietary trading. Moreover supervisors would have to review these banks' trading activities and would have the power and—if the pursuit of such activities compromised financial stability—the obligation to require the transfer of those activities to separate, ring-fenced subsidiaries unless the bank in question convinces them that it would not be justified.

Several measures also target credit rating agencies (CRAs). The Dodd–Frank Act enhances its regulation and creates an Office of Credit Ratings that will increase the governance of CRAs, prevent conflicts of interest and set rules to ensure their integrity. In the European Union, the CRD IV package aims at decreasing the reliance of financial institutions on CRAs, notably by developing internal credit opinions.

The use of complex and opaque derivatives such as collateral debt obligations and credit default swaps was a key element of the financial crisis. The G20 recommended that OTC derivatives should be cleared through central counterparties (CCP). In the EU legislation already deals with aspects of the problem. When fully implemented, transparency of financial firms' OTC derivatives will be increased by requiring detailed information on the contracts (for all derivatives) and the publication of aggregate positions by class of derivatives in CCPs. Central clearing is made obligatory for certain classes of derivatives and risk mitigation techniques will be applied to noncentrally cleared derivatives. The CRD III package contains enhanced rule for disclosure requirement of securitization exposures and higher capital requirements for re-securitization. In addition CRD IV includes an increase in own funds requirements for OTC derivatives and securities financing transactions. In the United States, the Dodd–Frank Act forces financial institutions to retain an economic interest in the credit risk of their asset-backed securities (usually a minimum of 5 percent) and increases reporting obligations. It also foresees bringing back OTC derivatives into CCPs.[9]

1.4   Contributions in This Volume

The economic literature on the financial sector was so far separated between contributions on regulation (e.g., see Dewatripont and Tirole 1994; Freixas and Rochet 1997) and contributions on taxation issues (e.g., see Bradford 1996; Honohan 2003). The financial crisis has urged economists to rethink fundamental questions on how governments should intervene in the financial sector, in particular at the interplay between public finance and banking. The studies that have emerged so far deal with key issues such as how to best design policies to cope with externalities in the financial system, or how to minimize tax distortions from a broader welfare perspective, thereby taking into account many specific elements of how financial markets operate. This volume contains contributions that fit into this new strand of literature. Thus it adds to two recent books on related issues. One is by Alworth and Arachi (2012). Alworth and Arachi are mainly concerned with the role that taxation played in the financial crisis and focuses on tax reform proposals developed in its aftermath. The interplay between taxation and regulation of the financial sector is acknowledged but not fully investigated. The other book is by Wymeersch, Hopt, and Ferrarini (2012), which explores regulation of the financial sector from a financial law perspective.

The contributions in this volume are divided into three groups. The first group, part I, contains contributions exploring the conceptual ground on the interplay between taxation and regulation of the financial sector. Chapters 2 and 3 provide an overview of the economic and political-economy issues regarding the taxation and regulation of the financial sector, respectively, authored by Michael Devereux and Reint Gropp. Three analytical chapters that address the choice between regulation and taxation to cope with externalities in the financial sector. Normative approaches to policy design are taken in chapter 4 by Brian Coulter, Colin Mayer, and John Vickers, who stress the advantages of capital regulation for loss absorption, and in chapter 5 by Jin Cao, who concludes that taxation in combination with liquidity and solvency requirements can improve allocative efficiency. Chapter 6 by Donato Masciandaro and Francesco Passarelli adopts a positive approach toward the notion of taxation versus regulation and explains why regulation has been a more popular way across the world to address externalities compared to taxation.

Part II looks more at the design of taxation of the financial sector. Chapter 7 by Ben Lockwood considers an optimal-tax problem on financial intermediation, and chapter 8 by Thiess Buettner and Katharina Erbe analyzes the welfare implications of the introduction of a financial activities tax in Germany. Julia Lendvai, Rafal Raciborski, and Lukas Vogel, in chapter 9, look into the impact of a financial transaction tax in Europe, using a dynamic stochastic general equilibrium model. Finally, chapter 10 by Guiseppina Cannas, Jessica Cariboni, Massimo Marchesi, Gaëtan Nicodème, Marco Petracco, and Stefano Zedda shows the implications of a financial activities tax and of bank levies on individual contributions to systemic risk, using a calibrated micro simulation model for banks in Europe. All these analyses help us better understand how tax and regulatory policy can contribute to mitigating preexisting distortions, avoiding another crisis or reduce its impact.

Part III contains studies on the actual behavior of financial institutions in response to taxation and regulation. Such empirical evidence is vital for policy design, as it determines the ultimate impact of prospective policies. The studies in this part exploit variations across countries and time or utilize quasi-experimental settings to identify how strong taxation affects outcomes. In chapter 11, Ruud de Mooij, Michael Keen, and Masanori Orihara assess the impact of the corporate tax bias toward debt on the probability of crisis via the higher debt ratio of banks. Chapters 12 and 13 by Gunther Capelle-Blancard and Olena Havrylchyk and by Timothy Goodspeed, respectively, explore who bears the incidence of the corporate tax on banks. They do so by estimating the impact on interest margins and wages. Chapter 14 by Ricardo Fenochietto, Carola Pessino, and Ernesto Crivelli estimates the impact of the bank transaction tax in Argentina on bank deposits. Finally, chapter 15 by Lawrence Kreicher, Robert McCauley, and Patrick McGuire assesses the impact of an expansion in the FDIC assessment base in the United States on managed liabilities.

1.5   The Interplay of Taxation and Regulation Policies for the Financial Sector

The recent financial crisis has highlighted the need for coordinating tax and regulatory policies for the financial sector to align their objectives and effects. The many changes described above are a testimony of the recognition by policy makers that serious changes had to be made. In practice, however, taxation and regulation do not necessarily share the same objectives and will influence each other's effects. In chapter 2, Michael Devereux offers a discussion of recently proposed new taxes on the financial sector, in particular the financial activities tax (FAT) and the financial services contribution (FSC or bank levy), in regards with their declared objectives. He starts by investigating the possible causes of the recent financial crisis, notably (1) the blurred distinction of liquidity and solvency problems, (2) the limited liability of share-holders and the presence of a too-big-to-fail subsidy, (3) the hubris of the sector that led to the inability to correctly assess the underlying risk of the financial instruments, (4) agency problems and remuneration structures that give shareholders and managers incentives to take excessive risks, (5) the tax distortions in the respective treatment of debt and equity financing, and (6) the exemption of the sector from VAT that could have contributed to the financial sector becoming larger than would otherwise have been the case. Devereux then moves to the declared rationales for new taxes, looking first to the desire that the sector contributes to the costs of the crisis, that it makes a fair and substantial contribution to public finances (given the VAT exemption) and that it could possibly finance a resolution fund, and discussing the merits, demerits and difficulties with the alternative taxes. Finally, he moves to their possible role in crisis prevention, conditional on existing regulations on capital requirements, and notes that although a minimum capital requirement does not necessarily reduce the measured risk to capital, it does reduce the nonmeasured risk relative to capital, decreasing externalities on creditors and taxpayers. A bank levy that is suffi-ciently high (under a threshold it would have no additional effect) would essentially have the same effect as an increase in the minimum capital ratio.

Focusing on bank taxes in chapter 3, Reint Gropp discusses the dif-ficulties policy makers will encounter when designing them. This is because the measurement of the contribution of individual institutions to systemic risk is a contentious issue, often based on past data and few observations. Hence such taxes have little chance to accomplish their Pigouvian objectives. Gropp argues that informational rents of banks create low competition on the market for loans for small busi-nesses and therefore the incidence of a bank tax is likely to fall on small businesses. He concludes that the focus should be on internalizing externalities rather than raising revenues or punishing banks for their past behavior, and that taxes are not necessarily the best instrument for this.

In chapter 4, Brian Coulter, Colin Mayer, and John Vickers compare the roles of taxation and regulation to internalize the negative externalities associated with systemic risk in the financial sector. When viewed as a classical externality problem, one might be tempted to argue that an optimal response to socially excessive risk taking by banks is to set a Pigovian tax. Such a tax would internalize the external costs in the behavior of banks and restore efficiency of private decisions. It would thereby not matter whether the revenue of these taxes flow into a special fund to bail out banks in case of failure, or into the general budget. Regulation in the form of a minimum capital requirement for banks, however, could achieve the same outcome as a tax. Indeed Coulter, Mayer, and Vickers show the conditions under which taxation and regulation are equivalent. These include an imperfect correlation of bank risks, an irrelevance of public versus private governance of banks, and no implicit guarantees for banks beyond what is collected from the bank levies. If these conditions are not met, Coulter, Mayer, and Vickers argue that regulation is typically superior compared to taxation. One reason is that taxation may increase debt ratios of banks as their cash flow shrinks, thus possibly exacerbating systemic risk. They therefore conclude that as the externality problem is of a different nature than the classical externalities related to pollution, capital requirements should play a central role in addressing systemic risk in the banking sector, rather than taxation.

In chapter 5, Jin Cao deals jointly with liquidity and solvency problems in the financial sector and how taxation and regulation address them. In the conventional banking literature, the two problems are clearly identifiable by market participants and can hence be addressed, respectively, by liquidity injections by the central bank against collaterals with certain future returns and by obligatory equity holding to eliminate bank losses. However, a remarkable feature of the crisis is the uncertainty between these two problems created by financial innovation that brings complexity and asymmetry of information on the real cause of the problem of financial institutions. In the bad states of the economy, when liquidity problems arise, banks freeze their lending activities because of the risk that the real issue is insolvency, which depresses the price of the collaterals. Traditional solutions no longer work and pure liquidity regulation is no longer sufficient to avoid costly bank runs. This liquidity gap is an extra cost for the bailout. Cao shows that between the two possible solutions—higher capital adequacy ratio and a bank tax on profit—the complementary bank tax that feeds a rescue fund offers a superior solution in terms of investors' expected return.

In chapter 6, Donato Masciandaro and Francesco Passarelli take systemic financial risk created by banks as a polluting activity that can be addressed by regulation and/or by taxation and study the political distortions that occur. Taxation lowers the difference between the private and the social costs of systemic risk. In the real world, however, regulation is often used while taxation is rarely adopted to cope with systemic risk. Masciandaro and Passarelli's positive political economy model explains this paradox. They show that when regulation is actually used, most of the sacrifices to decrease global systemic risk are borne by the larger polluters (i.e., the largest financial institutions) and the median voter will in this case opt for a level of regulation that is too strict. On the opposite, when taxation is chosen as the tool to address the risk, the smaller polluters will bear a disproportionally large share of the burden and the median voter will choose too lenient levels of taxation when portfolios are heterogeneous in their toxicity. Masciandaro and Passarelli show that under heterogeneity with a majority of low polluters, regulation is more likely to be chosen than taxation.

1.6   The Design of Taxes and Regulation for the Financial Sector

In chapter 7, Ben Lockwood assesses the taxation of savings intermediation services in a classical optimal-tax framework. His analysis offers fundamental insight into whether, conceptually, one should envisage taxes on financial intermediation. In fact, earlier authors have argued that intermediation between borrower and lender should remain untaxed, reminiscent to the Diamond–Mirrlees production-efficiency theorem. Lockwood sheds new light on the issue by exploring alternative second-best settings of the optimal-tax problem. He develops a dynamic general equilibrium model in which the government can employ taxes on consumption, income, profit and financial intermediation. Lockwood then solves for the optimal tax structure under a variety of assumptions. The first result is that financial services should be brought within the domain of the VAT, namely should be taxable yet as inputs fully credited. This result holds, irrespective of whether the government can utilize a 100 percent profit tax rate to tax away economic rent. The presence of this tax, however, does affect the optimal rate of tax. If a 100 percent profit tax is available, the optimal tax on financial intermediation is zero only in the steady state, while it can be positive away from that. If the 100 percent profit tax is not available, then the government will find it optimal to levy a positive tax on capital as an indirect way to tax rents. Interestingly, the optimal tax on financial intermediation is exactly equal to this tax on capital income. Hence the optimal tax might differ from the tax rate on other consumption.

In chapter 8, Thiess Buettner and Katharina Erbe explore the revenue and welfare effects two alternative ways to tax value added generated by the financial sector. The financial activities tax (FAT) is levied on a source basis on the sum of wages and profits of banks; the value-added tax (VAT) is levied on a residence basis on the interest margin of banks. Over the last decade several authors have explored the revenue and welfare losses caused by the exemption of margin-based financial services from the VAT. While conceptually appealing, however, eliminating the VAT exemption meets serious practical obstacles. Therefore some have started to consider alternative options that are practically feasible. One such alternative is the FAT, such as that proposed by IMF (2010). Using data for Germany, Buettner and Erbe find that a FAT rate of 4 percent would yield the same revenue as what they had estimated when the VAT exemption were removed, namely about 1.8 billion euro for Germany. If the revenue from the FAT would be used to cut other distortionary taxes as part of a revenue-neutral reform, the authors estimate that this would yield a welfare gain of about 1.5 billion euro.

In chapter 9, Julia Lendvai, Rafal Raciborski, and Lukas Vogel propose an original attempt to incorporate a financial transaction tax into a dynamic stochastic general equilibrium model with noise traders in order to study its effects on the volatility of financial and real variables and the long-term impact of such a tax on capital cost, investment and the economy. Their tax on equity transactions in a closed economy is shown to have a limited impact on volatility. Calibrated at a rate that would generate revenues of 0.1 percent of GDP, the equity transaction tax has a marked negative impact on the long-term level of economic activity with a decrease in long-term GDP by 0.2 percent. This result is driven by the increase in the expected before-tax equity premium and the subsequent fall in share prices. The increase in the cost of capital leads to a decrease in investment that is similar to the effects of an increase in the corporate income tax. Lendvai, Raciborski, and Vogel also offer an interesting comparison of the effects with those of an alternative tax on labor income and cuts in government spending. Finally, the discussion of their model, results, and possible extensions offer an interesting roadmap for future research in this nascent literature.

In chapter 10, Giuseppina Cannas, Jessica Cariboni, Massimo Marchesi, Gaëtan Nicodème, Marco Petracco, and Stefano Zedda use the SYMBOL model to estimate the individual contributions of European financial institutions to systemic risk. Their model is in the tradition of structural models approach to simulate losses affecting financial institutions, coupled with a direct financial contagion mechanism working through the interbank network. The authors propose four simulations under contagion and no contagion of losses to other financial institutions and under two levels of capital requirements. For each of these simulations, they compare their contributions to systemic risk with the amount they would pay under alternative versions of a financial activity tax or a bank levy. They show that avoiding contagion via, for example, a resolution fund and increasing capital requirements help diminishing systemic risk. When contagion is not avoided, all versions of the financial activity tax or bank levies perform about the same way. However, when contagion is avoided, the version with the broadest base (FAT1) is the best aligned to risk. Nevertheless, under the same conditions of contained contagion, bank levies outperform FATs in terms of their correlation with individual contributions of banks to systemic risk. Interestingly, increasing capital requirement reinforces the correlation. This result can be explained by the fact that the planned regulatory measures are able to contain the risks not linked to the size of the institutions such as leverage, leaving the remaining risk to be linked to size only. In conclusion, when contagion cannot be avoided, both FAT and bank levies perform equally but when an efficient resolution mechanism is put in place and allows avoiding contagion, bank levies—which are based on balance sheets (i.e., "stock") elements of financial statements—perform better than FAT—which are based on income statements (i.e., "flows") elements of financial statements—as counterpart to the systemic risk created by individual financial institutions. The more so, the broader is their base.

1.7   Evidence on the Efficacy of Taxation and Regulation

In chapter 11, Ruud de Mooij, Michael Keen, and Masanori Orihara empirically explore the link between the tax bias toward debt finance in banks and the likelihood of financial crises. Debt bias originates from the deductibility against corporate taxation of interest payments but not of the return to equity. This incentive applies, in principle, to all firms but is a particular concern in relation to financial institutions. By encouraging banks to finance themselves more by debt, this might have made them more vulnerable to shocks and so increased both the likelihood and intensity of financial crises. This potential link is now widely recognized, but analysis has not progressed beyond metaphor and speculation. De Mooij, Keen, and Orihara are the first to establish and quantify an empirical link between tax bias and the probability of financial crisis. The approach is to combine two elements in a causal chain. The first is that between the statutory corporate tax rate and banks' leverage. The second is that between the aggregate leverage of the financial sector and the probability of financial crisis. De Mooij, Keen, and Orihara find that tax bias is associated with significantly higher aggregate bank leverage and that this is associated with a greater chance of crisis. This gives a very different perspective on the nature and possible magnitude of the welfare costs associated with debt bias. Previous work, which has not reflected considerations of financial stability, has concluded that these are small. The implication of this chapter is that tax bias makes crises much more likely, and, conversely, that the welfare gains from policies to alleviate it can be substantial.

In chapter 12, Gunther Capelle-Blancard and Olena Havrylchyk empirically explore who bears the incidence of bank taxes. This is of great importance for the debate on bank levies as many of them are, at least in part, motivated by the desire to let banks pay a more substantial contribution to cover the cost of past and future bailouts. If banks would be able to shift the tax imposed on them toward their customers in the form of larger interest margins, this would challenge the aim of achieving such a more substantial contribution from the banking sector. Indeed earlier studies have found that taxes on banks are typically passed through to consumers. To explore the incidence question, Capelle-Blancard and Havrylchyk use a panel of European banks and estimate the systematic effect of the bank's corporate tax burden on their net interest margin. They control for possible endogeneity of the regressors and explore whether the impact is affected by the strength of market competition for which they use alternative measures. The results suggest that the pass-through of taxes into interest margins is so small that the incidence of taxes is largely borne by the banks themselves. This result is found for different degrees of competition, even in less competitive banking markets. The result contrasts that of previous studies, which, according to Capelle-Blancard and Havrylchyk, suffer from endogeneity or erroneous tax measurement.

In chapter 13, Timothy Goodspeed looks at the respective incidence of profit taxes, wage taxes, and regulations on financial institutions, focusing first on two important questions: first, whether there is an earnings premium in the sector, and, second, to which degree taxes and regulations influence wages in the sector. He uses a database of over half a million records of individual US citizens that combines data on their wages and characteristics and finds a wage premium of 45 percent in the banking sector relative to all industries. This wage premium could be explained by economic rents and by a higher average level of educational attainment in the sector. Next, Goodspeed exploits differences in bank tax rates and regulations across US states as well as differences between the standard corporate tax rate and the bank tax rate within states to look at their effects on wages. Clustering by states and controlling for individual characteristics of the workers and for regulatory and tax differences across states, he finds that while the corporate tax negatively affects wages in the manufacturing industry, the effect was either positive or null in the financial sector. Finally, the timing of deregulation bears importance in that wages in the sector are lower in those states that deregulated earlier, possibly indicating a higher elasticity of supply of banking services and/or more competition.

In chapter 14, Ricardo Fenochietto, Carola Pessino, and Ernesto Crivelli investigate the effects of the bank transactions tax introduced in Argentina in March 2001 as a mean to collect additional tax revenues during a period of economic crisis. Initially, the rate was 0.25 percent on debits and credits from bank accounts, then the tax was modified several times and remains today at a nominal tax rate of 1.2 percent, partly creditable to income taxes. Although the tax was successful at collecting revenue with tax collection slightly under 2 percent of GDP, the tax seems to have created nonnegligible disintermediation effects. Using various econometric techniques and controlling for concomitant regulatory changes between 1996 and 2010, Fenochietto, Pessino, and Crivelli find strong long-term negative effects of the tax on the level of deposits. Indeed their benchmark estimate tells us that a 0.1 percentage point net increase in the bank transactions tax leads to a 3 percent decrease in the long-term level of checking and saving deposits.

In chapter 15, Lawrence Kreicher, Robert McCauley, and Patrick McGuire utilize a change in the Federal Deposit Insurance Corporation

(FDIC) assessment base, which was part of the Dodd–Frank Act, to identify effects of bank taxes on bank behavior. The Act widened the assessment base for US chartered banks to include managed liabilities. Thus it can be interpreted as a corrective tax. The authors show that this additional tax was largely shifted to providers of wholesale funding. Moreover affected banks' balance sheets became markedly less dependent on managed liabilities and more dependent on deposits. The latter was precisely what might have been intended for a corrective tax. Kreicher, McCauley, and McGuire, however, identify an important side effect of the reform. US branches of foreign-chartered banks are not subject to the FDIC insurance and thus not affected by the reform. Compared to US-chartered banks (including subsidiaries of banks headquartered outside the United States) that are affected by the FDIC measure, Kreicher, McCauley, and McGuire find a significantly higher accumulation of claims on the Fed in the unaffected branches, suggesting a shift in dollar intermediation toward the latter. As these branches have less access to last-resort funding, this side effect could have reduced financial stability and offset the positive effect on US-chartered banks.

1.8   Conclusions

The fifteen chapters of this volume were prepared for the 2012 Venice Summer Institute on "Taxation of the Financial Sector," organized and sponsored by CESifo. The conference brought together experts in public finance and banking to discuss recent development and future directions in the taxation and regulation of the financial sector. All chapters have been subject to comments by the editors and discussants and a referee process. While some authors in this volume confirm earlier findings of the literature, others challenge them and introduce new considerations and avenues for future research. Some of those avenues are not covered in this volume, for example, liquidity regulation in complement to capital regulation, the effects of regulatory arbitrage and forbearance on the trade-offs between taxation and regulation, the optimal regulatory design of bankruptcy and resolution frameworks, the heterogeneity of financial institutions as well as the opacity of some segments of the sector and its impact on policy choices, the endogenous behavior of financial actors that can affect policy outcomes, or broad macroeconomic effects of taxation and regulation policies for the financial sector. Still the contributions in this volume innovate by exploring the interplays between taxation and regulation of financial institutions, highlighted by the development of the crisis, and by considering the design of taxes and regulation and assessing their efficacy in practice. We hope that this volume will be helpful for scholars and policy makers concerned with the regulatory and taxation aspects of the financial sector.

Notes

The authors thank Mathias Levin, Massimo Marchesi, Alienor Margerit, Ernesto Zangari, and four anonymous referees for their comments. The authors also thank Katja Gramann and Michael Stimmelmayr for the organization of the 2012 Venice Summer Institute, under the auspices and sponsoring of CESifo. The findings, interpretations, and conclusions expressed in this chapter are entirely those of the authors and should not be attributed to the European Commission, the International Monetary Fund, its members, or its board. All chapters in this volume are written in personal capacity of their authors and their conclusions should not be attributed to the European Commission or the IMF.

1. Two US government-sponsored enterprises active in the securitization of loans into mortgage-backed bonds. See Hemmelgarn and Nicodème (2012) and Hemmelgarn, Nicodème, and Zangari (2012) for an account of the developments leading to the crisis.

2. For background material on the IMF report, see Claessens, Keen, and Pazarbasioglu (2010).

3. For the developments of financial sector taxation in Europe, see http://ec.europa.eu/ taxation_customs/taxation/other_taxes/financial_sector/index_en.htm

4. This covers, inter alia, the annual and detailed publicity of remuneration policies, to align the pay incentives with the long-term objectives of the company, including at least 50 percent of variable remuneration in shares or equivalent instrument and at least 40 percent of this variable remuneration, which will be deferred over at least three to five years; a cap on cash bonuses of maximum 30 percent of total variable remuneration; and so forth. Moreover new regulations in the United States and European Union aim at increasing corporate governance in the financial sector and tackling the structure of remuneration. The CRD III package severely constrains the structure of remuneration in the sector, while the CRD IV heightens the rules and principles with regards to the composition, functioning and role of boards. The Dodd–Frank Act also foresees provisions with regard to remuneration such as submission of executive compensation to shareholder vote or the vote of shareholders on golden parachutes. As a result financial companies will have to better inform shareholders on their remuneration levels and structures.

5. Available at: http://www.esrb.europa.eu/shared/pdf/de_larosiere_report_en.pdf?ca 3072a98c6f009c4b1af0a0ae171ac6.

6. See EEAG (2012, p. 90). Following a recommendation of the ESRB, national macroprudential authorities have also been established in the EU member states and the ECB will also have macroprudential competences going forward in its capacity of single banking supervisor.

7. Further steps to increase consumer protection were foreseen in the Dodd–Frank Act, among which are a reform of the mortgage market to set standards, create bodies to protect borrowers and fight predatory practices; the setup of the Bureau of Consumer Financial Protection; stricter requirements for reporting for hedge funds; and so on.

8. See Independent Commission on Banking (2013).

9. See Felsenthal (2012) for a comparison of the EU and US provisions on OTC derivatives.

References

Alworth, Julian S., and Giampaolo Arachi, eds. 2012. *Taxation and the Financial Crisis*. New York: Oxford University Press.

Bradford, David F. 1996. Treatment of financial services under income and consumption taxes. In H. J. Aaron and W. G. Gale, eds., *Economic Effects of Fundamental Tax Reform*. Washington, DC: Brookings Institution Press, 437–64.

Claessens, Stijn, Michael Keen, and Ceyla Pazarbasioglu. 2010. Financial sector taxation: The IMF's report to the G-20 and background material. IMF, Washington, DC.

Dewatripont, Mathias, and Jean Tirole. 1994. *The Prudential Regulation of Banks* . Cambridge: MIT Press.

European Commission. 2011. Impact assessment accompanying the proposal for a Council Directive on a common system of financial transaction tax and amending Directive 2008/7/EC. SEC(2011)112. Brussels.

European Economic Advisory Group. 2012. *Banking Regulation: 11th EEAG Report on the European Economy*. Munich: CESifo.

Felsenthal, David. 2012. Regulation of OTC derivatives markets: EU vs. US initiatives. Available at: http://blogs.law.harvard.edu/corpgov/2012/09/23/regulation-of-otc -derivatives-markets-eu-vs-us-initiatives/.

Freixas, Xavier, and Jean-Charles Rochet. 1997. *Microeconomics of Banking*. Cambridge: MIT Press.

Getter, Darryl E. 2012. U.S. implementation of the Basel Capital Regulatory Framework. *Congressional Research Service Report for Congress*. Washington, DC: GPO.

Hemmelgarn, Thomas, and Gaëtan Nicodème. 2012. Can tax policy help to prevent financial crisis? In Julian S. Alworth and Giampaolo Arachi, eds., *Taxation and the Financial Crisis*. New York: Oxford University Press, 116–47.

Hemmelgarn, Thomas, Gaëtan Nicodème, and Ernesto Zangari. 2012. The role of housing tax provisions in the 2008 financial crisis. In Julian S. Alworth and Giampaolo Arachi, eds., *Taxation and the Financial Crisis*. New York: Oxford University Press, 61–87.

Herring, Richard. 2007. The rocky road to implementation of Basel II in the United States. *Atlantic Economic Journal* 35 (4): 411–29.

Honohan, Patrick. 2003. *Taxation of Financial Intermediation: Theory and Practice for Emerging Economies*. New York: Oxford University Press.

Independent Commission on Banking. 2013. The Vickers Report and the Parliamentary Commission on Banking Standards. London.

International Monetary Fund. 2010. A fair and substantial contribution by the financial Sector. Final report for the G-20. IMF, Washington, DC.

International Monetary Fund. 2013. Key aspects of macroprudential policy. Staff paper. IMF, Washington, DC.

Keen, Michael. 2011. Rethinking the taxation of the financial sector. *CESifo Economic Studies* 57: 1–24.

Kern, Steffen, and Sarah Lantz. 2012. Macro-prudential financial supervision in the US. The Financial Stability Oversight Council (FSOC). *Deutsche Bank Research*, April 12.

Liikanen, Erkki. 2012. High-level expert group on reforming the structure of the EU banking sector. Available at: http://ec.europa.eu/internal_market/bank/docs/high-level_expert_group/report_en.pdf.

PriceWaterhouseCoopers. 2011. Review of current practices for taxation of financial instruments, profits and remuneration of the financial sector. Taxation paper 31. European Commission.

Wymeersch, Eddy, Klaus J. Hopt, and Guido Ferrarini. 2012. *Financial Regulation and Supervision: A Post-crisis Analysis.* New York: Oxford University Press.

I   Interplay of Taxation and Regulation Policies for the Financial Sector

2 New Bank Taxes: Why and What Will Be the Effects?

Michael P. Devereux

2.1 Introduction

Since the beginning of the financial crisis numerous proposals have been made for new or increased taxes on banks and other financial companies. Many governments have individually taken action, and several official international bodies, including the IMF and the European Commission, have also been active in considering reform.[1] This chapter analyses some of the options for the taxation of banks and other financial companies that have been discussed, proposed and in some cases, enacted.

A starting point is to consider the objectives for new taxes on banks. The European Commission raised three possible objectives.

The first is that "taxes could indirectly and in addition to regulation contribute to the goal of improving the stability of the financial sector by dissuading it from carrying out certain risky activities."[2] Presumably the idea is to reduce the probability of default in individual banks or other financial companies, and in particular, in systemically important banks. This has been addressed partly through capital and liquidity requirements as part of the Basel III package (BCBS 2010), and partly in some countries by restrictions on the trading activities of some financial companies.[3]

A theme of this chapter is that to influence the behavior of banks through taxation is far from straightforward, and that any attempt to influence the behavior of banks must take account of financial sector regulations. It is possible that Pigouvian taxes may be more effective than regulations in correcting banks' behavior. But it seems implausible in practice that taxes could replace existing and planned new regulations. In this case the effects of taxes depend on such regulations. An important example, which I discuss in detail, is the effect of a levy based on bank liabilities. While appearing to create an incentive to use more equity capital, the tax may also interact with regulations to change a bank's asset structure, with uncertain effects on risk.

Second, the Commission argues that additional tax could be justified by the support given to the financial sector during the crisis, and the consequent negative impact on government debt. This appears to be a backward-looking, revenue-raising approach: the banks caused the crisis, and they should pay for the costs of recovery. As President Obama said, on proposing a new Financial Responsibility Fee: "My commitment is to recover every single dime the American people are owed."[4] The IMF was asked by the September 2009 G20 meeting "to prepare a report on how the financial sector could make a 'fair and substantial contribution' to meeting the costs associated with government interventions to repair it" (IMF 2010). This appears to express a similar sentiment. But it could also perhaps be interpreted in a wider sense, which links with the Commission's third objective.

That relates more specifically to ensuring that the financial sector makes a "fair and substantial contribution" to public finances. Distinguishing this from the second objective, the idea here appears to be to question whether in normal times, the financial sector pays its fair share of tax. What would be a fair share is, of course, difficult to judge. But more specifically, the Commission argues that since the financial sector is largely exempt from VAT, there may be a sense in which it is undertaxed relative to other sectors. As the Commission points out, the reason why the sector does not pay VAT is that it is administratively difficult to levy VAT on margin-based services. But two issues arise. The first is whether it is appropriate that intermediate goods and services produced by the financial sector to be subject to tax. The second is the more practical question of the extent to which exempting financial services actually reduces tax revenue, since VAT paid on inputs cannot be reclaimed. These issues are discussed below, together with some analysis of the form of tax that the IMF (2010) and Commission have in mind as a replacement for VAT: a financial activities tax (FAT).

A distinct fourth objective could also be considered. That also concerns revenue-raising, but more specifically in the context of raising funds to provide for a resolution mechanism in the event that a bank requires support in the future. The European Commission has been active in developing a new resolution mechanism within the European Union that has the aim of facilitating "the resolution of failing banks in ways which avoid contagion, allow the bank to be wound down in an orderly manner and in a timeframe which avoids the 'fire sale' of assets."[5] This chapter does not discuss the scope of such a resolution mechanism, but it does consider the issues that affect the design of a tax for such a purpose.

These differing objectives would give rise to rather different allocations of tax across different financial companies. The first objective seeks to impose higher tax on specific forms of activity within banks, related to improving the stability of the financial system. In principle, the appropriate tax could be based on leverage or the risk of a bank's assets. It might also be related to the extent of systemic interaction between each bank and the rest of the financial sector. A similar form of tax could be appropriate under the fourth objective; if the aim is to create funds for future resolutions, then one approach could be to charge a form of insurance premium. In this case, more fragile banks would pay a higher premium, and the base could be similar to that required under the first objective.

By contrast, the second objective would require a tax related to the costs imposed by an individual bank on the rest of society during the most recent financial crisis. For the third objective it would not necessarily be intended that the tax would influence behavior, or serve as an insurance premium. Instead, this tax would essentially raise additional revenue in an nondistorting way.

If these are the objectives, then there are also no shortage of taxes that have been proposed or enacted. Box 2.1 briefly summarizes the two options that this chapter discusses in detail, the financial securities contribution and the financial activities tax, drawing on IMF (2010).[6] The chapter proceeds by analyzing each of the objectives in turn.

Section 2.2 sets out a summary of the causes of the financial crisis. This is a necessary first step to analyzing and understanding the role of alternative policies designed to affect behavior in the financial sector: under the first, and possibly the fourth, objectives policy should be targeted toward the underlying causes of the crisis.

Section 2.3 discusses how taxes could be designed to meet the various objectives. The discussion begins with the revenue-raising objectives—the second, third and fourth objectives above. Section 2.4 raises the issue of whether a new tax could be introduced that could meet the first objective of enhancing the stability and efficiency of the financial system. This may also be relevant for the fourth objective. In this section I first consider the merits of inducing different behavior by banks through the tax system as opposed to regulation. I then consider

Box 2.1
Two forms of taxation

Financial Securities Contribution (FSC)

Various forms of a tax, or levy, on the liabilities of financial companies have been proposed. The version considered by the IMF (2010) would be paid by all financial institutions, and would initially be levied at a flat rate on a broad measure of the institution's liabilities or assets, excluding capital (tier 1 for banks), and with a credit in respect of insured liabilities, such as deposits.

Several countries have introduced a tax along these lines since the IMF report was published. These vary between countries in the precise definition of the tax base, the rate applied, and the use to which the revenue is intended to be put. For example, the United Kingdom introduced a bank levy in January 2011 on chargeable liabilities and equities less high quality liquid assets, for banks above a £20 billion threshold. The rate applied has risen several times since the tax was introduced; and there is a lower rate for long-term liabilities. Germany introduced a similar tax with effect from September 2011 on bank liabilities excluding deposits and capital, with a rate that rises with the size of the tax base, intended to reflect systemic risk. France introduced a tax in January 2011 based on the bank's minimum capital requirements, which depends on its risk-adjusted assets. Austria, Iceland, Latvia, Moldova, Portugal, Slovakia, and Sweden have all introduced similar taxes.

The motivation for these taxes differs. The IMF proposed that it be linked to a resolution mechanism, and that the levy would be intended to pay for any future government support for the sector. In some countries the fee is intended to accumulate in a resolution fund. In others it is intended to recover costs already incurred in the crisis. And it is generally also intended to enhance financial stability.[21]

Financial Activities Tax (FAT)

The IMF also considered various forms of a Financial Activities Tax. One possibility is to base the tax on profits and all remuneration of financial institutions. If all remuneration is included in the tax base, then the base would effectively be value added, and so could be seen as a substitute for VAT, which is not generally applied to financial activities. Some countries—for example, Denmark and Israel—operate a form of FAT for this purpose.[22] However, if the profit element is appropriately designed, and if the remuneration element is restricted to higher levels of remuneration, it could approximate a tax on economic rents earned in the financial sector, given that part of the rent is captured by high-earning executives. This form of taxation has not been embraced widely in response to the financial crisis, although Iceland introduced a tax on total remuneration plus profits above ISK 1 billion in 2012.

a specific form of tax on the liabilities of banks, and investigate what the effects of such a tax are likely to be in the context of the Basel system of capital requirements. Section 2.5 briefly concludes.

2.2 Underlying Causes of the Crisis

There were clearly many elements that contributed to the onset and scale of the financial crisis, and it is useful to detect them in order to identify policies that may help reduce the probability of future crises. I do so briefly and simply to set the scene, since many other contributions have already provided a comprehensive analysis of the causes of the crisis.[7]

Two key factors are liquidity and solvency. Banks use short-term debt to provide long term loans. The clear benefit to society is that funds can be pooled to allow investment in long-term illiquid assets, while meeting the expected demands for individuals' short term liquidity needs. However, as Diamond and Dybvig (1983) demonstrated, in such a situation any cost to the liquidation of long-term assets is likely to result in banks being inherently fragile, and susceptible to demands from short-term debtholders. The existence of deposit insurance reduces such fragility, as deposit holders are protected and hence less likely to create a bank run.

However, as King (2010) argues, although in 2007 "everyone thought that the crisis was one of liquidity ... it quickly became clear that it was in fact a crisis of solvency" (p. 8). The problem of insolvency was created by excessive leverage and risk, leading to low-equity to asset ratios.

The implication of such low-equity ratios is clear. Suppose that the equity to asset ratio is 4 percent. If the value of the assets held by the bank falls by more than 4 percent, then bank would be technically bankrupt: equity holders should be wiped out, and creditors should share what is left. So it is clear that both the risk of the bank's assets and the proportion of its assets that are financed by debt are crucial for solvency. This is why regulatory requirements for the capital ratio depend on risk-weighted assets: I discuss below whether existing and proposed regulations and taxes are sufficiently strict.

Several factors may have been involved in creating the situation in which banks held excessively risky assets, given their equity capital. Probably the key problem is the interaction of limited liability and the "too big to fail" subsidy. I discuss this in the next subsection, before considering other factors, including preferential taxation.

2.2.1   Limited Liability and the "Too-Big-to-Fail" Subsidy

Limited liability implies that the shareholders of a company gain from risk on the upside, but that their losses on the downside are limited. Hence limited liability can create the incentive both for high leverage and high risk, which improves the gamble available to shareholders. But this is true for the shareholders of any limited liability company. Other factors therefore need to be considered to see why banks succumbed to this risky behavior while companies in other sectors generally did not.

The key factor is the response of the debt-holders to greater risk on the asset side. Suppose that creditors are able to observe the strategy of the company, and to hold the company to a strategy after the lending has taken place. In general, these creditors will demand a rate of interest that compensates them for greater risk. In particular, as the risk to the bank assets increases, so does the downside risk to creditors, and so the interest rate charged will increase. Since shareholders have to pay the higher interest rate in the good state, there is no incentive for shareholders to take on extra risk.

A similar argument holds with respect to increasing leverage. As leverage increases, so does the risk to the creditors, and hence the rate of interest charged by the creditors. In principle, there is then no incentive for shareholders to increase leverage. This is simply the famous 1958 Modigliani–Miller theorem. A rise in the use of debt and a commensurate decline in the use of equity will increase the risk and required rate of return of both the debt and the remaining equity. But the overall cost of capital of the company will be unaffected.

So the existence of limited liability in itself does not necessarily induce more risky behavior, nor does it necessarily induce more leverage. But the conditions for this to hold are stringent. One is that there must not be a tax advantage to debt. A second is that the risk position of the bank must be observable to creditors, who must be able to adjust the interest rate in the light of the risk.

A third condition is that governments must not implicitly nor explicitly insure creditors. However, it is commonly suggested that that there was—and remains—implicit or explicit state support for the creditors of banks. Explicit insurance is commonly provided for deposit holders, and because of interconnectedness, allowing one large bank to default would have serious repercussions for other banks, in the tightly woven web of cross-bank lending and other holdings. This is commonly regarded as the "too-big-to-fail" phenomenon.

An implication of this is that creditors of "too-big-to-fail" banks evaluate their risk at a lower level than would otherwise be the case given the strategy pursued by banks of very low-equity ratios and high investment in risky assets. Ueda and Weder di Mauro (2010) estimated the benefits in terms of a funding cost advantage, with a range from 20 to 65 basis points.

2.2.2 Other Factors

Hubris

There are also alternative explanations. One possibility suggested by, among others, Mervyn King (2010) is that the proliferation of financial instruments, together with special investment vehicles and other factors, simply got out of hand, with buyers of financial instruments having little idea of their underlying risk. Ratings agencies—either through deliberate policy determined by their own incentive mechanisms, or simply because of miscalculation—were unable to offer appropriate advice. If creditors simply underestimated the risks that they were facing and hence charged rates of interest that were too low, this would create an incentive for banks to undertake excessive leverage and risky lending.

Agency Problems

A second alternative stems from the role of bankers rather than banks. Bank executives are in a similar position to shareholders in that they effectively have limited liability. Their downside risk is small, relative to the huge rewards that are available through very large bonuses. Large bonuses may be simply an indication of the interests of shareholders and executives being closely aligned. This does not, however, mean that we can rule out the possibility that executives were acting in their own interests rather than in the interests of the shareholders. This distinction could be important in devising strategies to reduce risk in the future.

There is evidence on both sides here. Sinn (2010) points out that senior bank executives are not unaccountable to investors and spend considerable time and effort to explain the strategies that the bank is employing. Nevertheless, executives earn truly gigantic bonuses. Is it really credible that these rewards represent optimal remuneration packages in the interests of shareholders? The degree of scarcity of managerial talent needed to motivate observed remuneration schemes seems too large to be empirically plausible.

An alternative is that there is a corporate governance and agency problem. Due to lack of information, or other agency problems, executives are able to capture a significant share of the profits earned. However, this is an explanation for a high generosity of remuneration, not for extremely high-powered incentives to take risks.

Costs of Equity Finance
Banks typically argue that equity finance is more expensive than debt finance, and that forcing banks to hold more equity would raise their costs, which in turn would raise the costs of their lending. It is generally accepted that by far the largest source of finance to the corporate sector in developed economies is internal finance in the shape of retained earnings. Of external finance, debt is used more heavily than new equity.[8]

There are many issues of agency and asymmetric information involved in external finance. Myers and Majluf (1984) suggested that asymmetry of information between management and external investors would lead to new equity being interpreted as a negative signal by outsiders, since managers will sell shares when they believe their shares to be overvalued. As a result managers will be reluctant to use new equity finance.

Hence, on the one hand, it is argued that a requirement to raise the capital ratio is more likely to be met in the short term by shrinking assets than by issuing new equity, even when the assets represent profitable investments. This is perhaps a caution against demanding too rapid a change in capital ratios. On the other hand, a regulation requiring additional equity presents a reason for issuing new equity which is clearly different from the Myers–Majluf argument. Adhering to new regulation by issuing new equity should reasonably not be viewed by the market as a negative signal.

Admati et al. (2010) and Hellwig (2010) consider various arguments that have been made to justify high leverage in banks. These arguments include: increased equity will increase funding costs since equity is more risky; increased equity requirements will lower the rate of return earned by banks; increased equity would be costly since debt is necessary for providing market discipline to managers; and increased equity would force banks to cut back on lending. They show that there is little evidence to support any of these propositions. Haldane (2010) demonstrates how leverage has significantly increased over the last few years: current levels are by no means the historic norm.

2.2.3   Tax Distortions
Deductibility of Interest for Corporation Tax
It is generally the case that corporation taxes are based on profits, including interest receipts but net of interest payments. For most companies this deductibility of interest payments creates an incentive to finance its activities through debt rather than equity—which typically does not receive any equivalent relief. The same is true for banks.

Such forms of corporation tax are not new: they have been in place for decades. If anything, there has been a move toward its restriction, in the context of combating tax avoidance schemes. Partly because these forms of taxation have been in place for some time, corporate taxation is not generally considered to have been a decisive factor in the lead-up to the crisis.[9] Another basis for this view is that the definition of what is "debt" and "interest" tends to be different for tax purposes and regulation.[10] Hence what is considered to be equity capital for regulatory purposes may receive favorable tax treatment. This implies that the favorable tax treatment of interest may not induce banks to reduce regulatory capital further.[11]

Exemption from VAT
The financial sector is generally exempt from VAT (historically because of the difficulties in identifying value added on margin-based instruments). This means that VAT is not charged on outputs, and VAT paid on inputs cannot be reclaimed. Broadly, evidence suggests that VAT revenue is lower than would be the case under full VAT treatment.[12] According to the IMF (2010), this could have contributed to the financial sector becoming larger than would otherwise have been the case.

Exemption is generally used because of the difficulties in identifying value added in margin-based instruments (e.g., borrowing and lending with a spread, but no explicit charge). But Lockwood (2010) suggests that in a general framework, the tax on savings intermediation should optimally be zero.[13] In this case there could be too much VAT charged on financial intermediation, since input VAT paid by banks cannot be claimed back by consumers, nor by business customers.

2.2.4   Why Did Regulation Fail?
Banks and other financial companies have been subject to capital requirement regulations especially in the Basel I and II agreements. It is nevertheless clear that these regulations failed to prevent the crisis. Detailed accounts of why these regulations were insufficient are

provided elsewhere (e.g., see Sinn 2010; Vives 2010a). However, in assessing the reform of these regulations, and the possible role of taxation as a replacement or complement to revised regulations, it is useful to identify briefly why they may have failed.

Under Basel I, assets are assigned to broad risk classes, and given weights for use in these ratios. For example, loans to firms were typically given a weight of 0.5, loans to normal banks a weight of 0.2, and sovereign loans a weight of zero. The Basel II accord introduced a much more flexible system of assigning weights to specific assets. Among other things, this permitted banks to hedge their lending with credit default swaps, and replace the risk weight of the debtor with that of the insurer. Overall, the result was that a tier 1 ratio could easily be four times larger than a simple equity asset ratio.

The problems of the system were exacerbated further by the accounting treatment of mark-to-market, which created procyclical effects. Consequently there is an incentive to reduce tier 1 capital in an upswing, making it more difficult to replace that capital in a downswing.

A further problem of the system was that significant parts of the financial system were not subject to the Basel regulations, in particular, hedge funds and special purpose vehicles. That latter were vehicles typically set up in tax havens, and whose assets did not appear on the balance sheet of the parent bank, even though in practice the parent was obliged to assume the risks of the special purpose vehicle.

This very brief review serves to highlight two factors: the level and the definition of the required capital ratio. Both factors require attention.

2.3 Taxation to Raise Revenue

At the start of this chapter I noted three variants of a rationale for raising additional tax revenue from banks and other financial companies:

• The financial sector was responsible for the recent financial and economic crisis and should be expected to make a significant contribution to meeting the costs of the crisis.
• The financial sector is exempt from paying VAT. This gives it a competitive advantage over other sectors which could be avoided or reduced by introducing an alternative tax.
• It is necessary to build a fund for a resolution mechanism to be used

in the future. The financial sector should pay a tax earmarked for such a fund.

I discuss each of these in turn.

Backward-looking Tax

The original US proposals for a "financial crisis responsibility fee" were explicitly related to paying for the bailout costs of the crisis through the TARP. Laeven and Valencia (2010) provide some evidence on the costs of bailouts to date. As might be expected, these costs vary considerably between crises and among countries. They also vary depending on what is included in the costs. For example, with respect to the financial crises in 2007 to 2009, Laeven and Valencia estimate that the direct fiscal costs were on average around 5 percent of GDP. In advanced economies, by the end of 2009, IMF (2010) suggests that the cost of direct support had amounted to only 2.8 percent of GDP. But Laeven and Valencia point out that the crises led to output losses of 25 percent of GDP, and a consequent increase in public debt of around 24 percent of GDP. The scale of the tax need to cover costs therefore depends critically on exactly what costs are to be covered.

In any case, the aim of reimbursing past costs deserves some comment. First, the effective incidence of taxes levied on banks now may not match the effective incidence of prior bailout payments. The implication of President Obama's remarks, cited above, is that individuals that benefited from the US bailouts should be those who repay that money in the form of higher taxes. But it is not enough to say, for example, that bank A received bailout funds, and therefore that bank A should face a tax payment now. First, this is because the benefits of the bailout were shared widely across the economy. Indeed the point of the bailout was not to protect individual banks but to protect the entire financial system, and beyond that, the entire economy. To that extent, virtually everyone in the economy must have benefited from bailouts.

Second, even from a narrower perspective, it cannot be the bank that ultimately bears the tax burden but individuals associated with the bank—its shareholders, employees, suppliers, and customers. Which of these individuals ultimately bears the tax burden depends on the type of tax levied, and the conditions in the various markets in which the bank operates. What is far from clear, however, is whether any tax levied post-crisis will be borne by the individuals who profited from the bailouts, or from the behavior of the bank before the bailout.

Even putting aside these considerations, what would be the appropriate form of a tax to reflect this backward-looking rationale? The principle would presumably be that cost should be borne by those who were most responsible for the crisis. This could perhaps be measured by use of bailout funds, though that would not reflect the systemic effect of the actions of any particular bank on the overall crisis. In any case, it is not clear that any of the tax bases summarized in the Introduction would constitute an appropriate base in this case.

A VAT Replacement

The second rationale is related to the instructions from the G20 to the IMF for considering taxes on banks: the IMF was charged to consider how the financial sector could make a "fair and substantial contribution" to public finances. The Commission's argument that the financial sector does not already do so is based primarily on the fact that it is exempt from VAT. I have already addressed whether this is a reasonable inference, based on the considerations from optimal tax theory. But leaving those considerations to one side, what would be an appropriate tax base to meet the objective of simply raising additional tax revenue from the financial sector?

One option would be to find ways of applying VAT to financial services.[14] But as an alternative to VAT, the IMF has proposed a financial activities tax (FAT), based on the sum of profit and remuneration for each bank. Since profit plus remuneration is equivalent to value added, this would be a natural candidate for an alternative form of tax, even though it would be administered in a very different way.

There are important technical details about how such an addition-based tax could be implemented that remain as yet unresolved, many of which are discussed, though not resolved, by Keen et al. (2010). One key issue is one of cascading: in the VAT system, VAT paid on inputs can be offset against VAT charged on outputs, which has the net effect that VAT ends up as a tax on sales to the final consumer. But there is no mechanism as yet for introducing something similar for the FAT, which would imply that there would be several levels of tax.[15] Keen et al. argue that this would be a reason for levying the FAT at a rate significantly below the VAT rate. In the design of a new tax, this does not appear very satisfactory. It would surely be better to attempt to design a tax with no underlying serious flaws than to introduce a new tax so likely to create such distortions that the rate needs to be kept low.

A second issue is international adjustment. VAT is levied on a destination basis: exports are tax free while imports are subject to taxes. Broadly, this implies that goods are taxed in the country in which they are consumed. This is a significant advantage for conventional VAT. The location of production is not distorted by tax, and if consumers are relatively immobile, then the location of consumption is also not be significantly affected.[16]

In principle, the FAT should follow this approach. Yet this would be more difficult to implement, since it implies, for example, that the sum of profit and remuneration must be reduced to the extent that sales take place abroad rather than at home. Yet even if this is done on an ad hoc basis, then there also needs to be a mechanism by which the value added relieved in the source country is taxed in the destination country. It is hard to see how this could be accomplished under an addition-method FAT. As a result it seems plausible only to levy the FAT as an origin-based tax. As such it will distort the location of production, in a similar way as conventional corporation taxes.

A third issue is which companies would be liable to the tax, and whether it is applied to all value added from financial transactions. A reasonable approach would need to ensure that income is not taxed both under a VAT and under a FAT. This could imply a complex allocation of income and expenditure to each category.

Although this version of the FAT is closest to a VAT, the IMF also considers other versions. Another possibility is that only remuneration to very high earners would be added to economic profit in the tax base. The definition of economic profit here is different from that normally used in corporation tax. In fact it is instead a tax on economic rent.

This could be implemented in several ways, but perhaps the most straightforward would be something comparable to existing corporation taxes, but which also gives relief for the opportunity cost of equity finance, known as an "allowance for corporate equity," or ACE (IFS 1991). This has been proposed in the literature as a replacement for existing tax systems, on the ground that it is neutral with respect to the financing decision (since debt and equity receive equivalent treatment) and the scale of investment (the effective marginal tax rate is zero, since it is a tax only on economic rent).

Such a tax could be implemented in addition to conventional, existing corporation taxes. The effect would be that the total marginal tax rate on economic rent would be equal to the sum of the rates of the two taxes, while a lower rate (from existing taxes) would be applied to other capital income. This would not remove the tax advantage to debt finance, but the new tax would not exacerbate that problem. An alternative would be to use such a tax to replace existing corporation taxes in the financial sector. However, in this case, to raise revenue in excess of what is already raised would require a very high rate, since it would be applied to a narrower tax base.

The narrow version of the FAT would be approximately the same as a corporation tax with an ACE allowance, plus a tax on workers with a very high remuneration. This high remuneration might also be considered a form of economic rent, to the extent that part of the economic rent of the company is captured by the management in the form of high remuneration.

The narrow version of the FAT, in principle, suffers to some extent from the same problems as the broader version. However, these problems are likely to be significantly smaller in the case of the narrower base. Very broadly, the narrower base would be a tax on economic rent, while the broader base would be a tax on economic rent plus all remuneration (i.e., value added). The crucial issue in determining the cascading effect here is whether the tax is passed onto the consumer through a higher price. We can assume that this happens in the case of VAT, and that the additional cost is offset against the VAT charged on the output. We can also assume that this happens in the case of the broad version of the FAT. But it is less clear that it would happen in the case of the narrower version, since a tax on economic rent is usually borne by the owner of the investment, rather than passed on in higher prices. If this is the case, then there would be no cascading effect.

Contrary to the view expressed by Keen et al. (2010), the international problem exists for an origin-based narrow FAT to the extent to which companies make discrete location choices, since even a tax on economic rent can affect discrete choices.[17] That is, if companies make location choices based on where they can earn the highest after-tax economic rent, then differences in the tax rate even on economic rent can affect those choices.

Of course, to raise the same revenue as the broader form of FAT, the rate charged would have to be higher. For relatively small tax revenues, the narrower tax base is attractive. However, if larger revenues are needed, then the implied tax rate required could be very high, and the broader tax base would be needed, even if it creates more distortions.

A still narrower version of the FAT is also considered by Keen et al. (2010). This would be a tax on very high returns, well above the normal return on equity. The idea here is that imposing such a tax on good outcomes would offset to some extent the relief that the government implicitly or explicitly offers in bad outcomes by bailing out creditors in the event of default. It would therefore induce banks to undertake less risky behavior. However, it is by no means clear that such a tax would have this effect. This depends on the extent to which a company or bank that in one period was liable to this tax was able to reduce its taxable income by undertaking more investment. Any allowance that the bank received for such additional investment would receive relief at the higher rate, and so an incentive for such additional investment could be created.

Financing a Resolution Fund

The third approach above was to consider a tax as raising revenue to fund future resolutions: a forward-looking use of the revenue. The IMF rightly argues that the financial sector should pay for fiscal support that it may receive in the future. In designing a tax to raise revenue for this purpose, there are two possible routes to consider, even leaving aside any deliberate attempt to modify behavior to reduce externalities.

The first route would be to attempt to design a tax that is as nondistorting as possible. This approach returns us to the discussion of the FAT above. The revenues from a FAT could be earmarked for a resolution fund, as well as making a general contribution to government finances. The use of the funds does not affect the issues discussed above.

The second route would be to attempt to design a tax or levy that is like an insurance premium. In this case the tax should fall more heavily on banks and financial companies that are more likely to require help from a resolution fund, and from those that are likely to require more substantial funds if that event occurs. That is, the tax should fall more heavily on companies that are larger, more fragile, and more systemically connected to the rest of the financial sector.

A tax designed on this basis would go well beyond the simple objective of raising revenue. By targeting companies that are more likely to require financial support, the tax would in turn be likely to have significant behavioral consequences. This may have beneficial consequences, but it raises the issue of the relationship of the relationship with existing regulations.

The behavioral consequences of the tax bring us to the first objective raised by the European Commission: to improve the stability of the financial sector. This is addressed in the next section, where I focus (in the second part) particularly on the Financial Securities Contribution (FSC). In particular, I analyze its likely effects, given existing Basel regulations.

2.4 Crisis Prevention

In the previous section I discussed the appropriate structure of taxes on the financial sector when the aim is to raise revenue in a relatively nondistorting way. I now turn to discuss the possibility that taxes may be used as a way of deliberately influencing the behavior of banks and other financial institutions, in particular to reduce the risk of a future financial crisis. A key issue in considering any form of tax designed for this purpose is its interaction with regulatory requirements.

Starting with a blank sheet of paper, it might be possible to design a tax that would make regulation unnecessary; and I discuss this possibility first. More realistically, though, any new tax would sit alongside existing and new regulations. It is therefore important to consider the impact of such a tax conditional on such regulations being in place.

2.4.1 Tax versus Regulation

Historically policies to deal with negative externalities arising in the financial system have taken the form of regulation, rather than taxes. However, since the crisis there has been a growing interest in introducing new taxes on banks.[18] In this section I address the basic principles involved in choosing between tax and regulation as a means of reducing externalities.

There is clearly a case for policy makers to intervene in a market that, left to itself, would generate harmful externalities on the rest of society. The classic example of such a market is one that creates pollution. But the need for regulation of banking shows that this is generally also thought to be true for banks as well. In considering intervention in such markets, policy makers have two possible tools, essentially affecting prices or quantities. We can translate this into taxes—affecting prices—or regulation—affecting quantities. Existing regulation of banks through capital requirements is a form of quantity control: banks are given a minimum capital requirement. A tax would follow a different route: by taxing or subsidizing alternative forms of finance, policy makers may induce banks to hold more capital.

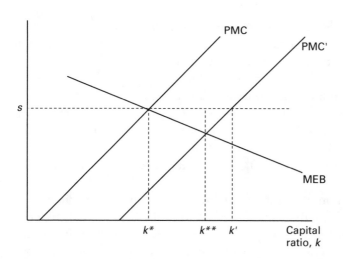

Figure 2.1
Illustration of subsidy versus regulation

The current mainstream view among economists about the relative merits of these two approaches stems from a contribution by Weitzman (1974). For example, Stern (2007) and Keen (2010) both apply Weitzman's model—to externalities from carbon emissions and from systemic risk in banking, respectively. It is therefore worth briefly commenting on this approach before questioning its application in banking.

The approach is illustrated in figure 2.1, taken from Keen (2010) though also used elsewhere. The upward-sloping lines show the marginal private costs (PMC) facing banks as the proportion of their funding in the form of equity capital, k, rises. The downward-sloping lines represent the marginal net external benefits (MEB) of increasing k. The initial social optimum is at k^*, where the initial PMC lines intersects with the MEB line.

Keen (2010) discusses the slopes of these lines in terms of a *failure externality* and a *bailout externality*. The failure externality reflects the probability of a bank falling into distress or failure, and the wider social costs if it does so. The greater is the sensitivity of this failure externality to the capital ratio, the steeper is the MEB line. The bailout externality reflects the benefits to banks due to a lower interest rate charged by creditors as a result of creditors expecting to be bailed out in the event of default. A larger bailout externality tends to flatten the MPC line, since it blunts the sensitivity of the cost of raising finance to the capital ratio.

With perfect information, a policy maker could ensure an outcome of k^* in two ways. He could subsidize the bank by paying a marginal subsidy of s to offset the banks private marginal costs (or impose a lump-sum tax, which is reduced at the margin by s). Or he could impose k^* as a minimum capital requirement.

However, now suppose that there is a change in the private marginal cost line to PMC'. Or PMC' might also be interpreted also as the "true" private marginal cost, known to the bank but not known to the policy maker (who believes that this cost is represented by the original line, PMC).

Under a minimum capital requirement of k^*, there is no change in the capital used by the bank. Even at PMC', the bank would prefer a capital ratio of less than k^*, since at this point private marginal costs are still positive. With a subsidy of s, however, the bank would instead choose capital ratio of k', where the combination of marginal cost and subsidy remains zero.

Neither of these outcomes is optimal, since the optimal position is at k^{**}. Conventional analysis compares the total welfare cost under each option. This depends on the relative slopes of the PMC and MEB lines. The position shown in the figure is that the distortion is lower with the subsidy, reflecting the fact that the PMC line is steeper than the MEB line. But this need not generally be true.

However, this analysis makes several implicit assumptions. Notably, as pointed out by Kaplow and Shavell (2002), the analysis assumes a linear subsidy schedule: that is, the marginal rate of subsidy is fixed.[19] Suppose instead that a nonlinear schedule were possible. We can expect the bank to take into account its private costs, but not the net social benefits, of a higher capital ratio. Then the optimal position could be achieved if the policy maker could set a marginal subsidy schedule (again possibly combined with a lump sum tax) equal to the MEB schedule. In effect, this would simply mean that the bank would fully incorporate the MEB schedule into its decision making.

In this case the policy maker would not need to know anything about private costs or benefits, but only to estimate the MEB schedule, reflecting the net marginal costs to society. Of course, to the extent to which the MEB schedule is measured with error, then the marginal subsidy would also contain error, and the outcome would not be efficient. But this would be the case with any intervention.

Note, though, that a lump-sum tax and marginal subsidy would not necessarily yield revenue equal to social costs. The subsidy would in principle be set to match the *marginal* social benefits and costs. The lump-sum element of the tax would then have to be determined so that the tax payment was equal to *average* social costs. To set the lump-sum tax correctly it would be necessary to know the schedules of both marginal costs and benefits.

Of course, both regulation and taxes face a problem in translating such macroeconomic analysis into a policy fit for individual banks. This is partly simply a scale problem. For example, if all banks faced the same nonlinear schedule, it would be necessary to divide the aggregate marginal external benefit between banks to derive the appropriate schedule for each bank. A similar problem exists for regulation. A more difficult problem is heterogeneity between banks: a bank which creates more systemic risk at the margin should in principle be taxed at a higher rate. But it is very difficult to implement a tax in which each bank faces a different tax rate. Dealing with differences between banks is perhaps less difficult for regulation: although even with regulation typically the same regulations apply to all banks within a jurisdiction.[20]

Finally, this theoretical analysis leaves to one side the fact that there is already a system of quantity regulation in place, supported by over 100 countries that have adopted the Basel system. By contrast, proposals for addressing banking externalities through taxes are new. Taking it as given that some form of regulation will continue along the lines of Basel III, as discussed below, a relevant question is whether there is a role of taxation as a correction mechanism *as well as* regulation. I discuss this further below, in the context of specific proposals.

2.4.2 Taxes in the Presence of Regulation

As described above, there have been considerable recent developments in regulations for capital adequacy through the Basel III proposals. At the same time, some of the taxes proposed in response to the financial crisis have also been designed to target the amount of capital held by banks. In this section I consider the likely effects of a tax on financial liabilities, along the lines of the financial services contribution proposed by the IMF, on the financing and lending activities of banks.

If taxation is to be used as an element of crisis prevention, then its precise design is important. To illustrate this, consider the financial securities contribution, as proposed by the IMF, a form of which has been enacted in Sweden and the United Kingdom. The IMF proposes a levy based on "a broad balance sheet base on the liabilities side, excluding capital … and possibly including off-balance sheet items, and with a credit for payments in respect of insured liabilities" (IMF 2010, p. 13).

The IMF proposes this base after considering a levy based on risk-weighted assets. It rejects the former on the grounds that such a levy could duplicate the effects of Basel regulations also targeted at risk of the asset side. This illustrates the problem of attempting to use two instruments. If the tax and the regulation are perfectly in alignment, then it seems likely that the tax would have no effect on behavior beyond what is required by regulation. But if they are not in perfect alignment, then the form of their interaction could be important.

To prepare for this discussion, let us first study the interaction between a regulation based on the tier 1 capital ratio and one which is in addition based on the capital asset ratio as in the Basel III system. Consider figure 2.2. The vertical axis shows a bank's sum of risk-weighted assets relative to total assets, R, and the horizontal axis the capital ratio, that is, the ratio of tier 1 capital to total assets (the inverse leverage ratio), k. The upward-sloping line marked Basel II reflects the trade-off permitted in the Basel II regulations between capital and risk-weighted assets. The inverse of the slope of this line is the tier 1 ratio,

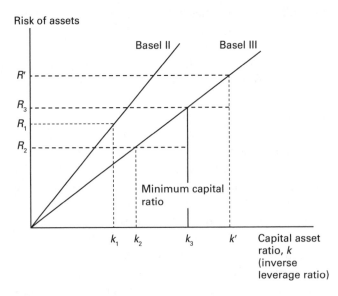

Figure 2.2
Effects of the FSC, given regulation

that is, the ratio of capital to risk-weighted assets. That is, a bank that increased the risk of its assets as measured in the Basel system would be required also to hold more capital. The line therefore represents a locus of points that are just acceptable to the regulator. We can assume, based on experience and the theoretical explanations for the incentive to gamble under limited liability, that banks would prefer a combination of lower capital and more risk: that is, they would prefer to be located toward the top left part of the diagram. However, given regulation, the bank is forced to choose a position either on the Basel II locus, or to the right of the locus.

Let us assume that the bank chooses the point (R_1, k_1). In practice, banks may choose to hold a buffer of additional capital to ensure that they do not easily cross the threshold due to small movements in asset values; however, we can neglect that possibility here.

The increase of the minimum tier 1 ratio according to Basel III pivots the locus to the right in a clockwise fashion, keeping the origin fixed, because more tier 1 capital is needed relative to total assets for any given share of risk-weighted assets in total assets. In the absence of further effects, let us suppose that given the new regulations, the bank moves to the point (R_2, k_2).

However, as noted above, the Basel III regulations also introduce a minimum constraint to the capital asset ratio. In the figure this constraint is assumed to be binding, at k_3 with $k_3 > k_2$. In effect, at the minimum capital asset ratio the maximum share of risk-weighted assets is R_3; above this level, the tier 1 ratio, as given by the Basel III line, becomes binding. As shown in the figure, as long as the bank continues to prefer to hold less capital and engage in more risky lending, then the effect of the leverage ratio will be likely to shift the bank from (R_2, k_2) not to (R_2, k_3) but to (R_3, k_3). This is still on the locus of acceptable points under the Basel III line. But it does not represent a safer combination of capital and risk as measured by the tier 1 ratio: rather, since it lies on the Basel III line, these two points represent an equally acceptable trade-off between risk-weighted assets and capital.

This may seem to imply that the minimum capital ratio does not serve any useful purpose. However, one rationale for the minimum capital asset ratio in Basel III is that there are important deficiencies in the Basel system of risk measurement. As noted above, loans to companies normally have a weight of 0.5, loans to banks have a weight of 0.2, and loans to governments are not counted at all. Given the crisis over sovereign debt, this set of weights is clearly unreasonable.

The leverage constraint in terms of the minimum capital asset ratio, k_3 in figure 2.2, has the effect of constraining the assets not included in the concept of risk-weighted assets. If the availability of equity capital is fixed, then a bank has to scale down its balance sheet to meet the higher required capital asset ratio. Doing so by reducing assets not included in the sum of risk-weighted assets, such as sovereign debt, would also raise the average risk of the remaining assets, and help the bank move toward (R_3, k_3). But it would reduce the overall risk, as the volume of assets such as government bonds, which are risky but not included in the sum of risk-weighted assets, is smaller at k_3 than at k_2. Thus, even though the minimum capital requirement does not change the measured risk relative to capital, it does reduce the non-measured risk relative to capital, which could mean lower externalities being imposed on the bank's creditors and on taxpayers.

This is demonstrated more formally in the appendix. There I first consider the case in which the bank holds only two types of assets—say loans to government, which have a risk weight of zero, and loans to firms, which have a positive risk weight. I measure the "default risk" of the bank as the probability that the value of its assets becomes lower than the value of its outstanding debt, in which case the bank would be technically bankrupt. This depends on the variance of the value of total assets, which in turn depends on the variance of the value of each asset and the covariance between them.

Suppose now that a minimum capital requirement is introduced, and that the bank aims to meet this requirement while maintaining its tier 1 ratio. It could do this by reducing its overall assets by selling sovereign debt, and using the proceeds to reduce debt, holding equity capital constant. As long as sovereign debt had a lower variance than lending to firms, then the average measured risk of the assets would increase, or equivalently, risk-weighted assets would increase relative to total assets. This would be consistent with a move from (R_2, k_2) to (R_3, k_3). The appendix demonstrates that the probability of bankruptcy would fall in this case, as long as there was a positive covariance between the returns of the two assets.

However, if we consider a more complex asset structure, then this result may not hold. In particular, the appendix also considers the case where there are three types of assets. The required move from (R_2, k_2) to (R_3, k_3) could again be achieved by selling assets and using the proceeds to reduce outstanding debt. But now there are additional options in choosing which asset to sell. As the appendix demonstrates, the probability of bankruptcy may rise or fall, depending on how the bank chooses to restructure its asset holdings.

Consider now a tax on a bank's balance sheet, net of its capital and augmented by off-shore operations. Suppose that we begin at point (R_3, k_3) and introduce the FSC. One possibility is that the new levy would have no effect: the bank would simply accept the additional cost, but that cost would not be sufficient to induce it to increase k.

The other possibility is that the levy is sufficiently high that the bank chooses to hold more capital than is required by the Basel regulations. As shown in the figure, this could move the bank to (R_3, k'). However, once again, if the bank prefers more risk in the sense of risk-weighted assets, then it can move back onto the tier 1 Basel III locus by investing in riskier assets, to reach (R', k').

This change therefore has exactly the same effects as that induced by the introduction of the minimum capital ratio. The share of risk-weighted assets in the bank's balance sheet will increase at the expense of other assets, though there is no change in the measured risk relative to capital. It is likely that the probability of default will be reduced, but this is not guaranteed.

The effects of the minimum capital requirement and the FSC have to be considered alongside existing regulations. It is possible to consider each of these as a reasonable attempt to overcome the deficiencies of the Basel risk-weighting system. But of course a more direct way to deal with this is to address these deficiencies directly.

2.5 Conclusions

This chapter discusses the case for introducing new taxes in the financial sector, based on two broad objectives. The first is straightforward: to raise revenue. But this could have three elements. It could be backward-looking—to reimburse governments and society for the cost of the last financial crisis; it could address the longer term problem that the financial sector may be undertaxed; and it could be forward-looking—to build a resolution fund ready for the next crisis. A second objective of a new tax in the financial sector could be to help make a future crisis less likely, by inducing banks and other financial companies to reduce leverage or to invest in less-risky assets.

This chapter analyses where these objectives lead in terms of introducing new taxes or modifying existing taxes. It focuses on two possible forms of taxation: the financial activities tax (FAT) and the financial services contribution (FSC). A tax that aims to raise revenue should normally do so in as neutral way as possible, without distorting choices of economic agents. The FAT comes closest to this objective. But the aim of inducing a more stable financial system necessarily must focus on changing the behavior of banks and other financial companies. The FSC is more attuned to this objective, but its effects are dependent on the form of financial regulation.

The financial activities tax (FAT), as recently proposed by the IMF, has two possible forms. In principle, this chapter favors a narrow base, including economic rents and remuneration of very highly paid employees (which are also akin to economic rents). This would, in principle, be nondistorting, except with respect to discrete investment decisions, but may require a relatively high rate, depending on the revenue requirements. This tax could be introduced alongside a conventional corporation tax on profits net of interest payments. If so, it would not correct the existing distortion in favor of debt finance, but it would also not worsen it.

At the other extreme, another version of the FAT would include all remuneration in the tax base. This would be similar to a tax on value added, and could be seen as a substitute for the lack of VAT in the financial sector. It too could be introduced alongside existing taxes. In this case there are a number of technical details about how the tax could be implemented that remain to be resolved. In the absence of their resolution, the tax could prove to have significant distorting effects.

One option for the second objective is the FSC, again proposed by the IMF. Basically this is a tax on the bank's balance sheet that exempts the equity capital and insured assets but includes off-balance sheet operations. Several countries have introduced such a tax. While this tax is partly designed to raise revenue, it is also clearly intended to reduce leverage.

In principle, such a tax could be a meaningful addition to a tier 1 capital regulation. It could induce a higher ratio of capital relative to all assets including government bonds, which are currently not included in the sum of risk-weighted assets in the Basel system. However, the FSC, like a minimum capital requirement such as included in Basel III, is independent of the risk of the bank's assets. It is likely that a bank would respond to a higher capital ratio—induced either by the FSC or by the minimum capital ratio—by increasing the risk of its assets, commensurate with tier 1 capital regulation. The benefit of higher capital would therefore be undermined, at least to some extent, by greater asset risk. After reacting to the tax, the measured risk relative to the capital may be as large as before.

In sum, additional tax revenue would be useful for many governments at present, and also in establishing a crisis resolution fund. Options for taxation include taxes, such as the FAT, that are intended to raise revenue in a relatively non-distorting way. They also include taxes, such as the FSC, which are intended to supplement regulation. The main case in favor of the latter stems from an attempt to overcome the deficiencies of existing regulation: its value may therefore depend on whether it is instead possible to reform the regulation directly.

Appendix: Effects of a Minimum Capital Ratio

Two Asset Case

The bank holds two assets, G of government bonds and F of loans to firms. Setting the size of total assets T to 1 implies that $G+F=1$. Only loans to firms are included in the measures of risk-weighted assets weights, with a weight of w_F. Hence total risk-weighted assets are $R = w_F F$. These assets are financed by equity of E and debt of D, so that $E+D=1$. The capital ratio is

$$k = \frac{E}{T} = E,$$

and the tier 1 ratio is

$$l = \frac{E}{R}.$$

The variance of one unit of government bonds is σ_G^2, and of one unit of loans to firms is σ_F^2. The covariance of one unit of each is σ_{GF}. The variance of the bank's total assets is therefore $V = G^2\sigma_G^2 + F^2\sigma_F^2 + 2GF\sigma_{GF}$.

Now consider a requirement to increase the capital ratio to a minimum level of k^*, leaving the tier 1 ratio unchanged. Assume that the bank holds E constant, but reduces D and hence the total value of the liabilities so that $T<1$. Since E has not changed, then holding the tier 1 ratio constant implies no change in risk-weighted assets, R. Hence the bank must sell government bonds and use proceeds to repay debt, with $\Delta G = \Delta D$, to reach new lower levels, G^* and D^*.

The new capital ratio is

$$k^* = \frac{E}{G^* + F} > k,$$

and the new variance of the assets is $V^* = G^{*2}\sigma_G^2 + F^2\sigma_F^2 + 2G^*F\sigma_{GF}$. If the covariance between G and F is positive, then the variance must fall, $V^* < V$. Since E is unchanged, the probability of default falls.

Three Asset Case

Now consider the case with a third asset, loans to other banks, B, so that $G+F+B=E+D=1$. Suppose that these loans to banks are also included in risk-weighted assets, with a weight of w_B, and that $w_F > w_B$. The sum of risk weighted assets is now $R = w_F F + w_B B$.

The variance of one unit of loans to banks is σ_B^2 and the covariances with other assets are σ_{GB} and σ_{FB}. The variance of balance sheet is therefore now $G^2\sigma_G^2 + F^2\sigma_F^2 + B^2\sigma_B^2 + 2GF\sigma_{GF} + 2GB\sigma_{GB} + 2FB\sigma_{FB}$.

Let us consider again a requirement to increase capital ratio to minimum level of k^*, leaving tier 1 ratio, l, unchanged. Assume again that E does not change, but that the value of assets and liabilities falls to $T<1$.

Again, holding E and l constant implies no change in R. However, the bank now has more options to reach k^*, while leaving l unchanged. Consider one option: to reduce B and raise F, with no change in G. In this case, to keep R unchanged, we require that $w_F dF + w_B dB = 0$. The change in total asset is

$$\Delta T = dB + dF = \frac{w_B - w_F}{w_B}dF < 0.$$

This raises k, as required.

The change in variance of balance sheet:

$$= \left\{2F\sigma_F^2 + 2G\sigma_{GF} + 2B\sigma_{FB}\right\}dF + \left\{2B\sigma_B^2 + 2G\sigma_{GB} + 2F\sigma_{FB}\right\}dB$$

$$= \left\{2\left[F\sigma_F^2 + G\sigma_{GF} + B\sigma_{FB}\right] - \frac{w_F}{w_B}\left[B\sigma_B^2 + G\sigma_{GB} + F\sigma_{FB}\right]\right\}dF.$$

This could be positive or negative, implying that the probability of default could rise or fall.

Notes

This chapter was originally prepared for the ETPF/CEPS Conference on Taxes and Behavior, in Brussels in April, 2011. It draws on earlier work by the author as part of the European Economic Advisory Group (EEAG). It was subsequently revised for the CESifo Summer Institute 2012 on Taxation of the Financial Sector. I thank my colleagues on the EEAG, members of the ETPF, conference participants, and especially Clemens Fuest, Michael Keen, Ben Lockwood, Ruud de Mooij, Gaëtan Nicodème, and John Vella for helpful discussions. The work was supported partly by the ESRC, through grant RES 060–25–0033.

1. See, for example, IMF (2010) and European Commission (2010a); the accompanying staff working document is European Commission (2010b).

2. European Commission (2010a, p. 3).

3. For example, through the Dodd–Frank Act in the United States.

4. White House press release, January 14, 2010.

5. See European Commission (2010c, d).

6. Two other forms of tax, not discussed here, are taxes on bonuses and on financial transactions.

7. See, for example, EEAG (2009), Sinn (2010), and Haldane (2011).

8. See Mayer (1988) and Tirole (2006).

9. See, for example, Hemmelgarn and Nicodeme (2010), IMF (2010), and Shackelford, Shaviro and Slemrod (2010).

10. See Devereux and Gerritsen (2010).

11. However, it is questionable whether financial intermediation should be subject to taxation (e.g., see Lockwood 2010).

12. De la Feria and Lockwood (2010).

13. Savings intermediation is here distinct from payment services provided by a bank, such as by checkbook, credit card, or other such facilities.

14. One well-known approach was proposed by Poddar and English (1997), but that has not yet been implemented.

15. Kerrigan (2010) proposes an allocation mechanism that could, in principle, address this problem.

16. There is a significant literature on the conditions under which destination- and origin-based VATs have equivalent effects (see Lockwood 2005; Auerbach and Devereux 2011).

17. See, for example, Devereux and Griffith (1998, 2003).

18. Recent theoretical contributions include Bianchi and Mendoza (2010), Jeanne and Korinek (2010), and Perotti and Suarez (2010).

19. Weisbach (2010) also points out that this analysis assumes that policy makers are not able to change the rate of subsidy, or required level of k, in response to new information.

20. The financial securities contribution (FSC) proposed by the IMF is a tax on liabilities. Imposed at a single rate on the value of liabilities, this would be a linear tax, and subject to the Weitzman analysis above. The IMF does consider the possibility that the rate could reflect the systemic risk of each bank, but IMF does not appear to consider a nonlinear schedule.

21. For example, see Hoban (2010) for the United Kingdom.

22. See Poddar (2003).

References

Admati, Anat R., Peter M. DeMarzo, Martin F. Hellwig, and Paul Pfleiderer. 2010. Fallacies, irrelevant facts, and myths in the discussion of capital regulation: Why bank equity is not expensive. Working paper series 86. Rock Center for Corporate Governance, Stanford University.

Auerbach, A. J., and M. P. Devereux. 2011. Consumption and cash-flow taxes in an international setting. Working paper 11/08. Centre for Business Taxation, Oxford University.

Basel Committee on Banking Supervision. 2010. *The Basel Committee's Response to the Financial Crisis: Report to the G20.* Basel: Bank for International Settlements.

Bianchi, J., and E. Mendoza. 2010. Overborrowing, financial crises and "macro-prudential" taxes. Working paper 16091. NBER.

De la Feria, R., and B. Lockwood. 2010. Opting for opting-in? An evaluation of the European Commission's Proposals for reforming VAT on financial services. *Fiscal Studies* 31 (2): 171–202.

Devereux, M. P., and A. Gerritsen. 2010. The tax treatment of debt and equity. In D. A. Albregtse and P. Kavelaars, eds., *Naar een Europese winstbelasting?* Deventer: Kluwer, 67–74.

Devereux, M. P., and R. Griffith. 1998. Taxes and the location of production: evidence from a panel of US multinationals. *Journal of Public Economics* 68: 335–67.

Devereux, M. P., and R. Griffith. 2003. Evaluating tax policy for location decisions. *International Tax and Public Finance* 10: 107–26.

Diamond, D. W., and P. H. Dybvig. 1983. Bank runs, deposit insurance and liquidity. *Journal of Political Economy* 91: 401–19.

European Commission. 2010a. Financial sector taxation. *European Commission COM(2010) 549* final. Brussels. European Commission.

European Commission. 2010b. Financial sector taxation. Staff working document, accompanying *Communication COM(2010) 549.* Brussels.

European Commission. 2010c. Bank Resolution Funds. *European Commission COM(2010) 254 final.* Brussels. European Commission.

European Commission. 2010d. An EU framework for crisis management in the financial sector. *European Commission COM(2010) 579 final.* Brussels: European Commission.

European Economic Advisory Group. 2009. The financial crisis. *The EEAG Report on the European Economy,* 59–122. Available at: www.ifo.de/portal/page/portal/DocBase _Content/ZS/ZS-EEAG_Report/zs-eeag-2009/eeag_report_chap2_2009.pdf.

Hemmelgarn, T., and G. Nicodeme. 2010. The 2008 financial crisis and tax policy. Working paper 20. European Commission DG for Taxation and Customs Union.

Haldane, A. 2010. *The $100 Billion Question.* London: Bank of England.

Haldane, A. 2011. *Control Rights (and Wrongs).* London: Bank of England.

Hellwig, M. 2010. Capital regulation after the crisis: Business as usual? Preprints of the Max Planck Institute for Research on Collective Goods. Bonn 2010/31.

Hoban, M. 2010. *Ministerial Statement—Bank Levy: Draft Legislation.* London: HM Treasury.

Institute for Fiscal Studies. 1991. Equity for companies: a corporation tax for the 1990s. IFS Commentary C026. Capital Taxes Group Institute for Fiscal Studies, London.

International Monetary Fund. 2010. *Financial Sector Taxation: The IMF's Report to the G20 and Background Material.* Washington, DC: IMF.

Jeanne, O., and A. Korinek. 2010. Managing credit booms and busts: A Pigouvian taxation approach. Working paper 16377. NBER.

Kaplow, L., and S. Shavell. 2002. On the superiority of corrective taxes to quantity regulation. *American Law and Economics Review* 4: 1–17.

Keen, M. 2010. The taxation and regulation of financial institutions. CESifo and IIPF Musgrave Lecture. Munich.

Keen, M., R. Krelove, and J. Norregard. 2010. The financial activities tax. In *Financial Sector Taxation: The IMF's Report to the G20 and Background Material.* Washington, DC: IMF.

Kerrigan, A. 2010. The elusiveness of neutrality: Why is it so difficult to apply VAT to financial services? *International VAT Monitor* (March–April): 103–12.

King, M. 2010. *Banking: From Bagehot to Basel and Back Again.* London: Bank of England.

Laeven, L., and F. Valencia. 2010. Resolution of banking crises: The good, the bad and the ugly. Working paper 10/146. IMF.

Lockwood, B. 2010. How should financial intermediation services be taxed?", Oxford University Centre for Business Taxation Working Paper 10/14.

Matheson, T. 2010. Taxing financial transactions: issues and evidence. In *Financial Sector Taxation: The IMF's Report to the G20 and Background Material.* Washington, DC: IMF.

Mayer, C. P. 1988. New issues in corporate finance. *European Economic Review* 32:1167–1189.

Miles, D. 2010. *Monetary Policy and Financial Stability.* Bank of England.

Modigliani, F. and M. Miller. 1958. The cost of capital, corporation finance and the theory of investment. *American Economic Review* 48 (3): 261–97.

Myers, S., and N. Majluf. 1984. Corporate financing and investment decisions when firms have information that investors do not have. *Journal of Financial Economics* 12: 187–221.

Perotti, E., and J. Suarez. 2010. *A Pigouvian Approach to Liquidity Regulation.* Amsterdam: University of Amsterdam.

Poddar, S. 2003. Consumption taxes: The role of the value-added tax. In P. Honohan, ed.,*Taxation of Financial Intermediation.* New York: Oxford University Press, 345–80.

Poddar, S., and M. English. 1997. Taxation of financial services under a value-added tax: Applying a cash-flow approach. *National Tax Journal* 50: 89–111.

Shackelford, D., D. Shaviro, and J. Slemrod. 2010. *Taxation and the Financial Sector.* Ann Arbor: University of Michigan Press.

Sinn, H.-W. 2010. *Casino Capitalism*. Oxford: Oxford University Press.

Stern, N. 2007. *The Economics of Climate Change: The Stern Review*. Cambridge: Cambridge University Press.

Tirole, J. 2006. *The Theory of Corporate Finance*. Princeton: Princeton University Press.

Ueda, K., and B. Weder di Mauro. 2010. The value of the too-big-to-fail subsidy to financial institutions. In *Financial Sector Taxation: The IMF's Report to the G20 and Background Material*. Washington, DC: IMF.

Vives, X. 2010a. Competition and stability in banking. In *Monetary Policy under Financial Turbulence, Proceedings of the Annual Conference of the Central Bank of Chile*, forthcoming.

Vives, X. 2010b. *Strategic Complementarity, Fragility, and Regulation*. IESE Business School.

Weisbach, D. 2010. Instrument choice is instrument design. University of Chicago Law School.

Weitzman, M. 1974. Prices vs. quantities. *Review of Economic Studies* 41: 477–91.

3 Taxes, Banks, and Financial Stability

Reint Gropp

3.1 Introduction

In the response to the financial crisis and its aftermath, in many countries numerous different "fees," "taxes," or "levies" on financial institutions have been discussed or implemented. The main objective of this chapter is to draw attention to the connection between the incidence of the taxes, namely who ultimately pays; the incentives for financial institutions based on the incidence of the tax; and what policy makers are trying to accomplish by imposing these taxes. I argue that combining banking theory with standard models of tax incidence can provide us with insight as to the desirability of such taxes. While I do not attempt to work out a full-fledged model of tax incidence for all types of financial institutions taxes proposed, it should be intuitively apparent from my discussion that small- and medium-size financial firms disproportionately will bear the burden of the tax, quite contrary to the intention of policy makers.

In the main I consider taxes directly levied on financial institutions. I will not review the more radical reforms of the IMF and others intended to reduce the incentives for leverage of financial and nonfinancial firms by abolishing the deductibility of interest, or, alternatively, allow the deductibility of a risk-free return on equity (IMF 2010; Keen and de Mooij 2012; Gu et al. 2012). These changes could have significant consequences not only for financial institutions but also for all nonfinancial firms. In addition other taxes related to ensuring financial stability have been proposed, notably Tobin taxes on short-term financial transactions and taxes on manager bonuses in banks. However, I omit these taxes from my discussion because they are levied either on financial markets or individuals' bonuses, rather than on financial institutions themselves. Also their incidence would differ substantially from the taxes discussed here, even though to some extent these taxes are envisaged to serve a similar purpose as the taxes discussed in this chapter.

Optimal tax theory tells us that a tax should be designed such that it raises a maximum amount of revenue with a minimum amount of distortion to decisions of economic agents. Yet taxes on financial institutions are not only motivated by a need to raise revenue but also by a need to discourage certain types of behavior by banks, especially those types of behaviors that create systemic risk. In this chapter, I define systemic risk as an externality arising from the actions of one financial institution but impacting other economic agents, including other banks and also firms and households.

Hence the type of taxes considered here are Pigovian taxes, meaning taxes that are intended to make the private parties involved feel the social burden of their actions. The parallel to the pollution produced by firms causing harm to other parties is obvious, and indeed these taxes are somewhat similar to the pollution taxes that exist in many countries. Likewise the excessive risks to parties outside the bank are costs that are supposed to be internalized by the bank. Therefore some of the same shortcomings and problems that have been identified in the literature on pollution taxes apply to these Pigovian taxes: First, how to precisely measure the externality, namely the extent to which the actions of a financial institution cause systemic risk. And second, the so-called reciprocal cost problem identified by Coase (1960). While I will discuss the first problem in more detail in section 3.3, I will only very briefly discuss the latter here.

Coase illustrated the reciprocal cost problem with the following example: The social harm gets worse, Coase argues, if only one offender pays for the social harm. If the smoke-emitting factory must pay for all its smoke, it will reduce its quantity of production or buy the necessary technology to reduce its smoke rate. With pollution abated, the air becomes cleaner, and the neighborhood may attract new residents. This immediately raises the marginal social cost of smoke, which would require a tax increase on the factory. Essentially every time the tax increases, the population increases, and the marginal cost of the status quo increases some more. In effect the factory is punished for making conditions good enough that people want to move to its vicinity. This story translates quite directly to the case of banks "emitting systemic risk" and the taxation of this emission. If banks are indeed discouraged from entering into activities (at a cost to them) that may cause systemic risk, other economic agents, in particular other banks, may increase their risk exposure to these banks, and other market participants may reduce their monitoring of these risks. In the banking literature, this would imply a reduction in market discipline, which unambiguously would have a systemic risk-increasing effect. The difficulty of identifying systemic risks ex ante adds to this problem. In the Coase example, people move near the factory. But this can increase the marginal social cost of contagion, as the financial system becomes more interconnected, and hence more prone to systemic risk. Ultimately, even though a bank has reduced activities that can result in systemic risk, the systemic risk from the institution that remains can lead to a further tax increase, as in the Coase example.

Coase (1960) concludes that the tax should not be changed once it is implemented in order to avoid burdening firms unduly with taxation. This problem is even trickier with regard to reducing the systemic risk emanating from financial institutions. At this point, because of space constraints I will leave this issue.

Besides issues pertaining to Pigouvian taxes in general, the literature has developed some criteria for such taxes from a regulatory perspective. It is argued that any such tax intended to raise funds for future bailouts, and also to reduce the likelihood of financial instability occurring, should at least satisfy the following three criteria , (Weder di Mauro 2010):

• *Private incentive compatibility* The tax should reduce the financial institutions' incentive to create systemic risk.
• *Public incentive compatibility* The tax should reduce public sector forbearance, meaning it should make it easier for the public sector to stick to ex ante commitments to not insure financial institutions.
• *Transparency* The tax should be transparent, easy to enforce and difficult to manipulate by financial institutions. In general, the opacity of financial institutions (Morgan 2002) has made it relatively easy for them to circumvent regulation. Similarly there is the concern that financial institutions would be able to relatively easily avoid the tax by engaging in activities akin to regulatory (or tax) arbitrage.

In the next section I discuss two types of taxes that have been proposed, one in the United States and the other in the European Union. In section 3.3, I examine in more detail the measurement problem of taxing financial institutions to reduce systemic risk. In section 3.4, I review some of the theory regarding the likely incidence of taxes on financial institutions; in section 3.5, I compare capital requirements and taxes; and in section 3.6, I conclude the chapter.

3.2 Two Proposals

3.2.1 Financial Crisis Responsibility Fee (US)

A financial crisis responsibility fee was announced by President Obama on January 14, 2010. The motivation for introducing the fee was the idea that "the financial sector should pay back for the bailouts it received in 2008/2009 financial crisis." Hence it would be a temporary tax. The fee would remain in place only as long as needed to cover the losses incurred in TARP. At the time of the announcement in January 2010, these losses were estimated to be $117 billion. In President Obama's proposal the tax rate was envisaged to be 0.15 percent of covered liabilities of financial firms with more than $50 billion in consolidated assets. In 2010 this applied to about fifty institutions in the United States, including banks, thrifts, insurance, and other companies with insured deposits and broker dealers, and additionally their domestic and foreign subsidiaries. The tax base is defined as follows:

Covered liabilities =Total assets – Tier 1 capital – FDIC assessed (insured) deposits

The tax was estimated to be in place for twelve years in order to cover the losses estimated in January 2010.

More recently the costs of recapitalizing banks have been reduced to $68 billion, and the costs may fall further. This would cut the implementation time of the tax in half. Faced with questions about whether the tax was still needed given the much lower than estimated costs of the bailouts, President Obama adjusted the objectives of the tax and argued that the fee would reduce the incentives toward "excessive risk-taking" by reducing the incentives to use (non–insured-deposit) leverage.

Overall, the tax would go some way to reduce the bias toward debt finance for financial institutions, although the current proposal makes no attempt to calibrate the appropriate tax rate based on some estimate of the bias. Its temporary nature could also create unwelcome incentives for banks' financing choices. The reason that the tax is still not implemented may be due to the fact that financial institutions lobbied extensively against it based on the argument that bank shareholders were viewed as being unfairly treated, relative to shareholders of other firms. Nevertheless, the tax is part of President Obama's 2013 budget proposal, although largely disappeared from discussion before and after the November 2012 election.

3.2.2   Systemic Risk Charge (EU)

In the European Union a similar tax has been under consideration. The tax base is broadly consistent with the financial crisis responsibility fee in the United States. The tax would be levied on all "systemically relevant institutions," yet to be determined. The tax rates would be calibrated such that they would offset the "too-big-to-fail" funding advantage that systemically relevant institutions are presumed to enjoy at the moment. Depending on each specific situation, this could amount to 0.3 to 0.7 percent of liabilities.

There are three basic differences from the US approach. The tax is envisaged to be risk sensitive, and varies as a function of systemic risk that emanates from the bank. The tax does not accrue to the general budget, but rather to a "systemic risk fund" that could be used to bail out banks in the future. The tax is not concerned with forcing banks to pay for bailouts that occurred in the past, but rather with funding for bailouts in the future. Unlike the US tax, it is envisaged to be a permanent tax.

3.3   How to Measure an Institutions' Contribution to Systemic Risk?

In order to design an efficient tax on financial institutions that raises revenues for future bailouts in proportion to the potential future cost and that discourages activities entailing externalities to the entire economy, it is necessary to measure the externality. At the current juncture there is no agreement in the academic literature on the correct approach for measuring a financial institutions contribution to system risk. I briefly sketch one popular approach in order to highlight the difficulties that might be encountered.[1]

Before doing so, I will describe two fundamental problems that can confound such measures. First, the measure is estimated based on historical data. Hence the estimate to which an institution is deemed to be systemic in the future is based on the degree to which the institution was systemic in the past. While this may not be an important problem in the context of a pollution tax, it could be central in the context of ascertaining the contribution to systemic risk of a financial institution. The reason is that while most financial crises may share a pattern, the nature of the systemic risk emanating from institutions is difficult to predict. For example, in 2006 few would have thought that subprime loans were an asset class that could result in the financial turmoil that we ultimately observed. Similarly few saw risks due to the funding structure of a bank. Hence, while any proposed measure may do an excellent job at documenting which institution for what reason was systemically central to the last crisis, this may not give a good indication for future crises.

Second, all measures are necessarily based on relatively few observations, since crises, by definition, are rare (or "tail") events. Furthermore, after a string of good news (e.g., in the period 2001 to 2006 leading up the crisis), the risk may seem tamed, but as a new tail event occurs, the estimated risk measure may sharply increase. This problem is pronounced if the data samples are short. Hence in the literature time-varying contributions to systemic risk have been proposed (e.g., see Adams et al. 2013). Time-varying contributions to systemic risk, however, are the most useful basis for assessing a systemic risk charge, since precisely when the institution is in trouble, it is asked to pay more tax, potentially tipping it over the edge. Thus when considering the two measures described below, one should keep these two caveats in mind.

Adrian and Brunnermeier (2010) propose CoVAR (Co-value-at-risk, where the "co" may stand for conditional, co-movement, or contagion). They start from the most common measure of risk used by financial institutions, the value at risk (VaR). The VaR focuses on the risk of an individual institution in isolation. The $q\%$-VaR is the maximum pecuniary loss within the $q\%$-confidence interval. However, a single institution's risk measure does not necessarily reflect systemic risk. Based on Brunnermeier et al. (2009), any systemic risk measure should identify the risk to the system imposed by individual institutions. The exact source of the risk to the system remains unspecified. It could be direct links among institutions in financial markets, for example, but not limited to the interbank market, or indirect links through banks' exposures to similar assets or asset classes. Brunnermeier et al. (2009) emphasize that systemic risk could also emanate from small institutions, if they are part of a herd, namely a group of banks with similar exposures. A group of several institutions that act alike can be as dangerous to the system as one large entity.

It would go beyond the scope of this chapter to explain in detail how CoVaR is estimated. In a nutshell, Adrian and Brunnermeier (2010) use quantile regressions to estimate the contribution of one institution's VaR to another institution's VaR based on weekly changes of the market value of total assets of publicly traded financial institutions in the United States. This is the contribution of a financial institution to systemic risk or "CoVaR." This measurement in turn is related to a number of balance-sheet characteristics of the institution, in order to ascertain which features of the institution make it particularly prone to generating an externality.[2]

In principle, one could use the estimated CoVaR as a basis for a decision on which banks should be deemed systemically important and the degree of systemic importance. Moreover Adrian and Brunnermeier (2010) document that some deposits that would constitute the base for the proposed taxes in both the European Union and the United States are indeed positively correlated with an institution's contribution to systemic risk (Adrian and Brunnermeier 2010, tab. 6). However, their analysis also suggest that insured deposits, which under the current US proposal would not be taxed, contribute significantly more to an institutions' CoVaR than most other liabilities that would be subject to tax. Furthermore other factors, in particular the degree to which the institution is exposed to maturity mismatches (i.e., whether long-term assets are largely financed with short-term liabilities) have a much larger impact on the institution's contribution to systemic risk than individual components of liabilities.

3.4   Tax Incidence

Theory, for which the classic reference is Harberger (1962; for a modern treatment, see Gravelle 2010), suggests that the ability of banks to shift the tax burden to their customers by widening margins should depend on two factors. One is the degree of competition: the more competitive the banking market, the lower the tax incidence on banks' customers, as banks would be unable to pass on the tax. Second is the demand elasticity of customers: the higher the elasticity of demand, the lower the tax incidence on banks' customers.

There is ample evidence of substantial differences in the extent of competition in banking across countries even within the European Union (see Corvoisier and Gropp 2002 for the European Union; Hannan and Berger 1991 for the United States). This indicates that despite a harmonization of tax base and rate, differences are inevitable in the incidence of the tax and competitive distortions across countries will occur, even within the European Union.

More fundamentally, to fully understand the effects such taxes can have, we need a theory of tax incidence for financial institutions that takes the differences of banks relative to nonfinancial firms into account. The starting point may be basic banking theory. Banking theory would predict large differences in the degree of competition and the elasticity of demand even within countries across different banking products. Corresponding empirical evidence is provided in Corvoisier and Gropp (2002). Based on banking theory, the degree of incidence on banks versus their customers will depend on the degree of asymmetric information between bank and customer, the role of natural monopolies (e.g., in payment systems) and their regulation, and the outside options of the customer, such as financial markets and mutual funds.

Relationship lending theory (Sharpe 1990; Rajan 1992), for example, would predict that small, opaque firms obtain credit from banks based on the following deal: the bank invests heavily in collecting soft, non-verifiable information about the firm and provides credit at an initially relatively low interest rate. As the firm matures and becomes profitable, the bank will extract some of that surplus generated by the firm in order to compensate for the initial subsidy. The story suggests that the demand elasticity of small firms with respect to the interest rate is very low: They are locked in, as any departure from their bank entails the presumption that the firm is of poor quality by other banks ("a lemon"). Other banks may not be willing to make the investment in generating soft information and hence may be unwilling to supply credit to the firm. Overall, relationship lending may result in an "ex post monopoly of information" of the incumbent bank. This results in low *effective* competition for borrowers with a high degree of asymmetric information, regardless of the number of competitors in a market.

In contrast to small firms, large firms can obtain funding from financial markets ("arm's-length funding"). Imposing a tax on banks implies that the relative competitive position of banks relative to financial markets worsens, since financial markets are not subject to tax. Asymmetric information and relationships are less important for large firms, and hence *effective* competition for loans to large firms is high, regardless of market structure, indicating that the demand elasticity for loans by large firms is very high. There will be little incidence on large firm funding.

These considerations suggest that overall the incidence of a tax as discussed or implemented in the European Union and the United States may largely fall on small- and medium-size enterprises. Recall just two of the main objectives, namely "to make banks pay for their bailouts (FCRF, US)" and "to reduce incentives to create systemic risk." If the incidence of the taxes is largely on small- and medium-size enterprises, not the banks but rather small businesses will pay for the bailouts. This in turn will raise the cost of capital for small firms with extensive unintended collateral damage to growth and employment at small firms, which in all European countries make up sizable share of total employment. Furthermore the incentive not to engage in activities creating systemic risk is reduced if at least part of the cost can be passed on to the customers of the bank.

3.5 Capital Requirements versus Taxes

In principle, one could design a quantity regulation (e.g., a staggered capital requirement) that would be equivalent to the taxes discussed in the European Union and the United States. Such regulation, however, would substantially affect a bank's equity and debt, as it forces the bank to reduce its leverage. This is different from a tax on liabilities of the bank, as it would only increase the cost of debt and leave the choice of funding to the bank. As the cost of debt generally is considered to be lower due to the tax deductibility of interest under the corporate income tax, a tax would simply offset this tax disadvantage by complementing the taxation of banks with a tax advantage to equity. Hence, in the context of capital requirements, the question of whether equity financing is more expensive than debt financing is an important one. Most observers would favor this argument, although recently this argument has also been rejected (see Admati et al. 2011).

Similar incidence concerns could be applied as in the case of taxes. The fundamental difference between the two approaches is who controls the funds. With the financial crisis responsibility fee in the United States, the general budget would receive the proceeds from the tax, presumably to offset the losses from the bank bailout. In the case of systemic risk charges, the recipient of the tax revenue would be a systemic risk fund (presumably a bank supervisory agency), which would invest the funds in some way. The exact nature of this investment may determine the overall success of the measure; for example, it has been proposed that the funds should flow back to the banks in the form of bonds that would convert to equity based on certain triggers relating to the health of the institution. With the capital requirements in the European Union, no revenue would be generated.

3.6   Conclusions

Bank-specific taxes, rather than more fundamental changes to the corporate income tax, such as eliminating the bias toward debt finance, are being widely discussed in the United States and Europe. But the practical implementation problems appear to be very large when designing a specific tax on financial institutions. There are problems both of adequately measuring an institution's contribution to systemic risk and of deciding on a suitable tax base. Unless properly designed such a tax has little chance of accomplishing the stated objectives of the policy maker and will either create substantial distortions in banks' decisions without reducing systemic risk or be easily circumvented. Indeed we need a more sophisticated theory of tax incidence in the context of the specific characteristics of financial institutions. I have sketched what such a theory could look like based on basic relationship banking theory. The result suggests that it is likely that the incidence of the tax will not be on the financial institutions but rather on small businesses, as the effective competition in the market for loans to small business would be low due to the informational rents of the incumbent bank.

In this regard it is apparent that policy makers need to focus on ensuring that banks internalize the externalities their produce, rather than on raising revenue or even "punishing" them for past misbehavior. Other tools at the disposal of policy makers, aside from taxes, may be more suitable to this task. In particular, bail-in bonds that shift the burden to existing debt holders and future equity holders may be a much less distortionary approach to ensuring that those that take the risk also bear the cost if the risk materializes. Moreover, because the course is unchartered with these taxes, a number of issues regarding the likely effects of these taxes on banks and banks' customers need to be more fully explored.

Notes

These remarks were prepared for the CES-IFO Conference on the taxation of financial institutions. Financial support from CESifo Venice summer institute is gratefully acknowledged. Comments from Ruud De Mooij and Gaetan Nicodème greatly improved this chapter.

1. There are others, for example, Acharya et al. (2010) on "systemic shortfall."

2. Note that their approach focuses on the externality to other financial institutions only, rather than on the externality to the real economy that may be generated by the failure

of an institution. To my knowledge, there is no measure in the literature that seriously tries to develop this broader concept of a financial institution's externality.

References

Acharya, V., L. Pedersen, T. Philippon, and M. Richardson. 2010. Measuring systemic risk. Working paper. Stern School of Business, NYU.

Adams, Z., R. Füss, and R. Gropp. 2013. Forthcoming. Spill-over effects among financial institutions: A state dependent sensitivity value at risk approach. *Journal of Financial and Quantitative Analysis*.

Admati, A., P. DeMarzo, M. Hellwig, and P. Pfleiderer. 2011. Fallacies, irrelevant facts, and myths in the discussion of capital regulation: Why bank equity is not expensive. Working paper. Stanford University.

Adrian, T., and M. Brunnermeier. 2010. CoVaR. Working paper. Princeton University.

Brunnermeier, M., A. Crocket, C. Goodhart, M. Hellwig, A. Perssaud, and H. Shin. 2009. The fundamental principles of financial regulation. Geneva Report on the World Economy 11.

Coase, R. 1960. The Problem of Social Cost. *Journal of Law and Economics* 3 (1): 1–44.

Corvoisier, S., and R. Gropp. 2002. Bank concentration and retail interest rates. *Journal of Banking and Finance* 26 (11): 2155–89.

Gravelle, J. 2010. Corporate tax incidence: Review of general equilibrium estimates and analysis. Working paper 2010–03. Congressional Budget Office.

Gu, G., R. de Mooij, and T. Poghosyan. 2012. Taxation and leverage in international banking. Working Paper 12/281. IMF.

Hannan, T., and A. Berger. 1991. The rigidity of prices: Evidence from the banking industry. *American Economic Review* 81 (4): 938–45.

Harberger, A. 1962. The incidence of the corporate income tax. *Journal of Political Economy* 70 (3): 215–40.

IMF. 2010. A fair and substantial contribution by the financial sector. Final Report for the G-20. IMF.

Keen, M., and R. de Mooij. 2012. Debt, taxes and banks. Working paper 12/48. IMF.

Morgan, D. 2002. Rating banks: Risk and uncertainty in an opaque industry. *American Economic Review* 92 (4): 874–88.

Rajan, R. 1992. Insiders and outsiders: The choice between informed and arm's length debt. *Journal of Finance* 47: 1367–1400.

Sharpe, S. 1990. Asymmetric information, bank lending and implicit contracts: A stylized model of customer relationships. *Journal of Finance* 45: 1069–87.

Weder di Mauro, B. 2010. Taxing systemic risk. Unpublished manuscript. University of Mainz.

4 Taxation and Regulation of Banks to Manage Systemic Risk

Brian Coulter, Colin Mayer, and John Vickers

4.1 Introduction

The systemic costs of bank failures are typically addressed by capital regulation rather than taxation. This contrasts with other externalities, where taxation is generally viewed as the least distortionary intervention. In the wake of the financial crisis, there has been extensive discussion about taxation to address systemic externalities in banking. This chapter argues that these proposals may have shortcomings and that the conventional preference for capital regulation over taxation has a sound underlying rationale.

The first reason for this is that approaches to externalities involving the principle that "polluters should pay" are imperfectly applicable to bank failures. At first sight, the effect of a bank failure on systemic instability appears to bear a close resemblance to that of a polluting firm on the environment. If banks' actions involve socially excessive risk-taking, they jeopardize the wider economy. A natural suggestion is to tax the marginal contribution of a bank's risk-taking to systemic instability so that banks internalize the costs they impose on the larger economy. But, if this Pigovian tax is imposed after the bank has "polluted" the system and become insolvent, it is uncollectible. The polluter in banking is not in a position to pay ex post.

Taxes can therefore only be levied ex ante, pre-crisis. The tax is then a levy requiring banks to pay for the costs to others when their failures have to be resolved. Equity capital requirements are also a kind of prepayment, requiring banks to post a minimum amount of equity funds. We show that under certain conditions there is an economic equivalence between ex ante levies ("taxation") and requirements that banks hold capital themselves ("regulation").

Three key assumptions are required for our equivalence results. First, losses are perfectly correlated across banks such that the risks are systemic not idiosyncratic in nature. If this assumption is violated, then the central pooling of capital by the government may have an insurance benefit over the private holding of capital by individual banks. But insofar as risks are idiosyncratic rather than systemic in nature, they can be insured through private markets rather than public insurance. The theoretical advantage of taxation in pooling capital therefore occurs when, from a social perspective, it is least needed. There is little pooling advantage in relation to systemic risks, which are our focus.

The second assumption is that the returns on funds must be independent of who owns or manages them. Thus funds invested by governments are as productively employed as those run by private investors. If this assumption is relaxed, then self-insurance could be beneficial to the extent that funds are more productively employed privately than publicly because, for example, moral hazard problems arise when banks' investment choices are insured by a pool of collectively held capital. Capital requirements on banks can in this regard be likened to deductibles on insurance contracts, limiting the moral hazard problems to which insured persons are otherwise prone.

The third assumption for the equivalence result is that there are no flows to or from the government—so no bailouts beyond collected levies and full reimbursement to equity holders of any levy funds not used in bailouts. In reality, contrary to this assumption, governments tend to get drawn into large-scale bailouts, the anticipation of which can distort ex ante risk-taking incentives. Taxation to fund future bailouts, and moreover the externalities associated with them, are nevertheless a double-edged sword. That is to say, unless levied in pure capital—which would be akin to capital regulation—the taxation increases debt funding needed per loan, which could exacerbate rather than diminish potential externality problems.

These findings suggest that taxation per se has limitations as an instrument to address systemic externalities, and that bank capital is of prime importance. This is not to reject the logic of Pigovian taxation. Rather, it is to say that in view of the special features of systemic externalities arising from bank failures, capital needs to be central to the policy approach.

The rest of the chapter is organized as follows. Section 4.2 has a short review of the literature on bank taxation and regulation. Section 4.3 discusses limitations of the pollution analogy, in particular the "polluter cannot pay" problem in the presence of bank failures. Section 4.4 is the central section of the chapter. It sets out a simple model and uses it to show the economic equivalence between capital regulation and taxation under the conditions outlined above. The implications of relaxing these assumptions are then considered. Section 4.5 analyzes (constrained) optimal taxation in the presence of anticipated bailouts and shows the double-edged nature of taxation that is not in the form of pure capital. Section 4.6 concludes by discussing some implications, and possible extensions, of the analysis in the context of current policy debates on bank regulation.

4.2 Literature Review

A seminal paper in the general '"taxation versus regulation" debate is Weitzman (1974), which compares price (i.e., tax) and quantity (e.g., quota) approaches to externality control when there is uncertainty about the curvature of the marginal cost and marginal benefit curves. In this chapter we focus on systemic externalities associated with bank failure and explore a different aspect of the "taxation versus regulation" question. The kind of regulation at issue is not quantity control but requirements on the funding pattern of producers, in particular the minimum proportion of equity in bank funding. The review of related literature in this section starts with taxation and then proceeds to regulation.

4.2.1 Taxation
The recent academic literature has proposed a number of different tax regimes. We classify these regimes into two different types: revenue-focused taxation and corrective taxation. Of course, the various tax regimes fall somewhere on a continuum between these two extremes. However, for illustrative purposes, we attempt to classify each proposal as one of these two.

First, we discuss revenue-focused taxation. The argument for revenue-focused taxation is that governments periodically need to invest large sums of money into the financial system. Taxation, it is argued, can make the financial system bear this cost. We describe the four most popular types of revenue-focused taxation regimes (for a further account, see Keen 2011).

First, a financial activities tax (FAT) is levied on the profit or rent generated by the bank. The FAT is designed to be as nondistortionary as possible in generating revenues. Shaviro (2012) describes one possible variant as a tax on all "supra-normal" profits and wages; alternate versions tax all profits and wages and thereby serve as a surrogate VAT.

Second, a financial services contribution (epitomized by the US Financial Crisis Responsibility Fee) taxes all outstanding bank debt. This tax has been recommended for both retributive purposes in the wake of the recent financial crisis, and also as a "neutralization" of the implicit subsidy given to bank borrowing by the too-big-fail guarantee.

Third, a financial transactions tax (FTT) is levied on the notional value of all executed financial transactions. This tax is generally accepted to be distortionary,[1] but its proponents suggest that the primary distortion will be a reduction in socially wasteful high-frequency trading.

Fourth, bank employee bonuses may be subject to taxation. Temporary taxes of this type were instituted in the United Kingdom and France, and a permanent 10 percent tax on bonuses exists in Italy.[2] The primary justification for bonus taxes is retributive.[3] Thanassoulis (2012) considers possible implications from intervening in bonus pay structures; however, he concludes that bonus taxation will have minimal macroprudential implications.[4]

While these proposed taxes all have some corrective impact, their central focus is on the generation of tax revenue. Next we focus our attention on corrective taxation: taxation that aims to change the behavior of banks with a view to reducing systemic risks. We cover four main interventions: statistical default risk taxes, liquidity-based taxes, market-based taxes, and debt-bias related action.

In one example of a statistical default rate tax, Acharya et al. (2010) propose a tax levied in proportion to the calculated default risk of a bank. This tax would encourage banks to reduce their probability of default. Acharya et al. (2010) suggest calculating the probability of default through a combination of historic data and current balance-sheet information. The authors create a measure of systemic expected shortfall (SES): the expected loss of a firm conditional on a left-tail event for the market for the whole. They report that SES had predictive power for the systemic problems caused by institutions' defaults in the most recent crisis, and suggest that it would in the future as well. A qualitatively similar proposal, CoVaR, is made by Adrian and Brunnermeier (2011).

Statistical default risk taxes have an advantage over other taxes in that they explicitly take account of systemic effects of default. This approach is thus directly corrective, whereas most other interventions are corrective only indirectly through considering firms' individual actions and default risks. The major disadvantage with these approaches, however, is the difficulty in calculating the tax base. While calculations of SES and CoVaR are theoretically possible, it is unclear that they are sufficiently well-defined (or sufficiently contemporaneous) to be used as a tax base.[5]

One proposed alternative to the complexity of statistical default risk taxes is the imposition of taxes that vary with a market parameter. Proponents of market-based taxes argue that the market can combine available information more efficiently and more accurately than any static calculation algorithm. In one of the most cited examples, Hart and Zingales (2009) recommend taxing banks in proportion to the spread on their credit default swap contracts (CDS). As a bank's risk increases, its CDS spread rises as well, placing a tax burden on the bank. Anticipating this, the authors argue, banks will have incentives to reduce the riskiness of their portfolios. Kocherlakota (2010) presents a similar proposal that accounts for the size of a default but necessitates the creation of a new traded security. A major concern with market-based default risk taxes is the potential for market manipulation by third parties and by the banks themselves.

Liquidity taxes, a third proposal, are perhaps less susceptible to manipulation. Banks' reliance on short-term funding exposes them to damaging runs. By shifting the funding structure of banks to decrease reliance on short-term funding, liquidity taxes aim to minimize possible contagion risk.

The "liquidity risk charges" recommended in Perotti and Suarez (2009) have received particular attention. Perotti and Suarez's recommendation is that "a unit of short-term funding should be taxed in proportion to its marginal contribution to a bank's contribution to systemic vulnerability." They propose a tax that is levied with high frequency (weekly or monthly) on the outstanding debt of a bank, multiplied by a factor representing the average time-to-maturity (and thereby refinancing risk) of the debt. The closer a bank-issued debt instrument is to maturity, the greater will be the bank's tax burden. This tax would impose an additional cost on banks for short-term financing and encourage them to utilize funding subject to less refinancing risk.

A similar proposal is raised by Shin (2010). Shin argues that the use of non-core liabilities (generally any financing that is not equity or deposits) spikes during booms because risk is underpriced. A tax on the use of these non-core liabilities would then serve as a countercyclical intervention. Additionally the tax would encourage banks to internalize the possible spillover effects of their risk-taking insofar as this is generally financed through non-core liabilities.

Liquidity taxes may also have the advantage that cross-country coordination is not as critically important as it is with certain other taxes (e.g., an FTT). However, there are definitional issues that plague liquidity taxes. It is unclear how to define "non-core liabilities," and unclear what constitutes "short-term debt." Liquidity taxes may also be vulnerable to circumvention by off-balance-sheet financing. Still, liquidity risk taxation, possibly for its ease of implementation, is one of the leading corrective taxes being considered by many countries.

A final set of proposed interventions focuses on the well-known bias caused by the asymmetric tax treatment of debt and equity. In general, even if we take into account personal tax rates on interest, dividends, and capital gains, we find that there is a tax incentive for banks to finance themselves with debt. This debt bias leads to significant amounts of leverage in the financial system. While it is generally agreed that debt bias was not uniquely responsible for the most recent crisis, it almost certainly contributed to it (e.g., Keen 2011; de Mooij and Keen 2012). The simplest way to remove the debt bias would be to eliminate the tax deductibility of interest payments. But this might be politically untenable (see Devereux 2011).

The primary alternative is an allowance for corporate equity (ACE). In its simplest form, this allows companies to deduct an amount equal to the outstanding value of their corporate equity multiplied by the risk-free rate from their tax payable, thereby providing an offsetting benefit to the issuance of equity. So instead of making neither debt nor equity tax deductible, an ACE makes them both tax deductible, at an obvious cost to public finances. A major difficulty in analyzing the ACE, moreover, is that scant data exist of such systems in practice. Keen and King (2002) outline the Croatian ACE system, but given the data quality problems, they are unable to draw firm conclusions. Indeed the Croatian ACE is no longer in existence. Klemm (2007) provides another overview of ACE data, focusing largely on Brazil. Its ACE, however, makes the payment of dividends tax deductible rather than equity, adding an additional distortion. With this, Klemm finds only very weak data that the ACE achieved its desired goal of reducing corporate leverage.

Therefore, while the ACE has a theoretical justification, it imposes a tax burden on a country for an unproved systemic benefit.

Next we overview the major types of proposed regulation.

4.2.2 Regulation

One of the most popular regulatory interventions requires that banks maintain a minimum proportion of equity financing. These equity capital requirements are often a function of the riskiness of the assets of the bank, as with the Basel system of risk-weighted assets (RWAs). As described in Admati et al. (2010), the mechanism through which equity capital requirements improve the stability of the financial system is straightforward. The greater the proportion of equity in a bank's funding, the greater the losses that it can withstand before becoming insolvent. Prior to the crisis, many banks had greater than fifty times leverage.[6] At this leverage, losses of even 2 percent cause insolvency. With more equity, larger shocks can be safely weathered. Also, by increasing the "skin in the game" of bank owners, equity capital requirements may mitigate moral hazard problems.

The role of equity capital requirements is supported by the results of Black et al. (1978). They consider the relationship between banks and governments as analogous to that between a debtor and creditor. Governments implicitly guarantee banks' debt for reasons of systemic stability, and are therefore analogous to final (albeit contingent) creditors. Black et al. (1978) argue that the optimal form of bank regulation should therefore mirror that which is seen in the private market between freely contracting creditors and debtors. The imposition of an equity capital requirement is analogous to mortgage lender requirements that homeowners maintain a certain level of equity in their homes. Risk-weighted equity follows in the same way: required equity is greatest for the riskiest borrowers.

A second form of explicitly macroprudential regulation is proposed by Morris and Shin (2008). The authors' liquidity regulation forces banks to maintain certain levels of liquidity, to ensure that they are able to meet short-term demands for cash.[7] Morris and Shin (2008) argue that liquidity requirements reduce the likelihood of bank fire sales because banks are more likely to have liquid assets on hand with which to settle short-term debts. As fire sales impose a negative externality on other market participants by driving down asset prices, this supports the solvency of all banks in the financial system. The authors also argue, however, that liquidity ratios must account for the systemic nature of certain instruments. The problem to which they draw attention is that of a struggling bank which cuts loans to other banks to meet its own liquidity requirement. By cutting loans to other banks, a bank may strengthen its own liquidity situation at the cost of depleting the liquidity of the entire system. Therefore Morris and Shin (2008) argue for liquidity requirements that provide systemic stability through encouraging banks to maintain sufficient liquidity on hand, and also by discouraging the payment of debts through the withdrawal of systemically important loans to other banks.

A third set of recommendations to improve the stability of the financial system focuses on bank competition. Keeley (1990) argues that bank charter values could serve as an undiversifiable asset that is valuable conditional on the continued solvency of the bank. High bank charter values would then encourage banks to act prudently, to safeguard their future value. Restrictions on bank competition, the argument goes, could achieve these high charter values and could theoretically improve financial sector stability. Actual equity has a significant advantage over the intangible equity of charter value, however, in that only the former is loss-absorbent. Also the possible benefit of high charter value could be offset by a different impact of competition. Boyd and De Nicolò (2005) argue that an uncompetitive banking sector leads to higher interest rates being charged. Higher interest rates attract riskier borrowers in a process they describe as "risk-shifting," such that a less competitive banking sector may be less stable. These results are combined by Martinez-Miera and Repullo (2010), who argue that there is not a monotonic relationship between bank competition and bank stability. As the relationship between competition and financial sector stability is mixed, there is no good case for competition-lessening regulatory interventions. Furthermore bank competition may already be artificially low because untreated too-big-to-fail problems distort competition in favor of large and complex institutions at the expense of others.

Many reform recommendations integrate a number of these possible interventions. The Squam Lake Report, for example, combines aspects of bank equity capital requirements, centralization of regulation, improved resolution processes, and many others (French et al. 2010).

In the next section, we discuss the "polluter cannot pay" problem and begin to draw our own complementary results on government intervention.

4.3 Polluter Cannot Pay

Banks that take on undue risk impose a probabilistic negative externality on the wider economy. Parallels are often drawn between this negative externality and the problem of pollution control. This suggests that
banks' risk-taking should be controlled in the same way as the actions
of potentially polluting companies: for example, through Pigovian
taxation. As stated succinctly by Kocherlakota (2010), "just as taxes are
imposed to deal with pollution externalities, taxes can also address risk
externalities," and "a well-designed tax system can entirely eliminate
the risk externality generated by inevitable government bailouts."

While pollution may be a useful analogy for thinking about banks'
contributions to systemic risk, there are several critical differences. One,
not considered in this chapter, is the problem of apportioning responsibility among multiple banks for bad systemic outcomes and measuring their respective contributions to it. The same issue could arise if,
say, several chemical plants were located on the same polluted river,
but it is much more complex in the financial context.

In this chapter we focus on the difference between the ex post solvency of "polluters." Whereas in standard settings companies generally remain solvent after polluting, this is not true of banks in a crisis.
Banks that generate systemic risk become insolvent in the process:
insolvency is the mechanism by which the "pollution" occurs. It follows
that forms of taxation or regulation in which the "polluter pays" after
the event do not work. Banks responsible for causing a crisis are unable
to pay any taxes imposed ex post.

We can illustrate the problem of the ex post imposition of taxation.
Suppose that a bank can invest in an asset costing 100 that either yields
150 or 0 with equal probability, or a riskless asset also costing 100 that
will be worth 100. It can finance its investment from deposits and
equity. Suppose that there is a state-run scheme that guarantees depositors the full value of their deposits in the event of bank failure in recognition of the positive social value associated with each unit of
deposits. There is no interest rate and the bank's shareholders and
depositors are risk neutral. Assume that individuals benefit from the
option to invest in informationally insensitive assets: deposits. Then it
is socially optimal for the bank to invest in the riskless assets funded
from as high a proportion of bank deposits as possible.

Contrast two sequences. In sequence 1, in period 1, the government announces a capital requirement and the bank selects its form of

financing. In period 2, it makes the investment choice and in period 3 the investment outcome is realized and the deposit insurance is paid if required. In sequence 2, in period 1, the government announces a tax rate and the bank selects its form of financing; in period 2, the bank makes its investment choice, and in period 3, the investment outcome is realized, the deposit insurance is paid if required, and the bank pays any tax due, if it can.

Sequence 1 The social optimum is achieved by the government setting a minimum capital requirement of 50 percent in which case the bank will earn the expected return of 0 percent on its equity capital.[8]
Sequence 2 The government sets a tax rate of just in excess of 50 percent on the holding of deposits, in which case the bank chooses the riskless asset funded from all equity and earns a zero return.

If the government sets a tax rate below 50 percent in sequence 2, then the bank chooses the risky asset funded entirely from deposits; the bank earns an expected return of zero (on the essentially zero equity investment), and the government expects to earn 25 less in tax revenue than it pays in insurance to depositors.[9] The reason that sequence 2 cannot achieve the social optimum with taxation is that there is a moral hazard problem regarding the bank's choice of investment. The tax on deposits can only be paid when the bank is solvent, which encourages the bank to select inefficiently risky investments in preference to riskless ones.

It is possible, in theory, to design a Pigovian tax that takes into account the likelihood with which a given bank is insolvent at the time of payment. However, banks are able to select their own assets, and thus to control the risks to which they are exposed. Clearly, any ex ante imposition of tax would encourage banks to take on greater risks than if the tax could be collected ex post. Therefore the "polluter cannot pay" problem generates significant problems for the imposition of an ex post levy on banks. "Polluter prepays" approaches will be considered shortly.

There is a further respect in which the pollution analogy is imperfect. In a standard pollution context, the imposition of taxation does not directly impact pollution production. Pollution is impacted indirectly, as taxation encourages firms to change their behavior. In a banking context, however, government imposition of taxes may also directly impact systemic risk, by changing the funding requirements of banks. This direct impact on "pollution" is absent from standard pollution analyses, but it will feature prominently in the analysis that follows.

4.4 A Simple Model of Bank Taxation and Regulation

We now set out a simple model and use it first to show an equivalence between two different types of "polluter prepays" policies: capital regulation and an up-front levy paid into a government-run crisis fund.

4.4.1 The Model

Consider an economy with a continuum of banks and a continuum of borrowers. Every borrower has access to a project that requires a unit bank loan to proceed. Banks make loans to a large number of borrowers, such that every bank is a portfolio of diversified loan assets.

Borrowers' projects succeed with (global) probability $p \sim F(p)$ on $[p_L, 1]$, where $0 < p_L < 1$. As banks make a large number of loans, this is also the proportion of projects that succeed at each bank. Let $X(R)$ be the number of projects of type R or better. Borrowers' projects of type R pay $(1 + R)$ if they succeed, and zero otherwise. The degree of systemic shock, p, is uncorrelated with R.

A borrower pays its bank $(1 + r)$ if and only if its project succeeds, so the number of projects financed is $X(r)$. Fraction k of each loan is financed by equity, and fraction $(1 - k)$ is financed by debt. The risk-free rate is zero and all agents are risk-neutral. There is perfect competition. Each bank finances many projects, so the law of large numbers applies. Bondholders receive gross return $(1 + b)$ if their bank is solvent, and receive the value of bank assets under bank insolvency. In the absence of any crisis fund (see later), there is a negative externality of γ times the extent of uncovered losses—that is, losses not absorbed by k or (if such exists) by the crisis fund.[10]

Banks are always solvent if

$$(1 + b)(1 - k) \le (1 + r)p_L. \tag{4.1}$$

Solvency is maintained in (4.1) because even in the worst state, bondholders get repaid in full. When solvency is guaranteed, in equilibrium, $b = 0$. Bondholders are not promised any excess repayment because they do not accept any risk. Then the rate charged to borrowers, r, must be such that the gross return to equity is unity:

$$(1+r)\bar{p} = 1, \tag{4.2}$$

where $\bar{p} \equiv E[p]$. So from (4.1) and (4.2) we see that there is an always solvent equilibrium if

$$k \geq 1 - \frac{p_L}{\bar{p}}. \tag{4.3}$$

When (4.3) is satisfied, banks hold sufficient capital such that bond-holders are completely insulated from losses. The first best is achieved in this case: the optimal r is given by (4.2) and negative externalities never arise.

In a Modigliani–Miller (MM) world, this outcome could be achieved. Banks would be indifferent to their financial structure, and so would not object to structures meeting (4.3). But MM does not hold. First, if there is any tax and/or subsidy advantage to debt over equity, no matter how small, banks want to minimize k. In fact tax systems do favor debt over equity, and moreover debt has a subsidy advantage over equity unless the probability of bailout is precisely zero (as is assumed for equity). Second, if debt providers cannot (or do not have an incentive to) observe a bank's choice of k, then the bank would deviate from a candidate equilibrium in which (4.3) holds. If a bank deviated by funding itself with less capital than (4.3), so that default was possible, then the expected return to each unit of debt would fall below 1. But the overall (private) return would not decrease, so the expected return to equity would exceed 1, making the deviation worthwhile for the holders of equity in these circumstances. Third, if we start from a situation where (4.3) does not hold, increasing k lowers the probability of default so confers a positive externality on bondholders, for which equity holders effectively pay. This is the debt overhang problem.

For several reasons we now consider the (much more common) situation in which (4.3) does not hold: banks maintain insufficient capital to shield bondholders from losses. Assume then that (4.1) does not hold and define $P(k) > p_L$ as the p such that with equity ratio k there is insolvency if and only if $p < P(k)$. The function $P(k)$ is defined implicitly by

$$(1 + b)(1 - k) = (1 + r)P(k). \tag{4.4}$$

Assume (for now) that there are no transfers to or from the government in any circumstance. Then overall, investors (i.e., bank bondholders plus equity holders) must get back unity on average per unit loan so that (4.2) continues to hold. Therefore $P(k)$ and b are related by

$$P(k) = (1 + b)(1 - k)\bar{p}. \tag{4.5}$$

Bondholders get back $(1 - k)(1 + b)$ per unit loan if $p \geq P(k)$. That is, as long as the bank is solvent, bondholders receive their promised amount. Otherwise, using (4.4), bondholders get

$$(1+r)p = \frac{p}{\bar{p}} = (1-k)(1+b)\frac{p}{P}$$

in state p. On average, because of risk neutrality, bondholders get back unity per unit of debt.

Therefore

$$1 = (1+b) - \frac{1}{(1-k)\bar{p}} \int_{P_L}^{P} (P-p)dF(p)$$

$$= (1+b) - \frac{1}{(1-k)\bar{p}} \int_{P_L}^{P(k)} F(p)dp. \tag{4.6}$$

For convenience, define

$$\phi(P) \equiv \int_{P_L}^{P} F(p)dp. \tag{4.7}$$

So $\phi(P)$ is a strictly increasing function with $\phi(p_L) = 0$ and $\phi(1) = 1 - \bar{p}$. From (4.6) we have

$$(1-k)b = \frac{\phi(P(k))}{\bar{p}}. \tag{4.8}$$

Combining with (4.5) it follows that

$$(1-k)\bar{p} = P(k) - \phi(P(k)), \tag{4.9}$$

so in turn

$$k\bar{p} = \int_{P(k)}^{1} [p - P(k)]dF(p)$$

$$= \int_{P(k)}^{1} [1 - F(p)]dp. \tag{4.10}$$

This implicitly defines P in terms of k. The greater the fraction of equity, k, the less likely insolvency becomes, so the lower is P.

The expected negative externality per project $z(k)$ is taken to be γ times the expected loss not absorbed by capital—that is, the loss in insolvency. In the absence of bailouts this expected loss is the difference between the contracted payment to bondholders, $(1 - k)(1 + b)$, and what they receive on average, that is, $(1 - k)$. So using (4.8) obtains

$$z(k) = \gamma b(1-k)$$

$$= \gamma \frac{\phi(P(k))}{\bar{p}}. \tag{4.11}$$

Then from (4.10),

$$z'(k) = \frac{\gamma F(P(k))}{1 - F(P(k))}.$$

Given externality $z(k)$, there is in a sense "too much lending." The bank does not internalize the negative externality created by the issuance of loans, because the losses conditional on default fall on the bondholders. We discuss below that while taxes can partially internalize the externality, they do not address the underlying problem of insufficient loss-absorbency.

4.4.2 Neutrality Result

The obvious policy to adopt in this setting is to require sufficient k to meet (4.3). Suppose, however, that such a requirement is impossible to achieve, perhaps for political reasons, and that for exogenous reasons k is insufficient to meet (4.3). In theoretical terms this is an unsatisfactory assumption, but given the manifest difficulties of raising banks' capital ratios, it leads to important and practically relevant questions for (second-best) policy analysis.

The aim of this subsection is to compare capital ratio regulation with "taxation" in the form of a levy to create a crisis fund. In particular, suppose that banks must prepay an amount s per unit bond, so $(1 - k)s$ per unit loan, into a crisis fund. A number of questions then arise: On what basis is s calculated? When and how is the fund disbursed? Who owns it if, or to the extent that, it is not disbursed? How is it invested in the meantime? Assume first that any payouts from the fund go to bondholders and that its residual value (all of it if no payouts) is returned to equity owners. Suppose that the fund is invested in the risk-free asset. Then (4.2) still holds, so r is as in the previous analysis.

The fund is then equivalent to a higher k. To see this, compare the situation with capital k and no crisis fund with that with capital $k_0 < k$ and a crisis fund as above with

$$s = \frac{k - k_0}{1 - k_0}. \tag{4.12}$$

(In the special case $k_0 = 0$, we have $s = k$.) Shareholders have to pay $(1 - k_0)s = (k - k_0)$ per unit loan into the crisis fund in addition to their capital of k_0 per unit loan, making k in total. Let b_0 be the return on bonds in this situation. Bondholders receive less than $(1 + b_0)$ only if

$$p < (1+b_0-s)(1-k_0)\bar{p}$$
$$= [(1+b_0)(1-k_0)-(k-k_0)]\bar{p} \qquad (4.13)$$
$$\equiv P_0,$$

say. Since bondholders get unity on average per unit of debt, we have that

$$1 = (1+b_0) - \frac{1+r}{1-k_0}\int_{PL}^{P_0}(P_0-p)dF(p)$$

$$= (1+b_0) - \frac{\phi(P_0)}{(1-k_0)\bar{p}}.$$

Rearranging the equation above yields

$$(1-k_0)b_0 = \frac{\phi(P_0)}{\bar{p}}. \qquad (4.14)$$

With (4.13), this gives

$$P_0 = (1-k)\bar{p} + \phi(P_0).$$

It is now apparent from (4.9) that

$$P_0 = P(k),$$

and moreover that

$$(1-k_0)b_0 = (1-k)b. \qquad (4.15)$$

From (4.11) we see that the externality is also the same in the two situations. Hence we have a neutrality result: capital ratio k with no crisis fund achieves the same economic outcome as capital ratio k_0 and levy s set as in (4.12).

4.4.3 Imperfect Correlation

Our neutrality result between taxation and capital ratio regulation is based on three key assumptions:

1. Banks face perfectly correlated risks of failure (there are no idiosyncratic failures).
2. Return on levy funds is independent of who owns or manages them.
3. No flows to or from government (neither taxes and nor subsidies).

We now consider deviation from the first assumption, and examine the implications of imperfect correlation in risks among banks. To do this sharply, we consider the extreme situation of bank-specific, but not aggregate, uncertainty in returns. If bank losses are not perfectly correlated, there is a risk-pooling benefit to holding capital centrally. Any capital held by an individual bank that does not default is effectively 'wasted' if others default. This capital could have been more useful if held centrally, and allocated to failing banks.

Consider an economy as above, but with $p_i \sim F(p_i)$ the proportion of bank i's loans that succeed. Therefore there is bank-specific but not aggregate uncertainty: the economywide proportion of projects that succeed is always $\bar{p}$. So this variant is a model of idiosyncratic but not systemic risk. In this situation a prepaid crisis fund of

$$\kappa = (1+r)\phi(\bar{p}) = \frac{\phi(\bar{p})}{\bar{p}} \tag{4.16}$$

per loan is sufficient to ensure no defaults. The banks with $(1 + r)p_i < 1$, that is, with $p_i < \bar{p}$, would receive funds. Their shortfall in total is κ. Note that

$$\kappa = \frac{\phi(\bar{p})}{\bar{p}} < \frac{1}{\bar{p}}(\bar{p} - p_L)F(\bar{p}) < 1 - \frac{p_L}{\bar{p}},$$

the last term of which is the capital ratio such that no bank had a shortfall. So it is evident that with uncorrelated returns across banks, a central fund can avert any shortfalls with less capital than with decentralized capital held in each bank. This is simply the insurance benefit—if capital is costly—of pooling capital. However, it raises a number of issues. First, if (as in the model) capital is not socially costly, there is no benefit. Second, an appropriately designed market mechanism might be able to achieve the same result. Third, who would operate the fund, and how? Finally, serious moral hazard problems could result from a crisis fund, whereas decentralized capital ownership has shareholders (more) on the hook for their bank's decisions. A crisis fund results in socialized bank losses, yet private bank gains: this encourages banks to take on undue risk.

In any event, the major concern in financial regulation is that of systemic risk: the concern that many banks sustain heavy losses simultaneously. The benefits of risk-pooling are least in that case, but it is when the crisis fund is needed most. Because systemic risk is the main subject of this chapter, we next return to the case of perfectly correlated returns across banks.

4.5 Taxes and Implicit Subsidies

We now relax another of the assumptions on which the neutrality result depends—that of no flows to or from government. This enables us jointly to consider taxation and anticipated bailouts. Suppose that there is a tax $t \geq 0$ per unit loan that is prepaid by banks, and that the government bears fraction $\lambda \geq 0$ of losses in insolvency. (Suppose that taxes and bailout subsidies are transfers to and from the exchequer, and that there is no specific crisis fund.) Each loan now requires $(1 + t)$ of funding, and, consistent with before, we let k denote the proportion that is capital.

It remains true that there is never insolvency if

$$1 - k \leq \frac{p_L}{\overline{p}}.$$

This is because bondholders, who supply $(1 - k)(1 + t)$ of funding per loan, can be repaid in full even in the worst state, when the gross return is $(1+r)p_L = (1+t)p_L/\overline{p}$. We assume, however, that there is insufficient capital to rule out insolvency, so bailouts might happen. Then the critical P below which there is insolvency is given by

$$(1 + b)(1 - k)(1 + t) = (1 + r)P. \tag{4.17}$$

The return to bondholders satisfies

$$(1 - k)(1 + t)b = (1 + r)(1 - \lambda)\phi(P).$$

With (4.17) this gives

$$(1 - k)(1 + t) = (1 + r)[P - (1 - \lambda)\phi(P)]. \tag{4.18}$$

Since the overall expected return to the private sector equals unity in equilibrium it must be that

$$1 + t = (1 + r)[\overline{p} + \lambda\phi(P)]. \tag{4.19}$$

The implicit subsidy is measured by $(1 + r)\lambda\phi(P)$. Combining (4.18) and (4.19), we get

$$1 - k = \frac{P - (1 - \lambda)\phi(P)}{\overline{p} + \lambda\phi(P)}. \tag{4.20}$$

As P increases from p_L to 1, the RHS of (4.20) increases monotonically from $p_L/\overline{p}$ to 1, so there is a unique P that satisfies (4.20) given k and λ. The RHS is also increasing in λ, so P is decreasing in λ as well as k.

But P is independent of t, which just scales things up. Expected losses from insolvency per unit loan are

$$(1+r)\phi(P) = \frac{1+t}{\lambda + \overline{p}/\phi(P)}, \qquad (4.21)$$

which is decreasing in k and in λ, and increasing in t. The implicit subsidy is naturally increasing in λ.

The special case of neutral tax and subsidy has

$$t = \frac{\lambda\phi(P)}{\overline{p}},$$

for then

$$t = (1+r)\lambda\phi(P)$$

and $1+r = 1/\overline{p}$ as in the previous analysis. The expected insolvency loss per unit loan is then $\phi(P)/\overline{p}$.

What is the optimal tax rate t given k and λ? To answer this, it is useful to allow for the possibility that there is a social value of public funds in addition to the externality cost of losses not absorbed by capital. The γ parameter above relates to the latter. Separately from that, let the social value of public funds be $1 + \beta$, so taxes/bailouts have welfare benefit/cost $\beta \geq 0$ per unit. A reason for $\beta > 0$ is that taxation distorts economic incentives, so bailouts are costly to the economy— rather than being welfare-neutral transfers—because they increase the taxes needed to restore the public finances to the condition that they would be in without the bailouts.

Expected welfare can be written as

$$W = \overline{p}\int_r^{R_{\max}} (1+R)[-X'(R)]dR - [1+(\beta\lambda+\gamma)(1+r)\phi(P)-\beta t]X(r)$$

$$= \overline{p}\int_r^{R_{\max}} (1+R)[-X'(R)]dR - [1+\beta(1-(1+r)\overline{p})+\gamma(1+r)\phi(P)]X(r),$$
$$\qquad (4.22)$$

using (4.19). From (4.21) it is apparent that choosing optimal t is equivalent to choosing r to maximize (4.22). Optimal r satisfies

$$\frac{(1+r)\overline{p}-1}{(1+r)\overline{p}} = \frac{\beta}{1+\beta}\frac{1}{\eta(r)} + \frac{\gamma}{1+\beta}\frac{\phi(P)}{\overline{p}}\left(1-\frac{1}{\eta}\right), \qquad (4.23)$$

where

$$\eta(r) \equiv -\frac{(1+r)X'(r)}{X(r)}$$

is the elasticity of demand for loans. This is a sort of Ramsey equation. On the LHS is a price/cost markup because $(1+r)\bar{p}$ is the effective "price" per loan and 1 is its cost. The first term on the RHS is an inverse elasticity formula. The second term, which captures negative externalities, is ambiguous in sign, depending on whether or not the elasticity $\eta > 1$. If $\eta > 1$, then the externality term has a positive effect on the optimal tax rate: higher t reduces the number of loans more than it increases funding per loan. But, if $\eta < 1$, then its effect is negative because the effect of higher t on funding per loan dominates the loan reduction effect. This is the "double-edged" nature of taxation as an instrument to curb the negative externalities arising from systemic bank failures.

4.6 Conclusions

Systemic banking crises generate large negative externalities, but the standard economics of pollution control do not apply to these externalities. For example, the principle of "polluter pays" for damage cannot work because banks are insolvent in a crisis. That shifts attention to the ex ante properties of taxation. The normal risk-pooling benefits associated with the central holding of funds do not apply in the context of correlated systemic risks and the moral hazard problems that central holding creates argue against it. Furthermore ex ante Pigovian taxes are a double-edged sword: for a given capital ratio they increase the debt funding needed per loan, and so may increase the scale of negative externalities in the event of a crisis. Thus the externality is directly and undesirably as well as indirectly and desirably affected by taxation. This issue, which is absent from standard externality settings, would not arise if taxes were levied in terms of capital alone. But, as our equivalence result illustrates, capital levies and the regulation of capital ratios have similar economic effects. The issue is not therefore "taxation versus regulation," since the two are fundamentally the same. Rather, the issue concerns the terms by which ex ante taxes are paid: unless pure capital, the double-edged aspect of taxation arises.

Most of our analysis is based on the theoretically arbitrary but realistic assumption that required capital ratios are fixed at too low a level. The first-best solution would be to raise capital and/or loss absorbency more generally, through contingent capital (e.g., CoCos) and bail-in able debt. Structural reform—as proposed in the US Dodd–Frank Act (2010), the UK Independent Commission on Banking Report (2011), and the Liikanen Report (2012)—in tandem with enhanced loss absorbency may further reduce the prospective damage from future banking crises and improve banks' ex ante incentives.

Notes

This chapter was prepared for the CESifo Summer Institute on Taxation of the Financial Sector. For helpful comments and discussion, we thank, without implication, Viral Acharya, Charles Calomiris, Michael Devereux, and Matthew Richardson.

1. See Vella et al. (2011) for a full discussion.

2. Simon Bowers, Jill Treanor, Fiona Walsh, Julia Finch, Patrick Collinson, and Ian Traynor, "Bonuses: The essential guide," *The Guardian*, February 28, 2013.

3. The justification for the imposition of the temporary taxes in the United Kingdom and France was partially macroprudential: it was argued that taxes on bonuses would incentivize firm managers to keep capital within the firm instead of distributing it to employees. This would be unlikely to apply for a permanent tax, though.

4. Thanassoulis (2012) suggests that regulation of bonus *structure* could have macroprudential implications, but taxation alone would not.

5. Statistical default rate taxes generally have the property that a firm's tax payable is impacted by the actions of other firms in the industry. If other firms take greater risks, then the systemic expected shortfall for a third-party firm likely increases, resulting in an increase in taxes payable for the firm. Economically, this is not problematic. Politically, though, it may not be tenable.

6. Simon Nixon, "G-20 protesters are aiming at wrong target," *Wall Street Journal*, April 2, 2009.

7. Liquidity regulation also satisfies the desired analogy between regulation and privately contracting creditors and debtors. Just as bank loan covenants require debtors to meet certain short-term solvency ratios, liquidity regulation forces banks to maintain a minimum proportion of liquid assets.

8. At 50 percent leverage, the equity returns 100 with 50 percent probability, which equals the equity capital invested of 50. The risky investment therefore yields the same expected return of zero as the riskless investment.

9. As the tax rate on deposits approaches 50 percent, the expected equity return on the risky investment falls to zero $[0.5 \ (150 - (100 \times 1.5))]$ on the optimal level of leverage of 100 percent. The government's expected revenue is $0.5 \times 100 \times 0.5 = 25$ and its expected payment to depositors is $0.5 \times 100 = 50$, the net subsidy of 25 compensating for the expected loss of 25 on the risky investment. Above a tax rate of 50 percent, the riskless investment yields a higher return of 0 percent at the optimal level of leverage of 0 percent.

10. A natural generalization of our analysis would be to make the negative externality term γ nonlinear to represent a greater proportionate cost of a major banking crisis. We use the linear formulation below for analytic tractability.

References

Acharya, V., L. Pedersen, T. Philippon, and M. Richardson. 2010. Measuring systemic risk. Working paper 10–02. Federal Reserve Bank of Cleveland.

Admati, A., P. DeMarzo, M. Hellwig, and P. Pfleiderer. 2010. Fallacies, irrelevant facts, and myths in the discussion of capital regulation: Why bank equity is not expensive. [Max Planck Institute for Research on Collective Goods.] *Preprint* 2010:42.

Adrian, T., and M. Brunnermeier. 2011. CoVaR. Working paper 17454. NBER.

Black, F., M. Miller, and R. Posner. 1978. An approach to the regulation of bank holding companies. *Journal of Business* 51 (3): 379–412.

Boyd, J., and G. De Nicolò. 2005. The theory of bank risk taking and competition revisited. *Journal of Finance* 60 (3): 1329–43.

de Mooij, R., and M. Keen. 2012. Debt, taxes, and banks. Working paper 12/48. IMF.

Devereux, M. 2011. New bank taxes: Why and what will be the effect? Working paper. Oxford University Centre for Business Taxation.

French, K., M. Baily, J. Campbell, J. Cochrane, D. Diamond, D. Duffie, and A. Kashyap. 2010. *The Squam Lake Report: Fixing the Financial System*. Princeton: Princeton University Press.

Hart, O., and L. Zingales. 2009. To regulate finance: Try the market. Available at: http://scholar.harvard.edu/hart/publications/regulate-finance-try-market.

Independent Commission on Banking. 2011. Final Report: Recommendations. London.

Keeley, M. 1990. Deposit insurance, risk, and market power in banking. *American Economic Review* 80 (5): 1183–1200.

Keen, M. 2011. Rethinking the taxation of the financial sector. *CESifo Economic Studies* 57 (1): 1–24.

Keen, M., and J. King. 2002. The Croatian profit tax: An ACE in practice. *Fiscal Studies* 23 (3): 401–18.

Klemm, A. 2007. Allowances for corporate equity in practice. *CESifo Economic Studies* 53 (2): 229–62.

Kocherlakota, N. 2010. Taxing risk and the optimal regulation of financial institutions. Economic policy paper 10–3. Federal Reserve Bank of Minneapolis.

Liikanen, E. 2012. *Final Report of the High-level Expert Group on Reforming the Structure of the EU Banking Sector*. Brussels.

Martinez-Miera, D., and R. Repullo. 2010. Does competition reduce the risk of bank failure? *Review of Financial Studies* 23 (10): 3638–64.

Morris, S., and H. Shin. 2008. Financial regulation in a system context. *Brookings Papers on Economic Activity* 39 (2): 229–74.

Perotti, E., and J. Suarez. 2009. *Liquidity risk charges as a macroprudential tool. Policy insight 40.* CEPR.

Shaviro, D. 2012. The financial transactions tax versus (?) the financial activities tax. Law and economics research paper 12–04. NYU.

Shin, H. 2010. Non-core liabilities tax as a tool for prudential regulation. Policy memo. Princeton University.

Thanassoulis, J. 2012. The case for intervening in bankers' pay. *Journal of Finance* 67 (3): 849–95.

United States Congress. 2010. *Dodd–Frank Wall Street Reform and Consumer Protection Act. Public Document H.R. 4173*. Washington, DC: GPO.

Vella, J., C. Fuest, and T. Schmidt-Eisenlohr. 2011. The EU commission's proposal for a financial transaction tax. CBT working paper. Oxford University.

Weitzman, M. 1974. Prices vs. quantities. *Review of Economic Studies* 41 (4): 477–91.

5   Insolvency Uncertainty, Banking Tax, and Macroprudential Regulation

Jin Cao

Now it is true that banks are very unpopular at the moment, but this (banking tax) seems very much like a case of robbing Peter to pay Paul.
—"Taxing the banks?" *The Economist*, July 20, 2011

5.1   Introduction

This chapter aims to discuss the role of banking tax, jointly with the other macroprudential policies in maintaining financial stability under the uncertainty between systemic liquidity and solvency shocks. First, I present the systemic risk that arises from two major problems in banking, illiquidity and insolvency problems. Then I show why conventional, one-handed regulatory policies fail to maintain financial stability under illiquidity and insolvency uncertainty, and how (or whether) banking tax helps restore constrained efficiency jointly with the other regulatory tools.

Illiquidity and insolvency are two major risks in banking. Illiquidity means that one financial institution is not able to meet its short-term liability via monetizing the future gains from its long-term projects—in other words, there's a mismatch between the time when the long-term projects return and the time when its liability is due, meaning it is "cash flow trapped" but "balance-sheet solvent." In contrast, insolvency of a financial institution generally means that liabilities exceed assets in its balance sheet, meaning it is not able to meet due liabilities even by perfectly monetizing the future gains from its long-term projects. These two problems have been separately studied in the literature for long time, and the policy implications seem to be straightforward: if the problem is just illiquidity, liquidity regulation with central bank's lender of last resort policy works perfectly—banks can get enough liquidity from the central bank with their long-term assets as collateral, since the high yields from these assets will return in the future with certainty; if the problem is insolvency, obligatory equity holding can be a self-sufficient solution for the banks to eliminate their losses.

However, one of the most remarkable features about the current crisis is the uncertainty between illiquidity and insolvency. Financial innovation in the past two decades does not only help improve market efficiency, it also creates high complexity (hence asymmetric information), which blurs the boundary between illiquidity and insolvency. The sophisticated financial products, as Gorton (2009) states, finally "could not be penetrated by most investors or counterparties in the financial system to determine the location and size of the risks." Such uncertainty brings new challenges to both market practitioners and banking regulators. On one hand, when there comes a liquidity shock, banks can neither get sufficient liquidity from the market nor central bank because the collateral, in the presence of insolvency risk, is no longer considered to be good. Therefore conventional liquidity intervention such as lender of last resort policy may fail. On the other hand, equity requirements may be inefficient as well because the coexistence of the two problems make equity holding even costlier.

Using a compact and flexible model, I address these new challenges. I attempt to shed some light on understanding the frictions in financial market and designing proper regulatory rules, especially on the role of the banking tax in stabilizing the banking sector. The model is an extension of Cao and Illing (2011). In this model illiquidity is the only risk, conditional with ex ante liquidity requirements for banks' entry to the financial market; a liquidity injection from the central bank fully eliminates the risk of bank runs when bad states are less likely. The outcome of such conditional bailout policy dominates that of equity requirements, since the banks have to incur a high cost of holding equity in order to fully stabilize the system. However, when insolvency is mixed with illiquidity and market participants cannot distinguish between the two, banks have difficulties in raising sufficient liquidity using their assets as collateral. This may have profound impacts on both equilibrium outcomes and policy implications. Because of the insolvency uncertainty, the price of risky assets as collateral will be depressed in the downturn, making it impossible for the banks to raise sufficient liquidity either from liquidity market or from the central bank: such a "liquidity gap" is the extra cost in the bank bailout. To cover such cost, regulators would need to raise the capital adequacy ratio in the normal time or tax the banks. These two practices have different welfare implications.

Section 5.2 presents the baseline model with real deposit contracts, where the fragility of banking comes from both illiquidity and insolvency risks. Section 5.2.3 presents the solution to the central planner's problem. Then section 5.2.4 characterizes the market equilibrium and shows how it deviates from the reference point, the central planner's solution. In section 5.3 the regulatory policies that have been proposed to fix the inefficiencies are carefully examined. The failure of liquidity regulation is analyzed in section 5.3.1, and this can be fixed by introducing banking tax. In section 5.4 an alternative solution of liquidity regulation complemented by equity requirements is discussed. Section 5.5 concludes.

5.2 The Model

We will start with a simple banking model that captures both illiquidity and insolvency shocks to the banks. At this stage it is assumed that all the deposit contracts are real, meaning the central bank as a fiat money issuer is absent.

5.2.1 Agents, Time Preferences, and Technology

In this economy there are three types of agents: investors, banks (run by bank managers), and entrepreneurs. All agents are risk neutral.[1] The economy extends over three periods, $t = 0, 1, 2$, and the details of timing will be explained in the next section. We will assume the following:

1. There is a continuum of investors each initially (at $t = 0$) endowed with one unit of resources. The resource can be either stored (with a gross return equal to 1) or invested in the form of bank deposits.

2. There is a finite number N of banks actively engaged in Bertrand competition for investors' deposits. Using the deposits, the banks as financial intermediaries can fund the projects which are run by the entrepreneurs.

3. There is a continuum entrepreneurs of two types, denoted by type $i, i = 1, 2$. Each type of entrepreneurs is characterized by the return R_i of their projects.

Type 1 projects (safe projects) are realized early at period $t = 1$ with a certain return $R_1 > 1$. Type 2 projects (risky projects) give a higher

Timing of the model

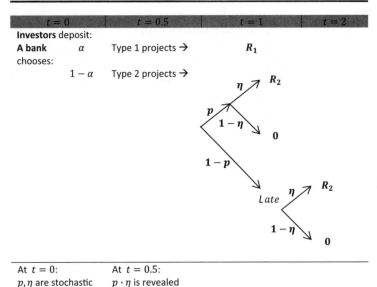

$t = 0$	$t = 0.5$	$t = 1$	$t = 2$

Investors deposit:

A bank α Type 1 projects → R_1
chooses:

        $1 - \alpha$ Type 2 projects →

At $t = 0$:   At $t = 0.5$:

p, η are stochastic $p \cdot \eta$ is revealed

Figure 5.1
Timing of the model

return $R_2 > R_1 > 1$. These projects may be realized at $t = 1$, but they may also be delayed until $t = 2$ or fail with zero return.

The exact payoff structure of type 2 projects is shown in figure 5.1. With probability p the projects are realized in $t = 1$. For those projects with early returns

- with probability η the project is successful, returning R_2;
- with probability $1 - \eta$ the project fails, returning 0.

With probability $1 - p$ the project is delayed until $t = 2$. For those projects with late returns

- with probability η the project is successful, returning R_2;
- with probability $1 - \eta$ the project fails, returning 0.

The values of p and η, however, are not known at $t = 0$. They will be only revealed between 0 and 1 at some intermediate period, call it $t = \frac{1}{2}$. In the following, we are interested in the case of aggregate illiquidity/insolvency shocks. We model them in the simplest way. Assume that p can take three values, $p_L < \bar{p} < p_H$, and that η can take three values as well, $\eta_L < \bar{\eta} < \eta_H$. To concentrate on the cases where there is a demand for liquidity, we assume that $\eta R_2 > R_1$ such that the expected overall return of the risky projects (no matter whether they are delayed or not) is higher than that for the safe projects, but $p\eta R_2 < R_1$ such that the early return from the risky projects is lower than the return from the safe projects. Therefore, although it is more appealing to invest on the risky projects, the banks still need to invest on the safe projects to meet the early withdrawal from the investors (to be explained later).

At $t = \frac{1}{2}$, $p \cdot \eta$, or the early return from the risky projects becomes public information. It can take two values, $(p \cdot \eta)_H$ and $(p \cdot \eta)_L$, but no player knows the exact values of p and η. Further assume that there can be only one shock at $t = 1$, that is, it may be either p or η that takes its "extreme" value, but not both.

Next assume that $(p \cdot \eta)_L = \bar{p} \cdot \eta_L = \bar{\eta} \cdot p_L < \bar{p} \cdot \eta_H = \bar{\eta} \cdot p_H = (p \cdot \eta)_H$, and that $(p \cdot \eta)_H$ occurs with probability π. Therefore (1) if one observes $(p \cdot \eta)_H$, it may come from p_H (with probability σ) or η_H (with probability $1 - \sigma$); (2) if one observes $(p \cdot \eta)_L$, it may come from p_L (with probability σ) or η_L (with probability $1 - \sigma$).

This setting captures the fact that both solvency and liquidity risks are relevant concerns in the banking industry. The value p is linked to liquidity: it defines how likely the cash flow is realized early, meaning the liquidity of the risky projects. The value η is linked to solvency: it defines the quality of the projects—or how likely the banks stay solvent.

Investors are impatient, so they want to consume early (at $t = 1$). In contrast, both entrepreneurs and bank managers are indifferent between consuming early ($t = 1$) or late ($t = 2$). To motivate the role of liquidity, we assume that resources of investors are scarce, in the sense that there are more projects of each type available than the aggregate endowment of investors. Due to the holdup problem[2] entrepreneurs can only commit to paying a fraction γ ($p < \gamma < 1$) of their return. Banks' role as intermediaries is justified by the fact that they have superior collection skills (a higher γ). In a frictionless economy (in the absence of a holdup problem) total surplus would go to the investors. They would simply put all their funds in early projects and capture the full return. However, the holdup problem prevents realization of such an outcome, creating a demand for liquidity. Since there is a market demand for liquidity only if investors' funds are the limiting factor, we concentrate on deviations from this market outcome. With investors' payoff as the relevant criterion, we analyze those equilibria coming closest to implement the frictionless market outcome.

Following Diamond and Rajan (2001), banks offer deposit contracts with a fixed payment d_0 (payable at any time after $t = 0$) as a credible commitment device so as not to abuse their collection skills. The threat of a bank run disciplines bank managers to fully pay out all available resources, pledged in the form of bank deposits. Deposit contracts, however, introduce a fragile structure into the economy: whenever investors have doubts about their bank's liquidity (the ability to pay investors the promised amount d_0 at $t = 1$), they run on the bank at the intermediate date, forcing the bank to liquidate all its projects (even those funding entrepreneurs with safe projects) at high costs. Early liquidation of projects gives only the inferior return $c < 1$. In the following, we do not consider pure sunspot bank runs of the Diamond–Dybvig type. Instead, we concentrate on the runs happening if liquid funds are not sufficient to pay out investors.

Limited liability is assumed throughout the chapter. All the financial contracts only have to be met with the debtors' entire assets. For the deposit contracts between investors and banks, when a bank run happens, only the early withdrawers receive the promised payout d_0^i; for the liquidity contracts between banks and entrepreneurs at $t = 1$, although in equilibrium the contracted interest rate is bid up by the competing banks to the level that the entrepreneurs seize all the return from the risky projects in the good state of the world at $t = 2$ (the details will be explained later), the entrepreneurs cannot claim more than the actual yields in the bad state.

5.2.2 Timing and Events

The timing and events of the model are shown in figure 5.1. At date $t = 0$, banks competing for funds offer deposit contracts with payment d_0 that maximize expected return of investors. Banks compete by choosing the share α of deposits invested in type 1 projects, taking their competitors choice as given. Investors have rational expectations about each bank's default probability; they are able to monitor all banks' investment. At this stage the share of type 2 projects that will be realized early is not known.

At date $t = \frac{1}{2}$, the return of type 2 projects that will be realized at $t = 1$, $p \cdot \eta$, is revealed, so does the expected return of the banks at $t = 1$. A bank would experience a run on if it cannot meet the investors' demand. If this happens, all the assets—even the safe projects—have to be liquidated.

Those banks that are not run trade with early entrepreneurs in a perfectly competitive market for liquidity at $t = 1$, clearing at interest rate r. Note that because of the holdup problem, entrepreneurs retain a rent—their share $1 - \gamma$ in the projects' return. Since early entrepreneurs are indifferent between consuming at $t = 1$ or $t = 2$, they are willing to provide liquidity (using their rent to deposit at banks at $t = 1$ at the market rate r). Banks use the liquidity provided to pay out investors. In this way impatient investors can profit indirectly from the investment in high yielding long-term projects. So banking allows the transformation between liquid claims and illiquid projects.

At date $t = 2$ the banks collect the return from the late projects and pay back the early entrepreneurs at the predetermined interest rate r.

5.2.3   The Central Planner's Constrained Efficient Solution

If all the agents are patient, it is ex ante optimal to allocate all the resources to the high-yield risky projects so that the expected aggregate return is maximized. However, because the investors are impatient and there is no way to reshuffle the output between periods, the central planner needs to take the investors' expected return as relevant criteria.

Since $p\eta R_2 < R_1$, in the absence of holdup problems, the central planner should only invest in safe projects, maximizing the output at period 1. But due to the holdup problem caused by entrepreneurs, the central planner can implement only a constrained efficient solution: she invests a share α on the safe assets, and α depends on the type of the risk.

Proposition 1 *The optimal solution for the central planner's problem is as follows:*

a. In the absence of aggregate risk, the planner invests the share

$$\alpha = \frac{\gamma - p}{(\gamma - p) + (1 - \gamma)\dfrac{R_1}{\eta R_2}} = \frac{1}{1 + (1 - \gamma)\dfrac{R_1}{\eta R_2 (\gamma - p)}}$$

in liquid projects and the investors' return is maximized at $\gamma E[R] = \gamma[\alpha R_1 + (1 - \alpha)\eta R_2]$.
In the presence of aggregate risk, the central planner implements the following state contingent strategy, depending on the probability π for $(p \cdot \eta)_H$ being realized: The planner invests the share

$$\alpha_H = \frac{1}{1 + (1 - \gamma)\dfrac{R_1}{\gamma E[R_2|(p \cdot \eta)_H] - (p \cdot \eta)_H R_2}},$$

in which $E[R_2|(p \cdot \eta)_s] = (p \cdot \eta)_s R_2 + [(1 - \bar{p})\bar{\eta} + (1 - \bar{p} - \sigma)(\eta_s - \bar{\eta})]R_2$ *(s $\in$ {H, L}), in liquid projects as long as*

$$\tilde{\pi}_2' = \frac{\gamma E[R_L] - \kappa}{\gamma E[R_H] - \kappa + \gamma E[R_L] - \gamma E[R_{L|H}]},$$

in which $\gamma E[R_s] = \gamma(\alpha_s R_1 + (1 - \alpha_s)E[R_2 | (p \cdot \eta)_s])$ *(s $\in$ {H, L}), $\kappa = \alpha_H R_1 +$ $(1 - \alpha_H)(p \cdot \eta)_L R_2$, $\gamma E[R_{L|H}] = \gamma(\alpha_L R_1 + (1 - \alpha_L)E[R_2 | (p \cdot \eta)_H])$), and the share*

$$\alpha_L = \frac{1}{1 + (1 - \gamma)\dfrac{R_1}{\gamma E[R_2|(p \cdot \eta)_L] - (p \cdot \eta)_L R_2}}$$

otherwise, that is, for $0 \le \pi < \tilde{\pi}_2'$.

Proof See appendix 5A.1. ∎

When there is no aggregate risk, meaning $p \cdot \eta$ is deterministic, the central planner implements the α that maximizes the investors' return. It can be seen that $\partial\alpha/\partial\eta > 0$; that is, when insolvency risk is less severe, illiquidity problem dominates so that more funds should be invested on the safe assets. Moreover $\partial\alpha/\partial p < 0$ implies that more funds should be invested on the safe assets when the long-term projects get more illiquid. In the presence of aggregate risk, the central planner faces the trade-off between reaping the high return from the risky projects in the good state (which corresponds to the lower α_H) and securing the return from the safe projects in the bad state (which corresponds to the higher α_L). The solution is hence a contingent plan that depends on the probability π.

2.4 Market Equilibrium

In this section I consider the market equilibrium when banks act as financial intermediaries. For the simplest case, if there is no aggregate uncertainty and $p \cdot \eta$ is deterministic, the market equilibrium of the model is characterized by the bank i's strategic profile (α_i, d_{0i}), $\forall i \in \{1, ..., N\}$ such that

- bank i's profit is maximized by

$$\alpha_i = \arg\max_{\alpha_i \in [0,1]} \gamma\left\{\alpha_i R_1 + (1 - \alpha_i)\left[p\eta R_2 + \frac{(1 - p)\eta R_2}{r}\right]\right\}; \tag{5.1}$$

- bank i makes zero profit from offering deposit contract d_{0i}

$$d_{0i} = \max_{\alpha_i \in [0,1]} \gamma\left\{\alpha_i R_1 + (1 - \alpha_i)\left[p\eta R_2 + \frac{(1 - p)\eta R_2}{r}\right]\right\}; \tag{5.2}$$

- it is not profitable to deviate from (α_i, d_{0i}) unilaterally;
- the market interest rate:
  - when the aggregate liquidity supply at $t = 1$ is equalized by the aggregate demand, $r \geq 1$;
  - when there is excess liquidity supply at $t = 1$, $r = 1$.

If there is no aggregate uncertainty, the market equilibrium is in line with the solution of the social planner's problem which is constrained efficient: banks will invest such that—on aggregate—they are able to fulfill investors' claims in period 1, so there will be no run.

Proposition 2 *If there is no aggregate uncertainty the optimal allocation of the social planner's problem is the same as the allocation of market equilibrium:*

a. All banks set

$$\alpha = \frac{\gamma - p}{(\gamma - p) + (1 - \gamma)\dfrac{R_1}{\eta R_2}} = \frac{1}{1 + (1 - \gamma)\dfrac{R_1}{\eta R_2 (\gamma - p)}};$$

b. The market interest rate $r = 1$.

Proof See appendix A5.2. ∎

The problem becomes complicated when there is aggregate uncertainty. When $(p \cdot \eta)_s$ $(s \in \{H, L\})$ is revealed in $t = \frac{1}{2}$, the expected return of the risky projects at $t = 2$ is given by

$$R_2^s = [(1 - \bar{p})\bar{\eta} + (1 - \bar{p} - \sigma)(\eta_s - \bar{\eta})]R_2, \tag{5.3}$$

in which σ is the probability that the shock to early return comes from a shock to p (or, a liquidity shock), and the aggregate expected return from the risky projects is

$$\begin{aligned}
E[R_2|(p \cdot \eta)_s] &= (p \cdot \eta)_s R_2 + [(1 - \bar{p})\bar{\eta} + (1 - \bar{p} - \sigma)(\eta_s - \bar{\eta})]R_2 \\
&= [\bar{\eta}\sigma + (1 - \sigma)\eta_s]R_2.
\end{aligned} \tag{5.4}$$

Since $\eta_H > \eta_L$, $E[R_2 | (p \cdot \eta)_H] > E[R_2 | (p \cdot \eta)_L]$.

If there's only illiquidity risk as in Cao and Illing (2008, 2011), the expected return from the risky projects is just R_2 (the only thing that matters is the timing of cash flow). Now with coexistence of insolvency risk, such return is determined by the probability and scale of insolvency, as (5.4) suggest. In good times, the confidence in the risky assets (more likely to have good quality) raises the expected return (hence asset price at $t = 1$), and vice versa.

The market equilibrium is then characterized in the following proposition:

Proposition 3 *The market equilibrium depends on the value of π, such that*

a. There is a symmetric pure strategy equilibrium such that all the banks set α_H as long as

$$\pi > \bar{\pi}_1 = \frac{\gamma E[R_L] - c}{\gamma E[R_H] - c} \ .$$

In addition
i. at $t = 0$ the banks offer the investors a deposit contract with $d_0 = \gamma E[R_H]$;
ii. the banks survive at $(p \cdot \eta)_H$, but experience a run at $(p \cdot \eta)_L$;
iii. the investors' expected return is $E[R(\alpha_H, c)] = \pi d_0 + (1 - \pi)c$.

b. There is a symmetric pure strategy equilibrium such that all the banks set α_L as long as $0 \leq \pi \leq \bar{\pi}_1$. In addition,
i. at $t = 0$ the banks offer the investors a deposit contract with $d_0 = \gamma E[R_L]$;
ii. the banks survive at both $(p \cdot \eta)_H$ and $(p \cdot \eta)_L$;
iii. the investors' expected return is $\gamma E[R_L] = d_0$.

Proof See appendix A5.3. ∎

Proposition 3 says that when π is low, the banks coordinate on the higher α_L to always be prepared for the bad state, while whereas π is high, the banks coordinate on the lower α_H to reap the high return in the good state because the risk of experiencing a bank run is rather low. The investors' expected return in equilibrium as a function of π is summarized in figure 5.2.

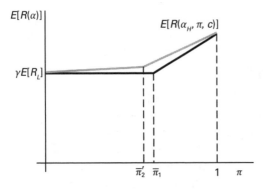

Figure 5.2
Investors' expected return ($E[R(\alpha)]$) in the market equilibrium. The gray line shows the planner's solution and the black line the market outcome subject to bank runs.

Comparing this solution with the solution of the central planner's problem, when the liquidity and insolvency problem coexist, we see that the inefficiency arises from the costly bank runs when π is high. Banking regulation is therefore needed to restore the efficiency. In the next section we will examine to what extend regulatory policies can cope with these inefficiencies.

5.3   Liquidity Regulation, Nominal Contract, and the Lender of Last Resort Policy

One standard policy to cope with liquidity shortage is to introduce liquidity regulation: Banks are required to invest a minimum level $\underline{\alpha}$ on the safe projects, and only those who observe the requirement will be offered the lifeboat when there's liquidity shortage. Usually such lender of last resort is the central bank that is able to create fiat money at no cost.

In this section we add the central bank as the fourth player into the model. The timing of the model is as follows:

1. At $t = 0$ the banks provide nominal deposit contract to investors, promising a fixed nominal payment d_0 at $t = 1$. The central bank announces a minimum level $\underline{\alpha}$ of investment on safe projects as the requirement for the banks' entry into the banking industry and the prerequisite for receiving liquidity injection.[3]

2. At $t = \frac{1}{2}$ the banks decide whether to borrow liquidity from the central bank. If yes, the central bank will provide liquidity for the banks, provided they fulfill the requirement $\underline{\alpha}$.

3. At $t = 1$, the liquidity injection with the banks' illiquid assets as collateral is done so that the banks are able to honor their nominal contracts, which reduces the real value of deposits just to the amount of real resources available at that date.

4. At $t = 2$ the banks repay the central bank by the return from the late projects, with gross nominal interest rate $r^M \geq 1$ agreed at $t = 1$.

Since the central bank doesn't produce real goods but rather increase liquidity supply by printing fiat money at zero cost, all financial contracts now have to be nominal, meaning one unit of money is of equal value to one unit real good in payment. The central bank's liquidity injection then inflates the nominal price by *cash-in-the-market principle* à la Allen and Gale (1998) — the nominal price is equal to the ratio of the amount of liquidity (the sum of money and real goods) in the

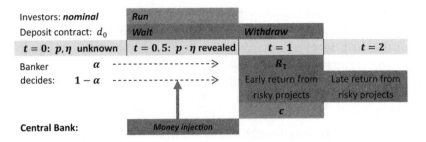

Figure 5.3
Timing of the model with a central bank

market to the amount of real goods. However, the welfare criterion is still based on the *real* goods received by the investors.

5.3.1 Liquidity Regulation with Conditional Bailout

In the presence of nominal contracts where the central bank is the lender of last resort, as Cao and Illing (2011) argue, the optimal policy is to restore the efficient allocation as that of proposition 1. Therefore the liquidity requirement $\underline{\alpha} = \alpha_L$ for $0 \le \pi \le \bar{\pi}_1$, and $\underline{\alpha} = \alpha_H$ for $\bar{\pi}_1 < \pi \le 1$. Moreover the troubled banks should get liquidity injection at the lowest cost, $r^M = 1$.

With $\underline{\alpha} = \alpha_L$ as a requirement for entry, the banks are obliged to hold sufficient liquidity when the illiquidity and insolvency risks are high, that is, when $0 \le \pi \le \bar{\pi}_1$. For $\bar{\pi}_1 < \pi \le 1$, with $\underline{\alpha} = \alpha_H$ the banks can meet the deposit contract with their real return at $t = 1$ if $(p \cdot \eta)_H$ is revealed:

$$d_0 = \alpha_H \gamma R_1 + (1 - \alpha_H)\gamma E[R_2 | (p \cdot \eta)_H] = d_0|_{(p \cdot \eta)_H}.$$

If $(p \cdot \eta)_L$ is revealed, the banks need liquidity injection to meet the nominal contracts. However, since r^M is bounded by 1, the central bank can only inject liquidity up to the expected return of the risky assets. Therefore the maximum nominal payoff the depositors can get is

$$d_0|_{(p \cdot \eta)_L} = \alpha_H \gamma R_1 + (1 - \alpha_H)\gamma E[R_2 | (p \cdot \eta)_L]$$
$$< d_0. \tag{5.5}$$

That is to say, the banks will still be run despite the promised lifeboat from the central bank, and the outcome is no different from that in the market equilibrium. The scheme fails to eliminate the inefficient bank runs at $\pi > \bar{\pi}_1$.

With both illiquidity and insolvency risks, the value of the risky assets is depressed when the bad state is revealed, which makes the banks unable to get as much liquidity as they may need. Therefore, in contrast to the models with pure illiquidity risk such as Allen, Carletti, and Gale (2014), pure liquidity regulation with conditional bailout is no longer sufficient to eliminate the costly bank runs.

5.3.2   Conditional Liquidity Injection with Banking Tax

The failure of pure liquidity regulation comes from the fact that the potential insolvency risk adds an extra cost to stabilizing the financial system. This implies that the regulator needs to find a second instrument for covering such cost, an additional banking tax or financial stability contribution: to the scheme in section 5.3.1 a tax has to be added at $t = 1$ if $(p \cdot \eta)_H$ is observed, and the troubled banks will be bailed out with liquidity injection plus the tax revenue if $(p \cdot \eta)_L$ is observed.

Such augmented scheme works as follows: At $t = 0$, a minimum liquidity requirement $\underline{\alpha}_T$ is imposed on all banks, and at $t = 1$, the banks are taxed away a fixed amount $T_H \geq 0$ out of their revenue if $(p \cdot \eta)_H$ is observed. The banks are bailed out with liquidity injection plus the tax revenue if $(p \cdot \eta)_L$ is observed, and in this case the banks pay no tax, $T_L = 0$.

To find the optimal policy, first consider the high values of π. To eliminate the bank runs, T_H should be so high that the central bank has just sufficient resource to cover the gap left by liquidity injection:

$$\underline{\alpha}_T \gamma R_1 + (1 - \underline{\alpha}_T)\gamma E[R_2 | (p \cdot \eta)_H] - T_H = \underline{\alpha}_T R_1 + (1 - \underline{\alpha}_T)(p \cdot \eta)_H R_2 - T_H,$$

$$= d_{0,T},\tag{5.6}$$

and

$$\underline{\alpha}_T \gamma R_1 + (1 - \underline{\alpha}_T)\gamma E[R_2 | (p \cdot \eta)_H] - T_H$$
$$= \underline{\alpha}_T \gamma R_1 + (1 - \underline{\alpha}_T)\gamma E[R_2 | (p \cdot \eta)_L] + T_H \frac{\pi}{1 - \pi}.\tag{5.7}$$

Equation (5.6) is no different from the social planner's problem for high π; therefore the liquidity requirement $\underline{\alpha}_T = \alpha_H$ when π is high. Equation (5.7) says that the tax revenue should be just sufficient to fill in the gap in the liquidity bailout,

$$T_H = (1 - \pi)\gamma(1 - \alpha_H)(E[R_2 | (p \cdot \eta)_H] - E[R_2 | (p \cdot \eta)_L]).$$

The depositors' real return in the bad state is

$$\alpha_H R_1 + (1 - \alpha_H)(p \cdot \eta)_L R_2 + T_H \frac{\pi}{1 - \pi}.$$

When π gets lower, it would be costly to stay with α_H. The regulator should switch to $\underline{\alpha}_T = \alpha_L$ when

$$
\begin{aligned}
\gamma E[R_L] &> \pi \big(\alpha_H \gamma R_1 + (1 - \alpha_H) \gamma E[R_2|(p \cdot \eta)_H] - T_H \big) \\
&\quad + (1 - \pi) \bigg(\alpha_H R_1 + (1 - \alpha_H)(p \cdot \eta)_L R_2 + T_H \frac{\pi}{1 - \pi} \bigg) \\
&= \pi \gamma E[R_H] + (1 - \pi)\kappa, \\
\pi &< \frac{\gamma E[R_L] - \kappa}{\gamma E[R_H] - \kappa} = \bar{\pi}'_{2T}.
\end{aligned}
\tag{5.8}
$$

The effectiveness of the scheme is summarized in the following proposition:

Proposition 4 *With liquidity regulation complemented by the procyclical banking tax, the bank runs are completely eliminated:*

a. For $\pi \in [0, \bar{\pi}'_{2T}]$, all the banks are required to invest a share of $\underline{\alpha}_T = \alpha_L$ on the safe assets, and no banking tax is necessary. The investors' expected real return is lower than the central planner's constrained efficient solution.
b. For $\pi \in (\bar{\pi}'_{2T}, 1]$, all the banks are required to invest a share of $\underline{\alpha}_T = \alpha_H$ on the safe assets. The banking tax T_H is charged at $t = 1$ when $(p \cdot \eta)_H$ is revealed, and the investors' expected real return is the same as the central planner's constrained efficient solution.

Proof See appendix A5.4. ∎

Figure 5.4 compares the investors' expected return under banking tax with market equilibrium outcome. By fully insured against illiquidity and insolvency risks, such regulatory scheme allows banks to take risks in a wider parameter range $(\bar{\pi}'_{2T}, 1]$, and the investors' welfare is improved by completely eliminating the costly bank runs.

However, in practice, such scheme with banking tax is certainly subject to implementation difficulties. The taxation revenue, or the safety funds, has to be accumulated to a sufficient amount before it is in need, meaning at the time when a crisis hits. Otherwise, when a crisis comes before the funds are fully established, the government must face a public deficit which can only be covered by the future taxation revenue. Usually raising public deficits implies political debates and

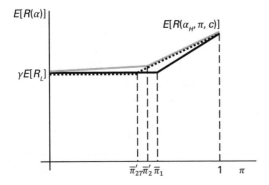

Figure 5.4
Investors' expected return ($E[R(\alpha)]$) under additional banking tax. The gray line shows the planner's solution, the black line the market outcome subject to bank runs, and the dotted line the regulatory outcome under a banking tax.

compromises, substantially restricting the effectiveness of such scheme. In this sense a "self-sufficient" solution such as equity holding may be more realistic, which is to be studied in the next section.

5.4   Insolvency Risk and Equity Requirement

As was shown above, with the coexistence of both illiquidity and insolvency risks, the scheme of liquidity requirement with conditional bailout only works if an additional cost is introduced. Such cost can be either "external," for example, establishing safety funds via taxation as the past section suggested, or "internal," for example, covering the cost with equity holdings.

Now suppose that an equity requirement is imposed to stabilize financial system in a way that all the losses will be absorbed by equity holders. Equity is introduced à la Diamond and Rajan (2005) such that the banks issue a mixture of deposit contract and equity for the investors. Assume that the equity holders (investors) and the bank managers equally share the profit, that is to say, in good times the level of equity k is defined as the ratio of a bank's capital to its assets

$$k = \frac{\dfrac{\gamma E[R_H] - d_{0,E}}{2}}{\dfrac{\gamma E[R_H] - d_{0,E}}{2} + d_{0,E}}, \quad d_{0,E} = \frac{1-k}{1+k}\gamma E[R_H],$$

where $d_{0,E}$ denotes the investors' return from deposits under equity requirements.

To see how equity holdings cushion illiquidity and insolvency shocks, remember that if banks are required to maintain the financial stability in a self-sufficient way, in all contingencies the depositors can only receive the same expected return as in the bad state. However, since there's a positive probability that the risky assets are simply illiquid, the expected future return from the risky assets can be higher, meaning the "fair" value of the risky assets (as the right-hand side of equation (5.5) shows) is higher. Therefore liquidity injection from the central bank may enable the banks to pledge for bailout funds up to the fair value of their late risky assets. However, as I argued in sections 5.3.1, 5.3.2, without imposing extra costs such as taxation, these bailout funds won't be enough for the banks to avoid the costly bank runs, as long as there's still a positive probability that the banks will be insolvent. The regulator can impose equity requirement to cover this part of the cost. Since the banks only need equity to cover the gap left over by liquidity injection, it'll be much less costly for the banks to carry equity.

The proposed regulatory scheme is as follows: First, all banks are required to invest $\underline{\alpha}_E = \alpha_H$ of their funds on safe assets at $t = 0$ for high π, and $\underline{\alpha}_E = \alpha_L$ for low π (the cutoff value of π is different from $\bar{\pi}_1$, and we'll compute it later); second, all the banks are required to meet a minimum equity ratio k for high π^A. The banks are bailed out by liquidity injection in the form of fiat money provision when the time is bad. In this case the regulator only needs to set k to fill in the gap after a liquidity injection when $(p \cdot \eta)_L$ is observed:

$$
\begin{aligned}
\frac{1-k}{1+k}\gamma E[R_H] &= \alpha_H\gamma R_1 + (1-\alpha_H)\gamma E[R_2|(p\cdot\eta)_L] \\
&= \gamma E[R_{H|L}] \\
&= d_{0,E},
\end{aligned}
\tag{5.9}
$$

where $\alpha_H R_1 + (1 - \alpha_H)E[R_2 \,|\, (p \cdot \eta)_L]$ is denoted by $E[R_{H|L}]$. The investors' deposit return is $d_{0,E}$. Then, when $(p \cdot \eta)_H$ is observed, the investors' real expected return is $[(1-k)/(1+k)]\gamma E[R_H]$. However, when $(p \cdot \eta)_L$ is observed, the investors' real expected return is $\kappa = \alpha_H R_1 + (1 - \alpha_H)(p \cdot \eta)_L R_2$, and the liquidity is injected for the banks to meet the nominal deposit contract. Therefore the investors' real expected return is the sum of the deposit return and the dividend from equity holding

$$
\begin{aligned}
&\frac{1-k}{1+k}\gamma E[R_H]\pi + (1-\pi)\kappa + \frac{\gamma E[R_H]-d_{0,E}}{2}\pi \\
&= \pi\gamma E[R_{H|L}] + (1-\pi)\kappa + \frac{E[R_H]-E[R_{H|L}]}{2}\gamma\pi.
\end{aligned}
\tag{5.10}
$$

For sufficiently low π the banks are required to hold $\underline{\alpha}_E = \alpha_L$, and the investors' expected return is $\gamma E[R_L]$. It pays off for the banks to choose α_L instead of α_H if they can get higher expected real return than (5.10), that is, when

$$\gamma E[R_L] > \pi\gamma E[R_{H|L}] + (1-\pi)\kappa + \frac{E[R_H] - E[R_{H|L}]}{2}\gamma\pi. \qquad (5.11)$$

The solution gives the cutoff value $\bar{\pi}_2''$, which can be solved from (5.11) when it holds with equality

$$\bar{\pi}_2'' = \frac{\gamma E[R_L] - \kappa}{\gamma \dfrac{E[R_H] + E[R_{H|L}]}{2} - \kappa}.$$

The effectiveness of the scheme is summarized in the following proposition:

Proposition 5 *With liquidity regulation complemented by equity requirements, the bank runs are completely eliminated. The investors' expected real return is lower than that under liquidity regulation complemented by the procyclical banking tax.*

Proof See appendix A5.5. ∎

The banks will experience liquidity shortage when $(p \cdot \eta)_L$ is revealed. Because of insolvency uncertainty, the expected return of the illiquid assets gets lower so that the banks cannot borrow sufficient liquidity from the central bank to repay the investors; the complementary equity holding is thus required to make up the gap. The investors will not run on the banks once the equity ratio is high enough to ensure they'll get fully repaid, as proposition 5 claims. However, because equity is costly, in the sense that investors need to share profit with bank managers, the investors' expected return is lower than that under liquidity regulation, which is complemented by the procyclical banking tax by which the tax revenue is fully repaid to investors in the downturn.

Figure 5.5 shows the numerical simulation results. In fully eliminating costly bank runs, we find that liquidity regulation, as complemented by equity requirements, improves investors' welfare for $\pi \in [\bar{\pi}_1'', \bar{\pi}_2'']$, as compared with the market equilibrium outcome. However, such a scheme is not useful for the case where the likelihood of crisis is very low, for $\pi \in (\bar{\pi}_2'', 1]$, since part of the banks' profit goes to the bank managers.

Figure 5.6 compares the investors' returns under all schemes. The outcome under the conditional liquidity injection in addition to the banking tax is much better, since all the profits that are levied as a banking tax will be returned to the investors through the bank bailout in the crisis. However, when the political cost is too high to impose an extra tax in the boom economy and raise the public deficit during its bust, combining liquidity regulation and the equity requirement will be a second-best alternative.

5.5 Conclusion

In the recent banking literature, illiquidity and insolvency shocks are usually isolated. Market participants are assumed to have perfect knowledge about the types of shock. This chapter attempts to model the fact that financial innovation makes it hard to tell whether a financial institution is illiquid or insolvent. Such uncertainty can affect the modeling of market equilibrium outcomes and significantly complicatethe regulator's course of action. To cover the extra cost arising from the banks' bailout, a banking tax or some additional regulatory capital holding will be necessary.

It is shown that the price of illiquid assets as collateral is inflated in the good state while depressed in the bad state. This explains why the market is awash with credit in good times, but the bank lending is frozen in bad times. To maintain financial stability, liquidity regulation must be complemented by equity requirements: Pure liquidity regulation is not sufficient to avoid inefficient bank runs in the bad state, since the collaterals are no longer considered to be good. Therefore banks also have to hold an additional equity buffer to cover the extra cost. An alternative complement to liquidity regulation is to introduce a banking tax, which is a reserve levied from the banks' profit in the boom and used to bail out the banks in the bust. However, raising new tax generally implies higher political cost, which is not covered in this model and left for future research.

To put banking tax to work, this chapter also shows that the tax rate should be related to the banks' illiquidity and insolvency risks, and all financial intermediaries should be involved. However, in reality, because of asymmetric information, the tax rate calculated by the regulators does not reflect true banking risks, and indeed there are shadow banks that are free from regulation. Such features in the banking industry allow banks to do regulatory arbitrage. Therefore a banking tax must be introduced along with any regulatory reforms, and more effort must to be made to help regulators better understand the incentive problems in banking.

Appendix A: Proofs for Propositions

Proof of Proposition 1
In the absence of aggregate risk, given $p \cdot \eta$, the social planner maximizes the investors' return by setting α such that

$$\alpha = \arg\max_{\alpha \in [0,1]} \gamma \left\{ \alpha R_1 + (1-\alpha) \left[p\eta R_2 + \frac{(1-p)\eta R_2}{r} \right] \right\},$$

and the interest rate r is determined by

$$r(1 - \gamma)[\alpha R_1 + (1 - \alpha)p\eta R_2] = \gamma(1 - \alpha)(1 - p)\eta R_2$$

with $r \geq 1$. Solve to get

$$\alpha = \frac{\gamma - p}{(\gamma - p) + (1-\gamma)\dfrac{R_1}{\eta R_2}} = \frac{1}{1 + (1-\gamma)\dfrac{R_1}{\eta R_2(\gamma - p)}}$$

with $r = 1$.

In the presence of aggregate risk, the social planner's optimal α may depend on π. First, solve for the α that maximizes the investors' return for each $\pi \in [0, 1]$. The gross interest rate offered to the entrepreneurs at $t = 1$ is no less than 1, and this implies that for any given α the investors' expected payoff is

$$E[R(\alpha)] = \pi \min\{\alpha R_1 + (1 - \alpha)(p \cdot \eta)_H R_2, \gamma(\alpha R_1 + (1 - \alpha)E[R_2 \,|\, (p \cdot \eta)_H])\}$$

$$+ (1 - \pi) \min\{\alpha R_1 + (1 - \alpha)(p \cdot \eta)_L R_2, \gamma(\alpha R_1 + (1 - \alpha)E[R_2 \,|\, (p \cdot \eta)_L])\},$$

which is a linear function of π. Define α_H as the α that equates $\alpha R_1 + (1-\alpha)(p \cdot \eta)_H R_2$ and $\gamma(\alpha R_1 + (1 - \alpha)E[R_2 \,|\, (p \cdot \eta)_H])$, and α_L as the α that equates $\alpha R_1 + (1 - \alpha)(p \cdot \eta)_L R_2$ and $\gamma(\alpha R_1 + (1 - \alpha)E[R_2 \,|\, (p \cdot \eta)_L])$. Solve to get

$$\alpha_H = \frac{1}{1 + (1-\gamma)\dfrac{R_1}{\gamma E[R_2 | (p \cdot \eta)_H] - (p \cdot \eta)_H R_2}}$$

and

$$\alpha_L = \frac{1}{1+(1-\gamma)\dfrac{R_1}{\gamma E[R_2|(p\cdot\eta)_L]-(p\cdot\eta)_L\,R_2}}\,.$$

Depict $E[R(\alpha_H)] = \pi\gamma E[R_H] + (1 - \pi)\kappa$ and $E[R(\alpha_L)] = \pi\gamma E[R_{L|H}] + (1 - \pi)\gamma E[R_L]$ as figure 5.5 shows, in which the intersection is denoted by

$$\tilde{\pi}_2' = \frac{\gamma E[R_L]-\kappa}{\gamma E[R_H]-\kappa+\gamma E[R_L]-\gamma E[R_{L|H}]}\,.$$

For any $\alpha \in (\alpha_L, 1]$,

$$E[R(\alpha)] = \pi\gamma(\alpha R_1 + (1 - \alpha)E[R_2 | (p \cdot \eta)_H]) + (1 - \pi)\gamma(\alpha R_1 + (1 - \alpha)E[R_2 | (p \cdot \eta)_L])$$

$$< \gamma E[R(\alpha_L)]$$

as shown by the dotted gray lines in figure 5.5. For any $\alpha \in [0, \alpha_H)$, $E[R(\alpha)] = \pi[\alpha R_1 + (1 - \alpha)(p \cdot \eta)_H R_2] + (1 - \pi)[\alpha R_1 + (1 - \alpha)(p \cdot \eta)_L R_2]$. Note that $E[R(\alpha)] < \kappa$ when $\pi = 0$ and $E[R(\alpha)] < \gamma E[R_H]$ when $\pi = 1$, as shown by the dotted black lines in figure 5.5.

For any $\alpha \in (\alpha_H, \alpha_L)$, $E[R(\alpha)] = \pi\gamma(\alpha R_1 + (1 - \alpha)E[R_2 | (p \cdot \eta)_H]) + (1 - \pi)[\alpha R_1 + (1 - \alpha)(p \cdot \eta)_L R_2]$. Denote $\alpha R_1 + (1 - \alpha)E[R_2 | (p \cdot \eta)_H]$ by $E[R_\alpha]$, and $\alpha R_1 + (1 - \alpha)(p \cdot \eta)_L R_2$ by κ'. Note that $\kappa < E[R(\alpha)] < \gamma E[R_L]$ when $\pi = 0$ and $\gamma E[R_{L|H}] < E[R(\alpha)] < \gamma E[R_H]$ when $\pi = 1$. Such $E[R(\alpha)]$ are depicted as the chain lines in figure 5.5.

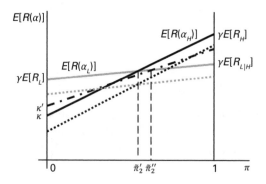

Figure 5.5
Investors' expected return for any $\alpha \in [0, 1]$. The gray line represents $E[R(\alpha_L)]$, the black line $E[R(\alpha_H)]$, the dotted gray line those $E[R(\alpha)]$ with $\alpha \in (\alpha_L, 1]$, the dotted black line those $E[R(\alpha)]$ with $\alpha \in [0, \alpha_H)$, and the chain line those $E[R(\alpha)]$ with $\alpha \in (\alpha_H, \alpha_L)$.

Suppose that the intersection between $E[R(\alpha)]$ and $E[R(\alpha_L)]$ is

$$\tilde{\pi}_2'' = \frac{\gamma E[R_L] - \kappa'}{\gamma E[R_\alpha] - \kappa' + \gamma E[R_L] - \gamma E[R_{L|H}]}.$$

To determine the value of $\tilde{\pi}_2''$, note that $\tilde{\pi}_2'' \gtrless \tilde{\pi}_2'$ only if

$$\frac{\gamma E[R_L] - \kappa'}{\gamma E[R_\alpha] - \kappa' + \gamma E[R_L] - \gamma E[R_{L|H}]} \gtrless \frac{\gamma E[R_L] - \kappa}{\gamma E[R_H] - \kappa + \gamma E[R_L] - \gamma E[R_{L|H}]}.$$

This is equivalent to

$$\gamma E[R_L](\gamma E[R_H] - \gamma E[R_\alpha]) + (\gamma E[R_\alpha] - \gamma E[R_L])\kappa + (\gamma E[R_L] - \gamma E[R_H])\kappa'$$

$$+ (\gamma E[R_L] - \gamma E[R_{L|H}])(\kappa - \kappa') \gtrless 0. \tag{5A.1}$$

Using the fact that $\gamma E[R_s] = \alpha_s R_1 + (1 - \alpha_s)(p \cdot \eta)_s R_2$ ($s \in \{H, L\}$), and replace α by the linear combination of α_H and α_L, $\alpha = \omega\alpha_H + (1 - \omega)\alpha_L$ with $\omega \in (0, 1)$, the sum of the first three terms in left-hand side of inequality (5A.1) turns out to be

$$\gamma E[R_L](\gamma E[R_H] - \gamma E[R_\alpha]) + (\gamma E[R_\alpha] - \gamma E[R_L])\kappa + (\gamma E[R_L] - \gamma E[R_H])\kappa' = 0.$$

Note that the last term in left-hand side of the inequality (5A.1) is

$$(\gamma E[R_L] - \gamma E[R_{L|H}])(\kappa - \kappa') > 0,$$

which implies that $\tilde{\pi}_2'' > \tilde{\pi}_2'$.

In figure 5.5 all the cases are combined to show the investors' expected return for any $\alpha \in [0, 1]$. The social planner's optimal solution is given by the frontier of the investors' expected return, which is a state-contingent strategy depending on the probability π. The planner invests the share α_H in liquid projects as long as $\tilde{\pi}_2' \le \pi \le 1$, and the share α_L in liquid projects as long as $0 \le \pi < \tilde{\pi}_2'$. ∎

Proof of Proposition 2
To show that the optimal allocation is indeed market equilibrium, one has to show that it is not profitable for any bank to deviate unilaterally. First, suppose that bank i deviates by setting $\alpha_i < \alpha$. By market-clearing condition, the interest rate r' is determined by

$$r'\{(1 - \gamma)[\alpha_i R_1 + (1 - \alpha_i)p\eta R_2] + (N - 1)(1 - \gamma)[\alpha R_1 + (1 - \alpha)p\eta R_2]\}$$

$$= \gamma(1 - \alpha_i)(1 - p)\eta R_2 + (N - 1)\gamma(1 - \alpha)(1 - p)\eta R_2.$$

Therefore $r' > 1$. For the nondeviators, the return for their depositors is

$$\gamma\left\{\alpha R_1 + (1-\alpha)\left[p\eta R_2 + \frac{(1-p)\eta R_2}{r'}\right]\right\}$$
$$< \gamma\left\{\alpha R_1 + (1-\alpha)\left[p\eta R_2 + \frac{(1-p)\eta R_2}{r}\right]\right\} = d_0 \text{ with } r = 1.$$

This means that they cannot meet the deposit contracts and the depositors will choose the deviator at $t = 0$. The deviator is able to offer at maximum

$$d_0' = \alpha_i R_1 + (1-\alpha_i)p\eta R_2 < \alpha R_1 + (1-\alpha)p\eta R_2 = d_0,$$

which implies that the deviator gets worse off;

Second, the bank i deviates by setting $\alpha_i > \alpha$. The rent seized by the deviator's early entrepreneurs exceeds the deviator's late return:

$$(1 - \gamma)[\alpha R_1 + (1 - \alpha)p\eta R_2] > \gamma(1 - \alpha_i)(1 - p)\eta R_2.$$

Therefore there will be excess aggregate liquidity supply at $t = 1$ and the interest rate for the liquidity market will remain to be 1. The deposit contract that the deviator is able to offer is at maximum

$$d_0' = \gamma[\alpha_i R_1 + (1-\alpha_i)\eta R_2] < \gamma[\alpha R_1 + (1-\alpha)\eta R_2] = d_0,$$

which means the deviator cannot get any depositor at $t = 0$. It is not a profitable deviation. ∎

Proof of Proposition 3

When banks coordinate on choosing α_H, they survive when $(p \cdot \eta)_H$ is revealed but experience bank runs when $(p \cdot \eta)_L$. The investors' expected return is $\pi\gamma E[R_H] + (1 - \pi)c$. When the banks coordinate on choosing α_L, they survive in both states, and the investors' expected return is $\gamma E[R_L]$. The investors' expected return is higher under α_H only if

$$\pi > \bar{\pi}_1 = \frac{\gamma E[R_L] - c}{\gamma E[R_L] - c}.$$

When $\pi > \bar{\pi}_1$, α_H is the symmetric pure strategy equilibrium because a bank cannot profit from unilateral deviation:

1. If the deviator chooses α_L, its investors' expected return is lower than that of its competitors.
2. If the deviator chooses $\alpha > \alpha_L$, its investors' expected return is $\gamma[\alpha R_1$

+ $(1 - \alpha)\eta R_2]$, which is decreasing in α. Therefore such strategy α will be outbid by α_L, and hence by α_H.

3. If the deviator chooses $\alpha_H < \alpha < \alpha_L$, it experiences a run when $(p \cdot \eta)_L$ is revealed (which is the same for banks with α_H) and when $(p \cdot \eta)_H$ is revealed its investors' expected return is $\gamma[\alpha R_1 + (1 - \alpha)\eta R_2]$ decreasing in α so that the expected return is lower than banks with α_H.

4. If the deviator chooses $\alpha < \alpha_H$, it will experience bank runs in both states, which makes such α an inferior strategy. ∎

Following similar approach, one can show that α_L is the symmetric pure strategy equilibrium for low π, that is, $0 \leq \pi \leq \bar{\pi}_1$.

Proof of Proposition 4

For $\pi \in (\pi'_{2T}, 1]$, equation (5.7) implies that the depositors' expected return is the same in both states; therefore bank runs are completely eliminated. Since $\kappa > c$, $\bar{\pi}'_{2T} < \bar{\pi}_2$, which means that $[0, \bar{\pi}'_{2T}]$ is a subset of $[0, \bar{\pi}_2]$ where α_L maximizes the depositors' expected return in the market equilibrium.

Equation (5.8) is exactly the same as $E[R(\alpha_H)]$ in figure 5.5, implying that the investors' expected real return is the same as the central planner's constrained efficient solution for $\pi \in (\pi'_{2T}, 1]$. ∎

Proof of Proposition 5

Equation (5.9) implies that the investors get the same nominal deposit returns in both states; therefore there will be no bank runs. The investors' expected real return

$$\pi\gamma\frac{E[R_H] + E[R_{H|L}]}{2} + (1 - \pi)\kappa,$$

which is linear in π, becomes κ when $\pi = 0$ and

$$\gamma\frac{E[R_H] + E[R_{H|L}]}{2}$$

when $\pi = 1$. Since

$$\gamma\frac{E[R_H] + E[R_{H|L}]}{2} < \gamma E[R_H],$$

such real return is below $E[R(\alpha_H)]$ (see the proof to proposition 1 above) for all $\pi \in (0, 1]$. ∎

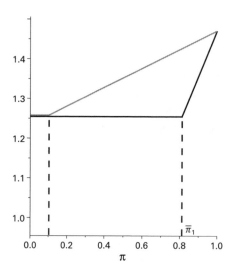

Figure 5.6
Investors' expected return (the y-axis, measured by the real output at $t = 1$) in equilibrium: Market economy (solid black line) versus economy with conditional liquidity injection and procyclical taxation (solid gray line). Parameter values: $(p \cdot \eta)_H = 0.36$, $(p \cdot \eta)_L = 0.24$, $\gamma = 0.6$, $R_1 = 1.5$, $R_2 = 4$, $c = 0.3$, $\bar{\eta} = 0.8$, $\eta_H = 0.9$, $\eta_L = 0.6$, $\bar{p} = 0.4$, $p_H = 0.45$, $p_L = 0.3$, $\sigma = 0.5$.

Appendix B: Results of Numerical Simulations

Figures 5.6, 5.7, and 5.8 present the numerical simulations for various regulatory schemes.

Notes

The author would like to thank Gerhard Illing, Lindsay Mollineaux, Gaëtan Nicodème, Ted Temzelides, and anonymous referees for very useful comments, as well as the participants of various seminars and conferences. The author acknowledges CESifo's support for the workshop "Taxation of the Financial Sector," at San Servolo, Italy, July 20–21, 2012. The views expressed in this chapter are those of the author and should not be attributed to Norges Bank.

1. Alternatively we may assume that all agents are risk averse; then due to uncertainty on the projects' return, the investors will ask for higher deposit rate d_0 and the banks will face higher refinancing cost r at $t = 1$. However, this does not change the nature of banking fragility in this model—that banks are subject to runs once a negative shock to early return gets revealed and the liquidity market gets frozen because of the insolvency uncertainty. In other words, the key results will not qualitatively change under risk aversion. So we will stay with risk neutrality throughout this chapter.

2. Since the entrepreneurs cannot commit to using their human capital on behalf of the banks, they will earn a rent from the return of the projects. That is, if the entrepreneurs

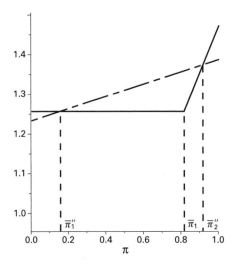

Figure 5.7
Investors' expected return (the y-axis, measured by the real output at $t = 1$) in equilibrium: Market economy (solid black line) versus economy with pure equity requirement (black chain line). Parameter values: $(p \cdot \eta)_H = 0.36$, $(p \cdot \eta)_L = 0.24$, $\gamma = 0.6$, $R_1 = 1.5$, $R_2 = 4$, $c = 0.3$, $\bar{\eta} = 0.8$, $\eta_H = 0.9$, $\eta_L = 0.6$, $\bar{p} = 0.4$, $p_H = 0.45$, $p_L = 0.3$, $\sigma = 0.5$. Note that the outcome under the equity requirement is superior to that of market economy for $\pi \in [\bar{\pi}_1'', \bar{\pi}_2'']$.

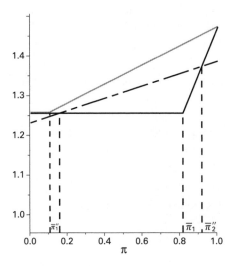

Figure 5.8
Investors' expected return (the y-axis, measured by the real output at $t = 1$) in equilibrium: Market economy (solid black line) versus economy with (1) conditional liquidity injection and procyclical taxation (solid gray line), (2) pure equity requirement (black chain line). Parameter values: $(p \cdot \eta)_H = 0.36$, $(p \cdot \eta)_L = 0.24$, $\gamma = 0.6$, $R_1 = 1.5$, $R_2 = 4$, $c = 0.3$, $\bar{\eta} = 0.8$, $\eta_H = 0.9$, $\eta_L = 0.6$, $\bar{p} = 0.4$, $p_H = 0.45$, $p_L = 0.3$, $\sigma = 0.5$.

walk away from the ongoing projects, the banks are only able to collect part of the return if they take over the projects because they don't have the human capital of running the projects. Therefore entrepreneurs can only commit to paying a fraction of their return. See Hart and Moore (1994) and Diamond and Rajan (2001) for more discussion.

3. Regulatory policies in this chapter are designed as entry requirements to avoid the time-inconsistency problem. Otherwise, banks would invest excessively on high-yield risky illiquid assets, and the central bank would be forced to bail them out ex post in the bad state to avoid socially costly bank runs, as discussed in Cao and Illing (2011).

4. For sufficiently low π the banks would coordinate on the safe strategy. There would be no bank runs and no need for liquidity injection, and hence no need for equity to cover the gap in bailout funds.

References

Allen, F., and D. Gale. 1998. Optimal financial crises. *Journal of Finance* 53: 1245–84.

Allen, F., E. Carletti, and D. Gale. 2014. Money, financial stability and efficiency. *Journal of Economic Theory* 149, 100-127.

Cao, J., and G. Illing. 2008. Liquidity shortages and monetary policy. Working paper series 2210. CESifo. Available at SSRN: http://ssrn.com/abstract=1090825.

Cao, J., and G. Illing. 2010. Regulation of systemic liquidity risk. *Financial Markets and Portfolio Management* 24: 31–48.

Cao, J., and G. Illing. 2011. Endogenous exposure to systemic liquidity risk. *International Journal of Central Banking* 7: 173–216.

Diamond, D. W., and R. G. Rajan. 2001. Liquidity risk, liquidity creation and financial fragility: A theory of banking. *Journal of Political Economy* 109: 287–327.

Diamond, D. W., and R. G. Rajan. 2005. Liquidity shortage and banking crises. *Journal of Finance* 60: 30–53.

Diamond, D. W., and R. G. Rajan. 2006. Money in the theory of banking. *American Economic Review* 60: 615–47.

Freixas, X., B. M. Parigi, and J.-C. Rochet. 2000. Systemic risk, interbank relations, and liquidity provision by the central bank. *Journal of Money, Credit and Banking* 32: 611–38.

Freixas, X., B. M. Parigi, and J.-C. Rochet. 2004. The lender of last resort: A twenty-first century approach. *Journal of the European Economic Association* 2: 1085–1115.

Gorton, G. 2009. The subprime panic. *European Financial Management* 15: 10–46.

Hart, O., and J. Moore. 1994. A theory of debt based on the inalienability of human capital. *Quarterly Journal of Economics* 109: 841–79.

6 The Political Economy of Containing Financial Systemic Risk

Donato Masciandaro and Francesco Passarelli

6.1 Introduction

The instability phenomenon represented by the financial system risk can be considered as a peculiar case of externality resulting from contagion effects (e.g., Acharya et al. 2007). The policy maker can enforce ad hoc regulation, directly limiting the possibility to trade toxic instruments or to build up high systemic risk portfolios (Claessens et al. 2010; Jeanne and Korinek 2010). Alternatively, taxation is an effective policy to curb systemic risk because it lowers the difference between private and social cost of systemic risk.

John Maynard Keynes (1936) can be considered the former proponent of systemic risk taxation, although he identified the security contracts as the main source of instability. James Tobin (1974, 1978) proposed to implement a tax on transactions in order to prevent the instability produced by exchange rate volatility (Eichengreen et al. 1995). A tax can be better calibrated in order to take into account the social benefit from a certain financial activity and social cost in terms of systemic risk (Goodhart 2010). The use of taxation to face financial instability, however, has been largely ignored in actual policy practice.[1] In the last decade several G20 countries imposed different forms of financial transaction tax, but with a general trend in reducing their application (Matheson 2011). Recent experiences confirm this trend. In the United States the 2010 Dodd–Frank Act focused on capital adequacy requirement instead of using taxation in order to contain the financial systemic risk. In the European Union the efforts to introduce a financial tax are so far frustrated by the impossibility to achieve consensus among all 27 member states, while the member states were able to define common guidelines on banking regulation to face systemic risks (Cortes and Vogel 2011). How is it that regulation is so frequent in financial markets, whereas taxation is quite rarely adopted to cope with systemic risk problems?

This chapter addresses this question and proposes a positive, political economy argument to explain the use of undertaxation instead of over regulation (Masciandaro and Passarelli 2012a–c; Alesina and Passarelli 2014). We treat systemic risk as a kind of "financial pollution." The default of a specific financial portfolio can induce negative and amplifying effects on the claims of other connected banking operations, producing a domino effect. In this way each portfolio owner can be characterized by a level of toxicity in terms of the system risk externalities produced. Policy could be used to curb systemic risk and affect individuals' portfolio choice, forcing costly changes. The way that sacrifices are distributed to reduce systemic risk, however, can be different based on the policy instrument used. We argue that regulation shifts most of the sacrifices to the large risk polluters. In contrast, a taxation system would force low-risk polluters to bear more of a share of the total sacrifice. All individuals, directly or indirectly, pollute by their portfolio choices. All such individuals would also support policy to reduce systemic risk pollution. Thus financial regulation or taxation are of general interest. Thus we use a majority rule voting model to study the policy decision.

We consider a population made of low-polluting portfolio owners. We show that the majority will choose a level of the policy (whether regulation or taxation) that is too harsh with respect to the socially efficient level of the policy. The reason is that the majority of low polluters choose the high level of policy in order to benefit from the externality reduction by large polluters, disregarding their sacrifices.

We also show that this same majority has an incentive to choose regulation instead of taxation in order to charge the majority a larger share of the total sacrifice. From a normative point of view, however, regulation is usually less efficient than taxation. In fact, if portfolio toxicity is easily detectable (i.e., the so-called measurement bias is sufficiently small) regulation has a too progressive effect, forcing big polluters to large and socially inefficient changes in their portfolios. Taxation can be better tailored to account for the actual amount of externality produced. Thus we could have cases where the social planner chooses taxation instead of regulation while the majority of low toxicity portfolio owners choose regulation. A double political distortion occurs when the majority chooses regulation but the socially efficient instrument is taxation; then that majority chooses a level of regulation that is too restrictive. This distortion is smaller when toxicity in a portfolio is not easily detectable. The reason is that in the presence of a relevant measurement bias, the effects of regulation become less progressive, and more similar to taxation. In this case a transaction tax has regressive effects. It is voted when the majority is composed of relatively large polluters, and the tax level is likely to be too low.

The existing literature suggests that the measurement bias induces policy makers to choose financial regulation in order to produce progressive effects in investors' risk-taking (Goodhart 2010; Claessens et al. 2010; Acharya et al. 2009). The measurement bias seems to be less likely when regulation is adopted. Regulation can be more detailed and easier to implement than taxes; moreover the use of soft information is easier in regulation than taxation. The use of the financial taxation has not followed so far a precise externality principle. Taxes in the financial industry have been used, for example, to implement a general taxation design (Lockwood 2010) to ensure that banks meet the direct financial costs of bailouts, or to facilitate the implementation of bankruptcy schemes (Claessens et al. 2010), and to facilitate macroeconomic policies in managing aggregate demand (Tobin 1978). Some reconfigurations of the tax system proposed on the financial sector have been based on taxes that differ from the systemic risk tax, such as ex post levies on banks and broadly based on funding or on profits, including taxes on banking bonuses. The political-economic perspective in this chapter offers a novel approach to the question of why regulation is systematically often preferred to taxation. Our argument is not alternative, but rather complementary, to those discussed in the current debate.

6.2   A Political Economy Model

Consider a continuum of agents, indexed by i, who make portfolio choices. Agents are heterogeneous in the systemic risk associated to their portfolios. Call x_i the risk of i's portfolio and let $F(x): [0, 1] \rightarrow [0, 1]$ be the distribution of x on the unit interval. In a sense x_i is a measure of the "pollution" produced by agent i, a measure of the "toxicity" of his portfolio ($x_i \in [0, 1]$). We say that i is a "low" type when x_i is low, and vice versa. A low (high) type is an investor who unilaterally chooses a small (large) amount of toxic instruments in his portfolio. $F(x)$ describes how systemic risk is produced across population. For example, a rightward slanted distribution means that there are relatively few big-risk producers, whereas the majority of investors prefer low amount of toxic instruments in their portfolios.

Call r_i the amount of systemic risk associated to i's *actual* portfolio choice, with $r_i \in R$. If an agent chooses a portfolio with an amount of systemic risk that is different from his type (i.e., $r_i \neq x_i$), then he bears a cost that we assume is increasing and quadratic in the distance between r_i and x_i:

$$c(r_i, x_i) = k \cdot (x_i - r_i)^2, \tag{6.1}$$

where $k \geq 1$ parametrizes cost convexity. For simplicity, we will assume in this chapter that $k = 1$.[2]

Let $\varepsilon(r_i)$ be the externality produced by i, where[3]

$$\varepsilon(r_i) = -r_i$$

The idea is that if an investor produces an amount of systemic risk that is lower than his type ($r_i < x_i$), he reduces the negative externality. Thus he generates a *social* benefit that spreads over the population, but he bears a *private* sacrifice given by (1). Let $G(r): [0, 1] \rightarrow [0, 1]$ be the risk distribution associated to investor's actual portfolio choices. Agent i's utility function is

$$U_i = -\int_0^1 r dG(r) - (x_i - r_i)^2. \tag{6.2}$$

Since any agent is infinitesimal in the population, the private benefit that he obtains from his own externality reduction is infinitesimal too. Hence nobody has an incentive to reduce unilaterally his portfolio's systemic risk below his type. Therefore $r_i = x_i$ for all i, and the equilibrium profile of portfolio choices is $G(r) = F(x)$. Ultimately, a free-riding problem emerges. Investors make portfolio choices with too much systemic risk production. This problem can be solved, at least partially, by regulation or taxation.

6.3   Regulating Systemic Risk

Financial regulation is any policy that directly limits the supply of instruments with given level of toxicity. Think, for example, of direct bans of instruments having with too much attached risk. Regulation can also significantly affect the design of certain financial contracts, with the aim of reducing potential toxicity. In synthesis, regulation has a strong impact on the availability of highly polluting instruments and a limited impact on the supply of instruments that do not pollute much. Agents who hold toxic instruments in their portfolios then have to make substantial changes. In other words, regulation forces them to make large adjustments from x_i to r_i. In contrast, agents who hold only low-pollution instruments will need to make only small adjustments.

Formally, we can capture this idea by assuming that regulation has a more than proportional impact on risk production. Let ρ be the policy parameter that measures the regulation level (with $0 \leq \rho \leq 1$). Once ρ is enforced an agent with x_i risk in his portfolio has to lower it down to r_i according to the following function:[4]

$$r_i \equiv r(x_i, \rho) = (1 - \rho \cdot x_i) \cdot x_i.$$

The decision regarding the level of the regulation parameter is made by majority voting, under open agenda procedure. The timing is the following: at time 1, given the distribution of types $F(x)$, individuals compute their preferences regarding ρ; at time 2, they select a Condorcet winner; at time 3, they choose their portfolios and their pollution levels, r_i.

The indirect utility function of an agent i is

$$U_i(\rho) = -\int_0^1 x - \rho \cdot x^2 dF(x) - \rho^2 x_i^4 .$$

Thanks to the convexity of the cost function, all U_i's are single peaked. Call ρ_i^* agent i's bliss point

$$\rho_i^* = \frac{\int_0^1 x^2 dF(x)}{2x_i^4} . \tag{6.3}$$

In the bliss point i equates the marginal private (and social) benefit of the regulation with the marginal private cost of complying with the regulation. Observe that bliss points are negatively related to types: heterogeneity in policy preferences is due to differences in types. Agents who pollute a lot want lenient regulation, and vice versa. The reason is that private benefits are the same for all, but for any level of regulation an agent with a very toxic portfolio bears a larger compliance cost. The median voter theorem applies: under the bare majority, the voting outcome is the bliss point of the median type, m:

$$\rho_m^* = \frac{\int_0^1 x^2 dF(x)}{2x_m^4} . \tag{6.4}$$

The social planner would prefer a possibly different regulation level. It would maximize total utility in the population, which in this case is $-\int_0^1 x - \rho \cdot x^2 dF(x) - \rho^2 \int_0^1 x^4 dF(x)$. Thus the socially optimal regulation is

$$\rho^* = \frac{\int_0^1 x^2 dF(x)}{2\int_0^1 x^4 dF(x)} . \tag{6.5}$$

The difference between ρ_m^* and ρ^* represents the political distortion due to voting. It is easy to see that the majority adopts a regulation level that is too restrictive when $x_m^4 < \int_0^1 x^4 dF(x)$. By Jensen's inequality, a median that is lower than the average always chooses too restrictive a regulation. Moreover overly restrictive regulations occur also when the median agent pollutes slightly above the average. The idea is that when people vote on financial regulation, a too restrictive level is rather easy to emerge. Even if the median voter pollutes more than the average polluter, he may prefer an overly restrictive regulation in order to force the minority to make substantial portfolio changes. This is because the progressive impact that regulation has on risk reductions forces top polluters to make large adjustments. Unlike the social planner, the median voter does not take into account the adjustment costs incurred by the minority. Most voters rather see regulation as a way to charge top polluters with the main burden of an externality reduction.[5]

6.4 Taxing Systemic Risk

A tax raises the private cost of systemic risk production. The problem with taxation as a policy instrument is that the risk and toxicity of a portfolio is usually not easy to measure. In this section we assume that systemic risk in any portfolio is measurable and can be taxed. There is no measurement bias. We will see what happens if this is not the case in the next section.

Let τ be the fixed tax rate of a proportional tax that is levied on risk production directly. Given τ, any investor optimizes his portfolio by choosing a risk level, such that the marginal cost of decreasing risk is equal to the tax (or the price) per unit of risk. Then $c'(x_i - r_i) = \tau$. The optimality condition is

$$r_i = x_i - \tau/2. \tag{6.6}$$

Given τ, all investors reduce the systemic risk in their portfolios by the same amount, $\tau/2$. Assume that tax proceeds are lump-sum redistributed out of a balanced government budget, and preferences are quasi-linear in money. Any individual is refunded an amount that is equal to the average tax burden, $\tau \cdot \bar{r}$. In this case indirect utility is

$$U_i(\tau) = -\int_0^1 r(x)dF(x) - \left(x_i - r_i(x_i)\right)^2 - \tau \cdot \left(r_i(x_i) - \bar{r}\right). \tag{6.7}$$

Observe that $U_i(\tau)$ is concave in τ. Thus maximizing (6.7) subject to (6.6) yields i's most preferred tax rate, τ_i^*:

$$\tau_i^* = 1 + 2(\bar{x} - x_i).$$

Higher types want lower tax rates. Since bliss points are inverse-monotone in types, the majority chooses the median's bliss point:

$$\tau_m^* = 1 + 2(\bar{x} - x_m). \tag{6.8}$$

What would the social planner choose? Social welfare is maximized if, for any agent, the after-tax private marginal cost equals the social marginal externality. Since the marginal externality is constant, the optimal tax must ensure that marginal costs are the same for all investors, provided that individual risk choice satisfies the optimality condition in (6.6). Then

$$\int_0^1 \varepsilon_r'(r)dF(x) = \int_0^1 c_r'(r, x)dF(x) \tag{6.9}$$

subject to $r = x - \tau/2$.

The solution yields the socially optimal tax rate, which in this case is one:

$$\tau^* = 1. \tag{6.10}$$

Observe that both sides of (6.9) are independent of i. This means that the *first best* is achieved with a linear tax. The government sells for one dollar any unit of systemic risk. Individual tax burden is proportional to the risk produced: $\tau^* \cdot r_i = r_i$. All investors bear the same marginal cost. Proceeds are lump sum redistributed. Per capita refund amounts to $\bar{r}$.[6] A linear tax is socially optimal when externalities are linear. If one removes this assumption, no big changes occur. The social planner can establish a nice nonlinear tax schedule such that the (variable) marginal externality produced by any agent equals the marginal tax rate. Finally, observe that the first best is achieved thanks to the government's ability to detect and tax actual systemic risk production.

Let us consider the political distortion. The tax chosen by the majority is higher (lower) than the social optimum occurs when the median type pollutes less (more) than the average:

$$\tau_m^* - \tau^* = 2(\bar{x} - x_m).$$ (6.11)

A low median has an incentive to fix too high a tax rate in order to make others pay a larger share of the pollution reduction cost. No political distortion occurs only if the median's risk production equals the average. This result on taxation of systemic risk parallels the well-known result in the public finance literature on income taxation (Meltzer and Richard 1981). The parallelism is due to the specific hypotheses on the linearity of ε and the functional form of c. Of course, the basic intuition that a low median tends to choose too high a tax rate, and vice versa, holds also with more general specifications of these two functions.

6.5 Taxing Transactions

The exact amount of toxicity of specific instruments and portfolios is not easy to measure. Taxes are often levied on distorted measures of the produced systemic risk. Consider the Tobin tax. The tax base is designated by the monetary amount of financial transactions made by an investor in a given time period. Investors who make the same amount of financial transactions pay the same amount of tax, independently of actual systemic risk produced. In this section we show that taxing a biased measure of the externality is not only socially inefficient but gives also rise to an additional form of "political" distortion.

In order to study a transaction tax, we need to specify how the tax is related to the risk produced. Suppose that systemic risk in a portfolio is proportional to two elements: (1) the number of toxic instruments included and (2) the portfolio size (i.e., the total monetary amount of the instruments in the portfolio). Assume that only the second element, not the first one, is proportional to the amount of transactions made by the investor in a specific time period. With a proportional transaction tax, an investor pays in proportion to the second factor only. Thus we can realistically assume that a tax that is proportional to financial transactions is de facto regressive with respect to the total externality produced. Denote with φ the transaction tax rate. Regressivity occurs if the amount of taxes per unit of systemic risk is decreasing in systemic risk. Assume that this amount is

$$\left(\varphi - \frac{1}{b} r_i \right),$$

where b parameterizes the measurement bias ($b \geq 0$). High values of b imply that transactions are a good proxy of risk and the measurement bias is limited, and vice versa. The amount of taxes paid by investor i on a portfolio that produces r_i units of risk is

$$\left(\varphi - \frac{1}{b} r_i \right) \cdot r_i .$$

Individual optimal risk choice equates the marginal cost from reducing risk with the marginal tax burden:

$$c'(x_i - r_i) = \varphi - \frac{2}{b} r_i .$$

Therefore the optimality condition for individual portfolio choice is the following:[7]

$$r_i = \frac{b}{b-1} \left(x_i - \frac{\varphi}{2} \right). \tag{6.12}$$

Individual indirect utility function is the same as (6.7). Taking (6.12) as a constraint in utility maximization, and solving for the transaction tax rate, we get the agents' bliss points, $\varphi_i^* = (b-1)/b + 2(\bar{x} - x_i) - 2/b(\bar{x} - 2x_i)$. Most preferred tax rates are decreasing in individual risk preferences. Despite regressivity, those who pollute more want lower transaction taxes, and vice versa. The median voter argument applies; thus the transaction tax chosen by the majority is the median's bliss point, φ_m^*:

$$\varphi_m^* = \frac{b-1}{b} + 2(\bar{x} - x_m) - \frac{2}{b}(\bar{x} - 2x_m).$$

The tax chosen by the social planner, call it φ°, would maximize social welfare, subject to individual optimization constraint in (6.12):

$$\varphi^\circ = \frac{b-1}{b} + \frac{2}{b} \bar{x} . \tag{6.13}$$

This tax rate is second best. Taxing transactions forces the government to adopt a tax that is de facto regressive in the externality, whereas the first best is a linear tax on risk with unit tax rate. Top-risk polluters do not pay enough taxes; their private marginal cost is too low, compared to marginal externalities, and vice versa, low-risk polluters pay too much. Compare (6.10) and (6.13). The difference between first and second best decreases in the measurement bias. If the ability to tax externalities through transactions is high (large b), then φ° is close to τ^*. The socially optimal transaction tax approaches the first best. Thus the measurement bias does not affect the social planner's choice. Finally, observe that the second term in the left-hand side of (6.13) is increasing in $\bar{x}$. This means that with a regressive tax, the optimal rate must be higher when the average type is larger because, on average, the marginal cost decreases.

The difference between φ_m^* and φ° in (6.13) gives an idea of what kind of political distortion occurs when transactions instead of risk are taxed:

$$\varphi_m^* - \varphi^\circ = -\frac{4}{b}(\bar{x} - x_m) + 2(\bar{x} - x_m). \tag{6.14}$$

This first term in the right-hand side of (6.14) is positively related to the relative position of the median voter. A high-risk median voter wants too high a tax rate. This might sound counterintuitive in a voting context, but consider that due to regressivity, the marginal cost of taxes decreases with type. Thus a high-risk median voter may be tempted by high taxes because he pays relatively less. This, of course, is not the end of the story, because the "usual" political distortion occurs. The latter is represented by the second term, which works in the opposite direction: a high-risk median voter wants a low tax rate because he pays a large amount of taxes.

Interestingly, the net political distortion depends on the measurement bias, namely the parameter b. Suppose that $x_m > \bar{x}$. If $b > 2$, then the tax is too low. This means that if the median voter's level of toxicity is lower than average, then the "usual" political distortion prevails. Moreover, when the measurement bias is sufficiently low, the temptation of a high-toxicity median voter to choose a high tax rate, exploiting regressivity, is dampened, and vice versa: with a low b (large measurement bias), a high-toxicity median voter chooses a very high tax because regressivity, rather than high position, has now a more decisive impact.

Let us compare the political distortion in the case of a transaction tax with that of a regulation. Consider the interesting case where transactions are not a good measure of risk, $b < 2$. Suppose that the median voter's transaction tax is lower than the average. In this case regulation would be too restrictive: a low-risk median voter who votes to charge a high-polluting portfolio the largest share of total cost would cause large social welfare losses. In contrast, when a tax is very low due to tax regressivity, a low-risk median voter must pay a large tax, so he would tend to prefer the low tax level.

Summing up, with both instruments majority voting yields a political distortion. However, the distortion is considerably different when voting concerns a tax rather than a regulation, especially if there is a problem of measurement bias. Regulation is likely to become more restrictive than restrictive taxes.

6.6 Voting on the Instrument

Let us now endogenize also the instrument choice. At the first stage, the majority chooses the instrument; at the second stage, they choose its level. Voters know that whatever the instrument, the level that will pass at the second stage is the one preferred by the median. Any voter compares his own utility in both cases, and chooses his most preferred instrument. At the first stage, the majority behaves as a Stackelberg leader: they select the instrument and let a possibly different majority choose the level at the second stage.[8]

Low-polluting investors prefer regulation to taxation because, given the level of the instrument chosen by the median voter at the second stage, with regulation they will have to make small adjustments, whereas with a tax they will have to pay a relatively large amount of money, due to regressivity. A top-polluting type has reversed preferences. If the number of investors who own low-toxicity portfolios is sufficiently large, then a majority on regulation will form. We do not need the median level of toxicity to be lower than average. If regulation has a strongly progressive impact, then even moderately high polluters will prefer regulation at the first stage—and vice versa, if regressivity of a transaction tax is strong (i.e., large measurement bias), more moderate polluters prefer the tax. A majority on a transaction tax in the presence of a measurement bias is more likely when the median voter produces a relatively large amount of systemic risk.

What is the best instrument from a normative viewpoint? Regulation is strongly progressive: the cost is concentrated on high-risk investors—and vice versa, a transaction tax yields regressive effects—thus the cost is concentrated on low polluters. With linear externalities, the socially optimal instrument is a tax if regressivity is not too high, that is, if the measurement bias is not too strong. Consider, however, that when the measurement bias causes strong regressivity or when the distribution is slanted toward top-polluting portfolios, a majority of voters would prefer regulation. In this case a double political distortion occurs. First, the majority select the wrong instrument: regulation instead of taxation. Second, the majority of low polluters choose too restrictive a regulation level.

6.7   Discussion and Extensions

The model we have presented in this chapter assumes that voters follow an open agenda procedure in which they are free to propose amendments to the status quo in pairwise voting and the winner becomes in turn the new status quo. This model typically yields a unique equilibrium when the threshold is the simple majority and the policy issue is one-dimensional, as in the case of voting on a tax rate. The political outcome is the bliss point of the median voter and the model predictions are quite clear. The same result is obtained assuming an electoral competition à la Hotelling.

Median voter models, however, often fail to produce an equilibrium when the issue has multiple dimensions. A realistic alternative is represented by models of probabilistic voting, in which the hypothesis is that citizens take into account not only candidates' platforms but also random factors that influence policy performance. These models predict that the policy is more favorable to the most mobile voters and that, if mobility is equal across groups, then the equilibrium outcome is also the social optimum. The advantage of probabilistic voting models is the ability to yield an equilibrium even when the policy issues are multidimensional. An extension of our model to this approach would be quite interesting. It would explain the circumstances in which policies involving the simultaneous use of regulation and taxation emerge as possible equilibria.[9] Our hunch is that if the most mobile group is represented by moderate types, who invest in average toxicity portfolios, then both candidates would have an incentive to propose a platform which includes a policy of strict regulation to contain the systemic risk produced by very high types and, at the same time, a moderate regressive taxation that forces to pay especially low types who invest in portfolios with limited toxicity. The advantage to the average types would be twofold: higher benefits for reducing the toxicity of high types, and high benefits from tax revenues on low types.

In this chapter we approach systemic risk contagion as a general interest policy. In a sense, everybody is interested in reducing systemic risk and, as a consequence of the policy, all investors must readjust their own portfolio or bear a cost. Another interesting extension of our political economy approach is represented by lobbying models, which apply to political situations in which groups have specific interests.[10] A well-known result in this literature is that lobbying can reduce uncertainty but not eliminate it entirely (Grossman and Helpman 1996). In fact banks do have information relevant to policy makers' decisions on the toxicity of specific financial instruments. Let us suppose a situation in which both low- and high-polluting financial intermediaries lobby the policy maker. Then some efficiency gains would be realized because the two interest groups would pull the policy maker in opposite directions.

In an electoral competition, lobbying is often aimed to influence a party's position and improve its chance of winning. Winning is a motive common to all interest groups. So all groups have a strong incentive to support the party that has more of a chance to win. This typically yields self-fulfilling prophecy or multiple equilibria. How can we apply this general result in our scenario? One possibility is the following. Suppose that citizens are more inclined to vote for taxation (i.e., a "party of taxes" exists and it has large popular support). Suppose also that there is one lobby of bankers whose first-best is regulation. In case of taxation, this lobby would prefer low instead of high taxes. Lobbying is more productive if contributions are given to the political party favoring taxes, in order to influence its position toward softer taxation. If, instead, the citizens' preferences for taxes are not strongly voiced, the bankers' lobby will support the party that proposes regulation.

6.8 Conclusion

In this chapter we presented a political economy argument to explain why taxation is infrequently used as a tool to curb financial systemic risk, a sort of Tobin tax paradox. We treated systemic risk contagion as an externality issue, and as a policy of general interest. When policies to reduce systemic risk are made by voting, the political aspects of the decision are quite relevant and may cause significant distortions. These distortions hinge on the distribution of costs for the externality reduction, which may be substantially different when taxation rather than regulation is adopted.

From a normative viewpoint, taxation is preferred by the social planner when actual risk production is easy to detect and be taxed, and when the systemic risks are evenly distributed across financial instruments and investors. Yet regulation is more effective when systemic risk grows at a fast rate with the portfolio size. Moreover, if risk production is private information, then a regulation that limits specific financial activities is more effective than a tax.

When it comes to voting, the outcome can be different. We showed that a majority of small portfolio owners who invest in low-risk instruments tend to choose regulation to the disadvantage of a minority of high-risk producers. For the same reason this kind of majority may prefer a regulation level that is too restrictive. A transaction tax is likely to have regressive effects. Small portfolio owners pay proportionally more than large, toxic portfolio owners. A tax voted by a majority of relatively large polluters is likely to be at a level that is too low to be a socially optimal level.

This political economy argument may help policy makers understand why taxes on risky financial instruments are usually rare and low whereas financial regulation is much more frequent. Of course, there might be other arguments that explain the policy making of financial systemic risk. For example, financial externalities have clearly international implications. In order to avoid tax evasion, a sufficient degree of coordination among countries is needed internationally. However, enforceability issues severely limit the set of available policy options in an international context. These are, of course, relevant extensions of our approach.

Notes

We thank Brian Coulter, Charles Goodarth, Carmine Guerriero, Gaëtan Nicodème, and Enrico Perotti for useful comments and suggestions. We gratefully acknowledge the financial support of Ceisfo for the 2012 Venice Summer Institute.

1. For comprehensive surveys, see IMF (2010), Caldari and Masini (2010), Honohan and Yoder (2010), Matheson (2011), and Hemmeigarn and Nicodeme (2012). For an analysis of the effects on instability, see Lendvai et al. (2012), Acharya et al. (2011), Morris and Shin (2008), and Perotti and Suarez (2011).

2. As it will become clear soon, $k = 1$ yields corner solutions for some subsets of the values of relevant parameters. This problem is mitigated with higher values of k, at the cost of additional algebra.

3. Linearity is a simplifying assumption. Below we discuss how things change if one removes it.

4. For computational convenience, our results are not contingent on this specification. One could obtain more realistic descriptions by assuming less "curved" relationships between x and r, for given ρ. But that would require more complex algebra.

5. It is easy to see that when the voting outcome is very restrictive regulation, the political distortion is larger when costs are more convex and when the median voter is in a relatively low-risk position with respect to the high-risk types.

6. Observe that thanks to quasi-linear preferences, this tax schedule solves the Mirrlees problem. This tax would be optimal even if types and individual costs were private information.

7. Without loss of generality, we assume that $b > 2/\varphi$. As a result of the transaction tax, each agent reduces the amount of risk in his portfolio.

8. With this kind of sequential voting choice there is no scope for strategic vote. For an exhaustive analysis of sequential bi-dimensional voting, see De Donder, Le Breton, and Peluso (2010).

9. For an excellent survey of the application of these models to progressive taxation and tax refoms, see Castanheira, Nicodème, and Profeta (2012).

10. For a classical survey, see Grossman and Helpman (2001).

References

Acharya, V., S. Bharath, and A. Srinivasan. 2007. Does industry-wide distress affect defaulted firms? Evidence from creditor recoveries. *Journal of Financial Economics* 85: 787–821.

Acharya, V., L. Pedersen, T. Philippon, and M. Richardson. 2009. Measuring systemic risk. Working paper. Stern School of Business, NYU.

Acharya, V., L. Pedersen, T. Philippon, and M. Richardson. 2011. Taxing systemic risk. In V. Acharya, T. Cooley, M. Richardson, and I. Walter, eds., *Regulating Wall Street*. Hoboken, NJ: Wiley, 121–41.

Alesina, A., and F. Passarelli. 2014. Regulation versus taxation. *Journal of Public Economics* 110: 147–56.

Caldari, K., and F. Masini. 2010. National autonomy, regional integration and global public goods: The debate on the Tobin tax. Working paper series 1. CREI.

Castanheira, M., G. Nicodème, and P. Profeta. 2012. On the political economics of tax reforms: Survey and empirical assessment. *International Tax and Public Finance, Springer* 19 (4): 598–624.

Claessens S., M. Keen, and C. Pazarbasioglu. 2010. The financial sector taxation. IMF.

Cortes B., and T. Vogel. 2011. A financial transaction tax for Europe? *Tax Review* 1: 16–29.

De Donder, P., M. Le Breton, and E. Peluso. 2010. Majority voting in multidimensional policy spaces: Kramer–Shepsle versus Stackelberg. Working paper 593. IDEI.

Eichengreen, B., J. Tobin, and C. Wyplosz. 1995. Two cases for sand in the wheels of international finance. *Economic Journal* 105 (428): 162–72.

Goodhart, C. A. H. 2010. The new emerging architectures of financial regulation. Mimeo.

Grossman, G. M., and E. Helpman. 1996. Electoral competition and special interest politics. *Review of Economic Studies* 63 (2): 265–86.

Grossman, G. M., and E. Helpman. 2001. *Special Interest Politics*. Cambridge: MIT Press.

Hemmelgarn, T., and G. Nicodème. 2012. Can tax policy help to prevent financial crisis? In J. Alworth and G. Arachi, eds., *Taxation and the Financial Crisis*. Oxford: Oxford University Press, 116–47.

Honohan, P., and S. Yoder. 2010. Financial transaction tax: Panacea, threat, or damp squib? Policy Research working paper 5230. World Bank.

IMF. 2010. A fair and substantial contribution by the financial sector. Final Report for the G-0. IMF, Washington, DC.

Jeanne, O., and A. Korinek. 2010. Managing credit booms and busts: A Pigouvian taxation approach. Working paper 12. Peterson Institute for International Economics.

Keynes, J. M. 1936. *General Theory of Employment, Interest Rates and Money*. New York: Harcourt Brace World.

Lendvai, J., R. Raciborski, and L. Vogel. 2012. Securities transaction taxes: Macroeconomic implications in a general equilibrium model. Mimeo. CESifo Conference on Taxation of the Financial Sector, Venice.

Lockwood, B. 2010. How should financial intermediation services be taxed? Working paper 3226. CESifo.

Meltzer, A. H., and S. F. Richard. 1981. A rational theory of the size of government. *Journal of Political Economy* 89 (5): 914–27.

Masciandaro, D., and F. Passarelli. 2012a. Financial systemic risk: Taxation or regulation? *Journal of Banking and Finance* 37 (2): 358–96.

Masciandaro, D., and F. Passarelli. 2012b. Regulation and taxation: Economics and politics. In J. Alworth and G. Arachi, eds., *Taxation and the Financial Crisis*. Oxford: Oxford University Press, 257–69.

Masciandaro, D., and F. Passarelli. 2012c. The financial transaction tax: A political economy view. *Inter Economics* 47 (2): 96–98.

Matheson, T. 2011. Taxing financial transactions: Issues and evidence. Working paper 11/54. IMF.

Morris, S., and H. S. Shin. 2008. Financial regulation in a systemic context. *Brooking Papers on Economic Activity* (fall): 229–74.

Perotti, E., and J. Suarez. 2011. A Pigouvian approach to liquidity regulation. *International Journal of Central Banking* 7 (4): 3–41.

Tobin, J. 1974. *The New Economics One Decade Older*. Princeton: Princeton University Press.

Tobin, J. 1978. A proposal for international monetary reform. *Eastern Economic Journal* 4 (3–4): 153–59.

II Design of Taxes and Regulation for the Financial Sector

7 How Should Financial Intermediation Services Be Taxed?

Ben Lockwood

7.1 Introduction

Financial intermediation services comprise a significant and growing part of the national economy. For example, financial intermediation services as conventionally defined in the national accounts include activities such as the taking of deposits and the granting of credit, financial leasing, investment in securities and properties by financial intermediaries, insurance and pension funding, and services ancillary to financial intermediation.[1] The EU KLEMS database shows that this sector comprised 6.5 percent of national output in the United Kingdom in 1997, increasing to 7.9 percent by 2007. The figures for the United States, using the same definition of financial intermediation services, are 7.3 percent in 1997, rising to 8.6 percent and for the eurozone, 4.8 percent, rising to 5.3 percent.[2] Even excluding insurance—which is beyond the scope of this chapter—financial intermediation is quantitatively important in OECD countries.[3]

The question of whether, and how, financial intermediation services should be taxed is a contentious one.[4] For example, within European Union countries, most financial services are currently exempt from VAT, and there is considerable debate about the possible benefits from bringing them into the VAT system (de la Feria and Lockwood 2010). Also the recent IMF proposals for a "bank tax" to cover the cost of government interventions in the banking system include a financial activities tax levied on bank profits and remuneration, one version of which—FAT1—would work very much like a VAT, levied using the addition method (IMF 2010).

In the policy literature on this topic, it is largely assumed that within a consumption tax system, such as a VAT, it is desirable to tax financial services supplied at the standard rate of VAT, and allow providers of intermediation services to claim back VAT that they pay on inputs (e.g., see Ebril et al. 2001). However, this policy prescription is at variance with a small academic literature on this topic (Grubert and Mackie 1999; Jack 1999; Boadway and Keen 2003), which suggests that while payment services should be taxed at the same rate as consumption, intermediation between borrower and lender should not be taxed at all. However, this literature is based on first-best arguments, namely finding the tax arrangement that does not drive a wedge between the household marginal rate of substitution and the marginal rate of transformation in production.

The objective of this chapter is to take a fresh look at this question, from a second best point of view, that is, when revenue has to be raised using distorting taxes. My focus is on the most important intermediation service—intermediation between borrowers and lenders.[5] I set up and solve the tax design problem in a dynamic general equilibrium model of the Chamley (1986) type, where the government chooses a tax on savings intermediation, as well as the usual taxes on consumption (or equivalently, wage income) and income from capital, to finance a public good, and where financial intermediaries, in the form of banks, are explicitly modeled. I assume that savings intermediation is not explicitly priced, but charged for via a spread between borrowing and lending rates set by competitive banks. This spread can be taxed, at a rate that may be different from the tax on consumption, and the tax system is parameterized so that some fraction θ of the tax paid by firms on financial intermediation inputs can be credited against the consumption tax charged by firms. In the case of a VAT, $\theta = 1$.

The main results are as follows. First, the tax paid by firms on financial intermediation inputs should be fully credited (i.e., the tax should be a VAT) when 100 percent taxation of profit is possible.[6] This is an example of the general Diamond—Mirrlees production efficiency result that intermediate inputs should not be taxed under these conditions. But at what rate should the VAT be set? Here I have two main findings. First, the optimal tax structure is generally indeterminate because the government has two instruments, a capital income tax and a financial intermediation tax, to control one target, the marginal rate of substitution between consumption in successive periods. My other finding is that from a tax administration point of view, the simplest optimal tax structure is where the capital income tax and the financial intermediation tax are equal.

In particular, when 100 percent taxation of pure profit is possible, the simplest optimal tax structure is to set both the tax rate on capital income and the tax rate on financial intermediation services equal to zero. In the more realistic case when there is an upper bound on the rate of profit tax of less than 100 percent, I show that a simple optimal tax structure is again to set the two taxes at the same rate. The sign of this common rate then depends on the properties of the production function; it can be positive or negative. Moreover this common rate is generally different from the optimal tax rate on consumption.

These results are quite different from the existing literature (see section 7.1.2), which generally finds that financial intermediation services should be untaxed. However, these are first-best models in which there is (implicitly) no revenue requirement. There the optimality of leaving financial intermediation services untaxed is derived just from the condition that the marginal rate of substitution in consumption is equal to the marginal rate of transformation. My results also differ from Auerbach and Gordon (2002), who find, using a rather different argument, that financial intermediation services should be taxed at the same rate as consumption.

The remainder of the chapter is organized as follows. Section 7.1.1 discusses some basic facts about the taxation of financial intermediation, and section 7.1.2 discusses related literature. Section 7.2 outlines the model and section 7.3 presents the main results. Section 7.4 considers the case without 100 percent profit taxation, section 7.5 considers other extensions, and section 7.6 concludes.

7.1.1 Size and Tax Treatment of Financial Intermediation Services

The figures quoted at the beginning of the chapter measure the overall size of the financial intermediation sector. To get an idea of the value of financial intermediation associated with the taking of deposits and the grant of credit only, we can look at FISIM.[7] FISIM is computed from the transactions between the banking sector and other sectors of the economy (e.g., nonfinancial firms and households). For each of these sectors, the loans from, and deposits with, the banking sector are measured and the margins made by the banking sector on these activities are calculated. Specifically, the margin per currency unit deposited is a reference rate minus the average rate of interest on deposits, and the margin per currency unit lent is the average rate of interest on loans minus a reference rate (Akritidis 2007). So FISIM can be calculated by sector, and also on loans and deposits separately. As my focus

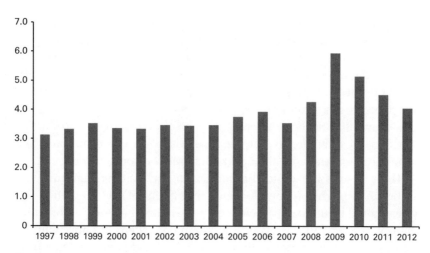

Figure 7.1
FISIM consumed by households as a percentage of household consumption expenditure, United Kingdom. The chart shows FISIM on loans (series IV8X) and deposits (series IV8W) consumed by households and nonprofit institutions serving households as a percentage of aggregate consumption (series RPQM). Source: Office of National Statistics, United Kingdom.

is primarily on taxation of the household sector, I show consumption of FISIM by households and nonprofit institutions serving households for the United Kingdom over the period 1997 to 2012.

This shows that consumption of FISIM by households is between 3 and 4 percent of total household expenditure in the United Kingdom over this period, not large but not a negligible fraction either. Also the financial crisis has had a positive impact on this figure, as banks have increased their spreads on loans to repair their balance sheets. So, overall, it can be seen that financial intermediation services are a significant and growing part of the economy in the United Kingdom. The picture is similar for other OECD countries.

As regards the taxation of financial intermediation services, in my theoretical analysis below, I assume that intermediation services can be taxed; specifically, that banks can charge taxes to households and firms separately on their consumption of intermediation services. It is recognized that in practice there are technical difficulties when those services are not explicitly priced (so-called margin-based services), because it is not straightforward to divide the value added between borrower and lender. In particular, this raises a problem for the use of a VAT via the usual invoice-credit method (Ebril et al. 2001). As a result the status quo in most countries is that a wide range of financial intermediation services are not taxed. For example, in the European Union, many such services are exempt as a result of the sixth VAT Directive.[8]

However, conceptually, the problems can be solved in several different ways. One administratively straightforward system would be to zero-rate sales to VAT-registered entities and tax sales to nonregistered entities, such as households, on an aggregate basis (Huizinga 2002). Alternatively, Poddar and English (1997) have proposed a cash flow VAT with tax calculation accounts; this is administratively more complex, but the increasing sophistication of banks' IT systems means that this solution is becoming practical. A recent study by the European Commission calculates that EU-27 tax revenue might rise by around 15 billion euro if intermediation services were brought into the VAT system, and taxed at the standard rate (European Commission 2011).

7.1.2 Related Literature

There is a small literature directly addressing the optimal taxation of borrower—lender intermediation and payment services, including work by Grubert and Mackie (1999), Jack (1999), and Boadway and Keen (2003). Using a simple two-period consumption—savings model, these papers agree on a policy prescription.[9] Given a consumption tax that is uniform over time, payment services should be taxed at this uniform rate, but savings intermediation should be left untaxed. The argument used to establish this is simple; in a two-period consumption—savings model with the same, exogenously fixed, tax on consumption in both periods, this arrangement leaves the marginal rate of substitution between current and future consumption undistorted, that is, equal to the marginal rate of transformation in production. Using a different approach, Auerbach and Gordon (2002) do not make a sharp distinction between payment services and savings intermediation, and argue that both activities should be taxed at the same rate as consumption.[10] More precisely, they show that a wage tax is equivalent to a uniform tax on consumption and intermediation services.

However, one could make three criticisms of this literature. First, taxes are taken as given. In particular, consumption taxes are assumed equal in both periods, and capital income taxes are set to zero. Combined with the (implicit) assumption of fixed labor supply in those models,[11] this amounts to a nondistortionary tax on labor income. In this setting, where lump-sum taxation is implicitly available, it is of course, optimal for the marginal rate of substitution in consumption to be equal to the marginal rate of transformation in production. It is then not very surprising that the tax on borrower—lender intermediation should be zero. Second, as taxes are not distortionary, there is no second-best tax design problem, so the question of trading off distortions generated by a tax on financial services against other distortionary taxes does not arise. Third, the production side of the economy is not explicitly modeled, so questions of distortions in input prices caused by taxes on financial services cannot be addressed.

Second, there is also a less closely related literature on the use of taxation to control "bad banks." The idea here is that while banks may engage in socially undesirable activities on both lending and deposit-taking margins, these should be corrected by Pigouvian taxes (or regulations) that apply directly to these decision margins. There has recently been surge of literature on such Pigouvian taxes (e.g., Acharya et al. 2010; Bianchi and Mendoza 2010; Keen 2010; Perrotti and Suarez 2011; Coulter, Mayer, and Vickers 2012). In my model, banks are merely producers that price intermediation services at marginal cost, so there is no role for Pigouvian taxes.

7.2   The Model

7.2.1   Households
The model is a version of the model of Atkeson, Chari, and Kehoe (1999), with savings intermediation by banks added to the basic structure. There is a single infinitely lived household with preferences over levels of a single consumption-capital good, leisure, and a public good in each period $t = 0, \ldots \infty$ of the form

$$\sum_{t=0}^{\infty} \beta^t \left(u\left(c_t, l_t\right) + v\left(g_t\right)\right), \tag{7.1}$$

where c_t is the level of consumption in period t, $l_t \in [0, 1]$ is the supply of labor hours, and g_t is public good provision. Utility $u(c, l)$ is strictly increasing in c, strictly decreasing in l, and strictly concave, and $v(g)$ is strictly increasing and strictly concave in g. Finally, $0 < \beta < 1$ is a discount factor.

In any period t, the household is assumed to pay an ad valorem tax τ_t^c on c_t, and also pays proportional taxes on labor and capital income. Using the well-known fact that a consumption tax is equivalent to a wage tax, we will assume, without loss of generality, that the wage tax is zero. Finally, for the moment, we suppose that the household has no profit income in any period: firms generate pure profits (for reasons explained in section 7.3.2 below), but these are assumed to be taxed at 100 percent. So, in any period, the budget constraint is

$$c_t\left(1+\tau_t^c\right)+k_{t+1} = w_tl_t +(1+\rho_t)k_t,$$

where ρ_t is the after-tax return to the household on savings, and w_t is the wage, and k_{t+1} is savings. Finally, $\rho_t =\left(1-\tau_t^r\right)r_t^h$, where r_t^h is the before-tax return on savings for the household, determined below, and τ_t^r is the capital income tax.

So, following Atkeson, Chari, and Kehoe (1999), the present value budget constraint of the household can be obtained by aggregating over per period budget constraints:

$$\sum_{t=0}^{\infty} p_t\left(c_t\left(1+\tau_t^c\right)+k_{t+1}\right) = \sum_{t=0}^{\infty} p_t\left(w_tl_t +(1+\rho_t)k_t\right), \tag{7.2}$$

where p_t is the price of output in period t. We normalize by setting p_0 = 1 and assume for convenience that $k_0 = 0$ i.e., initial capital is zero.[12] The first-order conditions for a maximum of (7.1) subject to (7.2) with respect to c_t, l_t, and k_{t+1}, respectively, are

$$\beta^t u_{ct} = \lambda p_t\left(1+\tau_t^c\right), \tag{7.3}$$

$$-\beta^t u_{lt} = \lambda p_t w_t, \tag{7.4}$$

$$p_t = (1 + \rho_{t+1})p_{t+1}, \tag{7.5}$$

where λ is the multiplier on (7.2), and we use (here and below) the notation that for any function $f(x_t, y_t)$, the partial derivative of f with respect to x_t is f_{xt}, the cross-derivative is f_{xyt}, and so on.

7.2.2 Banks
For simplicity, we assume 100 percent depreciation of the capital good. So in the standard version of this model, without financial intermediation, the household provides k_t units of the consumption-capital good to the firms in period $t - 1$, and firms (in aggregate) repay the k_t units of consumption-capital good to the household in period t, plus interest. In my version of the model, the k_t units of the consumption-capital good are deposited with a bank at $t - 1$, which can then provide this stock k_t to firms as an input to production. The firms repay k_t to the bank at t, plus interest, and finally, the bank repays k_t to the households, plus interest.

The cost of intermediating one unit of savings between the household and firm i is $\tilde{s}^i$ units of labor. We take $\tilde{s}^i$ as fixed, but possibly varying between firms. Variation across firms is realistic; lending is a complex process involving initial assessment of the borrower via such as credit scoring, structuring and pricing the loan, and monitoring compliance with loan covenants (Gup and Kolari 2005, ch. 9). The implications of endogenizing $\tilde{s}^i$ are discussed in section 7.5.2 below.

We can also suppose that the total intermediation cost $\tilde{s}^i$ can be divided by the bank between the cost of services provided to the household, s^h (e.g., safekeeping of deposits, liquidity) and cost of services provided to firm i (e.g., monitoring), s^i, that is, $\tilde{s}^i = s^h + s^i$. This is a realistic assumption because, in practice, any scheme (e.g., the tax calculation accounts of Poddar and English 1997) that implements a VAT on margin-based financial intermediation services must split the value added between borrower and lender. We will assume that banks can borrow and lend at a "pure" rate of interest r_t that will eventually be determined in equilibrium in the capital market. Finally, we will assume that banks are perfectly competitive and, combined with the constant returns intermediation technology, this implies that they make zero profit in equilibrium.

Last we will assume that a tax on intermediation services, or spread tax, is in operation at rate τ_t^s, which can be different from the rate τ_t^c on final consumption. Banks must break even on each of the two activities of providing services to households, and to firms separately; otherwise, a competitor bank could profitably undercut them. So, in equilibrium, the costs of intermediation $w_t s^i$, $w_t s^h$ plus the tax paid, are equal to the spreads $r_t^i - r_t$, $r_t - r_t^h$, respectively, where r_t^i is the rate at which firm i borrows and r_t^h is the rate of return on savings for the household; that is,

$$r_t^i - r_t = w_t s^i \left(1 + \tau_t^s\right), \quad r_t - r_t^h = w_t s^h \left(1 + \tau_t^s\right). \tag{7.6}$$

This is intuitive: the spread on both borrowing and lending is equal to the real resource cost plus the tax.

7.2.3 Firms

There are firms $i = 1, \ldots n$ that produce the homogeneous consumption good in each period.[13] Firm i produces output from labor and capital via the strictly concave production function $F^i\left(k_t^i, l_t^i\right)$, where k_t^i, l_t^i are capital and labor inputs.[14] Because firms may differ in intermediation costs s^i, firms face differences in the cost of capital, meaning firm i must repay $1 + r_t^i$ per unit of capital borrowed from the bank. So the profit of firm i is

$$F^i(k_t^i, l_t^i) - l_t^i w_t - (1 + r_t^i)k_i + \theta^i \tau_t^s w_t s^i k_i,$$

where $\tau_t^s w_t s^i k_i$ is the total tax paid on intermediation services by the firm, and θ^i is the fraction of the tax paid on intermediation services that the firm can claim against the tax paid on output. Of course, in the usual VAT system, $\theta^i = 1$. So substituting r_t^i from (7.6), we can write profit as

$$F^i(k_t^i, l_t^i) - l_t^i w_t - (1 + r_t + w_t s^i(1 + (1 - \theta^i)\tau_t^s))k_i. \tag{7.7}$$

Maximizing (7.7) with respect to k_t^i, l_t^i implies the first-order conditions:

$$F_l^i(k_t^i, l_t^i) = w_t, \quad F_k^i(k_t^i, l_t^i) = 1 + \tilde{r}_t^i, \tag{7.8}$$

where $\tilde{r}_t^i = r_t + w_t s^i(1 + (1 - \theta^i)\tau_t^s)$ is the cost of capital for firm i. Finally, the capital and labor market-clearing conditions are

$$\sum_{i=1}^n k_t^i = k_t, \quad \sum_{i=1}^n l_t^i + k_t s^h + \sum_{i=1}^n k_t^i s^i = l_t. \tag{7.9}$$

Conditions (7.8) and (7.9) jointly determine w_t and r_t, given household savings and labor supply decisions.

7.2.4 Discussion

The preceding model provides a general framework that encompasses some aspects of the specific models of taxation of financial services that have been developed so far (Auerbach and Gordon 2002; Boadway and Keen 2003; Jack 1999; Grubert and Mackie 1999). Specifically, ignoring payment services, which are not dealt with in this chapter, Boadway and Keen (2003), Jack (1999), and Grubert and Mackie (1999) are two-period versions of the model above,[15] with fixed taxes and (implicitly) fixed labor supply. Auerbach and Gordon (2002) is a finite-horizon version of the model with the additional feature [16] that there are n consumption goods in each period. Payment services are dealt with in a companion paper, Lockwood and Yerushalmi (2013).

7.3 Tax Design

We take a primal approach to the tax design problem. In this approach, an optimal policy for the government is a choice, in each period t, of all the primal variables in the model to maximize utility (7.1) subject to the capital and labor market-clearing conditions (7.9), and the aggregate resource and implementability constraints. The primal variables are consumption, labor supply, capital, the public good, and firm inputs. I am thus assuming, following Chamley (1986), that the government can pre-commit to a policy at $t = 0$.

The aggregate resource constraint says that total production must equal to the sum of the uses to which that production is put:

$$c_t + k_{t+1} + g_t = \sum_{i=1}^{n} F^i(k_t^i, l_t^i), \qquad t = 0, 1, \dots . \tag{7.10}$$

The implementability constraint ensures that the government's choices also solve the household optimization problem. I obtain this constraint by substituting the household's first-order conditions (7.3) to (7.5) into the household budget constraint (7.2). After some rearrangement, this gives the condition:

$$\sum_{t=0}^{\infty} \beta^t (u_{ct} c_t + u_{lt} l_t) = 0. \tag{7.11}$$

As is standard in the primal approach to tax design, we can incorporate the implementability constraint (7.11) into the government's maximand by writing

$$W_t = u(c_t, l_t) + v(g_t) + \mu(u_{ct} c_t + u_{lt} l_t), \tag{7.12}$$

where μ is the Lagrange multiplier on (7.11). We now assume that $u_{cl} \leq 0$, that is, that consumption and leisure are complements. Then it is possible to show that $\mu \geq 0$ at the solution to this tax design problem (see the appendix). If $\mu = 0$, the revenue from profit taxation is sufficient to fund the public good. We will rule out this uninteresting case, and so will assume that $\mu > 0$ at the optimum in what follows.

The government's choice of primal variables must maximize $\sum_{t=0}^{\infty} \beta^t W_t$ subject to (7.10) and (7.9). The first-order conditions with respect to c_t, l_t, k_t, g_t, k_{it}, and l_{it} are, respectively,

$$\beta^t W_{ct} = \zeta_t, \tag{7.13}$$

$$-\beta^t W_{lt} = \zeta_t^l, \tag{7.14}$$

$$\zeta_t^k = \zeta_{t-1} + \zeta_t^l s^h, \tag{7.15}$$

$$\beta^t v_{gt} = \zeta_t, \tag{7.16}$$

$$\zeta_t F_{kt}^i = \zeta_t^k + \zeta_t^l s^i, \qquad i = 1, ..., n, \tag{7.17}$$

$$\zeta_t F_{lt}^i = \zeta_t^l, \qquad i = 1, ..., n, \tag{7.18}$$

where ζ_t, ζ_t^k, and ζ_t^l are the multipliers on the resource constraint and the capital and labor market-clearing conditions at time t, respectively.

Moreover from (7.12),

$$W_{lt} = u_{lt}(1 + \mu(1 + H_{lt})), \quad H_{lt} = \frac{u_{lct} c_t + u_{lll} l_t}{u_{lt}}, \tag{7.19}$$

and

$$W_{ct} = u_{ct}(1 + \mu(1 + H_{ct})), \quad H_{ct} = \frac{u_{cct} c_t + u_{clt} l_t}{u_{ct}}. \tag{7.20}$$

Here H_{lt} and H_{ct} are standard formulas found, for example, in the primal approach to the static tax design problem (Atkinson and Stiglitz 1980). In particular, $-H_{ct}, H_{lt} > 0$ under our assumption $u_{clt} \le 0$.

We begin by characterizing the rate of tax on the consumption good via the following result, which is proved in the appendix:

Proposition 1 *At any date $t = 0, 1, 2, \ldots$, the optimal tax on final consumption in ad valorem form is*

$$\frac{\tau_t^c}{1 + \tau_t^c} = \left(\frac{v_{gt} - \alpha_t}{v_{gt}} \right) \left(\frac{H_{lt} - H_{ct}}{1 + H_{lt}} \right), \qquad \alpha_t = -\frac{u_{lt}}{w_t}. \tag{7.21}$$

Note that (7.21) is a formula for an optimal consumption tax that also appears in the static optimal tax problem, when the primal approach is used (Atkinson and Stiglitz 1980, p. 377). In particular, v_{gt} is the marginal benefit of \$1 to the government, and α_t is a measure of the marginal utility of \$1 to the household, so $(v_{gt} - \alpha_t)/v_{gt}$ is a measure of the social gain from additional taxation at the margin. So, the higher is this social gain, the higher is τ_t^c. Moreover the higher the degree of complementarity between consumption and leisure (i.e., the absolute value of u_{clt}), the higher are $-H_{ct}, H_{lt}$ and the higher is τ_t^c.

Now we turn to consider the question of whether tax paid on financial intermediation should be deductible by firms i.e., the choice of θ^i. From (7.17) and (7.18), we see that the marginal rate of substitution between labor and capital is

$$\frac{F_{kt}^i}{F_{lt}^i} = \frac{\zeta_t^k}{\zeta_t^l} + s^i, \qquad i = 1, ..., n, \tag{7.22}$$

which implies that

$$\frac{F_{kt}^i}{F_{lt}^i} - \frac{F_{kt}^j}{F_{lt}^j} = s^i - s^j . \tag{7.23}$$

However, from the first-order conditions for the firm, (7.8), we see that

$$\frac{F_{kt}^i}{F_{lt}^i} = \frac{1+r_t}{w_t} + s^i\left(1+\left(1-\theta^i\right)\tau_t^s\right), \tag{7.24}$$

which implies that

$$\frac{F_{kt}^i}{F_{lt}^i} - \frac{F_{kt}^j}{F_{lt}^j} = \left(s^i - s^j\right)\left(1+\left(1-\theta^i\right)\tau_t^s\right). \tag{7.25}$$

If $s^i \neq s^j$, and $\tau_t^s \neq 0$, equations (7.23) and (7.25) can only hold simultaneously if $\theta^i = 1$. So we have shown:

Proposition 2 *If there is heterogeneity in intermediation costs, ($s^i \neq s^j$, some i, j) and the rate of tax on financial services $\tau_t^s \neq 0$, then any date t, efficiency requires $\theta^i = 1$, that is, full deductibility of τ_t^s by firms.*

The intuition for this result is clear. Equation (7.23) says that the marginal product of capital net of true intermediation costs should be equal across firms, which of course is just the condition for capital to be allocated efficiently across firms. But condition (7.23) is generally not consistent with a nonzero τ_t^s when firms are heterogeneous. This is just an instance of the Diamond—Mirrlees production efficiency theorem. A tax on the bank margin is an intermediate tax on the allocation of capital, and given our assumptions (a full set of tax instruments, including 100 percent taxation of pure profits), this tax should be set to zero. Note also that when there is only one firm, this argument has no bite, and thus θ^i is left indeterminate.

We now turn to the question of how the taxes on capital income, τ_t^r and on intermediation services, τ_t^s, should be set. It can be shown, by straightforward manipulation of the first-order conditions to the optimal tax problem and the household and firm problems, that:

Proposition 3 *At all dates t = 1, 2, . . ., τ_t^r, τ_t^s solve*

$$A_t\left(1+r_t-w_ts^h\right) = 1+\left(1-\tau_t^r\right)\left(r_t-w_ts^h\left(1+\tau_t^s\right)\right), \tag{7.26}$$

where $A_t = \dfrac{1+\mu(1+H_{ct})}{1+\mu(1+H_{c,t-1})}\dfrac{1+\tau_t^c}{1+\tau_{t-1}^c}$.

The proof of this is in the appendix. Clearly, τ_t^r, τ_t^s are not uniquely determined from this single condition. Ultimately this is because the planner has two instruments, τ_t^r, τ_t^s for controlling the marginal rate of substitution between consumption at t and $t + 1$. However, we can use the following criterion to choose between solutions. Say that a solution τ_t^r, τ_t^s to (7.26) is *simple* if it solves (7.26) independently of the precise values of the economic data H_{ct}, w_t, r_t, and s^h. As the tax authority is unlikely to know these values, or at least to set taxes conditional on them, a simple solution is administratively convenient.

Now consider the steady state. Then $A_t = 1$, and therefore (7.26) becomes

$$(1 + r - ws^h) = 1 + (1 - \tau^r)(r - ws^h(1 + \tau^s)). \tag{7.27}$$

By inspection, the only simple solution to (7.27) is $\tau^r = \tau^s = 0$. The result that the interest income tax is zero is, of course, the classic result of Chamley (1986) and Judd (1985); our new result is that the rate of tax on financial services should be zero. So we have proved:

Proposition 4 *At the steady state, the only simple optimal tax system is where the tax on interest income, τ^r, and the tax on financial intermediation services, τ^s are both zero.*

Two comments can be made here. First, away from the steady state, $\tau_t^r = \tau_t^s = 0$ is generally not optimal. So proposition 4—along with proposition 6 below—makes precise the conditions under which the result of the existing literature that savings intermediation should not be taxed generalizes to a second-best environment; zero taxation of intermediation services requires (i) unrestricted taxation of profit and (ii) a steady state. Second, the celebrated result of Chamley (1986) and Judd (1985) that in the steady state, the tax on capital income is zero does not hold precisely in our model, as the planner has an additional tax instrument, τ_t^s. However, zero taxation of capital emerges if we also impose administrative simplicity.

7.4   Less Than Full Taxation of Pure Profit

Recall that we have to assume that firms have decreasing returns because they face different costs of capital. Therefore they generate pure profit. So far, we have made the strong assumption that 100 percent taxation of this profit is possible for the government. However, it is well known that this is a key assumption behind the classical Diamond–Mirrlees result that inputs are not taxed at the second-best optimum. Here we investigate to what extent our results generalize to the more realistic case where pure profit cannot be taxed at 100 percent. Ideally, we should model this via some kind of incentive constraint for managers or entrepreneurs that constrains a profit tax. However, that is beyond the scope of this chapter, and following a large literature in tax design, we just assume that the profit tax is fixed at some $\bar{\tau} < 1$.

The main change to the tax design problem is that now after-tax profit appears in the budget constraint of the household. This after-tax profit can be written as $(1 - \bar{\tau})\pi_t$, where π_t is aggregate before-tax profit

$$\pi_t = \sum_{i=1}^{n} \left(F^i - F_{lt}^i l_{kt}^i - F_{kt}^i k_t^i \right), \tag{7.28}$$

and so income in period t is now $w_t l_t + (1 + \rho_t)k_t + (1 - \bar{\tau})\pi_t$. It can then be checked that π_t also appears in the implementability constraint as follows:

$$\sum_{t=0}^{\infty} \beta^t \left(u_{ct}c_t + u_{lt}\left(l_t + (1 - \bar{\tau})\pi_t / w_t \right) \right) = 0. \tag{7.29}$$

From (7.28), and the fact that $w_t = F_{lt}^i$, we see that π_t / w_t only depends on l_t^i, k_t^i, $i = 1, \ldots, n$. So, the only first-order conditions to the tax design problem that change are (7.18) and (7.19). They change to

$$\zeta_t F_{kt}^i + (1 - \bar{\tau})\beta^t \mu u_{lt} \frac{\partial (\pi_t / w_t)}{\partial k_t^i} = \zeta_t^k + \zeta_t^l s^i, \quad i = 1, \ldots, n, \tag{7.30}$$

$$\zeta_t F_{lt}^i + (1 - \bar{\tau})\beta^t \mu u_{lt} \frac{\partial (\pi_t / w_t)}{\partial l_t^i} = \zeta_t^l, \quad i = 1, \ldots, n. \tag{7.31}$$

The first question is whether aggregate production efficiency holds, that is, whether $\theta^i = 1$. From (7.30) and (7.31) we can see that it is optimal to have (7.22) holding at the tax optimum *only* if the partial derivatives

$$\frac{\partial (\pi_t / w_t)}{\partial k_t^i}, \quad \frac{\partial (\pi_t / w_t)}{\partial l_t^i},$$

can be written $\kappa_i F_{kt}^i$, $\kappa_i F_{lt}^i$, respectively, for some common constant κ_i. It is easy to check that they cannot be written in this way.[17] All this implies in turn that we can no longer show that τ_i^s should be fully deductible, meaning $\theta^i = 1$. This is not surprising: generally, without

100 percent taxation of profit, and heterogeneous firms, it is well known that aggregate production efficiency does not hold at the solution to the tax design problem.

But with one firm, the question of the efficient allocation of capital across firms does not arise. So, to look at the key question of the optimal rate for τ_i^s, we assume just one firm; this way we can abstract from the question of whether τ_i^s can be deductible from firm costs. In fact, without loss of generality, we can assume full deductibility so that the cost of capital for the single firm is $\tilde{r}_t = r_t + w_t s^f$, where we replace s^i by s^f to emphasize that there is now a single firm. In this case we can prove the following analog of proposition 3. The proof follows the proof of proposition 3 closely, except that conditions (7.30) and (7.31) replace (7.18) and (7.19), and is thus omitted.[18]

Proposition 5 At all dates $t = 1, 2 \ldots$, τ_t^r, τ_t^s solve

$$A_t\left(1 + r_t - w_t s^h + B_t\right) = 1 + \left(1 - \tau_t^r\right)\left(r_t - w_t s^h\left(1 + \tau_t^s\right)\right), \tag{7.32}$$

where A_t is defined in proposition 3, and

$$B_t = w_t(1 - \overline{\tau})\frac{1}{1 + H_{lt}}\left(\frac{v_{gt} - \alpha_t}{v_{gt}}\right)\left((s^h + s^f)\frac{\partial\left(\pi_t/w_t\right)}{\partial l_t} - \frac{\partial\left(\pi_t/w_t\right)}{\partial k_t}\right).$$

Note that if 100 percent profit taxation is available, meaning $\overline{\tau} = 1$, then (7.32) reduces to (7.26). As before, τ_t^r and τ_t^s are not uniquely determined from this single condition. However, we can proceed as above by focusing on a solution where the interest income tax and the spread tax are equal. Assume a steady state, so that $A_t = 1$. Also assume that the two taxes are equal,[19] that is, $\tau^r = \tau^s/(1 + \tau^s)$. Substituting this into (7.32) gives

$$\frac{\tau^s}{1 + \tau^s} = \tau^r = (1 - \overline{\tau})\frac{1}{1 + H_l}\left(\frac{v_g - \alpha}{v_g}\right)\frac{w}{r}\left(\frac{\partial\left(\pi/w\right)}{\partial k} - (s^h + s^f)\frac{\partial\left(\pi/w\right)}{\partial l}\right). \tag{7.33}$$

This formula is quite intuitive. First, when 100 percent profit taxation is available, meaning $\overline{\tau} = 1$, it reduces to $\tau^r = \tau^s = 0$, consistently with proposition 4. Second, τ^r is nonzero only when it is socially desirable to tax more, meaning when $(v_g - \alpha)/v_g > 0$. Third, without transactions costs, the sign of τ_t^r is the same as the sign of $\partial(\pi/w)/\partial k$.

The intuition for the last point is as follows. If taxation is distortionary at the margin, the government would like to tax profit, as it is a nondistortionary source of tax revenue; more precisely, it would like to reduce π_t / w_t, as this relaxes the implementability constraint. It cannot do this directly. However, if a reduction in k_t reduces π_t / w_t, this can be done indirectly via taxing capital income. This is in line with results in Stiglitz and Dasgupta (1971) for the case of a static (one-period) economy. It is also similar to Correia (1996), who shows, in the context of the Chamley model, that if an untaxed (or incompletely taxed) third factor of production is complementary to capital in the production function, then capital income should be taxed positively.[20]

To get a feel for when τ will be positive, consider two cases. First, suppose that the production function is linear in labor, that is, $F(k, l) = F(k) + l$. Then it is easily checked that $\pi / w = F(k) - F'(k)k$, and then

$$\frac{\partial \left(\dfrac{\pi}{w} \right)}{\partial k} - \left(s^h + s^f \right) \frac{\partial \left(\dfrac{\pi}{w} \right)}{\partial l} = -F''(k)k > 0,$$

so from (7.33), the interest income tax and spread tax are both positive. But, if the production function is Cobb–Douglas, that is, $F(k, l) = k^\alpha l^\beta$, $\alpha + \beta < 1$, then $\pi / w = (1 - \alpha - \beta)\beta l$. In this case

$$\frac{\partial \left(\dfrac{\pi}{w} \right)}{\partial k} - \left(s^h + s^f \right) \frac{\partial \left(\dfrac{\pi}{w} \right)}{\partial l} = -\left(s^h + s^f \right)(1 - \alpha - \beta)\beta < 0,$$

so, again, from (7.33), the interest income tax and spread tax are both negative. To summarize:

Proposition 6 *Assume just one firm, and that the economy is in the steady state. Then an optimal tax scheme is to tax interest income and financial intermediation services at the same rate given by (7.33). This common tax can be positive or negative depending on the properties of the production function.*

7.5 Other Extensions

7.5.1 Unitary Taxation of Wage and Capital Income
In practice, many countries tax wage and nonwage income in a unitary way, according to a single progressive schedule.[21] In my simple model with linear taxes, unitary taxation of income simply means taxing both wage and capital income at the same rate. In the model above, there is no explicit wage income tax; it is implicitly defined via the budget

constraint via $\tau_t^w = \tau_t^c/(1+\tau_t^c)$. That is, if the government replaced a consumption tax at rate τ_t^c by a wage income tax at rate $\tau_t^c/(1+\tau_t^c)$, the real equilibrium in the model would be unchanged. So, with unitary taxation ($\tau_t^w = \tau_t^r$), we can replace $1-\tau_t^r$ by $1/(1+\tau_{tc}^c)$ in (7.25) to get

$$(1+\tau_t^c)A_t(1+r_t-w_t s^h) = 1+\tau_t^c + (r_t-w_t s^h(1+\tau_t^s)). \tag{7.34}$$

This condition is most easily analyzed in the steady state when $A_t = 1$. Then (7.34) can be easily solved for τ_t^s to give the following result:

Proposition 7 *Suppose that there is unitary taxation of wage and interest income. Then, at the steady state, optimal taxes τ^c and τ^s satisfy*

$$\tau^s = \left[1 - \frac{r}{ws^h}\right]\tau^c < \tau^c .$$

So we see that with unitary income taxation, the tax rate on intermediation services is no longer "simple," as defined above, because it depends on factor prices, and is no longer equal to τ_t^r. Rather, it is proportional to the tax on consumption, but is at a lower rate, and could be negative.

7.5.2 Endogenizing Savings Intermediation Services

We have thus far treated the service of savings intermediation by banks in rather "black box" fashion. In particular, we have treated s^i, the amount of intermediation services per unit of capital supplied to firm i, as exogenous. However, it is clear that banks supply several different kinds of intermediation services, notably liquidity services (Diamond and Dybvig 1983), and monitoring services (Diamond 1991; Besanko and Kanatas 1993; Holmstrom and Tirole 1997).

In this chapter, I do not attempt provide a fully microfounded version of these kinds of intermediation services, for several reasons. First, it is technically difficult to embed some explicit models of intermediation services into the dynamic optimal tax framework. Second, the payoff from doing so in terms of increased insights is not really proportionate to the increased complexity. In the end, bank intermediation activity, when explicitly modeled, may (or may not) have spillovers on the rest of the economy. If there are spillovers, then the optimal tax is a Piguovian one to internalize these spillovers. Ultimately this is because the government can use the interest income tax to control the household's marginal rate of substitution between present and future consumption, and so any tax on intermediation services is a free instrument that can be used to internalize externalities arising from bank activity.

These points are made formally in a previous version of the chapter (Lockwood 2010) where s^i is interpreted as the level of bank monitoring, along the lines of Holmstrom and Tirole (1997). In their framework, without monitoring, bank lending to firms is impossible because the informational rent they demand is so high that the residual return to the bank does not cover the cost of capital. So, as monitoring is costly, the socially efficient level of monitoring is that level which just induces to bank to lend. In the case where the bank is competitive, namely where the firm chooses the terms of the loan contract subject to a break-even constraint for the bank, an assumption commonly made in the finance literature, this is also the equilibrium level of monitoring. In this case, the savings intermediation should *not* be taxed because doing so will violate production efficiency. But, in the case where the bank is a monopolist, namely in that it chooses the contract, it will generally choose a *higher* level of monitoring than this in order to reduce the firm's informational rent. So, in this case, the optimal tax is a positive Pigouvian tax, set to internalize this negative externality.

7.6   Conclusions

This chapter has considered the optimal taxation of financial intermediation services in a dynamic economy, when the government can also use consumption and capital income taxes. The objective of this chapter has been to take a fresh look at this question from a tax design point of view. I set up and solve the tax design problem in a dynamic general equilibrium model of the Chamley (1986) type, where the government chooses taxes on savings intermediation, as well as the usual taxes on consumption (or equivalently, wage income) and income from capital, to finance a public good, and where financial intermediaries, in the form of banks, are explicitly modeled.

My main finding is that at the steady state, the only administratively simple optimal tax structure is to set the tax rate on financial intermediation services equal to the tax rate on capital income. When 100 percent profit taxation is available, this common rate is zero; in the more realistic case of less than 100 percent profit taxation, this common rate can be positive or negative, and is generally different from the optimal tax on consumption.

There are several obvious limitations of the analysis. The first, and most fundamental, is that the role of banks is not microfounded. This is clearly a topic for future work: some preliminary results in this direction are described in section 7.5.2. The second is the restriction to linear income taxation. The classic result of Atkinson and Stiglitz tells us that with nonlinear income taxation, commodity taxation is redundant, and more recently Golosov et al. (2003) have shown that this result generalizes to a dynamic economy. Their result would apply, for example, in a version of my model where households differ in skill levels, and without any financial intermediation. It is a topic for future work to introduce financial intermediation in this environment.

Appendix: Proofs of Propositions

Proof That $\mu \geq 0$

Suppose, to the contrary, that $\mu < 0$ at the optimum. Then, since $u_{llt} < 0$, $u_{clt} \leq 0$, and $H_{lt} > 0$, from (7.19) we have

$$W_{lt} = u_{lt}(1 + \mu(1 + H_{lt})) > u_{lt}. \tag{7A.1}$$

But from (7.15), (7.16), (7.19), and (7.8),

$$-\beta^t W_{lt} = \zeta_t^l = \zeta_t F_{lt}^i = \beta^t v_{gt} w_t. \tag{7A.2}$$

So, combining (7A.1) and (7A.2), we obtain

$$v_{gt} < -u_{lt}/w_t. \tag{7A.3}$$

But (7A.3) says that utility could be increased if \$1 of spending on the public good were returned to the household as a lump sum, contradicting the optimality of the policy. ∎

Proof of Proposition 1

From (7.14), (7.15), (7.19), and (7.8) we have

$$-\frac{W_{ct}}{W_{lt}} = -\frac{u_{ct}}{u_{lt}} \frac{1 + \mu(1 + H_{ct})}{1 + \mu(1 + H_{lt})} = \frac{\zeta_t}{\zeta_t^l} = \frac{1}{F_{lt}^i} = \frac{1}{w_t}. \tag{7A.4}$$

Moreover from (7.3) and (7.4),

$$-\frac{u_{ct}}{u_{lt}} = \frac{1 + \tau_t^c}{w_t}. \tag{7A.5}$$

Combining (7A.4) and (7A.5), we get, after some rearrangement,

$$\frac{\tau_t^c}{1+\tau_t^c} = \frac{\mu(H_{lt}-H_{ct})}{1+\mu(1+H_{lt})}.$$ (7A.6)

Also from (7A.2) we get

$$-W_{lt} = -u_{lt}(1 + \mu(1 + H_{lt})) = w_t v_{gt},$$

which implies that

$$\mu = \frac{1}{1+H_{lt}}\frac{v_{gt}-\alpha_t}{\alpha_t}, \quad \alpha_t = -\frac{u_{lt}}{w_t}.$$ (7A.7)

Combining (7A.6) and (7A.7) to eliminate μ, and rearranging, we get (7.21) as required. ∎

Proof of Proposition 3

From (7.14) and (7.21) we get

$$\frac{\beta^{t-1}W_{c,t-1}}{\beta^t W_{ct}} = \frac{1}{\beta\tilde{A}_t}\frac{u_{c,t-1}}{u_{ct}} = \frac{\zeta_{t-1}}{\zeta_t},$$ (7A.8)

where

$$\tilde{A}_t = \frac{(1+\mu(1+H_{ct}))}{(1+\mu(1+H_{ct-1}))}.$$

Next, using (7.17) and (7.18) to eliminate ζ_t^k and ζ_t^l in (7.15), we get

$$\zeta_t F_{kt}^i - s^i \zeta_t F_{lt}^i = \zeta_{t-1} + s^h \zeta_t F_{lt}^i.$$ (7A.9)

Then from (7A.9),

$$\frac{\zeta_{t-1}}{\zeta_t} = \left(F_{kt}^i - F_{lt}^i(s^i + s^h)\right) = w_t\left(\frac{F_{kt}^i}{F_{lt}^i}-(s^i+s^h)\right).$$ (7A.10)

But now from (7.24) with $\theta^i = 1$ we also have

$$\frac{F_{kt}^i}{F_{lt}^i} = \frac{1+r_t}{w_t}+s^i.$$ (7A.11)

Combining (7A.10) and (7A.11) gives

$$\frac{\zeta_{t-1}}{\zeta_t} = w_t\left(\frac{1+r_t}{w_t}-s^h\right).$$ (7A.12)

Next, combining (7A.12) and (7A.8), we get

$$\frac{u_{c,t-1}}{u_{ct}} = \beta\tilde{A}_t w_t\left(\frac{1+r_t}{w_t}-s^h\right).$$ (A.13)

Finally, from (7.3), (7.5), and (7.8), we get

$$\frac{u_{c,t-1}}{u_{ct}} = \beta(1+\rho_t)\frac{1+\tau_{t-1}^c}{1+\tau_t^c}$$

$$= \beta\left(1+\left(1-\tau_t^r\right)\left(r_t - w_t s^h\left(1+\tau_t^s\right)\right)\right)\frac{1+\tau_{t-1}^c}{1+\tau_t^c}. \qquad (7A.14)$$

Combining (7A.13), (7A.14), and eliminating $u_{c,t-1}/u_{ct}$, we get

$$A_t w_t\left(\frac{1+r_t}{w_t} - s^h\right) = 1+\left(1-\tau_t^r\right)\left(r_t - w_t s^h\left(1+\tau_t^s\right)\right), \qquad (7A.15)$$

where

$$A_t = \tilde{A}_t\frac{1+\tau_t^c}{1+\tau_{t-1}^c} = \frac{\left(1+\mu(1+H_{ct})\right)}{\left(1+\mu(1+H_{ct-1})\right)}\frac{1+\tau_t^c}{1+\tau_{t-1}^c}$$

as required. ∎

Notes

This chapter is a substantially revised version of part of an earlier paper of the same title (Lockwood 2010). I would like to thank Steve Bond, Michael Devereux, Clemens Fuest, Miltos Makris, Michael McMahon, Ruud de Mooij, David Ronayne, and seminar participants at the University of Southampton, GREQAM, the 2010 CBT Summer Symposium, and the 2011 IIPF Conference for helpful comments on an earlier draft. I also gratefully acknowledge support from the ESRC grant RES-060–25–0033, "Business, Tax and Welfare."

1. Financial intermediation comprises activities 65,66,67 in the ISIC/NACE system of national accounts. The definition of these activities can be found, for example, in the handbook NACE: REV.1, published by Eurostat.

2. Authors' calculations: financial intermediation comprises lines J65–67 in the EU KLEMS Growth and Productivity Accounts (http://www.euklems.net/index.html).

3. Data showing the size of intermediation services relating to the taking of deposits and granting of credit *only* are presented for the United Kingdom in section 7.1.2.

4. There are technical difficulties in taxing financial intermediation services; however, these difficulties are not insurmountable; see section 7.1.1.

5. I study taxation of payment services in a companion paper, Lockwood and Yerushalmi (2013).

6. Firms must make pure profit in equilibrium because they must have decreasing returns, and in turn because they possibly face different borrowing costs.

7. This is an acronym for "financial intermediation services indirectly measured."

8. The Sixth VAT Directive and subsequent legislation exempts a wide range of financial services from VAT, including insurance and reinsurance transactions, the granting and the negotiation of credit, transactions concerning deposit and current accounts, pay-

ments, transfers, debts, checks, currency, bank notes, and coins used as legal tender (Council Directive 2006/112/EC of 28 November 2006, Article 135).

9. Chia and Whalley (1999), using a computational approach, reach the rather different conclusion that payment services should be untaxed, but their model is not directly comparable to these others as the intermediation costs are assumed to be proportional to the *price* of the goods being transacted.

10. Auerbach and Gordon (2002) state: "transactions costs can include the real resources ... lost when investing these funds so that they will be available in a later period" (Auerbach and Gordon 2002, p. 412).

11. The exception here is Auerbach and Gordon (2002), where labor supply is variable. However, in their model the consumption tax is just assumed to be uniform, not optimized.

12. This implies that the government cannot set a first-period capital levy on fixed capital k_0 and thus simplifies the analysis (see Atkeson, Chari, and Kehoe 1999).

13. We can also assume, for convenience, that one unit of the consumption good can be transformed into one unit of the public good. This fixes the relative before-tax price of c_t and g_t at unity.

14. We assume that firms face decreasing returns, since with different costs of capital and the same wage, with constant returns, only the one firm with the lowest unit cost would operate, and this case is of limited interest.

15. A minor qualification here is that Boadway and Keen allow for a fixed cost of savings intermediation e.g., fixed costs of opening a savings account. They introduce a nonconvexity into household decision-making, which greatly complicates the optimal tax problem, and so I abstract from their work in this chapter.

16. Labor supply is available for only one period.

17. This can be seen from the fact that π_t/w_t depends on k_t^i and l_t^i via the term $(F^i - F_k^i \cdot k_t^i)/F^i - l_t^i$; differentiation of the latter with respect to k_t^i and l_t^i generate expressions that are not commonly proportional to F_k^i and F_l^i, even for special cases such as the Cobb—Douglas.

18. It is available on request.

19. The spread tax is expressed as a percentage of the cost of intermediation services, gross of the tax, and thus must be divided through by $1 + \tau^s$ to make it comparable to τ.

20. The exact conditions for $\tau_t^r > 0$ are somewhat different here to Correia (1996), as we assume that the third factor of production, which gives rise to pure profit, it is fixed supply, whereas in Correia (1996) it is in elastic supply. The latter assumption imposes an additional implementability contrsaint on the optimal tax problem.

21. A well-known exception here is the dual income tax system, which levies a proportional tax rate on all net income (capital, wages, and pension income less deductions) combined with progressive tax rates on gross labor and pension income. The dual income tax was first implemented in the four Nordic countries (Denmark, Finland, Norway, and Sweden) through a number of tax reforms from 1987 to 1993.

References

Acharya, V. V., L. H. Pedersen, T. Philippon, and M. Richardson. 2010. Measuring systemic risk. Working paper 1002. Federal Reserve Bank of Cleveland.

Akritidis, L. 2007. Improving the measurement of banking services in the UK National Accounts. *Economic and Labour Market Review* 5: 29–37.

Atkeson, A., V. V. Chari, and P. J. Kehoe. 1999. Taxing capital income: a bad idea. *Federal Reserve Bank of Minneapolis Quarterly Review* 23: 3–17.

Atkinson, A., and J. E. Stiglitz. 1980. *Lectures on Public Economics*. Cambridge: MIT Press.

Auerbach, A., and R. H. Gordon. 2002. *American Economic Review* 92: 411–16.

Besanko, D., and G. Kanatas. 1993. Credit market equilibrium with bank monitoring and moral hazard. *Review of Financial Studies* 6: 213–32.

Bianchi, J., and E. G. Mendoza. 2010. Overborrowing, financial crises and "macroprudential" taxes. Working paper 16091. NBER.

Boadway, R., and M. Keen. 2003. Theoretical perspectives on the taxation of capital and financial services. In Patrick Honahan, ed., *The Taxation of Financial Intermediation*. New York: Oxford University Press, 31–80.

Chamley, C. 1986. Optimal taxation of capital income in general equilibrium with infinite lives. *Econometrica* 54: 607–22.

Chia, N. C., and J. Whalley. 1999. The tax treatment of financial intermediation. *Journal of Money, Credit and Banking* 31: 704–19.

Correia, I. H. 1996. Should capital income be taxed in the steady state? *Journal of Public Economics* 60: 147–51.

Coulter, B., C. Mayer, and J. Vickers. 2012. Taxation and regulation of banks to manage systemic risk. Unpublished paper. University of Oxford.

de la Feria, R., and B. Lockwood. 2010. Opting for opting in? An evaluation of the European Commission's proposals for reforming VAT on financial services. *Fiscal Studies* 31 (2): 171–202.

Diamond, D. W. 1991. Monitoring and reputation: the choice between bank loans and directly placed debt. *Journal of Political Economy* 99: 689–721.

Diamond, D. W., and P. H. Dybvig. 1983. Bank runs, deposit insurance, and liquidity. *Journal of Political Economy* 91: 401–19.

Ebrill, L., M. Keen, J.-P. Bodin, and V. Summers. 2001. *The Modern VAT*. Washington, DC: IMF.

European Commission. 2011. Impact assessment accompanying the document proposal for a Council Directive on a common system of financial transaction tax and amending Directive 2008/7/EC. SEC(2011) 1102 final, vol. 6 (annex 5).

Golosov, M., N. Kocherlakota, and A. Tsyvinski. 2003. Optimal indirect and capital taxation. *Review of Economic Studies* 70: 569–87.

Grubert, H., and J. Mackie. 1999. Must financial services be taxed under a consumption tax? *National Tax Journal* 53: 23–40.

Gup, B. E., and J. W. Kolari. 2005. *Commercial Banking: The Management of Risk*, 3rd ed. Hoboken, NJ: Wiley.

Huizinga, H. 2002. Financial services—VAT in Europe? *Economic Policy* 17: 499–534.

Holmstrom, B., and J. Tirole. 1997. Financial intermediation, loanable funds, and the real sector. *Quarterly Journal of Economics* 112: 663–91.

International Monetary Fund. 2010. A fair and substantial contribution by the financial sector. Final Report for the G20. IMF.

Judd, Kenneth L. 1985. Redistributive taxation in a simple perfect foresight model. *Journal of Public Economics* 28 (1): 59–83.

Jack, W. 1999. The treatment of financial services under a broad-based consumption tax. *National Tax Journal* 53: 841–51.

Keen, M. 2010. Taxing and regulating banks. Unpublished paper, IMF.

Lockwood, B. 2010. How should financial intermediation services be taxed? Discussion paper 8122. CEPR.

Lockwood, B., and E. Yerushalmi. 2013. Taxation of payment services. Unpublished paper. University of Warwick.

Perrotti, E. and J. Suarez. 2011. A Pigovian approach to liquidity regulation. *International Journal of Central Banking* 7(4): 3–41.

Poddar, S. N., and M. English. 1997. Taxation of financial services under a value-added tax: Applying the cash-flow approach. *National Tax Journal* 50: 89–111.

Stiglitz, J. E., and P. Dasgupta. 1971. Differential taxation, public goods, and economic efficiency. *Review of Economic Studies* 38: 151–74.

8 FAT or VAT? The Financial Activities Tax as a Substitute to Imposing Value-Added Tax on Financial Services

Thiess Buettner and Katharina Erbe

8.1 Introduction

In the aftermath of the financial crises, interest in the taxation of the financial sector has been renewed. One issue that has continuously attracted the attention is the value-added tax (VAT) exemption of financial services, which is widely applied. The empirical literature has pointed at substantial revenue gains that a repeal of the VAT exemption might generate (Genser and Winker 1997; Huizinga 2002) and also the recent Mirrlees report notes the revenue potential (Mirrlees et al. 2011). Recent research has reconsidered the empirical evidence and found weaker revenue gains (Buettner and Erbe 2013) or even revenue losses (Lockwood 2011). Besides of revenue gains, also possible distortions of the VAT exemption of financial services are discussed in the literature. From a theoretical point of view, Auerbach and Gordon (2002) have argued that it is desirable to integrate financial services into the VAT base. Others have argued that consumption of financial services should not be treated like any other consumer good (e.g., Grubert and Mackie 1999; see also chapter 7 in this volume). Assuming that consumption of financial services does not show a particularly high degree of substitution with leisure, Buettner and Erbe (2013) provide an analysis of the welfare effects and find small welfare gains of a revenue-neutral repeal of the VAT exemption of financial services.

There are important practical concerns regarding VAT on financial services. A large part of financial services is paid implicitly through differences in the rate of interest paid on loans and deposits. In those cases no invoice exists that would allow banks to charge VAT. While administrative solutions may exist,[1] to the best of our knowledge, there is no country that imposes VAT on financial services.[2] Presumably practical concerns are the main reason why the current policy debate has moved on and discusses other means to raise taxes from the financial sector. Key proposals for the taxation of the financial sector are the financial transaction tax (FTT) (European Commission 2011) and the financial activities tax (FAT) (IMF 2010). The latter is closer to a VAT and its introduction might serve as a substitute to repealing the financial sector VAT exemption (Keen 2011). More specifically, a FAT imposed on wages and profits may cause an increase in the price of financial services, which would offset the implicit subsidization of financial services under VAT exemption. Since a price increase in financial services creates an incentive to outsource production to other sectors, a FAT might also offset the disincentive for in-house production associated with the VAT exemption (IMF 2010).

In this chapter we analyze revenue and welfare effects of implementing a FAT both from a theoretical and quantitative perspective, where we illustrate the effects with data for Germany. Our results point to somewhat lower revenue effects than indicated by the European Commission (2010). The Commission estimates a revenue gain of €4.5 bn for Germany in 2008 by levying a FAT rate of 5 percent on financial services, based on IMF data. Our estimate for this tax rate is lower and points to a revenue gain of about €2.2 bn for Germany in 2007. Comparing our findings with Buettner and Erbe (2013), who consider the effects of repealing the VAT exemption of financial services, we find that introducing a FAT rate of 4 percent would yield a similar revenue gain. If the revenue gain is used to lower the distorting taxes on labor, a welfare gain would result in an amount of about €1.5 bn, which is larger than in the case of VAT reform.

We proceed as follows. In section 8.2 we derive a theoretical model that allows us to quantify the effects of a FAT on a consistent basis. Section 8.3 presents the quantitative results for Germany. In section 8.4 we compare our results with those obtained for repealing VAT exemption and in section 8.5 we conclude.

8.2   Modeling Effects of a FAT Introduction

To assess revenue and welfare effects of imposing a FAT, we use a consistent theoretical model that includes multiple goods and some preexisting taxes, namely the VAT and other labor taxes. A similar approach is used by Buettner and Erbe (2013) to discuss the VAT exemption of financial services. Following the so-called addition method (IMF 2010), we levy the FAT on the sum of wages and profits of a financial institution. To keep the theoretical analysis simple, we focus on a single primary factor, labor. Later, in the empirical part, we take account of other inputs. The next subsection is concerned with the revenue effects, before we turn to the consequences for welfare.

8.2.1 Revenue Effects

To calculate the change in tax revenues caused by an implementation of a FAT, we compare before—and after—reform revenues. To simplify matters in this analysis, we ignore changes in the amount of unrecoverable input taxes arising under VAT exemption of financial services.[3] Noting that all private consumption, inclusive of taxes, is financed by labor income after taxes and assuming that all VAT rates are equal to the standard VAT rate τ, except for the tax on financial services, we can define tax revenues as

$$T = \tilde{\tau}_n p_n x_n + \tilde{\tau}_L L, \tag{8.1}$$

where x_n is the final consumption of financial services, priced with p_n. With the wage rate set to unity, L is labor income. Now

$$\tilde{\tau}_n = \frac{\tau_n - \tau}{1 + \tau}$$

captures the difference between the tax on final consumption of financial services and the standard VAT rate τ, and

$$\tilde{\tau}_L = \frac{\tau_L + \tau}{1 + \tau}$$

is the total tax on labor, inclusive of labor income taxes and VAT. The first term in (8.1) is negative and represents the implicit subsidy to the financial sector associated with the VAT exemption.

Using a prime to denote post-reform values, we can specify the tax revenue after introducing τ_{FAT}, modeled as a tax on the primary input labor, used in the financial sector: $T' = \tilde{\tau}_n p'_n x'_n + \tilde{\tau}_L L' + \tau_{FAT} L'_n$. Subtracting equation (8.1) gives the revenue change:

$$dT = T' - T = \tilde{\tau}_n \left(p'_n x'_n - p_n x_n \right) + \tilde{\tau}_L dL + \tau_{FAT} L'_n. \tag{8.2}$$

The revenue change is composed by three terms. If the value of the final output of financial services declines, the implicit subsidy associated with the VAT exemption of financial services is reduced. As a consequence the first term becomes positive, and we have a revenue gain. The second term represents the change in labor taxes due to the reform. The third term shows the revenue associated with the FAT evaluated at post reform conditions, where $L'_n = L_n + dL_n$.

The change in the labor demand by the financial sector is determined as follows. We employ a Cobb–Douglas production function, where

$$\frac{\partial F_n}{\partial L_n} = \alpha \frac{F_n}{L_n},$$

and α is the output elasticity of employment. Inserting this expression into the first-order condition for employment in the financial sector yields

$$p_n \alpha \frac{F_n}{L_n} = 1 + \tau_{FAT}.$$

Taking the total differential, noting that

$$\alpha = \frac{L_n}{X_n p_n}$$

in the absence of a FAT, and rearranging terms, we obtain

$$dL_n = \hat{p}_n L_n + \hat{X}_n L_n - \tau_{FAT} L_n,$$

where the hat denotes relative changes. Hence employment in the financial sector varies in proportion with the value of output except for the adverse effect of higher taxes on the primary input, labor, which works toward a decline in employment.

8.2.2   Welfare Effects

To determine the welfare effects, we start with a representative household's utility function:

$$u(x_1, x_2, \ldots, x_n, l),$$

where l is leisure, and x_i is final consumption of good i. The corresponding budget constraint is

$$\sum_{i=1}^{n} q_i x_i = (1 - \tilde{\tau}_L)(\mathcal{T} - l),$$

where $q_i = (1 + \tilde{\tau}_i) p_i$ is the (modified) consumer price for good i, $\mathcal{T}$ is the total time endowment of the household, and l is the demand for leisure. Maximizing utility yields the first-order conditions

$$\frac{\partial u}{\partial x_i} = q_i \lambda$$

and

$$\frac{\partial u}{\partial L} = -(1 - \tilde{\tau}_L)\lambda.$$

Taking the total differential of the objective function gives

$$\frac{1}{\lambda} du = \sum_{i=1}^{n} q_i dx_i - (1 - \tilde{\tau}_L) dL, \tag{8.3}$$

where $dL = -dl$ is the change in labor supply. Expression (8.3) indicates that welfare increases if the consumer's budget is expanded. With $q_i = (1 + \tilde{\tau}_i)p_i$ and $\tilde{\tau}_i = 0, \forall i \neq n$, we can reformulate the welfare effect using producer prices

$$\frac{1}{\lambda} du = \sum_{i=1}^{n} p_i dx_i + \tilde{\tau}_n p_n dx_n - (1 - \tilde{\tau}_L) dL. \tag{8.4}$$

As shown in the appendix, assuming profit maximizing firms, perfect competition, and full employment we can reformulate the welfare effect as

$$\frac{1}{\lambda} du = \tau_{FAT} dL_n + \tilde{\tau}_n p_n dx_n + \tilde{\tau}_L dL. \tag{8.5}$$

Since the FAT is a tax on producers, we have only indirect welfare effects through the changes in distorted markets. The first term on the right-hand side captures the welfare consequence of employment effects in the financial sector. It vanishes in an initial situation where no FAT exists. The second and third terms show the indirect effects on final consumption and on total employment, respectively.

Expression (8.5) allows us to calculate the deadweight loss associated with introducing a FAT, provided the tax revenue is redistributed in a lump-sum fashion to the household. Of course, we need to determine how total employment, as well as employment in the financial services sector n, are affected, and we need to specify the impact on the demand for financial services. Another consideration that may be important is to account for "recycling" the tax revenue through a revenue-neutral change in the labor tax rate; we will come back to this issue below.

Deadweight Loss Associated with Introducing a FAT
Using the Hicksian demands that

$$dx_n = \frac{\partial h_n}{\partial q_n} dq_n$$

and

$$dl = \frac{\partial h_{n+1}}{\partial q_n} dq_n ,$$

we can relate the change in the demand for leisure and in the demand for financial services to price changes. Noting that in a situation where initially no FAT is imposed, $\tau_{FAT} = 0$, and we have

$$\frac{1}{\lambda} du = \tilde{\tau}_n p_n \frac{\partial h_n}{\partial q_n} dq_n - \tilde{\tau}_L \frac{\partial h_{n+1}}{\partial q_n} dq_n. \tag{8.6}$$

To substitute the cross-price effect between consumption of leisure and good n, we follow Buettner and Erbe (2013) who utilize the discussion in Goulder and Williams (2003). With the labor supply elasticity

$$\varepsilon_L \equiv \frac{\partial L}{\partial (1 - \tau_L)} \frac{(1 - \tau_L)}{L_n}$$

and

$$\theta_n = \frac{\varepsilon_{n,n+1}}{\sum_{i=1}^{n} \sigma_i \varepsilon_{i,n+1}} - 1$$

as an indicator of the degree to which good n is a substitute to leisure— relative to all other goods, we can specify the impact on the demand for leisure by substituting this expression into equation (8.6) and inserting ε_{nn} for the own-price elasticity of the demand for financial services:

$$\frac{1}{\lambda} du = \frac{\tilde{\tau}_n}{1 + \tilde{\tau}_n} h_n \varepsilon_{nn} dq_n - \tilde{\tau}_L \varepsilon_L L \frac{h_n}{y} [1 + \theta_n] dq_n. \tag{8.7}$$

To evaluate the deadweight loss, we integrate over the tax induced change in consumer prices:

$$DWL_1 = \int_0^{q_n} \frac{1}{\lambda} \frac{du}{dq_n} dq_n - \int_0^{q'_n} \frac{1}{\lambda} \frac{du}{dq_n} dq_n = -\int_{q_n}^{q'_n} \frac{1}{\lambda} \frac{du}{dq_n} dq_n.$$

With

$$s_n = \frac{h_n q_n}{y}$$

we obtain

$$DWL_1 = -\frac{\tilde{\tau}_n}{1+\tilde{\tau}_n} q_n h_n \varepsilon_{nn} \hat{q}_n + \tilde{\tau}_L \varepsilon_L L s_n [1+\theta_n] \hat{q}_n. \tag{8.8}$$

Provided that we have an empirical estimate of the consumer price effect of introducing a FAT,

$$\hat{q}_n \equiv \frac{q'-q}{q},$$

as well as estimates of the elasticities $(\varepsilon_{nn}, \varepsilon_L)$ and the parameter θ_n, we can use this formula to compute the deadweight loss.

Welfare Gain of a Revenue-Neutral Change of Labor Income Taxes
The expression above for the deadweight loss rests on the assumption that revenue gains are distributed back to the household in a lump-sum fashion. An alternative way to use the funds is to reduce the distortive tax on labor income. This can be integrated in the above analysis by adding a welfare effect associated with the corresponding tax reduction. Following Buettner and Erbe (2013), we focus on the distortion associated with labor taxation, and approximate this welfare loss by

$$DWL_2 = \frac{1}{2}\left(\frac{\tilde{\tau}_L'^2}{1-\tilde{\tau}_L'} - \frac{\tilde{\tau}_L^2}{1-\tilde{\tau}_L} \right) L \varepsilon_L. \tag{8.9}$$

8.3 Quantification of FAT Effects Using German Data

To quantify the effects of the implementation of a FAT, we use German data for 2007. To highlight differences between FAT and VAT, we start by considering an implementation of a FAT with a rate of 19 percent, which is the standard VAT rate in the German system. Later we calculate the effects of an implementation of a FAT at more modest tax rates.

While proposals to implement FAT tend to use the cash flow in the financial sector (Keen, Krelove, and Norregaard 2010), our empirical analysis uses aggregate figures from the national accounts. For the calculation of the (producer) price effects we make use of the input–output table (see the appendix). In the national accounts the value of labor used in the financial sector relative to total output is the position *compensation of employees*, which amounts to €37.299 bn divided by the total *output produced by the financial sector* (€113.950 bn). Of course, while our theoretical model focuses on labor as the sole primary factor, a more comprehensive analysis would have to take account of the remuneration for other primary inputs, notably profits. This suggests that we add the *net operating surplus* to the tax base, which amounts to €10.260 bn.[4] Adding the capital input to the tax base, the question arises how this input will respond to the tax reform. With the simplifying assumption that the financial industry could substitute capital with inputs from other sectors in the same way as labor, we apply the same elasticity of input demand to both labor and capital inputs in the calculations below.

If the FAT rate is 19 percent after the reform, the quantitative results indicate the following:

- The price for financial intermediation services would increase by 7.66 percent.
- The price increases in the other sectors are small, in all cases they are less than 1 percent. The average price increase across all nonfinancial sectors amounts to 0.14 percent.

With the estimation of the price changes due to the implementation of the FAT, we can calculate the consequences for the tax revenue. For this purpose we use equation (8.2):

$$dT = \tilde{\tau}_n \left(\hat{p}_n \hat{x}_n + \hat{p}_n + \hat{x}_n \right) x_n p_n + \tilde{\tau}_L dL + \tau_{FAT} L'_n.$$

Three effects can be distinguished:

1. The first term is the change in tax revenue due to a change in the value of final demand at producer prices, which is calculated with −€0.177 bn (for the calculation, see the appendix). The negative sign results from the implicit subsidization of financial services as the total value of financial services increases. Hence the first term is a tax revenue loss.

2. The second term is the change in tax revenue due to a change in employment. The latter change is driven by the price change of financial services, which exerts income and substitution effects on labor supply:[5]

$$dL = -(\varepsilon_L - \varepsilon_Y) Ls_n \hat{p}_n = -0.06 \cdot €1180.43 \text{ bn} \cdot 0.018 \cdot 0.0766 = -€0.098 \text{ bn}.$$

The revenue implication is obtained by evaluating this decline in employment with an effective marginal labor tax rate of $\tilde{\tau}_L = 0.53$ percent (OECD 2008), which yields a revenue loss of $-€0.052$ bn.

3. The third term depicts the taxation of labor inputs and profits. Assuming that employment of all primary factors is equally affected by the reform, we arrive at a direct revenue effect of €7.690 bn.

The total revenue change with a FAT rate of 19 percent is a revenue gain of €7.461 bn.

The welfare effect can be quantified using equations (8.8) and (8.9), which are replicated for convenience.

$$DWL_1 = -\frac{\tilde{\tau}_n}{1+\tilde{\tau}_n} h_n q_n \varepsilon_{nn} \hat{q}_n + \tilde{\tau}_L \varepsilon_L L s_n [1+\theta_n] \hat{q}_n ,$$

$$DWL_2 = \frac{1}{2}\left(\frac{\tilde{\tau}_L'^2}{1-\tilde{\tau}_L'} - \frac{\tilde{\tau}_L^2}{1-\tilde{\tau}_L} \right) L \varepsilon_L .$$

The two terms associated with DWL_1 capture the welfare effects of a change in the consumer price of financial services. These effects amount to a small welfare loss of €0.032 bn. Note that this estimate is obtained under the assumption that consumption of financial services has the same substitution elasticity with leisure as other goods. More specifically, we have set $\theta_n = 0$. If financial services were more appropriate for the household to save time for consumption of leisure than other goods, θ_n might be larger than zero. In this case the welfare loss would be larger due to stronger responses in the labor market. DWL_2 is the effect of a compensating, revenue-neutral decline in labor taxation. According to our calculations the labor tax rate can be reduced by 0.896 percent to balance the tax revenue gains. Abstracting from minor preexisting distortions associated with VAT exemption and FAT, this would yield a welfare gain of €6.108 bn. Summing DWL_1 and DWL_2, we find that the total welfare effect is a gain of €6.076 bn.

Whereas the figures above are obtained by setting the FAT rate to 19 percent, figure 8.1 shows results for tax revenue and welfare effects for a range of FAT rates between 1 and 20 percent (see the appendix for numerical results). Figure 8.2 depicts the associated producer price increases. The figure also shows that the price changes in the other sectors are always very small. This supports our simplifying assumption, that only the producer price of financial services is affected by the reform.

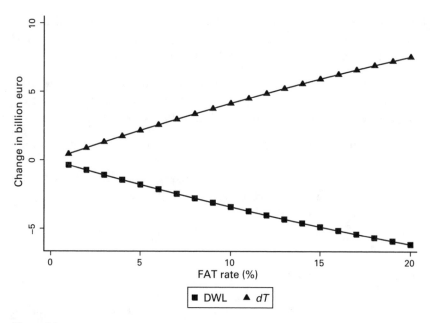

Figure 8.1
Revenue and welfare effects by FAT rate for German data in 2007

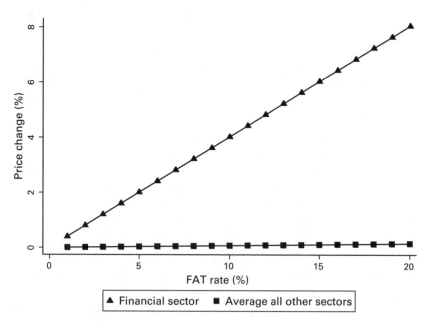

Figure 8.2
Price effects of different FAT rates for German data in 2007

Table 8.1
Effects of an implementation of a FAT versus repealing VAT in the financial sector

Change in . . .	FAT (19%)	FAT (4%)	VAT (19%)
Price	PP: +7.66%	PP: +1.61%	PP: −2.9%
	CP: +7.66%	CP: +1.61%	CP: +15.6%
Revenue	€7.461 bn	€1.792 bn	€1.698 bn
Welfare[a]	€6.076 bn	€1.490 bn	€1.028 bn

Source: FAT results: own computations; VAT results obtained from Buettner and Erbe (2013)
a. The welfare effect is based on the assumption that revenues are used to lower labor taxes.

8.4   Comparison with a VAT Reform

The VAT is a tax on sales minus deductable inputs, which includes goods and services purchased from other firms. This is the equivalent to wages plus profits taxed by the FAT. But under the VAT exemption of financial services some part of the value added of the financial sector is already taxed, at least indirectly. This indirect taxation in case of a FAT arises, since industries that use financial services as input are already subject to VAT. This is the reason why it has been proposed to implement FAT at lower rates than the VAT (Keen, Krelove, and Norregaard 2010).

Table 8.1 gives an overview on the comparison of the estimated effects of an implementation of a FAT at 19 percent, a more modest rate of 4 percent, and a repeal of the VAT exemption of financial services with a standard VAT rate of 19 percent. According to Buettner and Erbe (2013), repealing the VAT exemption results in a price change of the producer price of financial services by −2.9 percent, whereas the consumer price changes by +15.6 percent. The total tax revenue increases by about €1.7 bn, and the welfare gain is estimated with some €1 bn.

It may seem surprising, that similar tax rates of 19 percent yield so vastly differing results. According to our calculations, a FAT would generate a tax revenue gain of €7.5 bn, while imposing a VAT at the same rate on financial services generates only €1.7 bn. FAT is levied on all primary inputs used to produce financial services. In 2007, the labor input of the financial sector amounts to €37.299 bn. Adding profits, the tax base amounts to €47.599 bn. As we noted above, with VAT exemption of financial services some part of these inputs are already subject to VAT. Repealing the VAT exemption thus implies to collect additional taxes only from that part of financial services that constitutes final consumption, which is €35.630 bn in the German case. In addition, at least in Germany, the current exemption regime does not apply to all financial services. According to Buettner and Erbe (2013), a third of all final consumption of financial services is already subject to VAT. Hence repealing exemption would increase the VAT base only by two-thirds (€23.516 bn) of total final consumption of financial services. Moreover, due to unrecoverable input taxes, the financial sector already pays VAT on intermediate inputs. Hence repealing the VAT exemption is associated with an even weaker revenue gain. Buettner and Erbe (2013) quantify this revenue effect of unrecoverable input taxes with €1.955 bn.

From table 8.1 we can see that a FAT rate of 4 percent would generate similar results for revenue and welfare as repealing the VAT exemption at a VAT rate of 19 percent. Even at the lower FAT rate the price effects differ strongly. Whereas the VAT leads to a decline in the producer price, the FAT would be associated with a higher price. However, the consumer price of financial services would tend to increase much less with FAT.

If the FAT rate is chosen such that revenue implications are similar to those of repealing VAT exemption, the welfare consequences are slightly different. Since the VAT base is smaller, the associated consumer price effect of repealing VAT exemption is much larger than the price effect resulting from the introduction of a FAT. Therefore the welfare assessment looks better in case of the FAT.

Of course, our analysis has been based on the assumption that the increase in the cost of producing financial services associated with the FAT can be shifted to the final consumer. This assumption needs to be qualified, however, in an international context where taxing domestic consumers may have very different effects than taxing domestic producers. Repealing the VAT exemption would increase consumer prices of financial services regardless of whether purchased from domestic financial institutions or purchased from a competing institution with location in a country that does not impose VAT. Moreover producer prices may even be reduced—due to unrecoverable input taxes. Imposing FAT, however, implies to impose a tax burden at the source, namely at the location of the producer. But, if foreign producers of financial services do not face a FAT, it may be difficult to shift the burden of taxes to the consumer.

8.5 Conclusion

In this chapter we analyzed revenue and welfare effects of implementing a FAT. The analysis has not only dealt with theoretical issues but has also used the theoretical results in order to provide some quantifications that illustrate the effects for Germany. Following the IMF (2010), we discussed a rather broad concept of the FAT, that is, as a tax levied on the sum of wages and profits, and this bears some similarity with a tax on the value added of financial services (Keen 2011).

The European Commission (2010) calculates a revenue gain of about €4.5 bn for Germany in 2008 with a FAT rate of 5 percent. If we use this tax rate in our calculations, we obtain a revenue gain of only €2.2 bn for Germany in 2007, even though we include profits into the tax base. Using similar data, Buettner and Erbe (2013) consider the effects of repealing the VAT exemption of financial services. Accordingly, a VAT reform (with a VAT rate of 19 percent) would increase total tax revenues by some €1.7 bn. The quantification in this chapter suggests that introducing a FAT rate of 4 percent would yield a similar revenue gain.

It is tempting to confront our results with the practical experience with FAT. The IMF (2010) provides some information on three European countries that have some experience with FAT elements in their tax systems. Denmark levied a FAT rate of effectively 9.13 percent on labor costs until 2013 and increased it to 10.5 percent in 2013. Our result for a 9 percent FAT rate in Germany in 2007 would be €3.866 bn or 0.159 percent of German GDP. This is roughly consistent with the Danish experience, where comparable revenues from the financial sector amounted to €455 bn in 2008, which is 0.182 percent of GDP. Since 1968 France levies a payroll tax on firms that are not subject to VAT. The standard tax rate is 4.25 percent, but it increases with the payroll up to 13.60 percent. The generated tax revenue from the financial sector amounts to €9.605 bn in 2008 or 0.468 percent of GDP. Our result for a tax rate of 13 percent is €5.392 bn or 0.222 percent of GDP in 2007, which is much lower but still substantial. The IMF (2010) also discusses the case of Italy, but a comparison is difficult since there is insufficient information on the revenues generated by the financial sector.

The practical experience supports the view that imposing a FAT could serve as some substitute to repealing the financial service VAT exemption. Also the results from the welfare analysis favor FAT rather than a VAT reform. Our results show that if the revenue gain from a

FAT with a 4 percent rate is used to lower the distorting taxes on labor the welfare gain is approximately €1.5 bn, which is larger than the corresponding figure obtained for VAT reform. Of course, a FAT might exert additional distortions. A critical assumption made in our study is that the FAT burden is fully shifted to the consumer. With international competition in the banking sector the outlook would be less optimistic than our results suggest. For Europe, where this concern seems particularly relevant, this suggests to strive for a joint introduction of FAT among EU member states. With this caveat, however, the introduction of a FAT seems to offer a reasonable alternative to repealing the VAT exemption of financial services.

Appendix

Derivation of the Welfare Effect

This appendix shows how we can derive the expression for the welfare effect in equation (8.5). Inserting marginal products, we can express each sector's final demand change as

$$dx_i = \frac{\partial F_i}{\partial L_i} dL_i + \sum_{j=1}^{n} \frac{\partial F_i}{\partial X_{ji}} dX_{ji} - \sum_{j=1}^{n} dX_{ij}.$$

With F_i denoting the production function in sector i and X_{ji} denoting the input purchased by sector i from sector j, the first-order conditions for profit maximization of the firm are

$$p_i \frac{\partial F_i}{\partial X_{ji}} = p_j$$

and

$$p_i \frac{\partial F_i}{\partial L_i} = 1,$$

$\forall i \neq n$, and for sector n,

$$p_n \frac{\partial F_n}{\partial L_n} = 1 + \tau_{FAT}.$$

Substituting the first-order conditions into the final demand change for each sector, we have

$$p_i dx_i = dL_i + \sum_{j=1}^{n} p_j dX_{ji} - p_i \sum_{j=1}^{n} dX_{ij} \quad \forall i \neq n,$$

$$p_n dx_n = (1 + \tau_{FAT}) dL_n + \sum_{j=1}^{n} p_j dX_{jn} - p_n \sum_{j=1}^{n} dX_{nj}.$$

Summing over all changes in final demand obtains

$$\sum_{i=1}^{n} p_i dx_i = \sum_{i=1}^{n-1} dL_i + (1 + \tau_{FAT}) dL_n + \sum_{i=1}^{n} \sum_{j=1}^{n} p_j dX_{ji} - \sum_{i=1}^{n} \sum_{j=1}^{n} p_i dX_{ij},$$

and noting that changes in intermediate inputs wash out obtains

$$\sum_{i=1}^{n} p_i dx_i = \sum_{i=1}^{n} dL_i + \tau_{FAT} dL_n. \tag{8.10}$$

Inserting (8.10) into (8.4) and using

$$\sum_{i=1}^{n} dL_i = dL,$$

we get the welfare effect as in equation (8.5).

Price Effects of the Implementation of a FAT

Starting from the general expression for the producer price in sector i (assuming that there are no unrecoverable input taxes in sector n), we write

$$p_i = \sum_{j=1}^{n} a_{ji} p_j + b_i.$$

Total differentiation provides us with expressions

$$\hat{p}_1 = \sum_{i=1}^{n} \tilde{a}_{i1} \hat{p}_i,$$

$$\vdots$$

$$\hat{p}_{n-1} = \sum_{i=1}^{n} \tilde{a}_{i,n-1} \hat{p}_i,$$

$$\hat{p}_n = \sum_{i=1}^{n} \tilde{a}_{in} \hat{p}_i + \tilde{b}_n d\tau_{FAT}.$$

Hence the prices change due to price changes in the other sectors, and the price in the financial sector is additional affected by the taxation of the labor input. The relative producer price change is

$$\hat{p}_i = \frac{dp_i}{p_i}$$

and the value-based labor input coefficient is defined by

$$\tilde{b}_n = \frac{b_n w}{p_n},$$

where the wage rate is normalized to unity. $\tilde{a}_{in}$ is the value-based input coefficient, defined by

$$\tilde{a}_{in} = a_{in}\frac{p_i}{p_n},$$

where a_{in} denotes the technical input coefficient. Now we can solve this system of equations by using the transpose of the input index matrix $\tilde{A}_{n\times n}^T$:

$$\begin{bmatrix} \hat{p}_1 \\ \vdots \\ \hat{p}_n \end{bmatrix} = \left(I_{n\times n} - \tilde{A}_{n\times n}^T\right)^{-1}\begin{bmatrix} 0 \\ \vdots \\ 0 \\ \tilde{b}_n d\tau_{FAT} \end{bmatrix}. \tag{8.11}$$

In this setting the changes in producer and consumer prices are equal, because there is no additional tax on final consumption implemented.

Output Change of the Financial Sector

In the following we develop an expression for the change in the value of the output $X_n p_n$ of the financial sector. Starting from the value-based expression for inputs, produced by the financial sector and used by the other sectors:

$$p_n X_{ni} = p_i \tilde{a}_{ni} X_i.$$

Taking the total differential and rearranging yields:

$$dp_n X_{ni} + p_n dX_{ni} = p_i \tilde{a}_{ni} dX_i$$

$$\Rightarrow p_n \sum_{i=1}^{n} dX_{ni} = \sum_{i=1}^{n} p_i \tilde{a}_{ni} dX_i - \sum_{i=1}^{n} dp_n X_{ni},$$

$$p_n (dX_n - dx_n) = \sum_{i=1}^{n} p_i \tilde{a}_{ni} dX_i - \sum_{i=1}^{n} dp_n X_{ni},$$

$$p_n dX_n = \sum_{i=1}^{n} p_i \tilde{a}_{ni} dX_i - \sum_{i=1}^{n} \hat{p}_n p_n X_{ni} + p_n dx_n.$$

The first term on the right-hand side accounts for changes in input demands by the other sectors for financial services. The second term represents the reduction due to the price change of financial services, and the third term shows the change in private demand. Using $p_i dX_i = d(p_i X_i) - dp_i\, X_i$ and rearranging yields

$$p_n dX_n = \sum_{i=1}^{n} \tilde{a}_{ni}\left(d(p_i X_i) - dp_i X_i\right) - \sum_{i=1}^{n} \hat{p}_n \frac{X_{ni} p_n}{X_i p_i} X_i p_i + p_n dx_n \frac{dp_n}{dp_n} \frac{x_n}{x_n},$$

$$p_n dX_n = \sum_{i=1}^{n} \tilde{a}_{ni} d(p_i X_i) - \sum_{i=1}^{n} \tilde{a}_{ni} \hat{p}_i X_i p_i - \sum_{i=1}^{n} \hat{p}_n \tilde{a}_{ni} X_i p_i + \varepsilon_{nn} \hat{p}_n x_n p_n,$$

with

$$\hat{p}_i = 0 \quad \forall i \neq n,$$

$$p_n dX_n = \sum_{i=1}^{n} \tilde{a}_{ni} d(p_i X_i) - \tilde{a}_{nn} \hat{p}_n X_n p_n - \sum_{i=1}^{n} \hat{p}_n \tilde{a}_{ni} X_i p_i + \varepsilon_{nn} \hat{p}_n x_n p_n.$$

In the preceding formula most terms can be quantified using available statistics except for the output changes of the different sectors. Accordingly, we derive a quantifiable expression for the vector of output changes. We start by using the $(n \times n)$ value-based input index matrix $\tilde{A}$:

$$\left[I - \tilde{A}\right] \begin{bmatrix} d(p_1 X_1) \\ \vdots \\ d(p_n X_n) \end{bmatrix} = \begin{bmatrix} d(p_1 x_1) \\ \vdots \\ d(p_n x_n) \end{bmatrix}.$$

Rearranging and using the assumption that only p_n changes results in

$$\begin{bmatrix} d(p_1 X_1) \\ \vdots \\ d(p_n X_n) \end{bmatrix} = \left[I - \tilde{A}\right]^{-1} \begin{bmatrix} p_1 \dfrac{\partial x_1}{\partial p_n} dp_n \\ \vdots \\ p_{n-1} \dfrac{\partial x_{n-1}}{\partial p_n} dp_n \\ dp_n x_n + p_n \dfrac{\partial x_n}{\partial p_n} dp_n \end{bmatrix}.$$

Using Slutsky symmetry,

$$\left(\frac{\partial x_i}{\partial p_n} = \frac{\partial x_n}{\partial p_i} \right),$$

Table 8.2
Effects of FAT implementation at different rates

FAT rate (%)	Price change (%)	Change T	DWL_1	DWL_2	DWL
1	0.403	0.459	0.002	−0.385	−0.383
2	0.806	0.911	0.003	−0.763	−0.760
3	1.209	1.355	0.005	−1.133	−1.128
4	1.612	1.792	0.007	−1.496	−1.490
5	2.015	2.221	0.009	−1.852	−1.844
6	2.418	2.643	0.010	−2.201	−2.191
7	2.820	3.058	0.012	−2.543	−2.531
8	3.223	3.466	0.014	−2.877	−2.864
9	3.626	3.866	0.015	−3.205	−3.190
10	4.029	4.258	0.017	−3.525	−3.509
11	4.432	4.644	0.019	−3.840	−3.821
12	4.835	5.022	0.020	−4.146	−3.126
13	5.238	5.392	0.022	−4.446	−4.424
14	5.641	5.756	0.024	−4.740	−4.716
15	6.043	6.111	0.025	−5.027	−5.001
16	6.446	6.460	0.027	−5.307	−5.280
17	6.850	6.801	0.029	−5.581	−5.552
18	7.252	7.135	0.031	−5.848	−5.817
19	7.655	7.461	0.032	−6.108	−6.076
20	8.058	7.781	0.034	−6.362	−6.328

Source: Own computations using German data in 2007 (bn euro)

and inserting the cross price elasticities for financial services, ε_{ni}, gives a computable expression for the changes in outputs:

$$\begin{bmatrix} d(p_1X_1) \\ \vdots \\ d(p_nX_n) \end{bmatrix} = \begin{bmatrix} I - \tilde{A} \end{bmatrix}^{-1} \hat{p}_n x_n p_n \begin{bmatrix} \varepsilon_{n1} \\ \vdots \\ \varepsilon_{n(n-1)} \\ 1 + \varepsilon_{nn} \end{bmatrix}.$$

Quantification of FAT Effects for Different Tax Rates

Table 8.2 shows the price change in the financial sector, the change in tax revenue and the welfare effect (split up into the two effects) caused by the implementation of a FAT rate between 1 and 20 percent.

Notes

1. For instance, cash-flow taxation and tax calculation accounts use the accounts and balance sheets of the credit institutions to calculate a difference between the interest rate

for loans and deposits. Another solution may be zero taxation of B2B transactions, see Mirrlees et al. (2011).

2. New Zealand taxes insurance services with a cash-flow approach; see Cnossen (2013).

3. While views differ regarding the extent to which unrecoverable input taxes are significant, Buettner and Erbe (2013) provide estimates according to which a large part of the input taxes can actually be shifted to the taxed part of the financial sector.

4. Statistisches Bundesamt (2010, tab. 1.3).

5. With the parameters L = €1180.43 bn, s_n = 1.8 percent, $\varepsilon_L - \varepsilon_Y$ = 0.06 (average uncompensated labor supply elasticity reported by Keane 2011).

References

Auerbach, Alan J., and Roger H. Gordon. 2002. Taxation of financial services under a VAT. *American Economic Review* 9 (2): 411–16.

Buettner, Thiess, and Katharina Erbe. 2013. Revenue and welfare effects of financial sector VAT exemption. *International Tax and Public Finance,* published online, December 7, 2013.

Cnossen, Sijbren. 2013. A proposal to apply the Kiwi—VAT to insurance services in the European Union. *International Tax and Public Finance* 20 (5): 867–83.

European Commission. 2010. Financial sector taxation. Available at: http://ec.europa.eu/taxation_customs/resources/documents/taxation/gen_info/economic_analysis/tax_papers/taxation_paper_25_en.pdf.

European Commission. 2011. Proposal for a Council Directive on a Common System of Financial Transaction Tax and Amending Directive 2008/7/EC. Available at: http://ec.europa.eu/taxation_customs/resources/documents/taxation/other_taxes/financial_sector/com(2011)594_en.pdf.

Genser, Bernd, and Peter Winker. 1997. Measuring the fiscal revenue loss of VAT exemption in commercial banking. *Finanzarchiv* 54 (4): 563–85.

Goulder, Lawrence H., and Roberton C. Williams. 2003. The substantial bias from ignoring general equilibrium effects in estimating excess burden, and a practical solution. *Journal of Political Economy* 111 (4): 898–927.

Grubert, Harry, and Jim Mackie. 1999. Must financial services be taxed under a consumption tax? *National Tax Journal* 53: 23–40.

Huizinga, Harry. 2002. A European VAT on financial services? *Economic Policy* 17 (35): 497–534.

International Monetary Fund. 2010. A fair and substantial contribution by the financial sector. Final Report for the G-20. Available at: http://www.imf.org/external/np/g20/pdf/062710b.pdf.

Keane, Michael P. 2011. Labor supply and taxes: A survey. *Journal of Economic Literature* 49 (4): 961-1075.

Keen, Michael, Russell Krelove, and John Norregaard. 2010. The financial activities tax. In Stijn Claessens, Michael Keen, Ceyla Pazarbasioglu, and IMF staff, eds., *Financial Sector*

Taxation—The IMF's Report to the G–20 and Background Material. Washington, DC: IMF, 118–43.

Keen, Michael. 2011. Rethinking the taxation of the financial sector. *CESifo Economic Studies* 57 (1): 1–24.

Lockwood, Ben. 2011. Estimates from National Accounts Data of the revenue effect of imposing VAT on currently exempt sales of financial services companies in the EU. In: How the EU VAT Exemptions Impact the Banking Sector (PWC-Study). Available at: http://www.pwc.com/en_GX/gx/financial-services/pdf/2011-10-18_VAT_Study _final_report.pdf.

Mirrlees, J., Adam, S., Besley, T., Blundell, R., Bond, S., Chote, R., Gammie, M., Johnson, P., Myles, G., and J. Poterba. 2011. *Tax by Design: The Mirrlees Review*. New York: Oxford University Press.

OECD (2008), Taxing Wages 2006/2007, Paris.

Statistisches Bundesamt. 2010. Volkswirtschaftliche Gesamtrechnungen, Input-Output-Rechnung 2007. Fachserie 18 Reihe 2, Wiesbaden.

9 Assessing the Macroeconomic Impact of Financial Transaction Taxes

Julia Lendvai, Rafal Raciborski, and Lukas Vogel

9.1 Background

The banking and financial crisis of recent years has led to a broad debate on financial regulation to improve the resilience of the financial sector and reduce the likelihood of further crises. Given the costs that rescuing financial institutions has inflicted on taxpayers, the call for a contribution from the financial sector to the financing of crisis-intervention costs has also gained political voice and support (e.g., IMF 2010; Matheson 2011). Hence common objectives behind proposals to strengthen financial sector taxation are to recover part of the budgetary costs of the financial crisis from the financial sector, to charge the financial sector for the implicit bailout guarantee that many (too-big-to-fail) banks enjoy, and to correct behavior that might provoke or amplify financial crises.

The discussion on financial sector taxation focuses on three main types of instruments: (1) bank levies, which are taxes on financial institutions' balance sheets, (2) financial activity taxes (FAT), which are taxes on bank profits and remuneration packages, and (3) financial transaction taxes (FTT), which are taxes on transactions in financial instruments, in particular securities.[1] Forms of these financial sector taxes, such as taxes on bank profits or stamp duties, have been introduced in several countries as permanent or temporary measures (e.g., see Brondolo 2011; IMF 2010).

In September 2011 the European Commission issued a proposal for an EU-wide financial transaction tax. The aim of the proposal is to ensure that financial institutions make a fair contribution to the costs of the recent crisis, to create disincentives for socially unproductive transactions, and to avoid fragmentation of the internal market by uncoordinated measures at national level (European Commission

2012). The Commission proposes levying the tax on a broad set of secondary-market transactions (shares, bonds, derivatives) but exclude refinancing operations with central banks, most day-to-day transactions of private households and businesses (insurance contracts, mortgage lending, consumer credit, payment services), and currency transactions. The purpose of a broad tax base is to hinder tax evasion via the creation of alternative instruments and contain negative liquidity effects in certain parts of the market. A broad tax base also allows raising substantial revenue at low tax rates.

Against this backdrop, our chapter contributes to the discussion on the merits and drawbacks of an FTT. In particular, it concentrates on two key dimensions of the policy discussion: (1) the potential of such a tax to reduce the (nonfundamental) volatility of financial and real variables and (2) the long-term impact of the tax on capital costs, investment, and economic activity. Our interest and focus derives from the scarcity of integrated analysis on these two dimensions, especially the lack of an integrated treatment in a general-equilibrium framework.[2]

The general-equilibrium perspective, which is rather unusual in the public finance literature to date, is of interest for at least three independent reasons: (1) It illustrates the direct and indirect effects of taxation and their structural determinants. (2) It allows for a stylized comparison of the FTT with other standard taxes, in particular consumption taxes, corporate taxes and labor income taxes. Based on general-equilibrium models, macroeconomists have arrived at a hierarchy of taxes that ranks them by the size of distortions they create, with consumption taxes being the least and capital taxes the most distortionary. Placing the FTT in this hierarchy is a useful contribution to the policy debate. (3) The general-equilibrium framework enables economists to carry out proper welfare analysis that accounts for the level and volatility effects of FTTs.

Before we turn to the general equilibrium perspective, the next section reviews the existing research on the two dimensions of our interest. Most of this research has focused on one of the two aspects: the short-term volatility or long-term level effects; section 9.2 preserves this division. The discussion mainly concerns the effects of taxing equity. The analysis of taxes on financial derivatives or foreign-exchange transactions is beyond the scope of this chapter. In the following section we discuss the results of a general-equilibrium analysis of the impact of introducing an FTT on equity transactions. To the best of our knowledge, the underlying modeling work (Lendvai et al. 2012, 2013) is the first attempt to address the impact of equity transaction taxes in a DSGE framework. We show that the impact of the tax on financial and real sector volatility is limited, while the long-term impact in terms of higher capital costs and lower output is very similar to the impact of corporate income taxation.

The approach described in section 9.3 is only a first step in the process of incorporating FTTs into full-fledged general-equilibrium models. The modeling is stylized and misses details that might be relevant in the context of financial sector taxation. In section 9.4 we highlight several extensions that might affect the findings of the model in either direction and propose a list of issues that future research may want to pick up. Section 9.5 concludes.

9.2   A Bird's-eye View on Existing Literature

This section briefly summarizes existing work on the impact of transaction taxes or, more generally, transaction costs on market volatility and long-term levels of economic variables. Given the focus of the existing studies, the evidence is limited to effects on the volatility and long-term levels of financial variables. The link between financial and real variables remains unexplored in these contributions.

9.2.1   Transaction Taxes and Market Volatility

Transaction taxes would be beneficial from the regulatory perspective if these taxes reduced volatility in the financial and real sector of the economy to the extent that such volatility reflects nonfundamental ("noise") trading rather than an efficient adjustment to changes in economic fundamentals.[3] Curbing short-term financial trade is by some argued to reduce asset mis-pricing, nonfundamental market volatility, and the consumption of resources in socially unproductive zero-sum activities in this perspective (e.g., Stiglitz 1989; Summers and Summers 1989). Whether transaction taxes reduce the volatility in financial markets is foremost an empirical question. Transaction taxes and, more generally, transaction costs may reduce the "excess" volatility associated with nonfundamental shocks to return expectations. They may also increase the volatility of asset prices, however, by reducing market liquidity ("market thinning"). If taxing financial transactions reduces liquidity below the level where individual transactions have only negligible impact on asset prices, individual (fundamental and nonfundamental) transactions amplify asset price volatility compared to more liquid markets (e.g., Habermeier and Kirilenko 2003).[4] Given that discrimination between fundamental and nonfundamental transactions is difficult or impossible in practice, reducing the transaction volumes in financial markets does also not necessarily improve market efficiency from the volatility perspective. Furthermore, if all transactions are taxed at equal rates and independently of their respective risk profiles, transaction taxes are also unlikely to reduce risk-taking and fragility in the financial sector (Keen 2011).

Empirical studies on transaction taxes, or transaction costs, and market volatility are scarce and provide no clear evidence for a market-stabilizing impact of financial transaction taxes and, more generally, financial transaction costs. In fact Hau (2006) finds that increasing transaction costs have increased the volatility of individual share prices at short frequencies in the French stock market. Baltagi et al. (2006) find that the Chinese stamp tax has reduced trade volumes, increased market volatility and lengthened the time it takes for the stock market to absorb external shocks. Jones and Seguin (1997) find that declining transaction costs (i.e., the opposite of increasing transaction taxes or transaction costs) have increased trade volumes and reduced share price volatility in the NYSE. Note, however, that the existing empirical studies focus on transaction costs or taxes applying to subsegments of the financial market. The broad application of a transaction tax would narrow the scope for tax avoidance and could consequently reduce the negative impact on market liquidity and the related amplification of asset price volatility.

9.2.2   Long-Term Effects of Transaction Taxes

Besides the potentially ambivalent impact of transaction taxes on financial volatility, the second fundamental and controversial point in the policy and academic debate is the tax incidence, namely where will the tax burden finally be shifted, and what are the implications on the financing costs of firms, real investment, employment, and output in the longer term. The cost of capital for investors in the real sector increases to the extent that transaction taxes reduce the after-tax return and lower equity prices. Under decreasing returns to capital, higher capital costs reduce the capital stock, labor productivity, and real output in the long run. Moreover falling asset prices through primary-market taxation increase the cost of capital to be raised by new issuance of debt and equity. However, even if the tax excludes primary markets, secondary-market taxation may still significantly increase the costs of capital. Investors in debt or equity may, for instance, require premia on new issuance if lower secondary-market liquidity makes liquidating asset positions in the future and insuring against investment risks more difficult or expensive. Taxing secondary-market transactions may also reduce real investment when firms are credit-constrained as the decline in asset prices reduces the available collateral for investment loans.

Empirical studies on the impact of financial transaction costs or taxes on equity prices tend to support the view that transaction taxes lower equity prices and raise the cost of capital. Hu (1998) reports a negative impact of rising stamp-duty rates on stock prices in Asian markets. Umlauf (1993) estimates a share price decline by 5 percent in response to the announcement of the 1984 introduction of a 1 percent financial transaction tax in Sweden. In the opposite direction, Bond et al. (2005) find a positive impact of (announced) cuts in the UK stamp duty on the relative price of more frequently traded shares. The point estimates in Jackson and O'Donnell (1985) suggest that share prices rose by around 8 percent in response to the one percentage point reduction in the UK stamp duty in 1984. Westerholm (2003) estimates similar elasticities for the response of share prices to transaction costs in Finland and Sweden. These empirical studies do, however, not assess the propagation of the equity-price effect to real investment, capital and economic activity, which is captured in the general-equilibrium model discussed in section 9.3.

The general-equilibrium framework also allows a comparison with other taxes to assess the tax-related distortions relative to other instruments of revenue collection. Notably, the assessment of the long-term effects of financial transaction taxes might appear in a more favorable light if the former were less distortive than, for instance, corporate or labor income taxes. Implemented as a tax shift, levying transaction taxes could allow reducing other (more) distortionary taxes in this case.

9.3   Transaction Taxes in a DSGE Model

This section discusses the impact of an equity transaction tax (ETT) on financial markets and the macroeconomy in a dynamic stochastic general-equilibrium (DSGE) framework.[5] Empirical research and partial-equilibrium models have so far analyzed the impact of transaction taxes on (1) financial market volatility and (2) long-term financing costs separately; also the few contributions that tried to assess the implications of transaction taxes on the real economy did so outside the workhorse model that they used to assess the ETT's impact on financial variables. By contrast, the general-equilibrium approach can address the two dimensions within a single framework and directly links financial market dynamics to real sector volatility as well as long-term levels of economic aggregates.

The analysis of this section focuses on the general-equilibrium effects of a tax imposed on spot market equity transactions which is a tax akin to, for example, the UK stamp duty. The discussion is meant to illustrate ways in which linkages between the financial and nonfinancial sectors can be thought of. To keep the analysis tractable, the model abstracts from financial transaction taxes on other types of transactions such as foreign currency transactions or trade in financial derivatives.

9.3.1   A Brief Summary of the Model

While a general-equilibrium approach is warranted to analyze the macroeconomic impact of financial market taxation in a coherent way allowing for feedback effects across the entire economy, the assessment of financial transaction taxation in standard DSGE models proves to be challenging. First, standard models assume frictionless financial markets, a feature which precludes a discussion of macro-financial linkages in the economy. Second, DSGE models generally build on representative agents. If agents are homogeneous, however, each agent will hold identical portfolios and there is no incentive for trade among investors. Hence secondary financial market trade cannot be addressed in such a framework, nor can the taxation of secondary market transactions.

Therefore, to discuss the macroeconomic impact of the ETT in a DSGE model, it is necessary to depart from these two standard assumptions by allowing for (1) financial market frictions which make financial sector shocks and taxes matter for the real economy and (2) heterogeneity across agents who trade in financial markets, which leads to trade in financial assets among traders (secondary market trade).

For the first, we follow an influential recent contribution by Gertler and Karadi (2011) to assume that a part of households' savings is channeled from households to nonfinancial corporations via a sector of financial traders.[6] The friction that makes the financial sector's activity matter for the real economy is a leverage constraint for financial traders. The constraint originates from a moral hazard problem between depositor households and the traders. The leverage can be shown to depend on the share of funds that traders can irrecoverably divert as well as on the traders' future expected profitability. This leverage constraint puts an upper limit to the funds that traders can invest in corporate shares and thereby constrains the equalization of risk-adjusted returns across assets in the economy. Specifically, due to the limited funds that can be invested in assets, the returns on shares will remain relatively high (excess return) and the share price will be relatively low in the economy. Since the access to share issuance is necessary for firms to finance their productive capital, the financial sector's leverage constraint will have repercussions for economic activity in the model. Thereby, any shock that affects either financial traders' own capital or their degree of leverage will also be transmitted to the real economy through the leverage constraint.

Second, secondary financial market trade is introduced into this model by the "noise trader" approach based on De Long et al. (1990) and Shleifer and Summers (1990). The approach assumes that a share of traders is subject to changing sentiments about future asset returns ("noisy expectations"). The change in noise traders' sentiment is captured by a shock to their expectations, which generates trade between traders with noisy expectations and traders with rational expectations in the model. The noise trade is meant to capture nonfundamentals-based secondary financial market trade that policy makers arguably wish to target when introducing a financial transactions tax. The ETT in the model is introduced on noise-driven trade only, namely the tax base is restricted to the transactions triggered by noise shocks.

The fact that in our model all secondary financial market trade is driven by nonfundamental shocks and further that the ETT can be introduced on purely nonfundamentals-based financial trade is a simplifying assumption which is deliberately idealistic. It is meant to reflect the most favorable views on the effects of an ETT on the economy. Taxing nonfundamentals-driven trade only may potentially dampen nonfundamental fluctuations without restricting the adjustment to fundamental shocks. As the discrimination between fundamental and nonfundamental transactions is highly debatable in practical terms, the model is likely to introduce an upward bias for the potential gain from ETT imposition. It is unlikely that transaction taxes will be able to discriminate between fundamentals-based and noise trade in practice.

In practical terms, our model assumes a representative household that receives labor income and returns to savings and investment. The household can invest in risk-free government bonds or in corporate bonds and can save at the risk-free interest rate. It pays taxes on labor income and in the form of lump-sum taxes. Facing a dynamic budget constraint, the household maximizes lifetime utility, which depends positively on consumption and negatively on hours worked. Financial intermediaries collect deposits from non-owner households and collect capital investment from owner households and invest the money in traded corporate shares. They will receive a return on this investment in the form of dividends, which after deduction of the repayment of the loans (augmented by interest) to non-owner households will be paid to owner households. Financial intermediaries will seek to maximize the expected discounted return to their investments in shares. Financial intermediaries contain, however, a fixed share of noise traders who differ from rational traders in their expectations. Their expectations are affected by an additional noise shock (i.e., a white noise). The government collects an ETT on the difference between individual and average trading behavior, which limits the application of the tax to noise trading. This reflects the most positive possible design of the ETT as it does not affect price adjustments to changes in the fundamentals of the economy (TFP shocks in the model). Finally, firms maximize the present value of discounted dividends and pay corporate taxes on their profit. A full description of the model with parameterization can be found in Lendvai et al. (2013).

9.3.2 Intuition

To understand the intuition behind the results, note that a noise shock to traders' return expectations affects their demand for corporate shares. Unlike in models with a standard Euler equation on share returns, traders' ability to adjust their shareholding position in reaction to a noise shock is limited by the leverage constraint. In effect, equity returns and prices react to noise shocks and can move in either direction depending on the sign of the shock. In the case of positive noise, noise traders increase their demand for equity, which increases the share price. Via the firms' balance-sheet constraint, this leads to an increase in the level of capital and output. Negative noise shocks, by reducing the demand for stocks, have the opposite effect. The overall effect of the noise shock on the price level, capital, and output is hence ambiguous. However, the shock increases the volatility of financial and, potentially, real variables.

In contrast to stochastic noise shocks, introducing an ETT on noise trade always reduces the profitability of this trade and, in consequence, unambiguously reduces the demand for shares. In the case of positive noise, noise traders increase their demand for equity, which increases the share price. Imposing a tax on equity transactions will reduce the expected profitability of additional equity purchases. The required before-tax return increases and the share price remains below the share price in a zero-tax environment. A negative noise shock, in contrast, reduces the noise traders' demand for corporate equity. The decline in equity demand lowers the price of corporate shares. Levying a tax on equity sales reduces the expected profitability and the asset demand even further, so that the price of equity falls below the level that would prevail in a zero-tax environment. Consequently taxing transactions reduces share prices below their zero-tax level for positive and negative noise shocks alike. Finally, the impact of the ETT on the price of equity matters for physical investment and real sector activity because of the balance-sheet constraint of final goods producers.

At the same time, by reducing the profitability of noise trade, the ETT may potentially curb nonfundamentals-driven financial trading activity and thereby to also reduce excess volatility in the nonfinancial sector that is related to nonfundamental financial trade.

9.3.3   Main Findings

The model is calibrated to approximately match the empirical shares of demand components in GDP as well as certain characteristics of euro-area financial markets (see Lendvai et al. 2013 for details).

The results discussed show the impact of an ETT rate that generates additional revenues of 0.1 percent of GDP in line with the European Commission estimates of revenue that could be raised by taxing spot market transactions. Our results are approximately linear with respect to the targeted transaction tax revenue.

The simulation results suggest that introducing the ETT has a marked negative impact on the long-term level of economic activity (see table 9.1): apart from employment, the mean of every real economic variable is found to fall by between 0.2 and 0.6 percent. This is driven by the increase in expected before-tax equity premium and the subsequent fall in share prices.

Apart from the objective of raising additional tax revenue, the principal argument in favor of financial transaction taxes is the potential reduction of financially driven macroeconomic volatility. The model simulations yield mixed evidence for this argument. On the one hand, the simulation results confirm that introducing an ETT on noise trade

Table 9.1
Impact of the ETT

	Δmean (%)	Δstd (%)	$\Delta[100 * std(\ln x_t / \bar{x})]_{(pp)}$
Output	−0.22	0.00	0.01
Capital	−0.56	0.00	0.02
Investment	−0.56	−0.02	0.05
Consumption	−0.17	−0.01	0.01
Employment	−0.02	−0.05	0.00
Real wage	−0.20	0.00	0.01
Noise trade	−0.56	−0.57	0.00
Share price	−0.56	0.00	0.02
	Δmean (pp)	Δstd (%)	
Risk-free return	0.00	−0.25	
Return on shares	0.12	−0.16	
ETT revenue (% of GDP)	0.10		
Implicit ETT rate	0.07		

Note: Impact of the introduction of an ETT raising tax revenues by 0.1 percent of GDP. Δmean is the change in the variables' long-run average; results displayed as percentage changes (%) for macroeconomic aggregates and prices and as percentage point changes (pp) for the remaining variables. Δstd is the implied percentage change in the variables' standard deviation. The last column shows the percentage point change in the standard deviation of log-normalized variables where available.

reduces noise-trading activity and that it can thereby also reduce the volatility of financial returns (both risk-free and risky). However, the standard deviation of real economic variables is barely affected by the reduction of nonfundamentals-based trade in the model.

These numerical results for the impact of an ETT on long-term share prices and capital costs are qualitatively in line with the empirical studies discussed in section 9.2, which find a clear negative correlation between transaction costs/taxes and share prices but which do not address the impact of transaction taxes on real economic volatility (Bond et al. 2005; Jackson and O'Donnell 1985; Umlauf 1993; Westerholm 2003).

Comparing the impact of an ETT to that of the corporate income tax (CIT) and the labor income tax generating identical tax revenues, we find that the distortions introduced by the CIT are qualitatively and quantitatively very similar to those introduced by the ETT (table 9.2).[7] The labor income tax has less distortive long-run effects on economic activity than the ETT or CIT (see table 9.3).

Table 9.2
Impact of a corporate income tax increase

	Δmean (%)	Δstd (%)	$\Delta[100 * std(\ln x_t/\bar{x})]_{(pp)}$
Output	−0.20	−0.16	0.00
Capital	−0.50	−0.30	0.01
Investment	−0.50	−0.37	0.01
Consumption	−0.15	−0.06	0.00
Employment	−0.02	−0.24	0.00
Real wage	−0.17	−0.10	0.00
Noise trade	−0.50	−0.49	0.00
Share price	−0.50	−0.30	0.01
	Δmean (pp)	Δstd (%)	
Risk-free return	0.00	−0.01	
Return on shares	0.00	−0.02	
Corporate tax revenue (% of GDP)	0.10		
Corporate tax rate	0.01		

Note: Impact of corporate income tax hike raising tax revenues by 0.1 percent of GDP. Δmean is the change in the variables' long-run average; results displayed as percentage changes (%) for macroeconomic aggregates and prices and as percentage point changes (pp) for the remaining variables. Δstd is the implied percentage change in the variables' standard deviation. The last column shows the percentage point change in the standard deviation of log-normalized variables where available.

The similarity of the long-run macroeconomic impact of the ETT and the CIT comes from the fact that, ultimately, both increase the cost of capital investment. The corporate tax does so directly, whereas the ETT increases the cost of capital financing by decreasing the demand for corporate equity. As it turns out, if a tax increase is meant to raise a similar amount of revenue, as in our comparison, both taxes lead to quantitatively similar real effects.

There are two important differences between the ETT and the CIT, however. The first is their impact on the financial returns: while the ETT reduces the volatility of financial returns and increases the equity premium, these two variables are barely affected by the corporate tax. Second, the introduction of the ETT has very little impact on the volatility of real variables. In contrast, these volatilities are significantly reduced by the corporate income tax.

Table 9.3 illustrates that the labor tax is the least distortive among the three taxes considered. The level of output falls by 0.1 percent in the long term for the permanent tax rate increase generating additional

Table 9.3
Impact of a labor income tax increase

	$\Delta mean$ (%)	Δstd (%)	$\Delta[100 * std(\ln x_t / \bar{x})]_{(pp)}$
Output	−0.12	−0.12	0.00
Capital	−0.12	−0.11	0.00
Investment	−0.12	−0.12	0.00
Consumption	−0.14	−0.13	0.00
Employment	−0.12	−0.09	0.00
Real wage	0.00	0.01	0.00
Noise trade	−0.12	−0.11	0.01
Share price	−0.12	−0.11	0.00
	$\Delta mean$ (pp)	Δstd (%)	
Risk-free return	0.00	0.01	
Return on shares	0.00	0.01	
Labor tax revenue (% of GDP)	0.10		
Labor tax rate	0.002		

Note: Impact of a labor income tax hike raising tax revenues by 0.1 percent of GDP. $\Delta mean$ is the change in the variables' long-run average; results displayed as percentage changes (%) for macroeconomic aggregates and prices and as percentage point changes (pp) for the remaining variables. Δstd is the implied percentage change in the variables' standard deviation. The last column shows the percentage point change in the standard deviation of log-normalized variables where available.

tax revenue of 0.1 percent of GDP, which is half the output decline that occurs when raising identical revenue by the ETT or the CIT. Contrary to the ETT and the CIT, where the output decline is driven by falling levels of investment and capital, the negative output effect from higher labor taxation is driven by the decline in employment.

It is also instructive to compare the impact of an increase in the ETT with a cut in government expenditures as an alternative strategy to improve the primary government balance. Table 9.4 shows results for permanent expenditure cuts that achieve the same improvement in the primary balance. The impact of the cut in government expenditures depends on the extent to which these expenditures increase the productivity of private sector output. Two benchmark cases in macroeconomic literature are (1) entirely unproductive government spending and (2) productive government spending, where the elasticity of private output with respect to public capital equals the share of public investment in GDP.[8] As a third case we also add a higher degree of productivity to the simulation scenarios.

Table 9.4
Comparison of different fiscal measures

Instrument	$\Delta mean$ (% of GDP)
ETT	–0.22
CIT	–0.20
PTT	–0.12
Government spending	
Output elasticity* = 0	–0.07
Output elasticity*,** = 0.05	–0.20
Output elasticity* = 0.1	–0.34

Note: * indicates output elasticity with respect to government spending; ** corresponds to the share of public investment in GDP.

The results of the simulations show clearly that the long-term output losses generated by permanent government spending cuts largely depend on the productivity of the spending items. In the case of cutting unproductive spending, the output losses incurred are lower than those implied by the introduction of the ETT. Considering the public investment level to be optimal (i.e., case 2), the output losses are similar to those implied by the ETT. Finally, the output losses by spending cuts can exceed those implied by the ETT in case expenditures on highly productive public investment projects are cut.

Inversely, it is also possible to interpret these results by asking what would be the overall effect of spending revenues raised by the ETT on public investment projects. The answer that follows from the above discussion is that the overall impact can range from negative to positive depending on whether the projects eventually raise private productivity to a sufficient degree. Interestingly, calibrating the productivity of government investment based on the assumption that the current share of public investment expenditure in GDP is optimal, the overall impact of ETT-financed government investment (i.e., raising an ETT to finance additional government investment) is found to be roughly neutral. However, it should be pointed out that financing public investment of a given productivity by labor income taxes rather than the ETT will always generate more gains/less losses due to the lower degree of distortions introduced by the labor tax. Sensitivity checks across changes to the parametrization confirm the robustness of these results.

9.3.4 An Alternative Model Framework

Another model to analyze the impact of taxes on equity transactions is developed in Lendvai et al. (2012). The model shares main features of Lendvai et al. (2013) such as the objectives of households and firms and the production structure in the economy. Instead of financial intermediaries with Gertler and Karadi (2011) lending constraint, the model in Lendvai et al. (2012) introduces financial traders next to traditional infinitely lived worker-saver households. The financial traders borrow from households, invest in corporate equity and consume the investment return net of repayments to lender households. The traders' aim is to maximize their expected consumption, which implies maximizing expected investment returns. Lendvai et al. (2012) introduce two types of traders, namely "informed traders" with rational expectations and "noise traders" whose expectations are distorted by a white noise shock. Similarly to noisy information of financial intermediaries in Lendvai et al. (2013), noise trading in Lendvai et al. (2012) generates nonfundamental ("excessive") equity trade. Nonfundamental trade leads to nonfundamental volatility of equity prices and nonfundamental volatility in corporate investment given the financing constraint of firms in the real sector. To the extent that a tax on equity transactions (levied here on noise- and fundamental-driven transactions) reduces nonfundamental transactions and price fluctuations, the tax also stabilizes capital costs and corporate investment in the economy.

Contrary to Lendvai et al. (2013), the model in Lendvai et al. (2012) also includes resource costs of financial transactions. These resource costs take the form of output consumption analogous to the standard modeling of adjustment costs in DSGE models. The trading costs increase the economic costs of nonfundamental financial transactions (e.g., Stiglitz 1989; Summers and Summers 1989) compared to a model without transaction costs. At first sight, one may expect that the presence of transaction costs increases the real gain from reducing nonfundamental trading in financial markets. Transaction costs already reduce the amount of trading for given noise shocks, however. Hence one would expect the absence or presence of transaction costs to affect the total volume of financial transactions for given noise shocks without changing (much) the additional impact of ETT imposition on financial transaction.

In fact transaction costs and the ETT have similar effects on trading behavior. The main difference between adjustment costs and the tax is that adjustment costs consume resources and enter the resource con-

Table 9.5
Impact of the ETT in an alternative model version

	$\Delta mean$ (%)	Δstd (%)	$\Delta[100*std(\ln x_t/\bar{x})]_{(pp)}$
Output	−0.19	−1.18	−0.03
Capital	−0.43	−0.28	0.00
Investment	−0.42	−4.00	−0.13
Consumption	−0.02	−3.27	−0.12
Employment	−0.06	−8.33	−0.14
Real wage	−0.14	−0.48	−0.01
Noise trade	−8.40	−19.63	−21.91
Share price	−8.40	−10.00	−0.06
	$\Delta mean$ (pp)	Δstd (%)	
Risk-free return	0.00	−7.59	
Return on shares	1.25	0.43	
Transaction costs (% of GDP)	−0.06		
ETT revenue (% of GDP)	0.09		
Implicit ETT rate	0.14		

Note: Impact of the introduction of an ETT raising tax revenues by 0.1 percent of GDP. $\Delta mean$ is the change in the variables' long-run average; results displayed as percentage changes (%) for macroeconomic aggregates and prices and as percentage point changes (pp) for the remaining variables. Δstd is the implied percentage change in the variables' standard deviation. The last column shows the percentage point change in the standard deviation of log-normalized variables where available.

straint of the economy, whereas the ETT payments transfer resources from traders to the government budget and leave the overall resource constraint of the economy unaffected.

Results from the model in Lendvai et al. (2012) are reported in table 9.5 and can be compared to the Lendvai et al. (2013) results in table 9.1. The comparison shows both sets of results to be qualitatively and quantitatively similar. Long-term average values of real variables decline by similar magnitudes in both settings associated with the tax-related increase in corporate financing costs. The ETT reduces the price of traded equity and increases the average before-tax return on equity. The increase in the before-tax return on equity raises the financing costs of firms and reduces the average level of investment and capital. Average output, consumption and employment decline as well in response to the lower stock of capital, lower labor productivity and lower income. The decline in consumption and investment associated with similar average output reduction is more moderate in table 9.5, however, which derives from the fact that the transaction tax reduces financial trade and, hence, the resource costs of trading for the economy in this model variant.

Table 9.5 also shows a more pronounced ETT-related decline of real sector volatility compared to table 9.1. The stronger stabilization derives from the fact that financial traders consume investment profits period by period in the Lendvai et al. (2012) framework, whereas the profit of financial intermediaries is transferred to intertemporally optimizing households in Lendvai et al. (2013). The impact of noise shocks and related fluctuations in financial returns on aggregate demand is therefore stronger in the model underlying table 9.5. As a consequence the ETT-related reduction in noise-driven financial trade has stronger stabilizing effects on real sector variables.

9.4   Putting the DSGE Results into Perspective

In the benchmark model discussed in the previous section (Lendvai et al. 2013), the stock market provides financing for companies, and the ETT increases the cost of capital for firms by lowering the after-tax return to equity investment. Hence analyzing the impact of the tax on the cost of capital as the main channel by which an ETT affects the real economy is a natural way to assess its long-run effects (see also Hawkins and McCrae 2002). An additional advantage of this approach is that it allows for a stylized comparison with other distortionary taxes and with the effects of changes in public investment.

That said the effect on the cost of capital is not the only channel by which an ETT may affect economic activity. Economic models are simplifications of real-world processes and institutions. These simplifications are partly deliberate: they are aspects of the world that are kept aside to focus on the main channels and mechanisms of interest. Yet some of them are due to technical or conceptual problems with incorporating certain important features of the real world into a DSGE framework. This section situates our model-based analysis in the context of the academic and policy debate, in an attempt to identify relevant elements that would enrich and perhaps also modify the conclusions of our simple model. The following rather lengthy list should be viewed as a long-term research agenda in the field. At the current level of development of general equilibrium models incorporation of many of these elements would be very difficult.

Some channels that are absent from our model are likely to improve the assessment of the ETT in terms of lower financial and real volatility and more positive long-term output effects, whereas other elements might rather amplify short-term fluctuations and the negative impact on economic activity. Starting with the latter, transaction taxes are seen as introducing additional distortions between sectors and firms. An effect particularly associated with an ETT is that it distorts firms' financing decisions from equity toward debt. To the extent that some firms have easier access to debt financing than others, the ETT distorts the access to and the costs of financing across firms. It may also distort investment patterns between industries by disadvantaging sectors that rely more than others on risk capital in the form of equity. The effect is similar to the distortion introduced by the differential treatment of equity and debt in corporate income taxation. The empirical relevance of the financing distortion introduced by the CIT is discussed and illustrated in, for example, Feldstein (2006) and Johansson et al. (2008).[9]

A yet different margin is location decisions by firms, in particular, the impact of transaction taxes on the cross-border relocation of financial companies (to avoid the higher costs of transactions/intermediation) as well as nonfinancial firms (to decrease the financing cost of investment). The impact crucially depends on the selected tax base, namely whether transactions are taxed according to the place of origin of the underlying equity or according to the place of the transaction. Taxing transactions in equity issued by domestic firms disadvantages domestic nonfinancial companies as it raises their financing costs relative to foreign competitors, which may reduce domestic investment and activity and shift investment to foreign entities and locations (thereby also reducing the bases of corporate and labor taxes). Taxing transactions by the place of trading, regardless of the origin of the assets, provides incentives for the delocalization of financial services. Tax avoidance by delocalization may (further) increase the opacity of the financial sector and complicate effective financial regulation, which provides a strong case for an internationally harmonized approach.

Extending the discussion to financial transaction taxes (FTT) more generally, there are additional channels by which such taxes can affect the long-term economic performance and the short-term volatility of financial and real variables. Again, we focus on the channels that feature most prominently in the literature or public discussion. Several of these channels suggest additional negative economic effects of FTTs:

transaction taxes may cascade through the production chain, increase the costs of risk diversification and reduce market liquidity and price discovery. Other arguments point toward more benign effects of these taxes: an FTT may potentially reduce socially unproductive activities in the financial sector as well as the probability of the emergence of asset price bubbles.

To illustrate the cascading effect of transaction taxes, our model could be extended to include financial transactions as intermediate input or factor of production alongside capital and labor as proposed by Matheson (2011). The use of financial transactions as input varies across firms and sectors, so that transaction taxes will affect production costs across firms and sectors to a different degree, which in turn distorts production decisions. The evident example is the cascading effect of a general FTT that taxes all financial transactions between separate legal entities in the production process. Such tax would tend to favor the vertical integration of production chains, with the effect of restricting competition in intermediate goods markets and potentially also among final goods producers. The more atomistic the market, the higher are transaction costs under a cascading FTT.

Unlike the UK stamp duty or the ETT in our model, current proposals in Europe assume the financial transaction tax to be levied also on derivative transactions. In fact most of the estimated FTT revenue would stem from taxing derivative transactions (see European Commission 2012). While proponents of the tax argue that, especially in recent years, most derivative transactions have been detached from the hedging objective of firms and have rather speculative character (e.g., Schaefer 2012), there is little doubt that risk-hedging is still an economically important motive for derivative trading (Matheson 2011). Since European FTT proposals do not exempt risk-hedging transactions from the tax, the costs of hedging are bound to increase.[10] Quantifying the impact of the cost increase on the real economy would be of great relevance and interest, but is intrinsically very difficult. The problem is twofold. First, it is hard to quantify what proportion of trades in derivatives is driven by hedging motives. Second, economists still lack a proper modeling framework for hedging motives especially in general-equilibrium frameworks. Financial derivatives are absent from our model for exactly these reasons.

Another channel that could add to the detrimental effects of an FTT is the impact on market liquidity, which affects the impact of a given trade on asset prices (e.g., Kupiec 1996). Lower liquidity can have negative effects in the short and long term. First, lower liquidity increases the impact of individual transactions on asset prices and may decelerate the process of price discovery, which would increase asset price volatility and prolong periods of asset mispricing to the extent that, otherwise, prices would reflect fundamental factors (Matheson 2011). Second, lower market liquidity is likely to increase the liquidity premium required by traders, as less liquid markets make it more difficult to liquidate current asset positions when needed. A higher liquidity premium would further reduce asset prices beyond the impact of higher transaction costs on capital costs, leading to an additional increase in the cost of capital and an additional decline in economic activity. Again, incorporating liquidity effects in a general-equilibrium model is difficult since it requires giving up the notion of atomistic agents. It would be even more difficult to model the process of price discovery by financial institutions in such a framework.

However, the introduction of an FTT may also have additional positive effects that are neglected in the Lendvai et al. (2013) model. In contrast to the impact on hedging costs and market liquidity, two such effects seem easier to incorporate in a general-equilibrium framework. First, one can incorporate costs of financial market operations in the form of resource costs analogous to the standard modeling of adjustment costs or a production function for equity trading that uses labor and/or capital input to produce financial transactions. Resource costs of trading increase the economic costs of nonfundamental (but also fundamental) financial transactions and thereby allow for more real gains from less nonfundamental trade (e.g., Stiglitz 1989; Summers and Summers 1989). As discussed in section 9.3.4, the model in Lendvai et al. (2012) includes such transaction costs and obtains more moderate negative long-term real sector effects of levying an ETT, since ETT imposition reduces the resource costs absorbed in the financial sector. The imposition of an ETT leads to a small reduction in resource consumption by reducing the volume of noisy transactions, which cushions a little the negative long-term impact of the tax on the real economy.

From another angle, one can argue that relatively low marginal trading costs are a prerequisite for small ETT rates to have nonnegligible impact on the volume of financial transactions. If the marginal costs of financial trading were high, transaction volumes should not react strongly to nonfundamental events. Hence, transaction costs would mimic the ETT's corrective role in limiting nonproductive transactions (see also section 9.3.4).

A second element that may understate ETT-related gains in the model of section 9.3 is the separation between noise and rational traders. Our way of modeling noise/bubbles is very simple. Within the model the noise shock distorts only the expectations of noise traders. Other traders and agents remain rational in the sense that they adjust their responses to changes in the behavior of noise traders, but have themselves rational expectations. The effects in terms of the size and persistence of nonfundamental fluctuations would tend to be stronger if the noise traders also affected the expectations of previously rational traders in the economy, namely if noisy expectations were contagious. In our model a positive noise shock increases the equity demand by noise traders. The resulting share price increase reduces the equity demand by rational-expectation traders. The rational-expectation traders adopt contrarian behavior in this sense.

Borrowing from Christiano et al. (2010) a less simplistic setup could be developed in which boom–bust cycles are based on shared nonfundamental beliefs. This approach would incorporate contagion of optimism and pessimism in the economy and would let rational traders to (partly) follow noise traders and act in the same direction. The contagion mechanism would amplify nonfundamental volatility and prolong market deviations from fundamental prices, which might strengthen the benefits from volatility-reducing transaction taxes in terms of business-cycle stabilization.

The idea that an FTT may be useful in preventing asset price bubbles has been raised in the literature before. Scheinkman and Xiong (2003) put this hypothesis to a direct test and consider a transaction tax in a partial equilibrium model with two types of overconfident traders that trade in a generic financial asset. They demonstrate how differences in the valuation of the asset by the overconfident traders produce sizeable bubbles and show that transaction taxes reduce asset trade as in the model of section 9.3. Interestingly, however, the results suggest that the size of the bubble (understood as the difference between the actual asset price and its fundamental value) and the asset price volatility are little affected by the transaction tax.

Taken together, there is still too little theoretical and empirical research on the distortionary or corrective impact of financial transaction taxes in our view. In particular, we believe that there is room for analyzing these elements in a partial equilibrium setting. Embedding these aspects in a general-equilibrium framework appears still more difficult. Against this background, our modeling work aims at providing an initial, simplified but integrated discussion of the ETT's qualitative short-term and long-term effects rather than a quantitative assessment. The analysis provides interesting results, such as concerning the hierarchy of different taxes with respect to efficiency. Rather than being the final word, we hope the results may motivate further research in this area.

9.5 Conclusions

In this chapter we discussed the short-term and long-term macroeconomic impact of equity transaction taxes (ETT). Starting from a survey of theoretical arguments and empirical evidence on the volatility and level effects of transaction taxes, we provided simulation results from a general-equilibrium approach that suggest nonnegligible effects of the ETT on financial and real economic variables. The results have been placed in the context of the academic and policy debate to discuss the sensitivity of the simulation results with respect to modeling assumptions and the model structure and to relate our analysis of the ETT to the discussion of pros and cons of financial transaction taxes in general.

The simulation results suggest the ETT to reduce financial trading and dampen the volatility especially of financial sector variables. Volatility in the real sector is less affected by the transaction tax, partly due to the fact that real-sector volatility is also driven by fundamental shocks that are not dampened by the tax on the noise-driven part of financial market transactions. Introduction of the tax may also bring some efficiency gain as the amount of resources devoted to nonfundamental financial transactions in the economy declines. However, the size of the efficiency gain is rather limited for the low ETT rates considered in the chapter and envisaged in practice.

In an economy with financing constraints for real investors, the ETT does, however, also have negative side effects for financing costs, productive capital and output in the long run. In our example of a tax that would generate around 0.1 percent of GDP in revenue, long-term GDP could decline by about 0.2 percent. This long-term impact makes the distortive effects of the tax similar to those of corporate income taxation, which are above those of personal income and value-added taxes.

Overall, these results suggest that introducing an ETT may succeed in making the financial sector contribute to the costs of the financial crisis and in creating disincentives for socially unproductive transactions. At the same time the results indicate that achieving these objectives comes at the cost of a negative impact on economic activity.

Recent IMF studies (IMF 2010) reach similar conclusions. They also mention that alternative taxes, such as a financial activity tax or a bank levy, may be more effective tools to achieve the stated goals. The discussion of alternatives also builds on the observation that main contributing factors to the 2008 financial crisis—such as excess leverage, risk concentration, and financial innovations—are not directly linked to transaction costs/taxes. The deceleration of financial trading is not particularly effective in addressing financial complexity, excessive leverage, maturity/currency mismatch and systemic risk compared to more targeted tax or regulatory instruments (Hemmelgarn and Nicodème 2010; Matheson 2011).

Putting the results in the context of the policy debate, the limitations and simplifications in the model structure should be kept in mind. The tax considered in the model does not apply to trade in derivatives, which accounts for a large share of overall financial trade but is absent from the model. Even a very low tax rate could generate high tax revenues given the size of derivative trading.

Moreover the model looks at a closed economy with simple financial structure, which excludes a discussion of relocation effects (when entities or trading are moved abroad to avoid the application of the tax) and substitution effects (when entities change their portfolio structure to minimize the burden of the tax). In practice, broad application of the tax with respect to its geographical scope and the segments of the financial market covered would help minimizing these relocation and substitution effects.

Finally, the effects of an ETT on tax avoidance hinge on the technical design of the tax, such as the choice between taxing transactions by the origin of the underlying asset, the residence of the asset owner, and the place of trading. In principle, some of these issues could be addressed in a more complex multicountry general-equilibrium framework. The results that have been presented in this section are from a tractable model framework that avoids such complexity in favor of a better understanding of main transmission channels to the real economy.

Notes

We thank Ruud De Mooij, Ricardo Fenochietto, Thomas Hemmelgarn, Gaëtan Nicodème, and participants of the CESifo Summer Institute 2012 for very helpful comments and discussions. The views in the chapter are personal views of the authors and should not be attributed to the European Commission.

1. Matheson's (2011) category of *securities* transaction taxes broadly corresponds to our use of the term FTT. We prefer this nomenclature as it is used more frequently in the European public debate (e.g., Hemmelgarn and Nicodème 2010).

2. More generally, there has been a revival of academic interest in the field of financial taxation and regulation. Two main threads in this literature can be distinguished: a more theoretical discussion of the regulatory merits of taxing the financial sector and financial transactions especially in the context of the financial crisis (e.g., see Hemmelgarn and Nicodème 2010) and empirical work attempting to quantify the impact different transaction taxation schemes that were introduced in a number of countries. IMF (2010) and Matheson (2011) provide comprehensive surveys of the current state of policies and research. Nevertheless, as noted by Keen (2011), there is still little public finance literature on many important aspects of financial sector taxation that would guide policy makers in their choices.

3. On the concept of noise trading, see, for example, DeLong et al. (1990) or Shleifer and Summers (1990).

4. A number of partial-equilibrium heterogeneous-agent models (e.g., Demary 2006, 2010; Hanke et al. 2010; Mannaro et al. 2008; Kirchler et al. 2011; Pellizzari and Westerhoff 2009; Westerhoff and Dieci 2006) illustrate the impact of the microstructure of financial markets on the volatility effect of transaction costs or transaction taxes.

5. The following discussion and the results draw on the formal analysis in Lendvai et al. (2013).

6. The modeling of macro-financial linkages is a relatively new and, since the beginning of the financial crisis, rapidly expanding field in macroeconomic literature. The approach by Gertler and Karadi (2011) is one stylized way of modeling these linkages that has gained significant prominence, not least due to its simplicity and tractability. Our earlier paper (Lendvai et al. 2012) adopted a different approach to modeling the financial intermediation sector that captured the finite elasticity of demand for securities by the introduction of transaction costs. The findings from that model were virtually identical to the results obtained in the model we discuss in this chapter.

7. As it is standard in DSGE literature, it is assumed that the corporate income tax is levied on corporate income net of wage payments and capital depreciation. The model abstracts from various corporate-finance aspects of the CIT, such as dividend payout policy, debt-equity choices, incorporation decisions, and profit allocation.

8. As discussed in Baxter and King (1993), this benchmark corresponds to the optimal share of government investment in GDP. Empirically there are large uncertainties surrounding the productivity of government investment. For a recent contribution, see Leeper et al. (2010).

9. Endogenizing the firms' choice between equity and debt in the model underlying section 9.3 would require additional assumptions about the substitutability between both sources of financing and the heterogeneity of constraints across firms or sectors. Models that attempt to endogenize the equity-debt choice generally do so by assuming ad hoc economic costs of deviating from the optimal equity-debt mix or limited substitutability that determine the change in the financing mix in response to changes in the costs of debt and equity financing.

10. It is not clear whether such exemption would be feasible in practice. Schulmeister (2012) argues that the differentiation between speculation and risk hedging could be made operational by exempting all the trades in derivatives that are accompanied by a counter position on the spot market.

References

Baltagi, B., D. Li, and Q. Li. 2006. Transaction tax and stock market behaviour: Evidence from an emerging market. *Empirical Economics* 31: 393–408.

Baxter, M., and R. King. 1993. Fiscal policy in general equilibrium. *American Economic Review* 83: 315–34.

Bond, S., M. Hawkins, and A. Klemm. 2005. Stamp duty on shares and its effect on share prices. *Finanz-Archiv* 61: 275–97.

Brondolo, J. 2011. Taxing financial transactions: an assessment of administrative feasibility. Working paper 11/185. IMF.

Christiano, L., C. Ilut, R. Motto, and M. Rostagno. 2010. Monetary policy and stock market booms. Working paper 16402. NBER.

De Long, B., A. Shleifer, L. Summers, and R. Waldmann. 1990. Noise trader risk in financial markets. *Journal of Political Economy* 98: 703–38.

Demary, M. 2006. Transaction taxes, traders' behavior and exchange rate risks. Working paper 2006–13. Warwick Business School, Financial Econometrics Research Centre, Coventry.

Demary, M. 2010. Transaction taxes and traders with heterogeneous investment horizons in an agent-based financial market model. Economics—The open-access. *Open-Assessment E-Journal* 4: 1–44.

European Commission. 2012. Impact assessment accompanying the proposal for a Council Directive on a common system of financial transaction tax and amending Directive 2008/7/EC. Brussels.

Feldstein, M. 2006. The effect of taxes on efficiency and growth. Working paper 12201. NBER.

Gertler, M., and P. Karadi. 2011. A model of unconventional monetary policy. *Journal of Monetary Economics* 58: 17–34.

Habermeier, K., and A. Kirilenko. 2003. Securities transaction taxes and financial markets. *IMF Staff Papers* 50: 165–80.

Hanke, M., J. Huber, M. Kirchler, and M. Sutter. 2010. The economic consequences of a Tobin tax—An experimental analysis. *Journal of Economic Behavior and Organization* 74: 58–71.

Hau, H. 2006. The role of transaction costs for financial volatility: Evidence from the Paris bourse. *Journal of the European Economic Association* 4: 862–90.

Hawkins, M., and J. McCrae. 2002. Stamp duty on share transactions: Is there a case for change? *IFS Commentary* C: 89.

Hemmelgarn, T., and G. Nicodème. 2010. The 2008 financial crisis and taxation policy. Discussion paper 7666. CEPR.

Hu, S.-Y. 1998. The effects of the stock transaction tax on the stock market—Experiences from Asian markets. *Pacific-Basin Finance Journal* 6: 347–64.

IMF. 2010. A fair and substantial contribution by the financial sector. Final report for the G-20. Washington, DC.

Jackson, P., and A. O'Donnell. 1985. The effects of stamp duty on equity transactions and prices in the UK stock exchange. Discussion paper 25. Bank of England.

Johansson, A., Ch. Heady, J. Arnold, B. Brys, and L. Vartia. 2008. Taxation and economic growth. Working paper 620. OECD Economics Department.

Jones, C., and P. Seguin. 1997. Transaction costs and price volatility: evidence from commission deregulation. *American Economic Review* 87: 728–37.

Keen, M. 2011. Rethinking the taxation of the financial sector. *CESifo Economic Studies* 57: 1–24.

Kirchler, M., J. Huber, and D. Kleinlercher. 2011. Market microstructure matters when imposing a Tobin tax—Evidence from laboratory experiments. *Journal of Economic Behavior and Organization* 80: 586–602.

Kupiec, P. 1996. Noise traders, excess volatility and a securities transaction tax. *Journal of Financial Services Research* 10: 115–29.

Leeper, E., T. Walker, and S.-Ch. Yang. 2010. Government investment and fiscal stimulus. *Journal of Monetary Economics* 57: 1000–12.

Lendvai, J., Raciborski, R., Vogel, L., 2012. Securities transaction taxes: Macroeconomic implications in a general-equilibrium model. European Economy economic paper 450. European Commission.

Lendvai, J., R. Raciborski, and L. Vogel. 2013. Macroeconomic effects of an equity transaction tax in a general-equilibrium model. *Journal of Economic Dynamics and Control* 37: 466–82.

Mannaro, K., M. Marchesi, and A. Setzu. 2008. Using an artificial financial market for assessing the impact of Tobin-like transaction taxes. *Journal of Economic Behavior and Organization* 67: 445–62.

Matheson, T. 2011. Taxing financial transactions: Issues and evidence. Working paper 11/54. IMF.

Pellizzari, P., F. Westerhoff. 2009. Some effects of transaction taxes under different microstructures. *Journal of Economic Behavior and Organization* 72: 850–63.

Schaefer, D. 2012. Financial transaction tax contributes to more sustainability in financial markets. *Intereconomics* 47 (2): 76–83.

Scheinkmann, J., and W. Xiong. 2003. Overconfidence and speculative bubbles. *Journal of Political Economy* 111: 1183–1219.

Schulmeister, S. 2012. A general financial transactions tax: Strong pros, weak cons. *Intereconomics* 47 (2): 84–89.

Shleifer, A., and L. Summers. 1990. The noise trader approach to finance. *Journal of Economic Perspectives* 4: 19–33.

Stiglitz, J. 1989. Using tax policy to curb speculative short-term trading. *Journal of Financial Services Research* 3: 101–15.

Summers, L., and V. Summers. 1989. When financial markets work too well: A cautious case for a securities transaction tax. *Journal of Financial Services Research* 3: 261–86.

Umlauf, S. 1993. Transaction taxes and the behavior of the Swedish stock market. *Journal of Financial Economics* 33: 227–40.

Westerhoff, F., and R. Dieci. 2006. The effectiveness of Keynes–Tobin transaction taxes when heterogeneous agents can trade in different markets: A behavioral finance approach. *Journal of Economic Dynamics and Control* 30: 293–322.

Westerholm, J. 2003. The impact of transaction costs on turnover and asset prices: The case of Sweden's and Finland's security transaction tax reduction. *Finnish Journal of Business Economics* 2: 213–41.

10 Financial Activities Taxes, Bank Levies, and Systemic Risk

Giuseppina Cannas, Jessica Cariboni, Massimo Marchesi, Gaëtan Nicodème, Marco Petracco Giudici, and Stefano Zedda

10.1 Introduction

In the run-up and in the wake of 2007 financial crisis, the question of additional taxes on the financial sector taxation has been debated in academic and policy circles "as to how the financial sector could make a fair and substantial contribution toward paying for any burden associated with government interventions to repair the banking system" (IMF 2010). One of the drivers of this debate was the fact that the financial sector might be undertaxed, at least in the European Union, thanks to its compulsory exemption to value-added taxation (VAT).[1]

Among the various proposals, the introduction of a tax on profits and remunerations, called a "financial activities tax" or FAT (e.g., see Keen et al. 2010) would take up a role similar to VAT. The financial activities tax has, in particular, been considered as a possible option by the European Commission (2010a, b) in its Communication on Taxation of the Financial Sector. Buettner and Erbe (chapter 8 in this volume) find that a 4 percent FAT in Germany would generate similar revenues and welfare effects as the repeal of VAT exemption (at a rate of 19 percent) for the financial sector but with much smaller changes in consumer and producer prices. Another proposal introduced by several authors, and notably by the IMF (2010) that saw this as the first-best solution for the financial sector, is the financial stability contribution or bank levy. Several countries have implemented such a tax with various designs (see de Mooij and Nicodème, chapter 1 in this volume). Such a tax could also be designed to reduce risk when applied to uninsured liabilities.[2]

At the same time the banking sector is subject to various other regulatory proposals, aimed at strengthening its stability at the individual and systemic level such as Basel III and several policy initiatives in the

European Union (see section 10.3.3) and the United States (e.g., the Frank–Dodd Act). Those initiatives are particularly designed to strengthen the capital base of financial institutions and to decrease the risks of contagion. Financial and banking crises are indeed found to be extremely adverse in terms of output losses (Laeven and Valencia 2012) and policies to curtail the risks associated with financial crises are therefore high in the political agenda.

Therefore, a natural question to ask is whether a FAT or a bank levy would be a good proxy for a fee mirroring the individual contributions of banks to systemic risk (and possibly a contribution to a rescue or resolution fund), and how it would interact with other regulatory measures under the expected future regulatory scenario.

In order to investigate this question, we employ SYMBOL,[3] a microsimulation model of the banking system, to estimate contributions of individual banks within a large sample to total systemic losses under future capital requirements and resolution regimes and calculate the correlations of these contributions with alternative designs of FATs and bank levies. Under the regulatory scenarios, a capital requirement of 8 percent under a possibility of contagion is used as a proxy for the current situation while a capital requirement increased to 10.5 percent with curtailed risks of contagion is used as a proxy for the future regulatory design. A high correlation between the tax liability of financial institutions under a FAT or a bank levy and their individual contribution to systemic risk would indicate that the tax could be a serious candidate for a fee designed to reflect risk.

The literature on risk contributions of banks to systemic risk includes two approaches. The first one uses market data to investigate the correlation structure of returns and/or prices of assets of different institutions. It estimates the contribution of individual financial institutions to systemic risk using quantile regression. Systemic risk is generally measured as the change in system value at risk (e.g., Adrian and Brunnermeier 2011; Segoviano and Goodhart 2009; Acharya et al. 2012). The alternative approach uses structural models to simulate losses affecting financial institutions, via the value process of the banks' assets or a "stress test" on assets' values, and represents the channels of contagion between banks using estimated networks of interbank linkages, eventually in conjunction with interbank clearing algorithms (Upper and Worms 2004; Müller 2006; Cifuentes at al. 2005; Gauthier et al. 2012; Bluhm and Krahnen 2011; Bluhm et al. 2013).

The approach used in this chapter to calculate contributions to systemic risk broadly falls into the latter approach: SYMBOL is a structural model of the value of banks' assets which generates simulated losses for a sample of real banks, based on balance sheet and regulatory capital data. Additionally, as the model is based on individual banks, a direct contagion mechanism is modeled via the use of an interbank loans and deposits matrix. We define systemic risk as the total amount of funds which would be necessary to cover all nonequity creditors of defaulting banks, namely to cover all losses in excess of banks' capital. We then calculate the contribution to systemic risk based on the amount of funds necessary to cover expected losses generated by individual banks.

The simulation nature of SYMBOL also allows constructing counterfactual or "what if" scenarios based on future regulatory setups: losses in each scenario are distributed as implicitly defined by the Basel Regulation, correlated between banks, and based on proxies of assets' probability of default (PD) and actual values of the total capital. Based on the results of simulations we are able to construct the distribution of losses at the individual and aggregate levels and to define the contribution to risk as the average losses in excess of capital generated by each bank across all simulations.[4] Since we are not exclusively interested in tail events, we consider the whole distribution of losses.

Coming to the FAT, the tax is in essence a tax on the sum of profit and remunerations of the financial sector.[5] This tax has the features of being a good substitute for the VAT on the sector (because the sum of profit and remuneration is a good proxy for value added) and to present little distortions to the extent that it can be designed to mostly tax the rents of the sector. We compute the amounts of FAT that would be charged under three alternative designs to each bank in the sample. Finally, we calculate the correlations between the FAT charged to individual banks under each design and the individual risk from the SYMBOL simulations. We find that FAT1, the broader version of the base, is the best correlated with systemic risk and that regulatory improvements increase this correlation. This is mainly because FAT1 is the best correlated with the size of the institution, which appears to be a major determinant of the impact on aggregate risk. Several designs of bank levies are also tested. Broader versions of those levies appear to be best correlated to individual risks. Under a scenario of contagion, FATs and levies have similar performances. When contagion is contained, however, bank levies outperform FATs, mainly because of their stronger correlation with the size of financial institutions, a prime determinant of risk in this case.

The remainder of this chapter is organized as follows: Section 10.2 introduces the FAT and bank levy designs considered, section 10.3 illustrates the procedure to calculate risk contributions under future regulatory scenarios with the SYMBOL model, section 10.4 presents the main results, and section 10.5 concludes.

10.2 FAT and Bank Levies' Designs

In October 2010 the European Commission (2010a, b) evaluated options regarding the introduction of a harmonized financial sector taxation framework. Among these options, the European Commission considered a financial activities tax.

In its Impact Assessment of Financial Sector Taxation Proposals, the European Commission (2011a) considered three versions of the FAT. The first version, FAT1, defines the profit of financial institutions in cash-flow terms and adds the remunerations paid by the sector. FAT2 takes the same base for profit but only adds "excessive" remunerations, namely those above a defined threshold. Finally, FAT3 takes as tax base the sum of cash-flow profit above a defined return on capital and "excessive" remunerations.

To calculate the profit part of the financial activity tax, we would ideally have a cash-flow financial statement. This is not available to us. Nevertheless, we can use the information contained in the unconsolidated financial statements of banks as available in ORBIS.[6] The profit part of the FAT base is computed as a $R + F$ (i.e., real + financial transactions) base by adapting accounting profit to cash-flow profit. This is done by starting with the profit and loss before tax and distribution, subtracting the dividends received from subsidiaries (i.e., applying an exemption to avoid double taxation), adding the change in (nonequity) liabilities, subtracting the change in assets, except for change in cash hold and investment in subsidiaries. The labor costs part is the costs of personnel. As for the IMF's computation, the FAT1 is the sum of these two parts, the FAT2 takes the same cash-flow profit definition and 12 percent of labor costs,[7] and the FAT3 limits the cash-flow profit to what excesses 15 percent of total equity and adds it to 12 percent of the labor costs. It is important to note that the first two methods allow a loss-relief between the profit and the labor parts of the base, while the last method essentially put a floor of zero on the profit part. Hence the base of a risk-taxing FAT could in theory be larger than the base for the other two methods. In all cases an illustrative rate of 5 percent is applied to the base for 2009.

A bank levy is a tax on specific elements of the balance sheets of financial institutions and can hence take many forms. A first design could be a tax on total assets (i.e., the total of the balance sheet), which is a measure of the size of the bank. Another design may a tax on total regulatory capital, the sum of tier 1 and tier 2 capital. A third option would be a contribution on covered deposits. This is the system currently in place in all EU member states (and in many other financial systems in the world) under the deposit guarantee schemes that protect depositors up to EUR 100,000 per insured banks. Such schemes are commonly funded by fees paid by banks on deposits. An alternative design is to tax noninsured liabilities. Such an option that taxes total assets minus the covered deposits and tier 1 regulatory capital is expected to induce banks to switch their structure of assets toward more capital or covered deposits. Finally, a fifth option is to tax both covered deposits and uninsured liabilities—that is, all liabilities except for tier 1 regulatory capital.

10.3 Estimation of Risk Contributions

10.3.1 The SYMBOL Model

The main idea behind SYMBOL is to use the Basel formula for the foundation internal rating based (FIRB) loss distribution (BCBS 2004; Vasicek 1991, 2002) to estimate the average probability of default of the portfolio of assets of a bank and to numerically simulate future losses. The model estimates the distribution of losses at systemic level by simulating correlated losses in a banking system and aggregating losses in excess of available capital of defaulting banks. In this way SYMBOL estimates the distribution of losses passed over from the banking sector to the economy. Contagion effects between banks—the fact that bank failure can be driven by the default of others due to their interconnectedness—can also be taken into account using data on interbank exposures between banks.

More in detail, SYMBOL is based on the following steps:

1. Estimate the obligors' implied probabilities of default for each bank by inverting the Basel FIRB formula.

2. Using the same formula, generate a sample of loan losses via a Monte Carlo simulation.

3. Check which banks fail in the sample (when losses are in excess of capital).

4. Use the contagion model (and go back to step 3 to see which additional bank(s) fail because of contagion losses).

5. Once no additional bank fails, derive the final matrix of total losses for the economy (systemic losses).

In the first step, the implied probability of default of the banks' portfolio is estimated by inverting the Basel FIRB formula. This formula is used by many banks to estimate the risk of their portfolios and to calculate accordingly their minimum capital requirements K_n for each loan on the base of its probability to default, loss given default, size, and maturity. In unitary terms (1 euro loan) we have

$$K_n = \left\{ LGD_n \times N\left[\frac{\sqrt{R(PD_n, S_n)}N^{-1}(0.999) + N^{-1}(PD_n)}{\sqrt{1 - R(PD_n, S_n)}} \right] - LGD_n \times PD_n \right\}$$
$$+ [1 + (M_n - 2.5) \times B(PD_n)] \times [1 - 1.5 \times B(PD_n)]^{-1} \times 1.06,$$

where PD_n is the probability of default of the h asset in the bank portfolio; LGD_n is the loss given default, that is, the average loss expected on a defaulted loan; N and N^{-1} are the standard normal density function and its inverse, respectively; $R(PD_n)$ is the correlation between the assets in the banks' portfolio (as estimated by a specific formula on the base of the asset PD and size of the firm, S_n); M_n is the asset maturity; $B(PD_n)$ is another correction term based on the asset PD. The confidence level for value at risk (VaR) is imposed by Basel regulation at 99.9 percent.

The total capital requirement for the bank i is then obtained summing up the product of the unitary capital requirement times the amount of each loan:

$$K_i = \sum_n K_n \times A_n.$$

In the a formula above all variables (the totals for the bank, the values for each loan being evidently confidential) and parameters except $P\hat{D}_i$ are either available on public balance sheets (K_i, ΣA_n) or can be set at their default levels in the FIRB approach (LGD, R, M).[8] Thus the FIRB formula can be numerically inverted to obtain an estimate of the average implied probability of default of the obligors of each bank, $P\hat{D}_i$:[9]

$$\frac{K_i}{\sum_n A_n} = \left\{ LGD \times N \left[\frac{\sqrt{R(P\hat{D}_i)}N^{-1}(0.999) + N^{-1}(P\hat{D}_i)}{\sqrt{1 - R(P\hat{D}_i)}} \right] - LGD \times P\hat{D}_i \right\}$$
$$+ \left[1 - 1.5 \times B(P\hat{D}_i) \right]^{-1} \times 1.06,$$

where ΣA_n is the total value of assets detained by the bank (i.e., $K_i / \Sigma A_n$ is the MCR in relative terms).

In the second step SYMBOL generates a sample of loan losses via a Monte Carlo simulation. To this goal, the estimated probability of default $P\hat{D}_i$ is plugged back into the FIRB loss distribution, with all parameters set at their default values, to simulate individual bank's losses:

$$L_{ij}(z_{ij}, P\hat{D}_i) = \left[0.45\, N \left[\sqrt{\frac{1}{1 - R(P\hat{D}_i, 50)}} N^{-1}(P\hat{D}_i) \right. \right.$$
$$\left. \left. + \sqrt{\frac{R(P\hat{D}_i, 50)}{1 - R(P\hat{D}_i, 50)}} N^{-1}(z_{ij}) \right] - 0.45\, P\hat{D}_i \right]$$
$$\times \left(1 - 1.5\, B(P\hat{D}_i) \right)^{-1} \times 1.06,$$

where $i = 1,...,H$ banks, $j = 1,...,J$ simulations, $z_{ij} \sim N(0,1) \forall i, j$, and $\text{cov}(z_{ij}, z_{lj}) = 0.5\ \forall i \neq l$ (with i, l as bank indexes).

In the third step SYMBOL verifies which banks default due to the simulated losses. To this goal, losses are compared with the total capital of each bank including any excess capital held above minimum requirements: whenever the losses exceed capital, the bank is considered to default (see figure 10.1 for a graphical explanation):

$$L_{ij}(z_{ij}, PD_i) \geq CAP_i \Rightarrow \text{bank } i \text{ defaults} \quad \text{(no contagion case)}.$$

When at least one bank defaults, these 'excess losses' are recorded as 'no contagion losses'.

To include the contagion effects[10] in the absence of an effective intervention by resolution facilities,[11] exposures via the interbank market are used. Following the empirical literature, whenever a bank defaults, it is assumed that 40 percent of the amounts of its InterBank (IB) debits

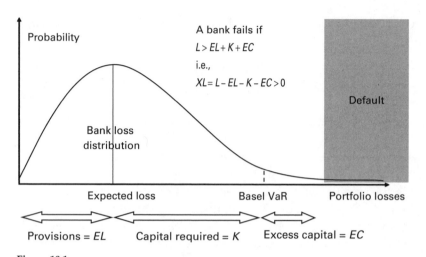

Figure 10.1
Loss distribution and default of banks. The first losses are absorbed by the bank provisions (*EL*), the next by the required capital (*K*), and further losses could be absorbed by excess capital (*EC*), when available. The tail risk, at the extreme right of the graph, is the portfolio losses that occur with a low probability but are very high in value and cannot be completely absorbed by provisions and capital of the financial institution, hence a default.

are passed as losses to creditor banks and distributed among them.[12] Missing a full interbank matrix, we estimate one using a maximum entropy criterion: the portion of losses absorbed by each 'infected' bank is proportional to its creditor exposure in the IB market. Whenever, with this additional loss, the simulation shows that another bank's losses exceed its capital, that banks is also considered to default, and so on until no additional bank defaults.

Therefore losses for each bank i in each j run in case of contagion become

$$L_{ij}^c\left(z_{ij}, PD_i, IB\right) = L_{ij}\left(z_{ij}, PD_i\right) + 0.4\sum_{h \neq i} D_h x_{ih}\left(IB\right),$$

where $D_h = 1$ if bank h defaulted, and 0 otherwise; x_{ih} are the elements of the maximum entropy interbank matrix. Considering this, bank i defaults when $L_{ij}^c\left(z_{ij}, \hat{PD}_i, IB\right) \geq CAP_i$.

The fact that the "contagion" results are based on the same starting seed in a random number generator and on the same simulation runs assures that differences in contagion results in simulation scenarios with contagion are only due to the effects of contagion.

Once at least 100,000 runs with at least one simulated default in the no contagion case are obtained the simulation is stopped. Systemic losses are then obtained by aggregating losses in excess to banks' capital over the entire population of banks in the considered banking system (e.g., one country):

$$L_j^{Syst} = \sum_{i=1}^{N} L_{ij} - CAP_i \quad \text{in the } no\ contagion \text{ case,}$$

$$L_j^{Syst,c} = \sum_{i=1}^{N} L_{ij}^c - CAP_i \quad \text{in the } contagion \text{ case.}$$

As in the current analysis we rely on a sample of banks (see the appendix), the distributions for the population of all banks in each member state are finally obtained by rescaling the distributions proportionally according to the ratio of total assets in the sample to the assets of the total banking sector in the member state.

10.3.2 Systemic Risk Contributions

Our methodology for calculating the contributions of individual banks $c(i)$ to systemic risk is a variation of the one proposed by Praschnik et al. (2001) and is such that $c(i)$ are directly proportional to total losses simulated for each bank in all simulation runs. The contribution of bank i to systemic losses is defined as the expected yearly loss for this bank and is estimated as its average loss over the whole set of simulations, as it follows:

$$c_i = \frac{\sum_{j=1}^{K} L_{ij}^{Syst}}{K},$$

where c_i is the risk contribution of bank i, expressed in money terms (i.e., EUR or USD), and

$$\sum_{j=1}^{K} L_{ij}^{Syst}$$

is the total of losses in excess of capital for bank i across all K simulations; for simplicity we drop the contagion/no contagion label.[13]

The contribution of each individual bank to the systemic risk as a share of the total can be expressed as

$$pc_i = \frac{c_i}{\sum_{h=1}^{H} c_h}.$$

10.3.3 Regulatory Scenarios

As a micro-simulation tool, SYMBOL can be used to simulate losses based on alternative settings attempting to capture the effects due to regulatory proposals. In this paper three distinct elements of the European regulatory framework related to banking stability and systemic risk are considered.

First, the Capital Requirements Directive (CRD IV),[14] which entered into force in July 2013 and translates into European regulation the rules proposed in the Basel III Accord, including new definitions of capital for regulatory purposes, a new set of capital requirements and the introduction of a capital conservation buffer of 2.5 percent of risk-weighted assets (RWA).

Second, on July 12, 2010, the Commission adopted a legislative proposal for a thorough revision of the Directive on deposit guarantee schemes.[15] It mainly deals with a harmonization and simplification of protected deposits, a faster payout, and an improved financing of schemes, as well as a substantial enlargement of the coverage (up to EUR 100,000).

Third, the European Commission has put forward a proposal for the introduction of an EU framework for bank recovery and resolution, including the creation of resolution funds in all member states that would help stopping contagion.[16]

These regulatory aspects are modeled by running SYMBOL under different "regulatory settings" and "contagion situations". In the current analysis, SYMBOL is run based on two alternative regulatory settings and two alternative contagion situations.[17]

The first setting regards the *level of regulatory capital* expressed as the minimum ratio of capital to RWA. Two different capital requirement settings are considered to evaluate the effects of the introduction or not of a mandatory "capital conservation buffer" for banks in Basel III. In other words, we distinguish between the situation where banks must hold a minimum capital equal to 8 percent of their RWA—considered as a proxy for the current situation—and the situation where a minimum capital conservation buffer of 2.5 percent is also requested, so as to reach at least a capital equal to 10.5 percent of RWA.

The second setting regards the *contagion situations*. They represent polar extremes of the effectiveness of interventions during the crisis. In the "best-case" situation, funds and facilities are assumed to be able to work in such a way that no additional losses due to liquidity or "fire sale" effects are generated, so that only economic losses due to defaults

Table 10.1
Scenario definition

		Capital setting		Situations	
Scenario number	Scenario label	No conservation buffer, capital ≥ 8% RWA	Conservation buffer, capital ≥ 10.5% RWA	Contagion	No contagion
1	080_c	X		X	
2	080_n	X			X
3	105_c		X	X	
4	105_n		X		X

in bank's portfolios need to be covered, that is, contagion effects are contained. In contrast, in the "worst-case" situation funds and facilities intervene, but they are not able to avoid liquidity and "fire sale" additional losses and to stop contagion. In sum, two situations are considered: one where intervention is perfectly effective in blocking contagion, and one where interventions are only able to reimburse losses but are not able to prevent contagion. As mentioned above, the second scenario assumes that 40 percent of the losses due to interbank exposures are passed to creditors.

The combination of these hypotheses yields four possible scenarios, represented in table 10.1. Scenario 1 represents a proxy for the current situation: banks do not hold a capital conservation buffer (i.e., they hold at least a capital of 8 percent of RWA) and DGS/RF are not effective/available in blocking contagion. In scenario 2, while the minimum capital stays at 8 percent of RWA, DGS/RF are effective in blocking contagion (no contagion). Scenario 3 and scenario 4 include the capital conservation buffer (i.e., banks hold at least a capital of 10.5 percent of RWA). Scenario 4 proxies the desired long-term regulatory setting where there would be a conservation buffer and where there would be no contagion.

10.3.4 Data Sample
SYMBOL, as a micro-simulation model, uses data from the balance sheet data of individual banks. The main data source is Bankscope, a proprietary database of banks' financial statements produced by Bureau van Dijk. The dataset covers a representative large sample of banks in 19 EU countries. Since at the time of preparing the analysis, the latest

available complete year of data was 2009, all data used refers to that year.

The data needed to run the model include minimum capital requirements, total capital, interbank deposits, and loans and total assets. When needed and possible, Bankscope data have been completed with public information on bank financial statements released by supervisory authorities and/or central banks. European Central Bank data has also been used to complete or correct the dataset (European Central Bank 2010a, b).[18]

For the purposes of simulation, we consider the stricter Basel III definition of capital to be relevant, while all regulatory capital is currently reported by banks according to the Basel II definition. In order to estimate capital ratios under the stricter Basel III definitions of eligible capital and RWA, we apply a corrective factor, namely the average changes in RWA and capital for each country and banks' size groups as estimated in the Basel III Quantitative Impact Study exercises conducted by EBA and CEBS.[19] After applying the correction, all banks which do not meet minimum capital requirements (8 percent or 8 percent plus a capital conservation buffer of 2.5 percent, see section 10.3.3 for details) are brought back to them (i.e., after corrections banks are allowed to hold a capital surplus but not a shortfall).

10.4   Results

10.4.1   Distribution of Excess Losses
Figure 10.2 shows some selected percentiles of the distribution of systemic losses under the various scenarios for a weighted average of the considered EU member states. The graph reports the cumulative distribution function of systemic excess losses.

It is clear that losses decrease moving from scenario 1 to scenario 2, and from scenario 3 to scenario 4, depending on the fact that contagion between banks is considered (scenarios 1 and 3) or not (scenarios 2 and 4). Moreover losses decrease when moving from a minimum capital ratio of 8 percent (scenarios 1 and 2) to a minimum capital ratio of 10.5 percent (scenarios 3 and 4).

10.4.2   Results for individual contributions to systemic losses
Unreported concentration curves of the distribution of individual percentage contributions to systemic losses for all banks in the sample—illustrating individual contributions for the whole set of cases (i.e.,

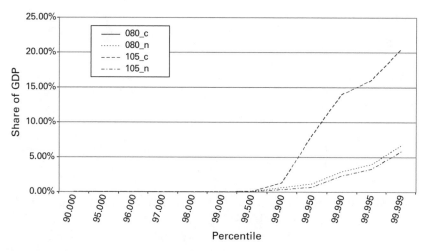

Figure 10.2
Simulated losses as share of GDP (contagion/no contagion cases, c/n). The vertical axis indicates the losses in percent of GDP, and the horizontal axis the inverted cumulated percentile of probability. Moving to the right, the level of probability gets lower, while moving upward loss gets higher. For example, losses representing 5 percent of GDP have a probability of about 0.25 percent under the scenario (8 percent, contagion) and a probability of 0.001 percent under the scenario (10.5 percent, no contagion).

without considering cases where losses exceed or are below the amount of funds available to DGS/RF) – have average yearly individual contributions that are usually much higher than the median, suggesting that there are few banks contributing most to the systemic risk.

This is not a surprising result as bigger banks (less numerous) tend to contribute relatively more to higher systemic losses, while smaller banks (more numerous) tend to contribute relatively more to lower systemic losses.

Table 10.2 tests the correlation between the individual contributions to systemic risk under each of the scenario and several balance sheet variables that can contribute to systemic risk. Adrian and Brunnermeier (2011) find that the contribution of an individual institution to systemic risk is correlated with leverage, the relative size, and maturity mismatch.

Each of the variables is indeed significantly correlated with systemic risk, although at various degree. Total assets appear the most correlated, in particular when contagion is contained. This confirms the conjecture above. Next maturity mismatch is proxied by the short-term funding ratio, defined as the ratio of short-term funding – excluding customer

Table 10.2
Correlation between individual contributions to systemic risk and balance sheet variables

Scenario	Total assets	RWA	STFR	Leverage
Contagion 8%	0.582***	0.482***	0.183***	0.078***
No contagion 8%	0.878***	0.891***	0.055***	0.044**
Contagion 10.5%	0.550***	0.422***	0.192***	0.085***
No contagion 10.5%	0.927***	0.874***	0.095***	0.078***

Note: *** significant at the 1 percent level, ** 5 percent level, * 10 percent level.

deposits – on regulatory capital. More stringent regulatory capital ratio increase its correlation with systemic risk but the absence of contagion goes in the opposite direction. It is worth mentioning that the Basel II FIRB formula and consequently the SYMBOL estimations are affected by the maturity of loans (not the maturity mismatch), as longer maturities are equivalent to higher PDs (see section 10.3.1). Finally, leverage, defined as one minus the ratio of equity to total assets, acts in the same way as maturity mismatch, although correlations are lower.

10.4.2 The FAT

Table 10.3 provides the coefficient of correlations between the three types of FAT and the four scenarios of systemic risk.[20] Several messages stand out. First, when contagion is not avoided, all versions of FAT perform in about the same way. Second, when contagion can be avoided, FAT1 is the best aligned to risk.[21]

As indicated in table 10.3, FAT1 is also the option that is best correlated with size, as measured by total assets, which may explain the results. Finally increasing capital requirement from 8 to 10.5 percent decreases the correlation between the contributions to FAT as measured by FAT1 and the contribution to systemic risk under contagion but increases this correlation when there is no contagion. This reveals the fact that under no contagion, higher capital requirements are able to contain the part of the risks that are not necessarily linked to the size of the institution (e.g., leverage), increasingly leaving the remaining risk to be linked to size only.

Last, more restricted definitions of the FAT base increase the correlation with maturity mismatch while none of the versions of the FAT is significantly correlated with leverage.

Table 10.3
Correlation between individual contributions to systemic risk and FATs

Scenario	FAT1	FAT2	FAT3
Contagion 8%	0.566***	0.529***	0.518***
No contagion 8%	0.600***	0.408***	0.342***
Contagion 10.5%	0.526***	0.500***	0.483***
No contagion 10.5%	0.630***	0.441***	0.373***
Total assets	0.714***	0.535***	0.448***
Risk-weighted assets	0.574***	0.383***	0.308***
ST financing ratio	0.059***	0.073***	0.081***
Leverage	0.014	0.027	0.029

Note: *** significant at the 1 percent level, ** 5 percent level, * 10 percent level.

Table 10.4
Correlation between individual contributions to systemic risk and bank levies

Scenario	Assets based	Total regulatory capital	Covered deposits	Noncovered liabilities	Noncovered liabilities + covered deposits
Contagion 8%	0.582***	0.432***	0.503***	0.588***	0.586***
No contagion 8%	0.878***	0.800***	0.886***	0.850***	0.877***
Contagion 10.5%	0.550***	0.389***	0.461***	0.560***	0.554***
No contagion 10.5%	0.927***	0.804***	0.901***	0.907***	0.928***
Total assets	1.000***	0.899***	0.896***	0.994***	0.999***
Risk-weighted assets	0.906***	0.953***	0.872***	0.878***	0.898***
ST financing ratio	0.102***	0.030	0.046**	0.122***	0.107***
Leverage	0.053	-0.005	0.066***	0.052***	0.058***

Note: *** significant at the 1 percent level, ** 5 percent level, * 10 percent level.

10.4.3   Bank Levies

As shown in table 10.4, of all five options of bank levies, taxing regulatory capital would provide the solution that performs the worst when the aim is to obtain a fee that reflects individual contributions to systemic risk. All other variants perform in a relatively similar way. When contagion is not contained, bank levies and FAT perform in ways that are very close in terms of their correlation to systemic risk. When contagion is contained, however, bank levies outperform FATs in their correlation to risk. Here again, the reason seems to be that when contagion cannot be avoided, both FAT and bank levies perform equally but when an efficient resolution mechanism is put in place and allows avoiding contagion, bank levies—which are based on balance sheets (i.e., "stock") elements of financial statements—perform better than FAT—which are based on income statements (i.e., "flows") elements of financial statements—as counterpart to the systemic risk created by individual financial institutions, the more so the broader their base. In such case their correlation with the size of the financial institutions, which is a prime determinant of risk in the absence of contagion, matters. Bank levies are also better correlated with maturity mismatch and leverage than FATs. An assets-based or a broad-base version (i.e., that simply excludes tier 1 capital) are found to display the higher levels of correlation. Increasing capital requirement improves the correlations when contagion is absent.

Note that those measures are static and do not include behavioral reactions of banks that could affect the structure of their balance sheets and hence both their contributions to risk and their levy. As seen before (see note 3), the direction of such change is ambiguous.

10.5 Conclusions and Policy Implications

The financial crisis has highlighted the potential contributions of banks, in particular, large banks, on systemic risk, also given the possibility of contagion of failing banks to other financial institutions. Several regulatory measures are being implemented to minimize this risk and its consequences for both public finances and economic growth. Among these are a strengthening of capital requirements and a funding of deposit guarantee schemes.

At the same time several options on how to increase the contribution of the financial sector to the cost of the crisis have been at the political agenda. One of the possible desired features of such a tax could be its ability to curb risk and/or to be in relation with the risk posed by individual institutions to the whole financial system. The possibility to introduce a bank levy or a financial activities tax (FAT), in their various versions, has been recently discussed by the IMF and the European Commission.

This chapter uses the SYMBOL model to estimate the contribution of each bank to systemic losses under alternative scenarios of capital requirements and (absence of) contagion. In parallel, we compute bank levies and FATs liabilities for individual banks under several alternative designs of the taxes and look at correlations between those liabilities and individual contributions to systemic risk. Of the three alternative designs of the FAT, the broader version (FAT1) is found to be the one that would be best correlated with individual risk under all scenarios of regulatory capital and contagion. This correlation is highest when contagion is contained and capital requirement increased. This is mainly due to the fact that FAT1 is the design that is best correlated with the size of the institution, which appears to be a major determinant of its impact on aggregate risk, the more so the higher the level of capital requirements. In the presence of contagion, bank levies display comparable correlations to individual banks' risk as do FATs. When contagion is contained, however, bank levies outperform FATs and display very high correlation to individual contributions to systemic risk. In particular, broad-based bank levies—thanks to their own correlation with banks' size—work particularly well.

As reported in this chapter, the absence of contagion is a prime determinant for decreasing the probability of losses, while increasing regulatory capital also provides an additional security, the more so if contagion cannot be contained. Measures to avoid contagion are therefore of prime importance, such as the presence of resolution funds. While any tax or government transfer could, in principle, finance those funds, the possibility of a tax that decreases individual contributions to systemic risk and/or is correlated with it could be of interest.

The effects of taxes on individual contributions to systemic risks are however beyond the scope of this paper as the current version of the SYMBOL model does not account for dynamic effects, which are left for future developments. Generally, well-designed bank levies could play a role in creating disincentives to leverage and, possibly, the size of financial institutions. A FAT could also, in theory, reduce the size of financial institutions to the extent that the tax is passed through into higher prices for financial services and that the demand for these services is sufficiently elastic. The pass-through into higher prices is more likely under the broader design of the FAT because for the same rate the tax would be higher but also because smaller designs of the FAT would increasingly target the economic rent and not the normal profit. A FAT would, however, normally have little effect on leverage.

In the absence of contagion, systemic risk is very much linked to the relative size of financial institutions. Hence bank levies whose design would be linked to the size of the institutions would be a logical choice as taxes that charge financial institutions in relation to their contribution to systemic risk.

Appendix: Description of the Sample of Banks for the SYMBOL Simulations

Table A.1
Description of the samples used for the simulations, data as of end 2009

	Number G1 banks	Number G2 banks	Sample % population[a]	Total assets (m€)	Total liabilities (m€)
BE	3	20	82.26%	878,336	829,934
BG*	0	24	94.77%	34,383	29,614
DK	3	96	71.05%	756,678	708,878
DE	6	1,476	64.19%	4,648,331	4,415,620
GR	3	13	71.42%	322,714	295,667
ES	8	135	73.95%	2,370,807	2,188,636
FR	17	178	102.59%	7,191,608	6,817,107
IE*	5	19	101.91%	1,221,181	1,155,789
IT	8	465	81.81%	2,827,051	2,556,174
CY (*)	0	15	80.80%	107,446	100,436
LV*	0	21	72.65%	19,088	17,037
LU	1	55	68.35%	465,539	441,916
MT	0	10	43.83%	18,076	16,225
NL	4	17	78.02%	1,680,455	1,600,687
AT	1	172	29.88%	306,457	282,380
PT	3	11	66.49%	323,762	297,421
FI	1	8	78.36%	290,500	275,621
SE	3	63	52.37%	455,355	422,301
UK	7	78	73.97%	4,278,074	4,074,946

Sources: (*) Central bank or supervisory authority; (+) estimated.

Note: Year 2009 is the latest year available in *Bankscope*, and even more important, 2009 is the year on which the Basel and the CEBS committee have based their Quantitative Impact Study exercises for the foreseen change on banks' capital and RWA when moving from Basel II to Basel III.

a. The sample of banks covered in each member states represents the indicated percentage of total assets for any member state as shown for 2009 in the 2010 ECB EU banking structures publication, computed as the amount of total assets for all banks minus total assets of branches from abroad. European Central Bank (2010a).

b. A correction factor for the volume of the interbank debt/credit has been applied to the following MS, to correct for the inclusion of some classes of debts certificates: GR (56.5 percent), FR (39.1 percent), IT (26.9 percent), LU (79.8 percent), and AT (48.4 percent). The correction factors employed have been estimated using the 2010 ECB *Banking Sector Stability*, table 11a.

c. Data on interbank credits was not available for BG and CY so equality of interbank debits and credits has been assumed.

d. The amount of funds for DGS/RF purposes is rescaled on the size of the sample (column 3).

Total interbank debt[b] (m€)	Total interbank credit[c] (m€)	Total covered deposits[(+)] (m€)	Total capital requirements (8% RWA) (m€)	Total capital (m€)	DGS/RF funds[d(+)] (m€)
184,888	160,678	260,890	23,413	48,401	2,516
6,521	6,521	14,074	2,239	4,769	223
143,362	92,279	118,179	23,749	47,800	2,168
1,086,016	790,975	1,093,841	125,452	232,711	20,096
43,441	20,313	135,758	16,781	27,047	1,511
348,780	226,113	542,332	115,565	182,171	7,874
842,666	779,727	1,550,504	245,024	374,500	22,850
276,738	148,729	147,145	44,121	65,392	3,488
188,375	195,958	476,963	97,416	270,876	7,816
53,067	53,067	22,661	4,883	7,011	537
5,943	2,609	3,995	1,127	2,050	58
169,984	161,827	103,441	11,485	23,622	1,321
5,222	2,689	6,893	760	1,851	58
319,699	398,659	314,059	46,903	79,768	5,091
50,382	39,692	71,381	14,656	24,077	860
43,561	34,505	82,952	17,704	26,342	1,121
54,361	79,820	48,998	7,968	14,879	1,024
97,604	122,872	75,383	16,356	33,054	1,314
743,978	691,049	464,241	110,757	203,129	12,313

Notes

The findings, interpretations, and conclusions expressed in this chapter are entirely those of the authors and should not be attributed to the European Commission. Neither the European Commission nor any person acting on behalf of the Commission is responsible for the use that might be made of this publication. An earlier version of this chapter appeared in the "Impact Assessment of the European Commission on Financial Sector Taxation" (European Commission 2011a). The authors thank Jin Cao, Philip Kermode, one anonymous referee, and the participants to the 2012 Venice Summer Institute hosted by CESifo for valuable comments.

1. See, for example, European Commission (2011a) and Huizinga (2002) who found an advantage that amounts to 0.15 percent GDP. Using a general equilibrium model for Germany in 2007, Buettner and Erbe (chapter 8 in this volume) find that repealing the VAT exemption for financial services would raise total tax revenues by EUR 1.2 billion, which at a 2007 GDP of 2,428.5 billion (AMECO database) represents about 0.05 percent GDP.

2. See, however, Devereux (chapter 2 in this volume) and Coulter, Mayer, and Vickers (chapter 4 in this volume) for counterarguments why such levy could actually increase risk, and Devereux, Johannesen, and Vella (2013) for empirical evidence that levies induce banks to hold more risky assets when the regulatory capital requirement is binding.

3. The SYMBOL model (SYstemic Model of Banking Originated Losses) has been jointly developed by the European Commission's Joint Research Centre, DG MARKT, and the University of Cagliari (see De Lisa et al. 2011). It should be noted that in De Lisa et al. paper the model is not yet named, as the SYMBOL acronym was adopted starting from 2012, when the model started being deployed in Impact Assessment work within the Commission.

4. This could seem more in line with CoVar-like indicators (e.g., Adrian and Brunnermeier 2011) used in the correlation/reduced form works, while normally structural models tend to employ a Shapley value methodology (Tarashev et al. 2010). However, this choice of the measure of systemic risk contributions is dictated by the fact that it is the most apt at measuring the optimal contribution to a possible rescue/resolution fund. This contribution would be based on the amount of resources the fund would need to dedicate to that institution in crisis events, reflecting its chance of participating to the event, independently of the banks' chance of contributing to starting the event itself. For a discussion on the different roles, see Tarashev et al. (2010).

5. For a description of the FAT, see Hemmelgarn and Nicodeme (2010, 2012).

6. Orbis is a database on financial statements of companies published by Bureau Van Dijk. Note that the sample can be biased toward large banks as financial information could be harder to obtain for smaller banks. Our version of Orbis contains 7,343 banks and 3,609 insurance companies for the EU27 (not all with exploitable financial information). For many banks, several variables necessary to compute FAT revenues are missing. Therefore they are estimated in the following way: For companies for which consolidated statements are available in Orbis, the missing variable of interest is replaced by the one from the consolidated statements, adjusted by the ratio of total assets between unconsolidated and consolidated statements. If the information is still missing, the same procedure is applied using country-level information on banking structures from the ECB publication *EU Banking Sector Stability* of September 2010. Our matching between

the FAT computations and the individual contributions to risk leaves us with 2,843 financial institutions for which we have the necessary information.

7. This is estimated to be 40 percent of the wage differential in the United Kingdom between the top 25 percent of earners in the financial sector and the top 25 percent earners in the rest of the economy. The 40 percent is based on the study by Philippon and Reshef (2009) for the United States who find that between 30 and 40 percent of the wage differential is rent. See Keen et al. (2010, p. 138). Note that Egger et al. (2012) found evidence of a wage premium in the financial sector that amounts to about 43 percent in the OECD.

8. See De Lisa et al. (2011) for technical details.

9. This is under the assumption that the loss distribution for all assets held by the bank can be approximated by considering as if all of them were loans. This assumption does not seem extreme given that the largest part of minimum capital requirements held by most banks is represented by credit risk capital.

10. Only domestic contagion is included in the current version of SYMBOL.

11. In the best-case scenario, a resolution fund operating in coordination with a liquidity facility would be able to neutralize contagion by absorbing a share of excess losses proportional to the size of a banks' interbank liabilities, while resolution and liquidity facilities are able to completely eliminate additional losses due to liquidation costs, fire sale effects, and market congestion.

12. A loss of 40 percent on the interbank exposure is coherent with economic research on this issue; see James (1991), Mistrulli (2011), and Upper and Worms (2004). The use of a matrix of exposures proportional to interbank credits is dependent on the fact that a bank-to-bank interbank lending matrix is not available to the Commission; however, sensitivity analysis conducted by the authors on this aspect points to the fact that the exact shape of the matrix is less important than total size of interbank market. See Zedda et al. (2012) for details. Gauthier at al. (2012, sec. 2.3) reach a similar conclusions on the impact of using maximum entropy matrices in this context. It is worth noting that contagion effects are sensitive to the two assumptions made: the 40 percent of interbank debits that are passed as losses to creditor banks in case of failure and the criterion of proportionality used to distribute these losses across banks.

13. Contributions are calculated by excluding the more extreme events above the 99.999th quantile, in order to exclude the influence of events at the leftmost tail that could be suffering excess variance due to undersampling.

14. Directive 2013/36/EU.

15. European Commission (2010d).

16. See European Commission (2010c, 2012). As far as deposit guarantee schemes and resolution funds are concerned, a possible amount of funds available to DGS + RF purposes is the maximum between 1.5 percent of a country covered deposits and 0.3 percent of the amount of liabilities, in line with discussion at the time when the simulations were run. Amounts of funds to be collected by each considered member state are reported in last column of table A.1 of the appendix. Figures refer to the sample of banks considered. As rules on the determination of the total amounts of funds available to DGS and RF in each MS are still under negotiation in the Council and the European Parliament, any rule adopted in the present study for simulation purposes cannot reflect the final form of the rule as it will eventually be implemented. It was therefore chosen to calibrate funds available to DGS/RF on the basis of SYMBOL results.

17. On top of this, SYMBOL is also able to include the possibility of a "no bail-in" or a "bail-in" framework. This distinction is not considered in this chapter.

18. Data from the ECB have been used for various purposes. For instance, in the Bankscope sample some values of key variables were missing for some banks. In some cases missing values have been filled in using estimations obtained from ECB aggregated data on banks' ratios such as the minimum capital ratio, the solvency ratio or the tier 1 ratio. Moreover ECB data have been used to estimate the size of the Bankscope sample and to rescale SYMBOL results across the entire population of banks in each country. Finally ECB data have been employed to validate the reliability of interbank data in Bankscope. For a description of Bankscope, see Bureau Van Dijk (2010), Bankscope—World Banking Information Source, Bureau Van Dijk.

19. The Basel Committee and CEBS have published anticipated average variations in bank capital ratios due to implementation of Basel III. In this report we have used the country-level confidential data on the estimated variations in banks' capital ratios that underlie published figures. See BCBS (2010) and CEBS (2010).

20. We ran additional (unreported) scenarios with capital requirements of 7, 9, and 10 percent. The results confirm that correlations increase with capital requirement under no contagion and decrease with capital requirement under contagion.

21. In theory, FAT3 would be designed to tax risk, but this rests on the hypothesis that high returns are due to higher risks. While this could be true, other factors may trigger higher returns such as a lack of competition or more efficient production methods (e.g., superior knowledge of markets, a more productive workforce, better management structures). In this latter case the tax could be a tax on talent rather than a tax on high risk.

References

Acharya, Viral V., Lasse H. Pedersen, Thomas Philippon, and Matthew P. Richardson. 2012. Measuring systemic risk. Discussion paper 8824. CEPR.

Adrian, Tobias, and Markus K. Brunnermeier. 2011. CoVaR. Working paper 17454. NBER.

Basel Committee on Banking Supervision (BCBS). 2004. *Basel II. International Convergence of Capital Measurement and Capital Standards: A Revised Framework.* Basel: Bank for International Settlements.

Basel Committee on Banking Supervision (BCBS). 2010. *Results of the Comprehensive Quantitative Impact Study.* Basel: Bank for International Settlements.

Bluhm, Marcel, Ester Faia, and Jan Pieter Krahnen. 2013. Endogenous banks' networks, cascades and systemic risk. Working paper 12. SAFE..

Bluhm, Marcel, and Jan Pieter Krahnen. 2011. Default risk in an interconnected banking systems with endogenous asset markets. Working paper 2011/19. CFS. .

Cifuentes, Rodrigo, Gianluigi Ferrucci, and Hyun Song Shin. 2005. Liquidity risk and contagion. *Journal of the European Economic Association* 3 (2–3): 556–66. doi:10.1162/jeea.2005.3.2-3.556.

Committee of European Banking Supervisors. 2010. *Results of the Comprehensive Quantitative Impact Study.* London: European Banking Authority.

De Lisa, Riccardo, Stefano Zedda, Francesco Vallascas, Francesca Campolongo, and Massimo Marchesi. 2011. Modelling deposit insurance scheme losses in a Basel 2 framework. *Journal of Financial Services Research* 40 (3): 123–41.

Devereux, Michael, Niels Johannesen, and John Vella. 2013. Can taxes tame the banks? Capital structure responses to the post-crisis bank levies. Paper presented at the CESifo conference on Public Sector Economics, Munich, March.

Egger, Peter H., Maximilian von Ehrlich, and Doina Radulescu. 2012. How much it pays to work in the financial sector? *CESifo Economic Studies* 58 (1): 110–39.

European Central Bank. 2010a. *EU Banking Structures (September 2010).* Frankfurt am Main: European Central Bank.

European Central Bank. 2010b. *EU Banking Sector Stability (September 2010).* Frankfurt am Main: ECB.

European Commission. 2010a. Taxation of the financial sector. SEC(2010)1166. Commission Staff working documents. Brussels.

European Commission. 2010b. Communication on taxation of the financial sector. COM(2010)549. Communications of the European Commission. Brussels.

European Commission. 2010c. Communication on bank resolution funds. COM(2010)254. Communications of the European Commission. Brussels.

European Commission. 2010d. Legislative proposal for a thorough revision of the Directive on Deposit Guarantee Schemes. COM(2010)369. Brussels:.

European Commission. 2011a. Impact assessment accompanying the document proposal for a Council Directive on a Common System of Financial Transaction Tax and Amending Directive 2008/7/EC, SEC(2011)1102. Brussels.

European Commission. 2011b. Proposal for a Council Directive on a Common System of Financial Transaction Tax and Amending Directive 2008/7/EC. COM(2011)594 final. Brussels.

European Commission. 2012. Proposal for a Directive of the European Parliament and of the Council establishing a framework for the recovery and resolution of credit institutions and investment firms and amending Council Directives 77/91/EEC and 82/891/EC, Directives 2001/24/EC, 2002/47/EC, 2004/25/EC, 2005/56/EC, 2007/36/EC and 2011/35/EC and Regulation (EU) No 1093/2010. COM(2012)280 final. Brussels.

Gauthier, Céline, Alfred Lehar, and Moez Souissi. 2012. Macroprudential capital requirements and systemic risk. *Journal of Financial Intermediation* 21 (4): 594–618. doi:10.1016/j.jfi.2012.01.005.

Hemmelgarn, Thomas and Gaëtan Nicodème. 2010. The 2008 financial crisis and taxation policy. Taxation paper 20. Directorate General Taxation and Customs Union, EC, Brussels.

Hemmelgarn, Thomas, and Gaëtan Nicodème. 2012. Can tax policy help to prevent financial crisis? In Julian S. Alworth and Giampaolo Arachi, eds., *Taxation and the Financial Crisis.* Oxford, UK: Oxford University Press.

Huizinga, Harry. 2002. A European VAT on financial services? *Economic Policy* 7 (35): 497–534.

International Monetary Fund. 2010. A fair and substantial contribution: A framework for taxation and resolution to improve financial stability. Report to the G20. Washington, DC.

James, Christopher. 1991. The losses realized in bank failures. *Journal of Finance* 46 (4): 1223–42. doi:10.2307/2328857.

Keen, Michael, Russell Krelove, and John Norregaard. 2010. The financial activities tax. In S. Claessens, M. Keen, and C. Pazarbasioglu, eds., *Financial Sector Taxation: The IMF's Report to the G-20 and Background Material.* Washington, DC: IMF, 118–43.

Laeven, Luc, and Fabian V. Valencia. 2012. Systemic banking crises database: An update. Working paper 12/163.IMF.

Mistrulli, Paolo Emilio. 2011. Assessing financial contagion in the interbank market: Maximum entropy versus observed interbank lending patterns. Journal of Banking & Finance, 35(5), 1114-1127.

Müller, Jeannette. 2006. Interbank credit lines as a channel of contagion. *Journal of Financial Services Research* 29 (1): 37–60. doi:10.1007/s10693-005-5107-2.

Philippon, Thomas, and Ariell Reshef. 2009. Wages and human capital in the U.S. financial industry: 1909–2006. Working paper 14644. NBER.

Praschnik, Jack, Gregory Hayt, and Armand Principato. 2001. Calculating the contribution. *Risk Magazine* (October): s25–s27.

Segoviano, Miguel A., and Charles Goodhart. 2009. Measuring systemic risk-adjusted liquidity (SRL): A model approach. Working paper 09/4. IMF.

Tarashev, Nikola, Claudio Borio, and Kostas Tsatsaronis. 2010. Attributing systemic risk to individual institutions. Working paper 308. BIS.

Upper, Christian, and Andreas Worms. 2004. Estimating bilateral exposures in the German interbank market: Is there a danger of contagion? *European Economic Review* 48 (4): 827–49.

Vasicek, Oldrich Alfons. 1991. Limiting loan loss probability distribution. KMV Corporation.

Vasicek, Oldrich Alfons. 2002. The distribution of loan portfolio value. *Risk* (Concord, NH) December issue, 160–12.

Zedda, Stefano, Giuseppina Cannas, Clara Galliani, and Riccardo De Lisa. 2012. The role of contagion in financial crises: An uncertainty test on interbank patterns. EUR Reports. Joint Research Centre of the European Commission.

III Evidence on the Efficacy of Taxation and Regulation

11 Taxation, Bank Leverage, and Financial Crises

Ruud de Mooij, Michael Keen, and Masanori Orihara

11.1 Introduction

The onset of the financial crisis of 2008 quickly prompted many assessments of the role that taxation might have played in its onset and impact.[1] Their consensus was clear, but vague: tax distortions did not trigger the crisis but might have increased vulnerability to financial crises. Prominent among the reasons given for this was "debt bias": the tendency toward excess leverage induced, in almost all countries, by the deductibility against corporate taxation of interest payments but not of the return to equity.[2] In encouraging firms to finance themselves by debt rather than equity, governments might have made them more vulnerable to shocks and so increased both the likelihood and intensity of financial crises. The point applies in principle to all firms, but is a particular concern in relation to financial institutions; and these are the focus here.

This potential link from tax design to financial crises is now widely recognized. But analysis has not progressed beyond metaphor and speculation. Shackelford, Shaviro, and Slemrod (2010, p. 784), for instance, stress "the possibility that the tax biases served ... as extra gasoline intensifying the explosion once other causes lit the match," and the European Commission that "The welfare costs related to debt bias might not be negligible [because] excessive debt levels increase the probability of default" (European Commission 2011, p. 7), with both the "might" and the "not negligible" leaving much doubt and imprecision.

This chapter aims to provide a first attempt to establish and quantify an empirical link between the tax incentives that encourage financial institutions (more precisely, banks, the group for which we have data) to finance themselves by debt rather than equity and the likelihood of financial crises erupting; and then to try to quantify the welfare gains that policies to address this bias might consequently yield.

The approach is to combine two elements in a causal chain. The first is that between the statutory corporate tax rate and banks' leverage. This has received substantial attention in relation to nonfinancial firms[3] but very little in relation to the financial sector. Keen and De Mooij (2012), however, show that for banks too a higher corporate tax rate, amplifying the tax advantage of debt over equity finance, should, in principle, lead to higher levels of leverage; the presence of capital regulations does not affect the usual tax bias applying, so long as it is privately optimal for banks to hold some buffer over regulatory requirements (as they generally do). Empirically too, Keen and De Mooij (2012) find that for a large cross-country panel of banks, tax effects on leverage are significant—and, on average, about as large as for nonfinancial institutions. These effects are very much smaller, they also find, for the largest banks, which generally account for the vast bulk of all bank assets. One task in this chapter is to explore these findings further, using data now available to extend coverage into the crisis period that began in 2008—enabling a comparison of tax impacts pre- and post-onset—and applying the same estimation strategy to country-level data for the OECD.

Importantly, the finding that tax distortions to leverage are small for the larger banks, which are massively larger than the rest, does not mean that the welfare impact of tax distortions is in aggregate negligible: even small changes in the leverage of very large banks could have a large impact on the likelihood of their distress or failure, and hence on the likelihood of financial crisis.

This is where the second link in the causal chain explored here comes in: that between the aggregate leverage of the financial sector and the probability of financial crisis.[4] We estimate such a relationship for OECD countries, applying the estimation strategy of Barrell et al. (2010) and Kato, Kobayashi, and Saita (2010) but, in contrast to these earlier studies, capture data on the recent financial crisis from Laeven and Valencia (2010). The results suggest sizable and highly nonlinear effects of aggregate bank leverage on the probability of financial crisis.

Combining the results from these two estimating equations enables simple calculations of the impact of a variety of tax reforms on the likelihood of financial crisis. Linking this in turn with estimates of the output loss that is historically associated with such crises gives some rough sense of the potential welfare gains from policies that mitigate debt bias in the financial sector. Putting aside the overarching debate as to the proper roles of taxation and regulation in addressing the potential for excess leverage in the financial sector,[5] we consider three tax reforms that would reduce the tax incentive to debt finance: a cut in the corporate tax rate; adoption of an Allowance for Corporate Equity form of corporate tax (which would, in principle, eliminate debt bias); and a "bank levy" of broadly the kind that a dozen or so countries have introduced since the crisis.[6]

All this gives a very different perspective on the nature and possible magnitude of the welfare costs associated with debt bias. Previous work, which has not reflected considerations of financial stability, has concluded that these are small. Gordon (2010) estimates the total efficiency loss from debt bias in the United States to be less than 1 percent of corporate income tax (CIT) revenue and concludes that "tax distortions from corporate financial policy are not an important consideration when setting tax policy." Weichenrieder and Klautke (2008) had put the marginal welfare loss from debt bias somewhat higher, but still only at 0.06 to 0.16 percent of the capital stock. The question here is whether considerations of financial stability imply much higher welfare losses—and the conclusion will be that it seems they do.

The next section of the chapter sets out our methodology and data (more details on the latter being in the appendix). Section 11.3 presents estimation results and section 11.4 reports simulations of the impact of the three reforms on the likelihood of a crisis and expected output. Section 11.5 concludes.

11.2   Methodology and Data

This section sets out the steps of the methodology sketched above: estimating the impact of the CIT rate on banks' leverage (subsection 11.2.1), estimating the effect of bank leverage ratios on the probability of a systemic banking crisis (subsection 11.2.2), and combining the two to explore the relationship between taxation and the likelihood of crisis (subsection 11.2.3).

11.2.1 Effect of Taxation on Leverage
The effect of the CIT rate on banks' leverage is estimated using both individual bank balance-sheet data and aggregate country-level data for the banking sector as a whole.

Bank-Level Data

These data are taken from Bankscope and include 82 countries for the period 2001 to 2011. They are similar to those used by Keen and De Mooij (2012), but here we use a slightly longer time series, which allows a distinction between pre- and post-crisis periods. Details and summary statistics are in appendix 1.

Following Keen and De Mooij (2012), the microdata are used to estimate dynamic panel regressions of the form:[7]

$$lev_{it} = \alpha + \beta_0 lev_{it-1} + \beta_1 tax_{it} + \beta_2' X_{it} + \alpha_i + u_t + \epsilon_{it}, \qquad (11.1)$$

where i identifies an individual bank, t the year, lev_{it} is the bank's leverage ratio for bank i in year t, tax_{it} is the statutory corporate income tax (CIT) rate that bank i faces in year t, X_{it} is a vector of controls (including total bank assets and its square, bank profitability measured by the return on assets (ROA), GDP growth, the inflation rate, and aggregate savings), and α_i and u_t are, respectively, bank- and time-fixed effects.[8] The lagged dependent variable allows for sluggish response. Attention focuses on the parameter β_1, which measures the contemporaneous response of bank leverage to the tax rate (the expectation being that $\beta_1 > 0$, as a higher tax rate increases the value of interest deductibility) and on $\beta_1 / (1 - \beta_0)$, which captures the long-run tax effect. Putting aside sluggish adjustment and focusing on the long-term relationship between taxes and leverage, results are also reported for the between-estimator:

$$\overline{lev}_i = \alpha + \gamma_1 \overline{tax}_{it} + \gamma_2' \overline{X}_i + \epsilon_i, \qquad (11.2)$$

where now γ_1 reflects the long-run tax effect of the CIT rate on banks' leverage, and the bar indicates a mean over time. As discussed below, some allowance is made for heterogeneity by running (11.1) and (11.2) separately for distinct subsets of banks.

Since the available evidence, and that developed below, links the likelihood of financial crisis to measures of overall leverage in the financial sector, some way is needed to aggregate the tax effects on individual banks' leverage into effects on aggregate leverage. This requires identifying any significant sources of heterogeneity in individual banks' responses. Keen and De Mooij (2012) explore various forms of heterogeneity by estimating a second-order polynomial with interactions of bank characteristics and the tax rate. Their results

Table 11.1
Partition of banks by size

Group	1	2	3	4	5
Percentile in assets	0–85	85–90	90–95	95–97.5	97.5–100
Asset share (%)[a]	13.4	4.6	8.6	8.7	64.7

a. The aggregate of assets of banks in the respective group, divided by aggregate assets of all banks.

suggest that responses differ only, but substantially, with bank size: large banks (which also tend to be more highly leveraged) are less responsive to tax than small banks. This is important at the macro level, since large banks generally account for a very large share of total banking assets in a country. That large banks are less tax-responsive than small may reflect a "too-big-to-fail" status that lowers their cost of debt finance, inducing them to become more highly leveraged and leaving less scope for tax effects. To allow for differences in effects by bank size, we split the sample of bank-years into five groups, according to asset size, as reported in table 11.1. Group 1, for instance, contains the 85 percent of bank-year observations with the lowest levels of assets (responses within finer partitions of this group giving very similar results); these account for only 13.4 percent of total assets. The largest 2.5 percent, in contrast, account for nearly two-thirds.

Effects of taxation on aggregate bank leverage are thus estimated by running separate regressions (11.1) or (11.2) for each of the size categories in table 11.1, and then using asset shares to calculate a weighted average effect, which approximates that on aggregate bank leverage.

Country-Level Data

The aggregated financial data come from *OECD Banking Statistics*, covering 29 countries over 2001 to 2009. Other macro-level control variables (used also in the bank-level regressions above), such as GDP growth, the inflation rate and aggregate savings, are taken from the IMF *World Economic Outlook*. Details and summary statistics are again in appendix A11.1.

The estimating equations are as in (11.1) and (11.2), but with i now identifying countries rather than banks. The controls include the same macro variables as in the micro specifications, along with the average return on assets held by banks.[9]

11.2.2 Effect of Leverage on the Probability of Banking Crisis

Our approach to estimating the impact of bank leverage ratios on the probability of a banking crisis follows Barrell et al. (2010) and Kato, Kobayashi, and Saita (2010),[10] but differs in using not the data on banking crisis constructed by Laeven and Valencia (2008) but the, updated data of Laeven and Valencia (2010), which includes information up to 2009 and so encompasses the start of the current crisis.[11] These data identify "systemic banking crises," defined as an event in which there are both (1) significant signs of financial distress (bank runs, bank losses, bank liquidation) and (2) significant policy interventions in banking (liquidity support, bank restructuring, nationalizations, guarantees, asset purchases, deposit freeze, bank holidays). Overall, they report eight OECD countries (and events) that meet the condition for a financial crisis. Laeven and Valencia (2010) also define events of "borderline systemic banking crisis," which occur when events 1 and 2 are judged to be almost met: this wider definition adds seven more events.[12] In the empirics, we assume that the banking crises last for two years.[13]

These data on the occurrence of crises are combined with aggregated balance-sheet data for banks provided in *OECD Banking Statistics*. The resulting sample covers 29 countries from 2000 to 2009. Details are in appendix A11.1.

As in Barrell et al. (2010) and Kato, Kobayashi, and Saita (2010), we estimate the logit model

$$\log[C_{it} / (1 - C_{it})] = \alpha + \delta_1 lev_{i,t} + \delta_2' Z_{i,t} + u_{it}, \tag{11.3}$$

where $C_{it} = 1$ if there is a systemic banking crisis (results being reported separately with and without borderline cases) and $C_{it} = 0$ otherwise. The main parameter of interest is δ_1, giving the impact on the odds of a crisis of a marginal increase in aggregate leverage; the expectation is that $\delta_1 > 0$. Drawing on previous results, the vector of controls Z includes the current account balance (in percent of nominal GDP) and two measures of bank liquidity (in percent of total assets): one includes variables on the asset side (cash, balances with the central bank and securities, etc.); the other includes variables on the liability side (such as customer deposits). Equation (11.3) is estimated by OLS and, to allow for possible correlation between *lev* and the error *u*, also by using as instruments the controls in the macro-level version of equation (11.1); that is, using in (11.3) not actual leverage but its predicted value from the leverage equation.

The two sets of regressions—for tax effects on leverage and leverage effects on crisis—are estimated separately: there is no apparent loss of efficiency in doing so since, estimating them as a system, the null of no contemporaneous correlation between the ϵ_{it} and the u_{it} cannot be rejected.

11.2.3 Simulating Tax Effects on the Probability of Crisis

The ultimate objective of the exercise is to simulate the impact of tax changes on the probability of a crisis. For this, we will simply combine various point estimates from the two sets of regressions just described. An alternative approach would be to simply substitute from the country-level version of (11.1) into (11.3) and so include the CIT rate directly as a regressor in modeling the probability of crisis. Doing so, the tax rate proves insignificant. This approach is problematic, however, for two reasons. First, the corporate tax rate might affect the probability of a crisis other than through an impact on bank leverage; one result reported below has the CIT rate appearing with a negative coefficient (which would tend to offset the positive effect expected though the leverage route), though the effect is not significant. The second difficulty is that the reduced form approach requires the additional identifying assumption, beyond those needed for the separate regressions, that $E[Z\epsilon] = 0$, so that the controls in the crisis regression are independent of the shock in the leverage equation. But it is not hard to think of reasons why this might fail: a shock to asset prices, for instance, might affect not only banks' leverage but also their liquidity.

11.3 Results

This section presents estimation results on the impact of the CIT rate on leverage (subsection 11.3.1) and the effect of leverage on the probability of a banking crisis (subsection 11.3.2).

11.3.1 Effect of Taxation on Leverage

Bank-Level Data

The results of estimating (11.1) and (11.2) using bank-level data are presented in table 11.2. Columns 1 and 2 use the dynamic specification of equation (11.1); columns 3 through 8 use the between-estimator of equation (11.2). In column 1, "tax (short-term)" refers to β_1 and "tax (long-term)" refers to $\beta_1 / (1 - \beta_0)$. Since about two-thirds of the

Table 11.2
Effect of tax on leverage: bank-level data

	(1)	(2)	(3)	(4)	(5)	(6)	(7)	(8)
Lagged leverage	0.67***	0.74***						
	(0.08)	(0.13)						
Tax (short-term)	0.08***	0.21						
	(0.03)	(0.03)						
Tax (long-term)	0.25***	0.21***	0.31***	0.17***	0.17***	0.18***	0.30***	0.14***
	(0.05)	(0.05)	(0.02)	(0.03)	(0.03)	(0.03)	(0.02)	(0.03)
Log of asset	0.05**	0.05*	0.17***	0.16***	0.18***	0.14***	0.14***	0.17***
	(0.03)	(0.03)	(0.00)	(0.01)	(0.01)	(0.01)	(0.00)	(0.01)
Squared log of asset	–0.00**	–0.00*	–0.01***	–0.01***	–0.01***	–0.00***	–0.00***	–0.01***
	(0.00)	(0.00)	(0.00)	(0.00)	(0.00)	(0.00)	(0.00)	(0.00)
ROA	–0.24***	–0.26***	–0.29***	–0.12***	–0.17***	–0.20***	–0.47***	–0.31***
	(0.03)	(0.09)	(0.02)	(0.03)	(0.02)	(0.03)	(0.02)	(0.05)
GDP growth	0.09**	0.01	0.06	–0.53***	0.57***	–0.09	–0.51***	–0.81***
	(0.03)	(0.05)	(0.07)	(0.09)	(0.09)	(0.11)	(0.06)	(0.08)
Inflation	–0.14***	–0.09	–0.63***	–0.47***	–0.90***	–0.50***	–0.51***	–0.36***
	(0.04)	(0.07)	(0.04)	(0.05)	(0.05)	(0.06)	(0.04)	(0.05)
Saving rate	0.00	0.03	0.10***	0.27***	0.06***	0.27***	0.17***	0.24***
	(0.01)	(0.04)	(0.02)	(0.03)	(0.02)	(0.04)	(0.02)	(0.03)
R^2			0.28	0.36	0.24	0.33	0.30	0.39
Observations	106,649	33,933	120,481	39,712	74,852	23,956	45,629	15,756
Arellano–Bond AR1	0.00	0.00						
Arellano–Bond AR2	0.04	0.21						
Hansen P-value	0.51	0.09						
US included?	Yes	No	Yes	No	Yes	No	Yes	No
Year	01–11	01–11	01–11	01–11	01–07	01–07	08–11	08–11

Note: Dependent variable is bank leverage, defined as total liabilities divided by total assets. Dynamic regressions (11.1) and (11.2) in the text are estimated by system GMM, with a maximum number of lags of two. Standard errors (between brackets) are heteroskedasticity-robust and clustered within countries. The between estimators (columns 3 through 8) are estimated by OLS. Tax (short-term) refers to β_1 in equation (11.1) and tax (long-term) refers to $\beta_1 / (1 - \beta_0)$ in equation (11.1) and γ_1 in equation (11.2). Standard errors on long-term impact are calculated by delta method. The rate of return on assets (ROA) is defined as the ratio of profit before tax to total assets. *, **, *** denote significance at the 10, 5, and 1 percent levels.

observations are for US banks, which may differ from others in ways not fully captured by fixed effects (e.g., in the extent of off–balance-sheet activities), results are reported in even-numbered columns when these are excluded. The sample is further divided to explore the potential difference between the pre- and post-crisis periods: columns 1 through 4 use all years available, columns 5 and 6 use only years 2001 to 2007, and columns 7 and 8 use only 2008 to 2011.

Consistent with theoretical prediction and the results of Keen and De Mooij (2012), the picture that emerges is of a strong positive association between the CIT rate and bank leverage: notably, the long-run coefficient is significant at the 1 percent level in all specifications. The long-run marginal impact lies between 0.14 and 0.31 and is similar between the dynamic and static specifications. The impact is also quite robust across different settings. Removing US banks from the sample (the even-numbered columns) typically gives somewhat smaller coefficients. Comparing columns 5 and 6 with columns 7 and 8 suggests, perhaps surprisingly, only minor differences between the periods before and after the onset of the 2008 financial crisis. The controls are generally significant and with plausible sign: larger banks are able to borrow more, more profitable banks have access to relatively cheap retention finance, and high savings are largely allocated at the margin to deposits. The negative effect of higher inflation is harder to explain: it may reflect a tightening of capital requirements to the extent that assets are valued for regulatory purposes at historic cost. The R^2 for the between-estimator ranges from 0.24 to 0.39. For the dynamic specification, the Arellano–Bond AR(2) statistic suggests that second-order serial correlation might be problematic in the first column. The Hansen statistic in columns 1 and 2 does not reject (at 5 percent) the null that the instruments are valid.

Table 11.3 reports estimated tax effects when the sample of banks is divided by size into the five groups of table 11.1. The underlying regressions include the same control variables as in table 11.2, use all years and banks, and use either the dynamic specification or the between-estimator; so the results are comparable to those in columns 1 and 3 of table 11.2. Tax effects decrease almost monotonically in banks' size, which is again consistent with Keen and De Mooij (2012). Indeed, with the dynamic-GMM estimator, the marginal coefficient is 0.26 (and highly significant) for the smallest banks but only 0.08 (and insignificant) for the largest. The between-estimator shows even more pronounced differences, with a coefficient of 0.36 for the smallest banks and –0.01 for the largest. Significance also drops with size, although

Table 11.3
Estimated tax effect on bank leverage for alternative size groups

Percentile (in assets)	0–85	85–90	90–95	95–97.5	Top 2.5
Asset share	13.4	4.6	8.6	8.7	64.7
Dynamic GMM estimator (long-term impact)					
Marginal impact coefficient	0.26***	0.17***	0.61	0.73	0.08
T-Value	4.68	3.74	0.53	0.63	0.26
Between estimator					
Marginal impact coefficient	0.36***	0.17***	0.15***	0.09***	−0.01
T-Value	16.00	5.66	5.60	2.66	−0.24

Note: Estimates as in specifications, columns 1 and 3, of table 11.2 for alternative size groups as in table 11.1. *** denotes significance at 1 percent.

less so for the between-estimator, where most results remain significant, including for larger banks.

Treating asset shares as exogenous, an unbiased estimator of the effect of the CIT on aggregate financial leverage is given by the asset-weighted average of the marginal coefficients in table 11.3. This gives implied aggregate tax responsiveness of 0.11 for the GMM estimators and 0.08 for the between estimates—quite a narrow range.[14]

Country-Level Data
Table 11.4 reports results using country-level data. Again, we remove US banks in the even-numbered columns. Columns 1 and 2 use all years, while columns 3 and 4 are for 2001 to 2006 and columns 5 and 6 for 2007 to 2009.

Like the bank-level data, the country-level data suggest that the CIT exerts a positive impact on the aggregate leverage ratio of banks. The statistical significance of the effect varies between models, however, from being significant at 1 percent level in column 2 to statistically insignificant in columns 3 and 5. Perhaps surprisingly, there is no systematic difference in tax effects before and after the financial crisis. The R^2 ranges from 0.44 to 0.54. Removing US banks from the sample leads to larger estimated tax effects, the opposite of the finding for country-level data. In the full sample the marginal impact of the CIT rate is 0.04 (column 1); excluding US banks, it increases to 0.06 (column 2). This is close to but somewhat lower from the simulated aggregate impact from the bank-level estimates in table 11.3. In the simulations below, and taking account too of the results for the bank-level data, we report results for tax effects on aggregate leverage in the range of 0.04 to 0.15.

Table 11.4
Effect of tax on leverage: country-level data

	(1)	(2)	(3)	(4)	(5)	(6)
Tax (long-term)	0.04*	0.06***	0.03	0.04**	0.02	0.09*
	(0.02)	(0.02)	(0.02)	(0.02)	(0.06)	(0.05)
ROA	−1.77***	−1.75***	−2.15***	−2.09***	−1.16***	−1.16***
	(0.19)	(0.20)	(0.23)	(0.23)	(0.41)	(0.39)
GDP growth	0.09	0.09	0.09	0.08	0.14	0.13
	(0.08)	(0.08)	(0.08)	(0.08)	(0.12)	(0.12)
Inflation	−0.15***	−0.15***	−0.18***	−0.17***	−0.16	−0.15
	(0.03)	(0.02)	(0.03)	(0.03)	(0.12)	(0.12)
Saving rate	0.13***	0.11***	0.12***	0.12***	0.11***	0.07*
	(0.02)	(0.02)	(0.03)	(0.03)	(0.04)	(0.04)
$R2$	0.50	0.51	0.54	0.53	0.44	0.52
Observations	253	244	199	192	54	52
US included?	Yes	No	Yes	No	Yes	No
Year	01–11	01–11	01–07	01–07	08–09	08–09

Note: Dependent variable is bank leverage in percent of total bank assets. Standard errors are heteroskedasticity-robust but not clustered. Tax (long-term) is the coefficient on the CIT rate. The rate of return on assets (ROA) is defined as the ratio of profit before tax to total assets. *, **, *** denote significance at the 10, 5, and 1 percent levels.

11.3.2 Effect of Leverage on the Probability of Banking Crisis

Table 11.5 presents estimation results for the logit model of equation (11.3), exploring the impact of bank leverage on the odds of a financial crisis. Columns 1 through 4 present results from simple OLS regressions, while column 5 instruments leverage by its predicted value from the macro regression in column 1 of table 11.4. Columns 1, 2, 3, and 5 count as crisis events both the "systemic" and the "borderline systemic" banking crises reported in Laeven and Valencia (2010), while column 4 counts only the former. Column 2 includes the CIT rate as an explanatory variable; column 3 excludes the United States.[15]

The effect of leverage on the probability of crisis is positive in all columns of table 11.5 but significant only under the broader characterization of crises (i.e., not in column 4). Excluding the United States increases the impact and significance of the leverage variable. This positive impact of leverage on the probability of banking crisis is consistent with previous studies (Barrell et al., 2010; Kato, Kobayashi, and Saita, 2010). Other control variables have expected signs—lower bank liquidity on the liability side and higher current account deficits are

Table 11.5
Effect of leverage on the odds ratio of a banking crisis

	(1)	(2)	(3)	(4)	(5)
Leverage	31.47**	31.58**	40.19***	42.42	139.27***
	(13.66)	(13.76)	(14.60)	(32.03)	(49.52)
Tax		−2.40			
		(4.22)			
Liquid assets	−1.19	−1.61	−1.26	−2.36	1.56
	(3.58)	(3.33)	(3.98)	(5.09)	(4.91)
Liquid liability	−4.82**	−4.48**	−5.39**	−3.96*	−5.63***
	(1.99)	(1.96)	(2.23)	(2.25)	(2.41)
Current account	−14.36***	−13.03**	−15.59***	−2.97	−30.18***
	(5.24)	(5.30)	(5.87)	(4.42)	(9.01)
Observations	240	240	231	240	240
Crisis/border	Both	both	both	crisis	Both
US included?	Yes	yes	No	Yes	Yes
Estimator	OLS	OLS	OLS	OLS	IV
R^2	0.14	0.14	0.18	0.13	0.30

Note: Dependent variable is the odds ratio of a banking crisis (logit). Standard errors are heteroskedasticity-robust and clustered within countries. Columns 1 through 4 use OLS, and column 5 instruments leverage by its predicted value from column 1 of table 11.4. "Crisis/border" indicates, respectively, whether observations are used for both the systemic and the borderline systemic banking crises or for only systemic banking crises.

significantly associated with higher probability of crisis—though liquidity on the asset side is generally insignificant. As mentioned above, the CIT rate enters with a negative but insignificant coefficient.

To interpret the size of the leverage coefficient in table 11.5, we transform it into a marginal impact on the probability of crisis. Since the logit model is nonlinear, the impact of a change in the leverage ratio on the probability of a financial crisis depends on the initial leverage ratio. Table 11.6 reports the simulated marginal impact (i.e., the impact of one percentage point change in the leverage ratio on the probability of crisis, measured in percent) for alternative values of the initial bank leverage ratio, based on columns 1 and 5 of table 11.5. All variables other than leverage are evaluated at their means. For comparison, the last two columns show the comparable marginal impact coefficients reported in Barrell et al. (2010) and Kato, Kobayashi, and Saita (2010).

Clearly, the marginal impact of bank leverage on the probability of a crisis increases rapidly, and increasingly rapidly, at higher levels of leverage. Taking the specification of column 1 in table 11.5, for instance, at initial leverage of 88 percent—which is the mean leverage in the

Table 11.6
Marginal impact of leverage on the probability of banking crisis

Initial leverage (%)	(1)	(5)	Barrell et al.	Kato et al.
88	0.3	0.0	1.7	0.6
90	0.5	0.0	2.7	1.1
92	0.9	0.5	4.3	1.9
94	1.5	7.3	6.9	3.2
96	2.6	34.8	NA	NA

Note: Columns 1 and 5 refer to regressions in columns 1 and 5 of table 11.5. Marginal impacts are measured in percent.

micro sample—an 1.0 percentage point increase in leverage increases the likelihood of a crisis by 0.3 percentage points; evaluated at an initial leverage ratio of 94 percent—close to the median in the macro sample—it increases the likelihood of crisis by 1.5 percentage points, around five times as much; and when leverage is initially 96 percent—as in many of the countries that experienced a crisis—the impact is an increased chance of crisis of 2.6 points. The implied effects at higher leverage ratios are even much stronger in the specification of column 5 of table 11.5. At the same time, according to this specification, the marginal impact is negligible at a leverage ratio of 0.88. Hence the marginal impact coefficient in column 5 is considerably more convex in the leverage ratio than it is in column 1. These results, which are not out of line with those of Barrell et al. (2010) and Kato et al. (2010), suggest that the marginal impact of leverage on the probability of crisis is small at low levels of leverage, but larger and possibly much larger at high levels of leverage.

Figure 11.1 shows the implied, highly nonlinear relationship between the initial leverage ratio and the probability of crisis, using the results from table 11.5. (Loosely speaking, figure 11.1 thus shows the integral of the marginal impacts reported in table 11.6.) While the likelihood of crisis is essentially independent of leverage, and while this remains below 90 percent or just above, the chances of a crisis increase rapidly, and increasing fast, at higher leverage.

11.4 Policy Simulations

The results of the previous section established two links in the chain described in the introduction: between the CIT rate and aggregate leverage in the banking sector; and between that aggregate leverage

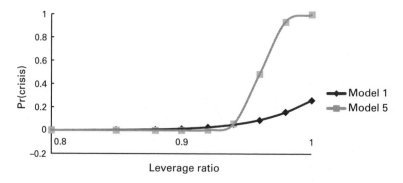

Figure 11.1
Relationship between initial leverage and the probability of banking crisis

and the probability of a financial crisis. The first part of this section brings together these two links to infer a relationship between the CIT rate and the chances of crisis. The second explores the implied welfare gains from a variety of policies to mitigate the debt bias in banks' financing decisions.

11.4.1 Taxation and the Likelihood of a Banking Crisis

The result in the previous section suggest that a 1.0 percentage point reduction in the CIT rate reduces the aggregate leverage ratio of banks by somewhere between 0.08 and 0.11 percentage points—though slightly less when inferred from macro data, so that we consider a range between 0.04 and 0.15; and that the impact of a marginal increase in leverage on the likelihood of crisis depends quite sensitively on its initial level. Taking this range of values for tax responsiveness and illustrative initial leverage ratios of 90, 93, and 96 percent (respectively: the level prevalent in some the low-leveraged countries in the sample, the mean in our sample, and a level prevalent in some of the high-leveraged crisis countries before the 2008 crisis), we combine these values in table 11.7 to arrive at the implied increase in the probability of crisis associated with a one percentage point increase in the statutory CIT rate, using the two sets of estimated relationships as in table 11.6 (corresponding to columns 1 and 5 of table 11.5).

Bearing in mind that a 1 point change in the CIT rate is quite a modest change, the effects are by no means inconsiderable, at least at high initial leverage ratios. For instance, at an aggregate leverage in the banking sector of 96 percent, increasing the corporate tax rate from 25 to 26 percent would increase the likelihood of crisis by between 0.1 and

Table 11.7
Marginal impact of tax on the probability of banking crisis

	Assumed marginal impact on leverage		
	0.04	0.08	0.15
Initial leverage (%)	Estimates of column 1 of table 11.6		
90	0.02	0.04	0.07
93	0.04	0.09	0.17
96	0.10	0.21	0.39
Initial leverage (%)	Estimates of column 5 of table 11.6		
90	0.00	0.00	0.01
93	0.08	0.16	0.29
96	1.39	2.78	5.22

0.39 points using the estimate from column 1 of table 11.6, and by between 1.39 and 5.22 points using that from column 5 of table 11.6. And this occurs, it should be stressed, even though the tax-responsiveness of larger banks is low. If the initial leverage ratio is low, however, the effects are quite modest: at an aggregate leverage in the financial sector of 90 percent, a higher corporate tax rate raises the likelihood of a crisis hardly at all.

11.4.2 Welfare Gains from Policies to Reduce Debt Bias in the Financial Sector

The link between taxation and the risk of crisis established above enables an assessment of three policies that would reduce the tax incentive for banks to finance themselves by debt rather than equity:

• *A ten-point cut in the CIT rate*   Given the convexity of the relationship between leverage and the changes of crisis, the effect of this more substantial reform is not simply ten times that in table 11.7 (but in general rather less). The simulations reported below (for all reforms) take account of this nonlinearity by extrapolating a series of small changes.

• *A "bank tax" of 10 basis points*   Since the crisis, 13 or so countries have introduced some form of levy on banks. While these differ in significant ways, the most typical form—broadly along the lines of the financial stability contribution proposed by IMF (2010)—is a charge on liabilities other than insured deposits. For instance, the United Kingdom has implemented a levy of 7.8 basis points (10.5 basis points from January 2013) on short-term nonsecured liabilities. Such a charge

is modeled here by transforming it into an equivalent tax on the flow of interest payments: assuming an interest rate of 4 percent, a bank levy of 10 basis points corresponds to a tax on interest of 2.5 percent (=10/400); so is modeled as a reduction in the CIT rate of 2.5 percent.
• An "allowance for corporate equity"(ACE) form of corporate tax   By providing a deduction for the normal return to equity, this would, in principle, eliminate the corporate-level tax bias toward debt finance.[16] It is in this respect equivalent, given the deductibility of interest, to reducing the corporate tax rate to zero. We simulate this reform as a 28-point reduction in the CIT rate, this being the mean value of the CIT rate in our panel.

The implications of these reforms for aggregate leverage are readily estimated using the results above. We suppose, as before, that a one percentage point reduction in the CIT rate reduces banks' aggregate leverage by somewhere between 0.04 and 0.15. This means, for instance, that the bank levy of 10 bp would reduce financial leverage by between 0.1 and 0.4 percentage points, for example from 93 percent to 92.9 or 92.6. Eliminating debt bias altogether with an ACE would reduce leverage by 2.2 percentage points under what we shall take to be the central estimate of 0.08: say, from 93 to 90.8; with the upper bound estimate of 0.15, leverage would fall by 4.2 percentage points.

These leverage effects can then be translated into impacts on the likelihood of crisis along the lines of table 11.7. To give some sense of the welfare implications, table 11.8 transforms these implied changes in crisis probabilities into expected effects on output, which will in turn depend, for the reasons discussed above, on the initial level of leverage.[17] Laeven and Valencia (2010) report that the mean output loss of a financial crisis, measured as the cumulative loss in GDP relative to the pre-crisis trend over a four-year period, averaged 23 percent over the period 1970 to 2009. Multiplying the change in crisis probability associated with the three policy reforms by this expected output loss of 23 percent gives an annual expected GDP gain associated with that policy reform.[18] Table 11.8 reports such estimates for three alternative assumptions on tax responsiveness of leverage, two of the initial levels of leverage in table 11.7 (93 and 96 percent), and using the same two estimates of the impact of leverage on the likelihood of crises as before (from columns 1 and 5 of table 11.6).

Table 11.8 shows that the implied welfare impact of tax reforms that ease debt bias in the financial sector can be substantial. For instance,

Table 11.8
Simulated four-year cumulative expected output gain of three tax reforms

	(1) CIT cut	(2) Bank levy	(3) ACE	(1) CIT cut	(2) Bank levy	(3) ACE
Initial leverage ratio 93 percent of assets						
	Impact of leverage column 1			Impact of leverage column 5		
Tax impact 0.04	0.1	0.0	0.3	0.2	0.1	0.4
Tax impact 0.08	0.2	0.1	0.5	0.3	0.1	0.4
Tax impact 0.15	0.3	0.1	0.7	0.4	0.2	0.5
Initial leverage ratio 96 percent of assets						
	Impact of leverage column 1			Impact of leverage column 5		
Tax impact 0.04	0.2	0.1	0.6	3.2	0.8	8.1
Tax impact 0.08	0.5	0.1	1.1	6.1	1.6	11.9
Tax impact 0.15	0.8	0.2	1.6	9.9	3.0	13.3

Note: "CIT cut" refers to 10 percentage point reduction in the CIT rate, "bank levy" refers to 10 basis point bank levy on all liabilities (2.5 percent lower debt bias), and "ACE" refers to allowance for corporate equity to neutralize debt bias (assuming an initial 28 percent CIT).

taking the central estimate for the tax impact on bank leverage of 0.08, eliminating debt bias through an ACE gives an expected GDP gain of between 0.5 and 11.9 percent. This is a large range, but both numbers are far larger than the very small deadweight losses reported in the literature for nonfinancial firms—and indeed large by the normal standards of tax analysis. The implication is that the most important social costs of debt bias likely originate not from the Harberger triangles that previous discussions have focused on but from the impact on financial sector risks, especially in countries where leverage ratios are already high.

Of the three reforms, it is the ACE that gives the largest gains—which is as one would expect, since it alone entirely eliminates the debt bias. The impact of a ten-point CIT cut, however, can also be sizable, but again especially at higher leverage ratios: at an aggregate bank leverage ratio of 93 percent, it is estimated to yield a cumulative expected GDP gain over four years of between 0.1 and 0.4 percent; at leverage of 96 percent, this effect may go up to 9.9 percent. The bank levy of ten basis points, however—a rate at the upper end of those observed, in practice—has much smaller effects, except when both tax responsiveness and initial leverage are high: even so, the estimated gain in expected GDP can rise to 3 percent.

These results raise more questions for policy design that can be addressed here. Prominent among these is whether, given the wider revenue loss they would otherwise imply, a reduced corporate tax rate and, more particularly, an ACE, could be applied only to the financial sector, where the welfare gains appear greatest. Clearly, applying differential corporate tax treatment to different sectors brings its own risk of creating avoidance opportunities and distortions of a kind not addressed here—for which reason it is usually considered bad policy. Perhaps the particularly tight regulations to which the financial sector is subject could substantially mitigate these risks (e.g., of nonfinancial activities conducted through financial institutions). If, however, sectoral differentiation through the corporate tax is ruled out—and, no doubt, the suggestion of lighter corporate taxation in the financial sector could be politically problematic—the implication would seem to be that a corrective case could be made for bank levies at substantially higher rates than at present.

11.5 Conclusion

The analysis here is in several respects simplistic and limited. In particular, the analysis deals with leverage in the banking sector itself, not in shadow banks where leverage ratios might have been particularly high and financial risks large. Moreover we have not uncovered a direct link between tax incentives favoring debt finance and the probability of financial crisis. But the evidence presented here does suggest the real possibility of such a connection. If debt bias leads to higher aggregate bank leverage than would otherwise be the case—and it seems that it does—and if higher aggregate bank leverage makes financial crisis more likely—and it seems that it does—then debt bias increases the chances of financial crisis. This in turn can imply welfare gains from mitigating debt bias far higher than the small amounts found in previous work: noticeably more, in some of the calculations reported here, than one percent of GDP. Regulation, of course, has historically had the dominant role in addressing such problems of excess leverage in the financial sector, and the higher and tighter capital and other requirements of Basel III should to some degree reduce the welfare costs of debt bias. How much comfort is taken from this will depend on one's evaluation of these reforms. What the evidence assembled here suggests, however, is that the tax incentive encouraging banks to use debt finance is not just an inelegant inconsistency with regulations intended to do the exact opposite, but a potential risk to be recognized, and, as need be, addressed, in the pursuit of financial stability.

Appendix Data

This appendix describes the data used in the exercises above. We first discuss the bank-level data used in the regressions for bank leverage, then the country-level data used for both the macro leverage regression and the crisis regression.

Bank-Level Data

The data collection process for individual banks is similar to that in Keen and De Mooij (2012). We take individual banks' balance sheet from Bankscope, constructed by Bureau van Dijk, worldwide CIT rate data from KPMG's corporate and indirect tax survey 2011, and country-level control variables from the IMF *World Economic Outlook*. Our observations consist of active commercial banks, savings banks, and cooperative banks. We use data from unconsolidated balance sheets. Our final observations contain data from 82 countries between 2001 and 2011. This is two years longer than in Keen and De Mooij (2012). We drop observations for which leverage exceeds unity. We keep observations when all the variables in table A11.1 are available. The number of total bank-year observations is 120,481. The number of banks is 13,356, and the panel is unbalanced. Note that 80,769 observations (67 percent of the total) are for US banks. Table A11.1 reports summary statistics.

Variables are defined as follows. "Leverage" is the individual banks' total liabilities divided by total assets. The mean leverage is 0.881. This is similar to the value in Keen and De Mooij (2012), suggesting that banks' overall capital structures had not changed greatly changed since the onset of the financial crisis. "Tax" refers to statutory CIT rate, the sample average of which is 36.7 percent. If we exclude US banks, the mean and median tax rates are 0.322 and 0.332, respectively. The average log of total assets is 12,210, implying an average asset value of 1.35 billion US dollars. The rate of return on assets (ROA) is defined as the ratio of profit before tax to total assets. The average value of ROA is 1.0 percent, with considerable variation ranging from −314.8 percent to 315.4 percent. The mean GDP growth rate, inflation rate, and saving rate are, respectively, 1.7, 2.7, and 17.4 percent.

Table A11.1
Summary statistics of data in the leverage regression using micro data

	N	Mean	Median	Standard deviation	Min	Max
Leverage	120,481	0.881	0.904	0.096	0.071	1.000
Tax	120,481	0.367	0.400	0.055	0.000	0.421
Log of asset	120,481	12.210	12.041	1.570	2.477	21.567
Squared log of asset	120,481	151.560	144.995	39.842	6.133	465.147
ROA	120,481	0.010	0.009	0.040	−3.148	3.154
GDP growth	120,481	0.017	0.019	0.027	−0.177	0.183
Inflation	120,481	0.027	0.022	0.025	−0.035	1.087
Saving rate	120,481	0.174	0.152	0.058	−0.041	0.535

Country-Level Data

Aggregated balance-sheet data of the country's banks from the *OECD Banking Statistics* are used to construct leverage and liquidity measures. Data on current account balances are from the *IMF World Economic Outlook*. Other variables such as GDP growth rate are collected as explained in the previous subsection. Coverage is between 2001 and 2009, which is a shorter period than for the micro level data, reflecting the unavailability of aggregated banks' financial information for 2010 and 2011. For most countries, information is available on the aggregated balance sheet of all banks. Four countries (Greece, Hungary, Portugal, and Turkey) report their balance sheets separately for commercial banks, saving banks, and cooperative banks; for these, we aggregate across these three kinds of banks. Only observations for which all the variables in table A11.2 are available are retained, giving a sample of 29 countries with 253 observations.

Following Barrell et al. (2010) and Kato, Kobayashi, and Saita (2010), we define variables as follows. "Asset liquidity" is measured as cash and balances with the central banks plus securities divided by assets; "liability liquidity" is measured as consumer deposits divided by assets; the current account balance is measured as the current account divided by nominal GDP. Other variables are defined in the same way as for the micro data.

Note that the mean leverage ratio in table A11.2 is higher than in table A11.1. This is because large banks tend to be more highly leveraged than small banks and account for a large share of total assets in a country. The average tax rate in table A11.2 is lower than that in table

Table A11.2
Summary statistics of data in the regressions using macro data

	N	Mean	Median	Standard deviation	Min	Max
Leverage	253	0.930	0.934	0.024	0.862	0.973
Asset liquidity	253	0.238	0.233	0.088	0.087	0.512
Liability liquidity	253	0.536	0.518	0.161	0.218	0.956
Current account balance	253	−0.007	−0.008	0.062	−0.159	0.164
Tax	253	0.286	0.290	0.069	0.125	0.421
ROA	253	0.009	0.009	0.008	−0.048	0.031
GDP growth	253	0.023	0.026	0.033	−0.143	0.105
Inflation	253	0.032	0.025	0.049	−0.026	0.685
Saving rate	253	0.219	0.222	0.056	0.051	0.404

A11.1; this is because many of the bank-year observations in table A11.1 refer to countries with a relatively high CIT rate (e.g., United States, Japan, and Germany), which thus carry a much larger weight in the average of table A11.1 than in that of table A11.2.

Notes

The views expressed here are those of the authors and should not be attributed to the IMF, its Executive Board or management, or to the Ministry of Finance Japan. We are grateful to Michael Devereux, Jaime Jaramillo-Vellejo, Gaëtan Nicodème, Lev Ratnovski, four anonymous referees, and participants in the CESifo Summer Workshop in Venice for helpful comments and suggestions.

1. Including IMF (2009a), Lloyd (2009), Slemrod (2009), Shackelford, Shaviro, and Slemrod (2010), and Hemmelgarn and Nicodème (2010). See also the contributions in Arachi and Alworth (2012).

2. De Mooij (2012) provides an overview of debt bias and possible policy responses to it.

3. See, for instance, the meta-analyses of De Mooij (2011) and Feld, Heckemeyer, and Overesch (2011).

4. There is evidence too that higher levels of leverage amplify output losses when crises occur, but this aspect is not explored here.

5. See, for instance, Keen (2011a, b), Devereux (2013), and Coulter, Mayer, and Vickers (2013).

6. Estimates of the kind reported here could in principle also be used to inform the calibration of corrective taxes on bank liabilities along the lines analyzed by Acharya et al. (2012) and Keen (2011b).

7. The dynamic equation is estimated using the system GMM estimator of Arellano and Bover (1995) and Blundell and Bond (1998) to address both inconsistencies arising from

correlation of the lagged dependent variable with the fixed effects and the weak instrument problem due to the persistence of taxes. The between-estimator uses OLS.

8. The regressions do not explicitly control for regulatory variables, but these are likely to be largely captured by the bank fixed effects. Keen and De Mooij (2012) include capital requirements in their regression and find that, although they matter, they do not negate the impact of taxes on leverage.

9. Aggregating the micro-level specification would imply that the product of banks' aggregate assets and a Herfindahl index of their concentration should also be included. In the absence of data, however, this is not captured in the macro regressions.

10. Some studies have used alternative indicators to explore similar relationships. For instance, Ratnovski and Huang (2009) explore the effect of capital ratios on stock price declines of large banks; IMF (2009b) analyzes the impact of alternative indicators of bank capital ratios on the likelihood of governmental intervention. Neither study finds robust significant effects.

11. Laeven and Valencia (2012) provide a further update of their database, with information up to 2011. There are no countries, however, for which a crisis began in 2010 or 2011, and the banking data from the OECD that we use are in any event available only up to 2009.

12. The crisis events refer to the United States in 2007 and Austria, Belgium, Denmark, Germany, Ireland, Luxembourg, and the Netherlands in 2008. The borderline cases refer to France, Greece, Hungary, Portugal, Slovenia, Spain, and Sweden in 2008. Other crisis events identified in Laeven and Valencia (2010), including, for instance, the United Kingdom are not part of our dataset.

13. Second crisis year observations are therefore not independent and are eliminated from the sample in the regressions.

14. With the further (and not entirely plausible) assumption that the estimated coefficients are independent across size groups, the standard standard errors of the estimated aggregate effect is $\left(\sum \text{var}(\hat{\beta}_i)(\omega_i)^2\right)^{1/2}$. This gives t-values of 0.53 and 1.91 for, respectively, the dynamic and between estimators; thus only the between estimate is significant, and only at 10 percent.

15. Adding the tax variable changes very little when added to columns 3 through 5; using lags for the independent variables reduces the significance of the leverage variable.

16. Further discussion of the ACE is in De Mooij (2012), and evidence of its impact in practice, which does tend to suggest some impact on leverage, is reviewed in Klemm (2007). There are, it should be noted, other forms of corporate tax which would also eliminate debt bias, such as a comprehensive business income tax (CBIT) —which would simply deny interest deductibility—or the $R + F$ cash flow tax of the Meade Committee (1978). These though tend to raise particular difficulties, practical or political, in their application to the financial sector: the CBIT, for instance, would presumably exempt interest received, so largely eliminating any tax liability for traditional banks.

17. This approach simplifies in ignoring the revenue implications of the various reforms, as would be appropriate if revenue could be raised and disposed of in lump-sum fashion.

18. While a case could be made for discounting these losses, since they accrue over time, acting in the opposite direction is that the approach here also ignores the losses that undoubtedly occur beyond the four-year horizon.

References

Acharya, Viral, Lasse Pedersen, Thomas Philippon, and Matthew Richardson. 2012. Measuring systemic risk. CEPR discussion paper 8824.

Arachi, Giampaolo, and Julian Alworth, eds. 2012. *Taxation and the Financial Crisis*. New York: Oxford University Press.

Arellano, Manuel, and Olympia Bover. 1995. Another look at the instrumental variable estimation of error-components models. *Journal of Econometrics* 68: 29–51.

Barrell, Ray, E. Philip Davis, Karim Dilruba, and Iana Liadze. 2010. The impact of global imbalances: Does the current account balance help to predict banking crises in OECD countries? National Institute of Economic and Social Research discussion paper 351, United Kingdom.

Blundell, Richard, and Stephen Bond. 1998. Initial conditions and moment restrictions in dynamic panel data models. *Journal of Econometrics* 87: 115–43.

De Mooij, Ruud A. 2011. The tax elasticity of corporate debt: A synthesis of size and variations. Working paper 11/95. IMF.

De Mooij, Ruud A. 2012. Tax biases to debt finance: Assessing the problem, finding solutions. *Fiscal Studies* 33 (4): 489–512.

European Commission. 2011. Growth-friendly tax policies in member states and better tax coordination in the EU. Annex to the European Growth Survey 2012, COM(2011) 815 final, *http://ec.europa.eu/economy_finance/publications/european_economy/2012/ee-2012-6_en .htm*.

Feld, Lars P., Jost H. Heckemeyer, and Michael Overesch. 2011. Capital structure choice and company taxation: A meta-study. Working paper 3400. CESifo.

Gordon, Roger H. 2010. Taxation and corporate use of debt: Implications for tax policy. *National Tax Journal* 63: 151–74.

Hemmelgarn, Thomas, and Gaëtan Nicodème. 2010. The 2008 financial crisis and tax policy. Working paper 20. European Commission Directorate-General for Taxation and Customs Union. Brussels.

International Monetary Fund. 2009a. *Debt Bias and Other Distortions: Crisis-Related Issues in Tax Policy*. Washington, DC: IMF.

International Monetary Fund. 2009b. Responding to the financial crisis and measuring systemic risk. *Global Financial Stability Report*. IMF. Washington, DC: IMF.

International Monetary Fund. 2010. A fair and substantial contribution by the financial sector: Final report for the G-20. Staff paper. IMF. https://www.imf.org/external/np/ g20/.../062710b.pdf

Kato, Ryo, Shun Kobayashi, and Yumi Saita. 2010. Calibrating the level of capital: The way we see it. Working paper series 10-E-6. Bank of Japan.

Keen, Michael. 2011a. Rethinking the taxation of the financial sector. Musgrave lecture. *CESifo Economic Studies* 57: 1–24.

Keen, Michael. 2011b. The taxation and regulation of banks. Working paper 11/206. IMF.

Keen, Michael, and Ruud De Mooij. 2012. Debt, taxes and banks. Working paper 12/48. IMF.

Klemm, Alexander. 2007. Allowances for corporate equity in practice. *CESifo Economic Studies* 53: 229–62.

Laeven, Luc, and Fabian Valencia. 2008. Systemic banking crises: A new database. Working paper 08/224. IMF.

Laeven, Luc, and Fabian Valencia. 2010. Resolution of banking crises: The good, the bad, and the ugly. Working paper 10/146. IMF.

Laeven, Luc, and Fabian Valencia. 2012. Systemic banking crises database: An update. Working paper 12/163. IMF.

Lloyd, Geoffrey. 2009. Moving beyond the crisis: Using tax policy to support financial stability. Mimeo. OECD.

Meade Committee. 1978. *The Structure and Reform of Direct Taxation: Report of a Committee Chaired by Professor J. E. Meade.* London: George Allen and Unwin.

Ratnovski, Lev, and Rocco Huang. 2009. Why are Canadian banks more resilient? Working paper 09/152. IMF.

Shackelford, Douglas A., Daniel Shaviro, and Joel Slemrod. 2010. Taxation and the financial sector. *National Tax Journal* 63: 781–806.

Slemrod, Joel. 2009. Lessons for tax policy in the Great Recession. *National Tax Journal* 62: 387–97.

Weichenrieder, A., and T. Klautke. 2008. Taxes and the efficiency costs of capital distortions. Working paper 2431. CESifo.

12 The Ability of Banks to Shift Corporate Income Taxes to Customers

Gunther Capelle-Blancard and Olena Havrylchyk

We task the IMF to prepare a report ... as to how the financial sector could make a fair and substantial contribution toward paying for any burdens associated with government interventions to repair the banking system.
G20 Leaders' statement, Pittsburg Summit, September 25, 2009

My commitment is to recover every single dime the American people are owed. ... I'm proposing a Financial Crisis Responsibility Fee to be imposed on major financial firms until the American people are fully compensated for the extraordinary assistance they provided to Wall Street.
President Barack Obama, January 14, 2010

12.1 Introduction

The recent financial crisis has given rise to intense discussions about the costs and merits of bank taxation (International Monetary Fund 2010; European Commission 2010, 2012a, 2012b). In light of this debate, several EU countries (Austria, France, Germany, Hungary, Sweden, United Kingdom, etc.) have introduced fees and taxes that vary according to their base and purpose. Regardless of the tax purpose, one of the most important questions is the tax incidence: who bears the effective burden? Imposing a tax on banks does not mean that banks will ultimately pay because, a priori, banks could pass on the burden of the new taxes to their customers by raising interest rates on loans and lowering interest rates on deposits, hence, increasing the cost of intermediation.

Despite the importance of the tax incidence question, the empirical literature on the banking sector is rather scarce (see table 12.1). As it was not possible to examine the impact of specific bank's taxes, a few studies analyze tax incidence of the existing corporate income taxes on different bank performance measures, most often on net interest

Table 12.1
Previous tax incidence studies applied to the banking sector

Studies	Sample	Data	Dependent variables	Variables of interest	Econometric method
Demirgüç-Kunt, and Huizinga (1999)	80 Countries (1988–1995)	Bankscope (5,841 banks)	NIM, before-tax profit	Implicit tax rate	Cross section, weighted least squares
Demirgüç-Kunt, and Huizinga (2001)	80 Countries (1988–1995)	Bankscope (5,391 banks)	NIM, before-tax profit	Average implicit tax rate, statutory tax rate	Cross section, OLS
Albertazzi and Gambacorta (2010)	10 OECD countries (1981–2003)	OECD & IMF (macro data)	NIM, noninterest income, provisions, before-tax profit	Statutory tax rate	Dynamic panel, GMM
Huizinga et al. (2011)	38 Countries (1998–2008)	Bankscope (9,729 banks	NIM, before-tax profit	Statutory tax rate, double taxation of dividends and Interests	Cross-section, OLS
Chiorazzo and Milani (2011)	EU (1990–2005)	Bankscope (8,000 banks approx.)	NIM, before-tax profit	Taxes/total assets	Dynamic panel, GMM

margins (NIM). Demirgüç-Kunt and Huizinga (1999, 2001) analyze bank level data for 80 countries (1988–1995) and find that a large part of bank taxes is passed on to banks' customers by increasing the spread between lending and deposit rate. In a more recent study Huizinga et al. (2011) focus on international banks and find that double taxation is almost fully reflected in the interest margins charged by foreign subsidiary banks. Albertazzi and Gambacorta (2010) analyze country level data in the OECD for the period 1981 to 2003 and find that 90 percent of the corporate income tax is passed by banks to their customers by raising lending rates. A similarly high pass-through is found by Chiorazzo and Milani (2011) for a sample of the EU banks for the period 1990 to 2005. Thus the literature, although relatively small, seems to have reached a consensus and as stated by the European Commission in its impact assessment, "overall, available studies suggest that financial companies are able to pass on taxes to their customers" (European Commission, 2012b).

Yet this conclusion is somewhat surprising. Indeed the theoretical literature on corporate income tax incidence is less clear than what the evidence above suggests: who pays corporate income taxes is one of the most debated questions in public finance (see Auerbach 2006). Partial equilibrium analysis suggests that corporate income tax is *not* shifted forward to customers, since it does not affect the maximization function of the firms.[1] This is different from a tax levied on banks' balance sheets, which could be shifted to customers with the lowest elasticity of demand (Capelle-Blancard and Havrylchyk 2013). More-over most of the general-equilibrium models consider that the burden of the corporate income tax is borne by factor income and not by the customers, and recent empirical research on incidence of corporate income taxes in the nonfinancial sector focuses on the effect on owners of capital or employees, but *not* on the customers.

Our study has two objectives. First, we would like to revisit the above-noted empirical evidence on the pass-through of the corporate tax burden on NIM because their results appear to contradict the theory, and we argue that previous empirical studies suffer either from the endogeneity problem or from erroneous specification of the tax burden variable. Second, we would like to investigate the impact of market competition and banks' market power on the ability of banks to shift taxes to their customers. Such focus is warranted by the existing evidence that banks operate in the environment of the monopolistic competition and enjoy large markups (Claessens and Laeven 2004; Angelini and Cetorelli 2003; Maudos and Fernández de Guevara 2004; Fernández de Guevara et al. 2005). To measure market power and competition, we rely on a battery of measures, such as market structure variables (i.e., Herfindal index and banks' market share) and indicators bor-rowed from the industrial organization literature, such as the Lerner index and the Panzar and Ross h-statistic. For our study, we rely on a dataset of 1,411 European commercial banks over the period 1992 to 2008. Contrary to earlier studies, we find no evidence that banks are able to shift taxes to their customers by widening the spread between lending and deposit rates. This holds even for uncompetitive markets and for banks with large market power.

The remainder of the paper is organized as follows. Section 12.2 provides descriptive statistics on banks' taxation and describes our dataset. Section 12.3 presents the econometric model. Section 12.4 discusses the results. Section 12.5 concludes.

12.2　Data

In this study we use data on individual banks from the Bankscope's database (Bureau Van Dijk). This database provides harmonized banks' financial statements (balance sheets and income statements) worldwide. The same database is used, for instance, by Demirgüç-Kunt and Huizinga (1999, 2001), Huizinga et al. (2011), and Chiorazzo and Milani (2011). We restrict our sample to commercial banks that operated in 17 European countries (Austria, Belgium, Denmark, Finland, France, Germany, Greece, Ireland, Italy, Luxembourg, Netherlands, Norway, Portugal, Spain, Sweden, Switzerland, and United Kingdom) for the period between 1992 and 2008.

Bankscope contains balance-sheet and income data for a large number of European public and private banks, but not all of them are available for the whole period and detailed observations are often missing. For a given bank and year, when a useful observation is missing, we drop all the corresponding bank-year observations. In addition we get rid of outliers by deleting the first and the last percentiles of the distribution of the following variables: NIM, equity, tax/profits, LLP, and costs. Alternatively, we perform an ad hoc cleaning of the database, controlling graphically for outliers. The method to handle outliers has no impact on the results (the two methods only differ for a dozen of observations). We present results for the first treatment of the database. Last, we restrict our sample to banks for which the profit and taxes are positive for a given year for the reasons explained later. The sample we use in this study contains 1,411 banks or 7,938 bank-year observations. Descriptive statistics are provided in appendix (tables 12A.1 and 12A.2).

We aim to investigate how taxes are passed on to banks' customers by increasing the spread between lending and deposit rates. Thus our first variable of interest is the net interest margin (NIM), calculated as the bank's net interest revenue (interest income less interest expense) over total assets. The series is characterized by a mean of 2.2 percent and a standard deviation of 1.28 percent. Since banks can also shift taxes by charging higher fees and commissions, we test the robustness of our results with net fees and commissions, calculated as net fees and commissions over total assets.

The second main variable in our analysis is a proxy for bank taxation (TAX). In this study we are interested in the implicit tax rate, as opposed to the statutory corporate income tax rate. Statutory corporate income tax rate have been used by Demirgüç-Kunt and Huizinga (2001) and Albertazzi and Gambacorta (2010). However, there is evidence that the statutory tax rate does not reflect the genuine fiscal burden. First, the amount of taxes that banks have to pay depends not only on the corporate income tax rate but also on the tax base, as well as specific fiscal rules (in particular, the regimes of tax carry back and carry forward). Second, given that international banks may take advantage of their cross border activities to shift their profits to minimize tax payments, the statutory tax rate does not reflect the real burden of taxation (Demirgüç-Kunt and Huizinga 2001). Next, we present a number of figures to support our decision to rely on implicit tax rates and not statutory ones.

Figure 12.1a compares the statutory corporate income tax rate and the implicit bank tax rate for the 17 European countries between 1994 and 2008. Bar charts represent statutory corporate tax rates; small horizontal lines correspond to weighted average values of the effective bank tax rate while vertical lines show the second and the third quartiles over the whole period. Data on statutory corporate income tax is taken from OECD, while the implicit bank tax rate is calculated with Bankscope database. In all countries, except Italy, the statutory tax rate is higher than the implicit tax rate. The weighted average ratio of tax expenses to profit in our sample varies from 19 percent in Portugal to 44 percent in Italy; this is a larger range than for statutory tax rates (21 to 42 percent). Similarly the standard deviations are 5 and 6 percent for statutory and implicit tax rates. Portugal appears to be an outlier in a sense that the implicit tax rate is much lower than the statutory rate (19 and 35 percent). Figure 12.1b presents two scatterplots. The first one indicates that the correlation between the statutory corporate tax rates (on the x-axis) and the weighted average implicit bank tax rates (on the y-axis) is weak, which supports our decision to rely on implicit tax rates. The second scatterplot represents the weighted average implicit tax rates on the x-axis, computed with our sample, and the implicit tax rates computed using aggregated OECD data over the same period on the y-axis. R^2 of this relationship equals to 64 percent, which indicates that the strength of this relationship is high and gives us confidence that our sample is representative. Figure 12.1 has already shown that the differences between tax rates are often more important between

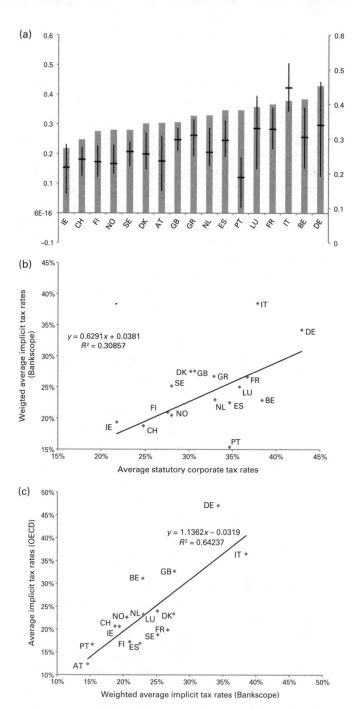

Figure 12.1
Statutory and implicit tax rates in 17 European countries. (a) Average statutory corporate tax rate (bar charts) and the implicit bank tax rate (the horizontal line correspond to the weighted average value and the vertical line to the second and the third quartiles) over the period 1994 to 2008; (b) relationship between average statutory corporate tax rates and average implicit tax rates computed with the OECD and Bankscope data.
Sources: Bankscope; Huizinga et al. (2011); author calculations

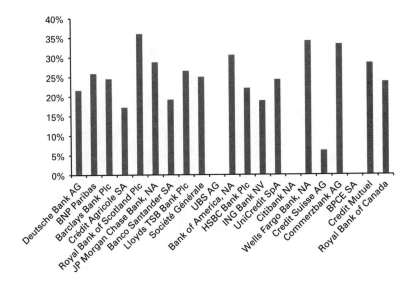

Figure 12.2
Average implicit tax rates for the largest banks in Europe and North America, 2005 to 2010
Sources: Bankscope; for UBS, Citibank, and BPCE, the average implicit tax rate is negative and, consequently, not reported; author calculations

banks within a country than between countries. Figure 12.2 further supports this claim by documenting a considerable variation of implicit tax rates between large banks from the same country.

In figure 12.3 we show the evolution of statutory and implicit tax rates over the observed period of 1992 to 2008. Both rates have decreased as countries have chosen to decrease the tax burden on enterprises. However, the implicit tax rate remains consistently below the statutory rate. These results (which rely on Bankscope data) are corroborated by the OECD data that allows seeing that declining implicit tax rates constitute a long-term trend. In fact profits of the financial sector in OECD countries have grown at a higher rate than banks' income taxes, leading to a sharp decrease of the implicit tax rate, from 40 percent in the late 1980s to 20 percent before the crisis (figure 12.4).

Since implicit tax rates reflect better the banks' tax burden, most recent studies rely on implicit tax rates. For example, Chiorazzo and Milani (2011) compute it as the ratio of tax expenses to total assets. The problem is that such measure can lead to a spurious regression between NIM and tax-to-assets ratio, because both dependent and independent variables are constructed with assets in the denominator. Hence they are related to each other by construction. Second, the inclusion of this

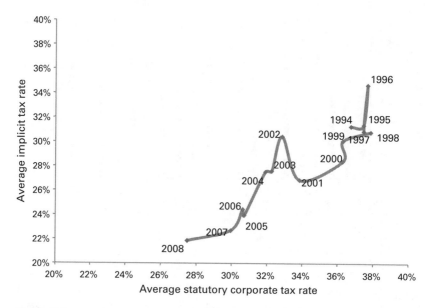

Figure 12.3
Evolution of implicit and statutory tax rates over 1994 to 2008. Represented are the weighted average statutory corporate tax rate and the weighted average implicit bank tax rate over the period 1994 to 2008 for the whole sample.
Sources: Bankscope; author calculations

variable could lead to the simultaneity bias, since both NIM and tax-to-assets ratio are simultaneously influenced by economic conditions and profit opportunities that are difficult to control for. Although the endogeneity stemming from this simultaneity problem can be corrected econometrically by the system GMM, the first problem would remain.

In contrast, Demirgüç-Kunt and Huizinga (2001) compute the implicit tax rate for each bank by dividing paid taxes by before-tax profits. Importantly, they average this variable for each bank over the observed period in order to preclude that a positive relationship between before-tax profitability and the tax rate simply reflects an increasing marginal taxation of bank profits. The drawback of such approach is that this variable is time invariant. Hence such regression cannot be estimated with fixed effects at the bank level, and moreover this variable takes the role of the fixed effect and can include any bank characteristic that is not captured by other explanatory variables, thus suffering from the endogeneity problem due to missing variable bias.

In this study we compute the implicit tax rate, calculated as the ratio of tax expenses to before-tax profits computed for each bank and each

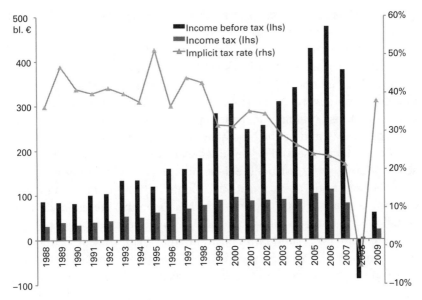

Figure 12.4
Bank implicit tax rates for the main OECD countries. Countries included are Austria, Belgium, Canada, Denmark, Finland, France, Germany (until 2008), Ireland (since 1995), Italy, Luxembourg, Norway, Netherlands, Portugal, Sweden, Switzerland, the United Kingdom (until 2008), and the United States.
Sources: OECD (Bank Profitability Statistics—Income Statement and Balance Sheet); author calculations

year. This ratio is directly comparable with the statutory tax rate because it has the same denominator. Since this variable only makes sense if profits and taxes are positive, we restrict our sample to profitable institutions that pay taxes. The ratio of taxes to profits should be less influenced by economic conditions than the ratio of taxes to assets, thus limiting endogeneity problems due to simultaneity.[2] As it is time variant, we can rely on different econometric techniques, such as system GMM estimator to tackle its potential endogeneity related to the fact that it is constructed from the same balance sheet as NIM.

12.3   Methodology

12.3.1   The Econometric Model
We propose to investigate whether the burden of taxation is passed through by banks to their customers by following literature on NIM determinants and estimating the following models:

$$NIM_{i,t} = \alpha + \beta \, NIM_{i,t-1} + \gamma \, Tax/profits_{i,t} + \delta \, X_{i,t} + \lambda_t + \varepsilon_{i,t}, \tag{12.1}$$

where *NIM* is the net interest margin (calculated as the difference between interest income and interest expenses, relative to total assets), *tax/profits* is the implicit tax rate (i.e., the ratio of tax expenses to before-tax profits), X is a set of controls, and λ_t is a time dummy. The set of controls X is composed of macroeconomic variables (GDP growth, inflation) and several bank characteristics: capital ratio (equity over total assets), risk (value of loans loss provisions over total assets), cost efficiency (measured by the ratio of noninterest expenses to assets), and size (log of total assets). For variables that divide a flow variable on a stock variable, we construct the denominators as the mean of the variable between t and $t - 1$. Exact variable definitions, data sources and descriptive statistics are reported in the appendix. We estimate this equation by relying on the system GMM estimators developed in Arellano and Bond (1991) and Blundell and Bond (1998). We test the robustness of our results with *Fees* as dependent variable (calculated as net fees and commissions relative to total assets).

12.3.2 Source of Heterogeneity: Market Power and Competition

We next proceed to investigate a potential heterogeneity between banks in the pass-through depending on the market power and competition:

$$NIM_{i,t} = \alpha + \beta\, NIM_{i,t-1} + \gamma\, Tax/profits_{i,t} + \theta\, Tax/profits_{i,t} * Z_{i,t}$$
$$+ \delta\, X_{i,t} + \lambda_t + \varepsilon_{i,t}, \tag{12.2}$$

where $TAX_{i,t} * Z_{i,t}$ is an interaction variable between $TAX_{i,t}$ and different measures of market power and competition, $Z_{i,t}$.

Market Share and Market Structure Indicators

Assuming that more concentrated markets lead to less competition (structure–conduct–performance paradigm), the easiest way to measure market competition is to rely on market structure measures, and hence we include bank's market share (in terms of assets, loans, or deposits) and the Herfindhal–Hirschman index (HH). HH index is a commonly accepted measure of market concentration and is defined as the sum of the squares of the market shares of each bank within the country. HH index ranges from 0 to 1. An increase in HH index is associated with a decrease in competition. This index is also computed in terms of assets, loans, and deposits.

Similarly we allow for taxation to accord with bank size, as bank size has served as an important threshold in taxation decisions. In most countries that have implemented or consider implementing a bank levy

(United States, United Kingdom, France, and Germany), small banks are exempt from a levy or pay a lower rate.[3] Theoretically, such progressive taxation is related to the moral hazard caused by the bailout of too-big-to-fail financial institutions. Another underlying reason for such progressive taxation is to ensure that banks do not pass taxes to their clients: if large banks decide to increase their lending rates, borrowers can go to smaller banks. Such approach assumes that bank size and market power are synonymous.

Alternatively, the theory of contestable markets suggests that one can have competitive markets even in concentrated systems, whereas collusive actions can be undertaken even in the presence of many firms (Claessens and Laeven 2004). Hence one should consider measures that econometrically estimate the actual conduct of banks (Panzar and Rosse h-statistic) or actual margins (Lerner index). The actual behavior of banks is related not only to the market structure but also to entry barriers, activity restrictions, and the degree of the competition from other forms of financial intermediation. The actual margins might additionally reflect the quality of the countries' information and judicial system.

Lerner Index

Lerner index is defined as $(p-mc)/p$ where p is the price of assets and mc is the marginal cost of assets. The Lerner index ranges from 0 to 1; the higher the index, the higher the market power. The price of assets is the sum of interest income, other operating income, net fees and commissions and noninterest expenses, relative to total assets. We compute marginal costs relying on the stochastic frontier approach that is assumed to take a translog function. Hence we measure how close a bank is to the cost frontier by following Fang, Hasan, and Marton (2010):

$$TC_{i,t} = f(X_{i,t}, P_{i,t}, Z_{i,t}) + v_{i,t} + u_{i,t}, \tag{12.3}$$

where $TC_{i,t}$ is total operating cost, $X_{i,t}$ represent output (total assets), $P_{i,t}$ input prices (price of borrowed funds, labor, and physical capital), and $Z_{i,t}$ fixed inputs (equity).

Panzar and Rosse h-Statistic

Our final measure of market competition is the h-statistic introduced by Panzer and Rosse (1987) to test for the existence of monopoly equilibrium. It is equal to the sum of the factor price elasticities of a banks' reduced-form revenue equation, which is estimated as follows (Claessens and Laeven 2004):

$$R_{i,t} = \alpha + \beta_1 \, pdep_{i,t} + \beta_2 \, plab_{i,t} + \beta_3 \, pcap_{i,t} + \gamma X_{i,t} + \lambda_t + \varepsilon_{i,t}, \qquad (12.4)$$

where $R_{i,t}$ is the bank revenue, measured by the ratio of interest income to total assets (in log), $pdep_{i,t}$ is the price of deposits, measured by the ratio of total interest expenses to total funding (in log), $plab_{i,t}$ is the price of labor, measured by the ratio of personnel expenses to total assets, $pcap_{i,t}$ is the price of capital, measured by the ratio of other operating expenses to fixed assets (in log), X is a set of controls composed by the ratio of loans to total assets (log), the ratio of equity to total assets (log) and the size of the bank (log of total assets). λ_t is a year dummy. We compute h-stat as the sum of β_1, β_2, and β_3. We run this equation separately for each country.

In computing h-stat, we quantify what will be the percentage change in equilibrium revenues resulting from a 1 percent change in all factor prices. Under monopoly, an increase in input prices increases marginal costs, reduces equilibrium output, and consequently lowers total revenues. Under perfect competition, an increase in input prices raises both marginal costs and total revenues by the same amount. Accordingly, the h-statistic is interpreted as follows: h-stat < 0 indicates monopoly, $0 < h$-stat < 1 monopolistic competition and h-stat $= 1$ perfect competition.

Our different proxies for market power and competition are expected to be connected, albeit not perfectly correlated. For instance, in Claessens and Laeven (2004), the correlation between the h-statistic and the market concentration (computed as the total market share of the fifth largest banks in each country) is of 38 percent. In our sample, estimates lead to similar relationships. Thus the correlation (at the country level) between the HH index and the Lerner index is of 10 percent, while the correlation between the Lerner index and the h-statistic is of 35 percent (in absolute value). These statistics confirm both the difficulty of measuring market power and the need for a large set of proxies.

12.4 Empirical Results

12.4.1 Impact of Taxation on Nominal Interest Margins

Before proceeding to the estimation of our baseline model (12.1), we present four different specifications of the model that differ with respect to the measure of taxation burden and econometric technique (table 12.2). Following Demirgüç-Kunt and Huizinga (1999), in column 1 we

Table 12.2
Impact of taxes on NIM and fees margin

	NIM					Fees
	(1)	(2)	(3)	(4)	(5)	(6)
NIM $_{t-1}$				0.57***	0.57***	
				(0.08)	(0.05)	
Fees $_{t-1}$						0.44*
						(0.26)
Tax (average)	0.01***					
	(0.0009)					
Tax/profit		0.004***	0.003		0.001	0.009
		(0.0007)	(0.005)		(0.0009)	(0.0008)
Tax/assets				0.49***		
				(0.18)		
Equity	0.03***	0.02***	0.02***	0.04***	0.04***	0.03***
	(0.003)	(0.002)	(0.002)	(0.01)	(0.009)	(0.01)
Costs	0.59***	0.58***	0.32***	0.14***	0.29***	0.48*
	(0.015)	(0.02)	(0.02)	(0.05)	(0.05)	(0.25)
Size	−0.001***	−0.001***	−0.002***	0.0001	−0.00004	0.0003***
	(0.0007)	(0.0007)	(0.0002)	(0.0002)	(0.0001)	(0.0001)
LLP	0.006***	0.006***	0.0002	0.003***	0.002***	0.001**
	(0.0006)	(0.0006)	(0.00)	(0.0007)	(0.0005)	(0.0006)
Assets share	0.01***	0.009***	−0.008*	0.0008	0.004*	−0.009**

Table 12.2
(Continued)

	NIM				Fees	
	(1)	(2)	(3)	(4)	(5)	(6)
	(0.003)	(0.003)	(0.004)	(0.002)	(0.002)	(0.004)
HHI assets	−0.005	−0.005	−0.003*	−0.003*	−0.007***	0.002
	(0.003)	(0.003)	(0.001)	(0.002)	(0.002)	(0.004)
GDP growth	0.03***	0.03***	0.02***	0.02***	−0.005	0.03**
	(0.01)	(0.01)	(0.005)	(0.005)	(0.006)	(0.01)
Inflation	0.03***	0.03***	0.03***	0.007*	0.03***	−0.03**
	(0.01)	(0.01)	(0.006)	(0.004)	(0.009)	(0.01)
Constant	0.02***	0.02***	0.04***	−0.0004	0.002	−0.006***
	(0.001)	(0.001)	(0.001)	(0.003)	(0.002)	(0.001)
Country dummies	Yes	Yes	No	No	No	No
Year dummies	Yes	Yes	Yes	Yes	Yes	Yes
Observations	7,938	7,938	7,529	7,938	7,938	7,793
Number of banks	1,411	1,411	1,345	1,411	1,411	1,398
R^2	0.52	0.52	0.33			
Arrelano–Bond test AR (2) P-value				0.29	0.43	0.13
Hansen test				0.27	0.17	0.13
Number of instruments				46	30	36
Lags for GMM instruments (NIM_{t-1})				3	1	6
Lags for GMM instruments (other variables)				2–3	1–2	1–5

Notes: Standard errors appear in parenthesis. Estimation of models 1 to 2 is performed with OLS; model 3 estimates panel data with fixed effects for banks, and models 4 to 5 estimate two-step Arrelano–Bover estimator (system-GMM) with robust standard errors. ***$p < 0.01$, **$p < 0.05$, and *$p < 0.1$.

measure the tax burden by the implicit tax rate averaged over the observed period, and to ensure comparability of the results, all variables are contemporaneous and the model is estimated with OLS. The specification in column 2 differs from column 1 insofar as we do not average the implicit tax rate and thus keep it time variant. The results of these two specifications are broadly in line with Demirgüç-Kunt and Huizinga (1999): we find a positive coefficient in both of these models, suggesting that banks pass through their taxes to customers by increasing interest margins. As these models are estimated with simple OLS, they do not attempt to control for endogeneity. Thus, in column 3 we present the specification with lagged bank characteristics and estimate it with bank level fixed effects. The results show that even after such control for endogeneity, the effect of banks' taxes on NIM is no longer statistically significant.

Column 4 reports the specification where the tax burden is measured as a ratio of paid taxes over total bank's assets, which corresponds to the definition introduced by Chiorazzo and Milani (2011). To ensure comparability of the results, we also estimate our model with Arrelano–Bover system GMM. This method allows us to estimate a dynamic model of NIM and to control for endogeneity of the tax variable. In line with Chiorazzo and Milani (2011) we find that in a short-run banks shift 49 percent of their taxes to customers by widening their interest margins. However, as mentioned earlier, such regression might suffer from two problems. First, NIM and tax-to-assets ratio can be correlated by construction because they both contain assets in denominator and this problem cannot be corrected with Arrelano–Bover system GMM. Second, the model suffers from simultaneity bias if we do not control sufficiently for profit opportunities that effect at the same time interest margins and profits. Even though this problem can be corrected theoretically with system GMM, it is more prudent to choose an explanatory variable that suffers less from endogeneity problems, as we propose to do it in the next model.

Hence in column 5 we report the results of our preferred specification and econometric methodology: The tax burden is measured as an implicit tax rate (paid taxes divided by before-tax profits) and the model is estimated with system GMM to control for any potential endogeneity (Arellano and Bover 1995; Blundell and Bond 1998). We consider NIM_{t-1}, equity, and tax/profits as endogenous variables, in line with Chiorazzo and Milani (2011). As suggested by Roodman (2009), we introduce year dummies, but we omit country dummies that might bias the results in system GMM if the number of time periods is small. As instrument proliferation can overfit endogenous variables, fail to expunge their endogenous components, and weaken the power of the Hansen test to detect this very problem, we attempt to limit the number of instruments by limiting the number of lags and collapsing them. Our choice is different for NIM_{t-1} and other endogenous variables (equity and tax/profits), and we report our separate choices and number of instruments at the bottom of table 12.2. We also show that our model passes the Hansen test of over-identifying restrictions and Arellano–Bond test of residuals' autocorrelation of order 2 at 1 percent significance level.[4]

According to this specification, the coefficient of the *tax/profits* variable is not statistically significant, and thus we do not find that banks are able to shift their tax burden to customers by widening the wedge between the lending rate and the deposit rate. As it is explained above, our results contradict earlier findings because they do not control for endogeneity (Demirgüç-Kunt and Huizinga 1999) or are biased due to the erroneous construction of the measure of tax burden (Chiorazzo and Milani 2011). If we apply the same approaches as these earlier papers, we are able to reproduce their results, suggesting that our findings are not driven by sample differences.

As far as other control variables are concerned, they have the expected sign and our results are in line with earlier empirical studies on NIM determinants (Demirgüç-Kunt and Huizinga 1999 or Claeys and Vander Vennet 2008). The positive sign of the ratio of bank's equity over total assets is consistent with the fact that the financing cost of well-capitalized banks is lower. The ratio of loan loss provisions over total assets has a positive and significant effect, which supports the idea that NIM is a compensation for risk taking. Similarly we observe that higher costs and larger market share in assets widen NIM as well. As to macroeconomic controls, we find that an increase of the inflation rate increases significantly the NIM, as banks raise their lending rates faster than deposit rates. Finally, we show that in more concentrated markets, NIM is lower, which can be surprising if one associates market concentration with the strength of competition. However, such naïve approach is often questioned after Claessens and Laeven (2004) have shown that concentration and competition are not necessarily related, and are sometimes even positively correlated (more concentrated markets are more competitive).

Impact of taxes on NIM breakdown by country

	FR	DE	IT	SH	LU	ES, PT, GR	DK, FI, NO, SE	AT, BE, NL	GB, IE
NIM_{t-1}	0.45***	0.61***	0.76***	0.65***	0.79***	0.37**	0.81***	0.91	0.73***
	(0.09)	(0.21)	(0.15)	(0.19)	(0.06)	(0.16)	(0.11)	(0.65)	(0.17)
Tax/profit	0.003	0.003	0.003	0.008	-0.004	0.001	0.01	0.01	0.005
	(0.003)	(0.002)	(0.002)	(0.03)	(0.002)	(0.004)	(0.008)	(0.01)	(0.02)
LLP	0.002	0.002	0.0009	0.0003	0.002***	0.0008	0.005	0.003	0.001
	(0.002)	(0.001)	(0.003)	(0.002)	(0.0007)	(0.002)	(0.003)	(0.003)	(0.003)
Costs	0.39***	0.19*	0.29*	0.01	0.02	0.72***	0.13	-0.05	0.32*
	(0.08)	(0.12)	(0.15)	(0.11)	(0.06)	(0.27)	(0.09)	(0.3)	(0.19)
Equity	0.02	0.05	0.01	-0.003	0.06***	0.005	0.08***	0.08	-0.006
	(0.02)	(0.04)	(0.03)	(0.02)	(0.01)	(0.03)	(0.03)	(0.08)	(0.0358)
Size	-0.0008	0.0001	-0.0001	-0.0003	0.0006**	-0.0002	0.0009*	0.0008	-0.0003
	(0.0006)	(0.0005)	(0.0006)	(0.0004)	(0.0003)	(0.0005)	(0.0005)	(0.001)	(0.0005)
Assets share	-0.01	-0.03	0.008	-0.002	-0.04**	0.004	-0.003	-0.005	-0.0002
	(0.02)	(0.03)	(0.01)	(0.004)	(0.02)	(0.01)	(0.003)	(0.02)	(0.01)
GDP growth	-0.16	-0.11	0.35	-0.13	-0.05	0.06*	0.03	0.01	-0.001
	(0.40)	(0.08)	(0.68)	(0.21)	(0.05)	(0.03)	(0.03)	(0.04)	(0.02)
Inflation	-0.13	0.02	0.49	-0.12	-0.14	0.009	-0.04	0.01	0.002
	(0.49)	(0.09)	(0.98)	(0.22)	(0.65)	(0.06)	(0.03)	(0.03)	(0.006)
HHI assets	-1.31*	-0.07	0.32	0.003	-0.04	0.005	-0.002	-0.008	-0.002
	(0.74)	(0.05)	(0.49)	(0.05)	(0.54)	(0.02)	(0.003)	(0.01)	(0.01)
Constant	0.08	0.003	-0.04	0.01	0.002	0.004	-0.01	-0.01	0.003
	(0.05)	(0.009)	(0.06)	(0.009)	(0.004)	(0.008)	(0.009)	(0.02)	(0.006)
Observations	1,080	755	1,059	1,031	854	842	778	660	750
Number of banks	193	169	185	188	134	143	118	139	132

Note: Standard errors appear in parenthesis. Estimations are performed with two-step Arrelano–Bover estimator (system-GMM) with robust standard errors. Year dummies are included; ***$p < 0.01$, **$p < 0.05$, and *$p < 0.1$.

Finally, in column 6 we test the robustness of our results with *fees* as dependent variable. Besides the difference in the dependent variable, the specification is identical to column 5. Our results show that higher taxes do not lead to wider fees margin; hence we confirm our previous findings that banks do not shift taxes to their clients.

12.4.2   Accounting for Bank Heterogeneity

As we discussed at the start of this chapter, the theory suggests that the degree of the competition could affect the ability of banks to shift their tax burden by widening the NIM. Benefiting from market power allows compressing interest expenses on funding as well as increasing interest rates on loans. To account for such phenomena, we interlink our measure of implicit tax rate with different indicators of market power and competition. We first discuss the results of table 12.4, where we look at the effect of size, market share, and HH index in terms of assets, loans, and deposits. Our results show the coefficient on *tax/ profits* is still not significant, and we find no effect of bank size or market share on the ability of banks to shift their taxes. At the same time we find that banks in more concentrated markets are more likely to pass taxes to their clients. Importantly, we confirm our earlier findings that NIM is lower in more concentrated markets. Considered together, these findings do not allow us to associate market concentration with weak competition, since theoretically weak competition should result in both wider NIM and higher pass-through of taxes.

Given the ambiguity of our findings, we propose to use alternative measures of market competition and market power by relying on indicators borrowed from the industrial organization literature, such as Panzer and Rosse (1989) *h*-statistic and Lerner index. Our results, reported in table 12.5, do not show that these variables influence the ability of banks to shift taxes to customers. At the same time the inclusion of the Lerner index affects the significance of *tax/profits* variable, which becomes significant at 10 percent level. This change is due to a different data sample, as the construction of the Lerner index requires data on a large number of variables and, consequently, shortens the number of available banks and observations in our sample.

12.5   Conclusions and Policy Recommendations

Our study investigates the ability of banks to shift their tax burden to customers by widening their net interest margins. The question of tax

Table 12.4
Effect of taxes on NIM, depending on size, market power, and market concentration

	Size	Market share (assets)	Market share (loans)	Market share (deposits)	HHI (assets)	HHI (loans)	HHI (deposits)
	(1)	(2)	(3)	(4)	(5)	(6)	(7)
NIM_{t-1}	0.85***	0.85***	0.85***	0.85***	0.83***	0.83***	0.82***
	(0.05)	(0.04)	(0.05)	(0.05)	(0.05)	(0.05)	(0.05)
Tax/profit	-0.02	-0.002	-0.003	-0.002	-0.006	-0.007	-0.007
	(0.01)	(0.00)	(0.00)	(0.00)	(0.00)	(0.00)	(0.00)
Equity	0.007	0.007	0.007	0.007	-0.004	-0.003	-0.004
	(0.02)	(0.02)	(0.02)	(0.02)	(0.02)	(0.02)	(0.02)
Costs	0.11**	0.11**	0.11**	0.11**	0.14***	0.14***	0.14***
	(0.04)	(0.04)	(0.04)	(0.04)	(0.05)	(0.05)	(0.05)
Size	-0.0006	-0.0002	-0.0002	-0.0002	-0.0002	0.0002	-0.0002
	(0.00)	(0.00)	(0.00)	(0.00)	(0.00)	(0.00)	(0.00)
LLP	0.001**	0.001**	0.001**	0.001**	0.001**	0.001**	0.001**
	(0.00)	(0.00)	(0.00)	(0.00)	(0.00)	(0.00)	(0.00)
Assets share	0.006**	-0.005	-0.007	-0.007	0.004**	0.006***	0.004**
	(0.00)	(0.01)	(0.01)	(0.01)	(0.002)	(0.002)	(0.002)
HHI assets	-0.004	-0.003	-0.005	-0.003	-0.04*	-0.04*	-0.04*
	(0.00)	(0.00)	(0.00)	(0.003)	(0.02)	(0.03)	(0.02)
GDP growth	0.006	0.004	0.005	0.004	0.005	0.003	0.003
	(0.00)	(0.00)	(0.00)	(0.00)	(0.00)	(0.00)	(0.00)

Table 12.4
(Continued)

	Size	Market share (assets)	Market share (loans)	Market share (deposits)	HHI (assets)	HHI (loans)	HHI (deposits)
	(1)	(2)	(3)	(4)	(5)	(6)	(7)
Inflation	0.006	0.006	0.007	0.006	0.007	0.008	0.008
	(0.00)	(0.00)	(0.00)	(0.00)	(0.00)	(0.00)	(0.00)
Tax*size	0.002						
	(0.00)						
Tax*share assets		0.04	0.05	0.04			
		(0.05)	(0.05)	(0.05)			
Tax*HHI assets					0.14*	0.16*	0.14*
					(0.08)	(0.10)	(0.07)
Constant	0.006	0.001	0.002	0.002	0.004	0.004	0.004
	(0.005)	(0.00)	(0.00)	(0.00)	(0.00)	(0.00)	(0.00)
Observations	7,938	7,938	7,934	7,937	7,938	7,934	7,937
Number of banks	1,411	1,411	1,411	1,411	1,411	1,411	1,411
Arrelano–Bond test AR (2) P-value	0.723	0.697	0.696	0.700	0.918	0.943	0.882
Hansen test	0.175	0.184	0.194	0.178	0.18	0.202	0.211
Number of instruments	35	35	35	35	34	34	34
Lags for GMM instruments (NIM_{t-1})	2–4	2–4	2–4	2–4	3–4	3–4	3–4
Lags for GMM instruments (other variables)	3–4	3–4	3–4	3–4	3–4	3–4	3–4

Notes: Standard errors appear in parenthesis. Estimations are performed with two-step Arrelano–Bover estimator (system-GMM) with robust standard errors. Year dummies are included; $***p < 0.01$, $**p < 0.05$, and $*p < 0.1$.

Table 12.5
Impact of taxes on NIM, depending on h-statistics and Lerner index

	h-Statistic	Lerner
	(1)	(2)
NIM_{t-1}	0.60***	0.74***
	(0.05)	(0.13)
Tax/profit	0.002	0.02*
	(0.004)	(0.01)
Equity	0.05***	0.13***
	(0.00)	(0.04)
Costs	0.26***	0.03
	(0.05)	(0.12)
Size	1.54e-05	0.001**
	(0.00)	(0.00)
LLP	0.002***	0.0007
	(0.00)	(0.00)
Assets share	0.004*	−0.002
	(0.00)	(0.00)
HHI	−0.007***	−0.0004
	(0.002)	(0.00)
Lerner		0.00
		(0.00)
GDP growth	−0.002	0.02*
	(0.01)	(0.01)
Inflation	0.02**	0.001
	(0.01)	(0.01)
Tax*h-statistic	−0.001	
	(0.01)	
Tax*Lerner		−0.0001
		(0.00)
Constant	0.001	−0.02***
	(0.00)	(0.00)
Observations	7,938	4,401
Number of banks	1,411	1,057
Arrelano–Bond test for AR (2) P-value	0.428	0.898
Hansen test of joint validity of instruments	0.126	0.199
Number of instruments	33	31
Lags for GMM instruments (NIM_{t-1})	1,1	1,1
Lags for GMM instruments (other variables)	1,2	2,2

Notes: Standard errors appear in parenthesis. Estimations are performed with two-step Arrelano–Bover estimator (system-GMM) with robust standard errors. Year dummies are included; ***$p < 0.01$, **$p < 0.05$, and *$p < 0.1$.

incidence is important inasmuch as one would like to know who bears the burden of banks' taxation: shareholders, employees, or customers. If banks are able to pass their taxes to clients, an increase in taxes would increase borrowing costs for enterprises and borrowers without diminishing banks' profits. This would be contrary to the objective of policy makers who would like to tax banks to recuperate bailout costs related to the crisis and to tax banks' economic rents due to implicit bailout guarantees in the future.

Our results show that banks, on average, do not pass their taxes to clients by widening their net interest margins and this lack of tax incidence is not affected by market competition and banks' market power. This suggests that the burden of banks' taxes would be effectively born by banks (shareholders or employees). Our findings differ from other studies that find a large pass-through because earlier studies do not control for endogeneity (Demirgüç-Kunt and Huizinga 1999) or suffer from the erroneous construction of the tax variable (Chiorazzo and Milani 2011).

From the policy perspective, taxing banking profits appears to be a good idea because there is no tax incidence and the tax does not distort banking spreads. However, two caveats apply. First, taxing profits might motivate banks to apply fiscal optimization tools to diminish profits or to shift them to countries with lower corporate tax rates. Hence policy makers have to take measures to prevent the erosion of the tax base. Second, it is important to emphasize that Bankscope database allows us to calculate NIM, market power, and the degree of the competition on an aggregated basis, overlooking the market segmentation (retail vs. wholesale, urban vs. rural areas, etc.). As some market segments are less competitive than others, the figure for an average pass-through hides the fact that even an average bank might shift all its taxes to customers that are "locked in," such as individual borrowers and SMEs, while sparing large enterprises that are more mobile. Thus more research is needed with the disaggregated data for different types of customers.

Appendix: Variable Description and Descriptive Statistics

Table 12A.1
Descriptive statistics for the whole sample (7,938 observed)

Variables	Description	Restrictions	Mean	Standard deviation	Min	Max
NIM	Bank's net interest revenue less interest expenses over total assets	]−0.05; 0.11[	2.2%	1.3%	0.2%	6.0%
Fees	Bank's net fees and commissions over total assets					
TAX	Bank's taxes over before-tax profit	]0; 1[	31.2%	14.7%	0.1%	98.8%
Assets	Bank's total assets (in million euros)		25,182	104,918	11	2,150,536
Deposits	Bank's deposits over total assets	–	78.6%	13.9%	0.0%	98.2%
Equity	Bank's equity over total assets	]0; 1[	8.0%	4.8%	1.3%	29.9%
Cost	Bank's noninterest expenses over total assets	]0; 0.2[	1.2%	0.8%	0.1%	4.0%
Loan loss Prov.	Bank's loan loss provisions over total assets	]−0.25; 1[	12.7%	15.1%	−25.0%	100.0%
ROE	Bank's before-tax profit over total assets	> 0	11.0%	17.5%	0.0%	700.9%
ROA	Bank's before-tax profit over total assets	> 0	0.8%	0.7%	0.0%	10.0%
Market share [a]	Bank's total assets as a share of banks' total assets in a country (within the sample)	—	1.3%	4.2%	0.0%	70.9%
HH index [a]	Herfindhal–Hirschman index of banking market concentration	—	9.3%	7.2%	2.6%	52.3%
Lerner index [a]	Bank's market power	—	25.6%	13.4%	−51.7%	81.6%
h-Statistic [a]	Panzer and Rosse's (1987) index of banking market competition	—	63.0%	15.9%	35.9%	89.5%
GDP	Real gross domestic product growth rate	—	2.5%	22.9%	−2.3%	11.3%
CPI	Rate of consumer price index inflation	—	2.1%	1.2%	−13.8%	20.6%

Source: Banskope
Author calculations. For variable that divide a flow variable on a stock variable, we construct the denominators as the mean of the variable between *t* and *t*–1.

Table 12A.2 provides a breakdown of our sample of banks by the country of location. See table 12A.1 for the definition of the variables.

Table 12A.2
Number of observations and mean values by country of residence

	Observations	NIM	Tax	Assets (th. euros)	Deposits	Equity	Cost	Loan loss pProv.	ROE	ROA	Market share	HH index	Lerner index	h-Statistic	GDP growth	Inflation
AT	257	2%	24%	10,351	7.6%	79%	1.3%	15%	12.3%	0.9%	1.3%	9.1%	24.5%	72.3%	2.3%	2.0%
BE	210	2%	31%	50,492	5.1%	87%	1.0%	8%	20.9%	0.6%	2.5%	11.6%	18.1%	89.5%	2.3%	1.9%
CH	1,033	2%	24%	16,821	10.3%	73%	1.2%	14%	16.8%	0.9%	0.6%	21.1%	18.5%	45.0%	1.8%	1.0%
DE	793	2%	34%	26,262	7.2%	83%	1.2%	18%	11.9%	0.7%	0.4%	4.0%	27.1%	61.2%	1.6%	1.6%
DK	510	4%	26%	8,098	11.0%	80%	1.9%	10%	11.4%	1.3%	1.3%	16.1%	34.4%	35.9%	2.1%	2.1%
ES	573	3%	30%	28,135	8.5%	83%	1.3%	14%	12.6%	1.0%	1.4%	8.4%	29.7%	67.0%	3.5%	3.2%
FI	43	1%	23%	41,391	6.0%	68%	0.7%	6%	12.1%	0.8%	14.9%	30.5%	23.3%	82.0%	3.8%	1.7%
FR	1,090	3%	33%	30,450	7.2%	80%	1.5%	13%	11.1%	0.8%	0.4%	5.2%	20.5%	81.8%	2.1%	1.7%
GB	683	2%	30%	63,941	9.1%	80%	1.1%	9%	10.9%	0.9%	0.8%	4.4%	27.3%	52.6%	2.8%	2.9%
GR	115	3%	31%	19,512	8.3%	83%	1.6%	18%	12.7%	1.1%	9.3%	16.7%	21.7%	87.7%	3.8%	4.2%
IE	97	2%	22%	38,608	6.0%	79%	0.8%	10%	13.4%	0.8%	7.3%	11.8%	28.6%	74.6%	6.7%	3.5%
IT	1,074	3%	45%	18,059	8.1%	68%	1.6%	15%	9.1%	0.7%	0.7%	5.4%	26.5%	53.9%	1.4%	2.6%
LU	854	1%	33%	5,923	4.9%	87%	0.6%	9%	72.1%	0.6%	1.1%	3.6%	18.2%	83.6%	4.4%	2.0%
NL	214	2%	26%	51,870	6.7%	76%	0.8%	10%	9.2%	0.7%	2.6%	19.5%	19.7%	54.6%	2.8%	2.1%
NO	100	2%	23%	13,322	7.2%	75%	0.9%	5%	9.4%	0.9%	5.9%	14.9%	14.5%	46.9%	3.4%	2.0%
PT	163	2%	19%	13,062	7.6%	80%	1.2%	18%	9.2%	0.8%	3.9%	9.0%	21.4%	81.6%	2.6%	3.1%
SE	129	2%	26%	35,099	8.7%	76%	1.2%	6%	10.9%	0.9%	5.0%	16.7%	31.3%	50.3%	2.7%	1.5%
Total	7,938	2%	31%	25,182	8.0%	79%	1.2%	13%	18.5%	0.8%	1.3%	9.3%	23.9%	63.0%	2.7%	2.1%

Sources: Banskope; author calculations

Notes

The authors thank Agnès Bénassy-Quéré, Vincent Bouvatier, Jézabel Couppey-Soubeyran, Michael Devereux, Iftekhar Hasan, Stéphane Gauthier, Christa Hainz, Laetitia Lepetit, Ruud de Mooij, Gaëtan Nicodème, Alain Trannoy, and Christian Valenduc for helpful comments, and also thank Claire Labonne for research assistance.

1. Corporate tax rate does not have any direct impact on the behavior of banks given that the optimization problem (that includes setting prices and quantities) is the same whether there is a corporate tax or not. However, as clearly stated by Albertazzi and Gambacorta (2010), corporate tax may have an impact on demand for loan (i.e., the higher the corporate tax, the lower the number of projects with a positive NPV) and on the cost of equity (i.e., the higher the corporate tax, the lower the net rate of return accruing to outside investors).

2. If banks were always profitable and were not able to shift taxes across time periods due to tax regimes that allow the carry back and carry forward for profits, the tax-to-profit ratio would be independent of economic conditions.

3. In this regard, the statement of President Obama on January 14, 2010, was very clear: "[The fee] will not be a cost borne by community banks or small firms; only the largest firms with more than $50 billion in assets will be affected."

4. In table 12.3 we re-estimate this model for several countries or group of countries.

References

Albertazzi, U., and L. Gambacorta. 2010. Bank profitability and taxation. *Journal of Banking and Finance* 34 (11): 2801–10.

Angelini, P., and N. Cetorelli. 2003. The effects of regulatory reform on competition in the banking industry. *Journal of Money, Credit and Banking* 35 (5): 663–84.

Arellano, M., and S. Bond. 1991. Some tests of specification for panel data: Monte Carlo evidence and an application to employment equations. Review of Economic Studies 58 (2): 277–97.

Arellano, M., and O. Bover. 1995. Another look at the instrumental variable estimation of error-components models. *Journal of Econometrics* 68: 29–51.

Auerbach, A. 2006. Who bears the corporate tax? A review of what we know. In ed. J. M. Poterba, ed., *Tax Policy and the Economy*, vol. 20. Cambridge: MIT Press.

Blundell, R., and S. Bond. 1998. Initial conditions and moment restrictions in dynamic panel data models. *Journal of Econometrics* 87: 115–43.

Capelle-Blancard, G., and O. Havrylchyk. 2013. Incidence of bank levy and bank market power. Working Paper 2013–21. CEPII.

Chiorazzo, V., and C. Milani. 2011. The impact of taxation on bank profits: Evidence from EU banks. *Journal of Banking and Finance* 35: 3202–12.

Claessens, S., and L. Laeven. 2004. What drives bank competition? Some international evidence. *Journal of Money, Credit and Banking* 36: 563–83.

Claeys, S., and R. Vander Vennet. 2008. Determinants of bank interest margins in Central and Eastern Europe: A comparison with the West. *Economic Systems* 32 (2): 197–216.

Demirgüç-Kunt, A., and H. Huizinga. 1999. Determinants of commercial bank interest margins and profitability: Some international evidence. *World Bank Economic Review* 13 (2): 379–408.

Demirgüç-Kunt, A., and H. Huizinga. 2001. The taxation of domestic and foreign banking. *Journal of Public Economics* 79: 429–53.

European Commission. 2010. Financial sector taxation. Taxation paper 25. Brussels.

European Commission. 2012. Tax elasticities of financial instruments, profits and remuneration: Review of the Economic Literature. *Taxation Paper 30*.

European Commission, 2012. Review of current practices for taxation of financial instruments, profits and remuneration of the financial sector. Taxation paper 31. Brussels.

Fang, Y., I. Hasan, and K. Marton. 2010. *Efficiency of banks in transition: Recent evidence from South and Eastern Europe.* Research discussion paper. Bank of Finland.

Fernández de Guevara, J., J. Maudos, and F. Pérez. 2005. Market power in European banking sectors. *Journal of Financial Services Research* 27 (2): 109–13.

Huizinga, H. P., J. Voget, and W. Wagner. 2011. International taxation and cross-border banking. Discussion paper 8436. CEPR.

International Monetary Fund. 2010. A fair and substantial contribution by the financial sector. Final report for the G-20. IMF.

Maudos, J., and J. Fernández de Guevara. 2004. Factors explaining the interest margin in the banking sectors of the European Union. *Journal of Banking and Finance* 28 (9): 2259–81.

Panzer, J., and J. Rosse. 1987. Testing for "monopoly" equilibrium. *Journal of Industrial Economics* 4: 443–56.

Roodman, D. 2009. How to do xtabond2: An introduction to difference and system GMM in Stata. *Stata Journal* 9 (1): 86–136.

13 The Incidence of Bank Regulations and Taxes on Wages: Evidence from US States

Timothy J. Goodspeed

13.1 Introduction

This chapter focuses on two questions. First, I ask whether there is an earnings premium in the financial sector. Next, I examine the issue of tax and regulatory incidence by estimating the degree to which banking regulations and company taxes on banks influence wages in the banking sector.

To do this, I examine data on wages gathered at the individual level from the Integrated Public Use Microdata Series (IPUMS). The US part of this database consists of more than fifty high-precision samples of the American population drawn from fifteen federal censuses and from the American Community Surveys of 2000 to 2010. The wage data correspond to the American Community Survey for 2003. Using these data, I am also able to control for a number of individual level variables known to affect wages, such as age, sex, education level, and race. I am also able to identify the industry of the worker and the state in which they reside.

I combine this information on individuals and industries with information on US states. Most US states tax banks as part of the corporate income tax. It should be noted that the rules applying to banks with respect to the corporate income tax base can differ from those applying to other companies. This is due to the nature of the financial business—profits are generated by the difference between interest paid and interest received, and losses on bad loans are a normal part of doing business. Nevertheless, the specifics with respect to banks differ across countries, as detailed in Price-Waterhouse-Coopers (2012), and in some countries there is little difference between the tax as applied to banks and other corporations. In the United States there is no difference between banks and other companies with respect to thin-capitalization rules, while in the United Kingdom and Switzerland such rules are applied differently for banks and in other countries such as France, Greece, and Spain, banks are exempted from thin-capitalization rules. For the United States the main difference for the banking sector is that there is an allowance for reserves for loan losses; this allowance is accompanied by specific rules to limit potential abuse.

As noted in section 13.3, the tax base applied to banks differs across US states. When the tax base for US states is accounting profit, states usually start with a bank tax base that closely follows the taxable income that the taxpayer is required to report to the US Treasury for federal corporate tax purposes, but the tax rate differs across states. The top marginal rate on banks is often the same as the top corporate tax rate in a state. I will examine differences in bank tax rates across states as well as any differences between the corporate tax rate and bank tax rate within a state. In addition I will examine banking regulations, and their differences across states in what follows.

With respect to a financial sector earnings premium my results suggest a raw 45 percent premium in the financial sector. With respect to incidence, my main findings are that the corporate tax negatively affects wages in the manufacturing sector, while the company tax on banks has either positive or no effect on wages in the banking sector. This latter result is somewhat surprising though it is consistent with Huizinga, Voget, and Wagner (2011), who find that home country corporate income taxation of foreign-source bank income is almost fully passed through to higher interest margins charged abroad, and Capelle-Blancard and Havrylchyk (chapter 12 in this volume) who similarly find taxes on banks are passed through to consumers. The result might have to do with specifics of the banking industry such as market power, labor mobility, or more traditional elasticity concerns. The timing of US state bank deregulation is found to have important effects on current wages in the banking sector. Wages in the banking sector are lower in states that deregulated earlier. This might be due to a more elastic supply of banking services and capital in deregulated states or less market power in a more competitive environment.

The chapter is organized as follows. Section 13.2 offers a short literature review concentrating on incidence. Section 13.3 briefly discusses the origins and history of US state bank taxation and regulation. Section 13.4 describes our data and offers several tables describing the banking sector differences across US states. Section 13.5 presents my data with respect to the question of the wage premium in the financial sector.

Section 13.6 offers a regression analysis of incidence in the banking sector using cross-state variation. Section 13.7 concludes.

13.2 Literature Review

The incidence of taxation is a fundamental part of the study of public finance. Who bears the burden of a tax boils down to a question of elasticities. Despite this simple proposition, the empirical identification of the incidence of a tax can be complex, notably for the corporate tax, on which there is little agreement.

The standard theoretical analysis of the incidence of company taxes begins with the general equilibrium model of Harberger (1962). The model posits a perfectly competitive economy with a taxed corporate sector and an untaxed noncorporate sector, and with factors of production moving freely between the two sectors. There is some question about whether Harberger's formulation is the appropriate framework for thinking about the incidence of a tax on banks. This is because banks are financial intermediaries, not really producers of final products. Nevertheless, the banking services that the financial sector provides will be affected in much the same way as in Harberger's analysis and factors of production used in producing banking services will also be affected in the same fundamental way. It thus seems appropriate to begin to think about the incidence of a corporate tax in the banking sector by working through the lessons of Harberger's analysis as applied to banks.

A tax on the banking sector will cause two sorts of reactions, dubbed the output and factor-substitution effects by Miezskowski (1967). First, to the extent that the demand for banking services is not perfectly elastic, a tax on banks will increase the price of banking services paid by consumers. The amount by which the price of banking services increases and the quantity of banking services falls depends on the elasticity of demand for (and supply of) banking services. If demand is completely inelastic, consumers of banking services will bear the entire burden of the tax, and neither capital nor labor in the banking sector bears any of the burden. In the less extreme case, the higher price of banking services leads to a fall in the equilibrium quantity. As fewer banking services are provided in the economy, factors that produce banking services will be fewer in demand and will cease to be employed in the banking sector. As the model is one of full employment, these factors must be absorbed in the other sectors of the economy. If the banking sector is capital intensive relative to the rest of the economy, large amounts of capital relative to labor must be employed in other sectors. This leads to a relatively large fall in the return to capital.

The second reaction caused by the tax on the banking sector is dubbed the factor-substitution effect. To the extent that labor and capital are substitutes, the fact that capital is now more expensive results in a substitution of labor for capital employed in the banking sector. As capital leaves and is re-employed where it is valued less, the economywide return to capital falls.

Incidence in an open economy with tax competition is discussed in a number of relevant papers, such as Gordon (1986), Razin and Sadka (1991), Zodrow and Mieszkowski (1986), and Wilson (1986). Tax competition in this framework will result in low tax rates on mobile factors, and the incidence will fall on immobile factors. Taxes on capital will lead to capital flight and a reduction in the capital–labor ratio, which decreases productivity and hence wages in the long run. It also follows that if capital is taxed more heavily in one sector, as suggested in Mieskowski and Zodrow (1985), the marginal product of labor and wages could rise in the less heavily taxed sector.

In sum, labor will tend to bear less of the burden of a tax on banks (1) the more inelastic is the demand for banking services, (2) the more capital intensive is the banking sector relative to the rest of the economy, (3) the easier it is to substitute labor for capital in the financial sector, and (4) the more mobile is labor relative to capital in the banking sector.

Differing regulatory environments across states are likely to affect the elasticity of supply of banking services. States that deregulated early would likely experience a more elastic supply of banking services, making it more likely for any tax to be passed on to labor in those states. Indeed the banking literature has established strong links between US state regulatory environments and economic growth (Jayaratne and Strahan 1996). I try to account for such factors in my empirical analysis.

Standard tax incidence models all rely on the assumption of perfectly competitive markets. It might be that the financial sector is not perfectly competitive, and this opens up the possibility of economic rents being earned in the financial sector. Philippon and Reshef (2009) find evidence of economic rents in the financial sector that can explain a wage premium of up to 50 percent in that sector. Egger, von Ehrlich, and Radulescu (2012) examine the earnings premiums of executives and find a premium of 43 percent in the financial sector. My wage data complement these studies on earnings premiums. Unlike Egger, von Ehrlich, and Radulescu (2012), I take the wage component of all employees, and unlike Philippon and Reshef, also at the individual level. My results show a wage premium of a similar magnitude. I find a raw 45 percent premium in the financial sector, without correcting for differences in human capital or other factors that influence relative wages.

My regression analysis focuses on the impact of corporate taxes in the banking sector. Some recent papers, surveyed by Gentry (2007), have attempted to estimate the degree to which corporate taxes are borne by labor, including Desai, Foley, and Hines (2007), Felix (2007), Felix and Hines (2009), Arulampalam, Devereux, and Mafinni (2010), and Altshuler and Liu (2011). These papers have generally found that corporate taxes lower wages, indicating that corporate taxes are partially borne by labor (Desai, Foley, and Hines estimate labor bears about 60 percent of the corporate tax). I follow the general empirical approach of these papers, but I concentrate on differences in the incidence of company taxes in the banking sector.[1]

13.3   US State Taxation and Regulation of Banks

Historically, banks in US states have been subject to unique tax regimes. Sylla, Legler, and Wallis (1987) indicate that taxation of banks by the states became an important revenue source when passage of the US Constitution forbade import and export taxes and state issuance of currency. Rather than create their own money, states turned to chartering banks that could create money. States created revenue by investing in banks (buying shares) and by taxing banks. As stakeholders, states had incentives to increase bank rents, and often did so by placing geographical restrictions on banks. For instance, as noted in Kroszner and Strayhan (1999), states gained no revenue from out of state banks and hence prohibited out of state banks from operating in their territory.

McCray (1987) discusses some of the important legislative history. In its landmark 1819 *McCulloch v. Maryland* decision, the US Supreme Court limited state taxes on national banks to taxes on real property or the value of banks shares unless authorized by Congress; states also applied this to state-chartered banks. Congress explicitly granted taxation of real property and the value of bank shares in the National Bank Act of 1864, and also limited the maximum tax on banks. In 1923 and 1926 Congress amended the National Bank Act to allow taxation of national banks with headquarters in a state (and by extension to home state-chartered banks) on income in one of three ways: (1) by including bank share dividends in the taxable income of a shareholder, (2) by imposing a net income tax, and (3) by levying a franchise tax according to or measured by net income.

In 1976 Congress removed all restrictions on state bank taxation (other than discrimination), but many states continue to apply a unique tax on banks. States mainly tax the financial sector as part of the state corporate income tax, but often separate out the financial sector with a franchise tax. The franchise tax uses as a base either corporate income or intangible assets (shares). When corporate income is used as the base, the tax is effectively the corporate income tax even though it is called a franchise tax. According to Fox and Black (1994), franchise taxes are popular because the income from US government securities only can be included in the tax base if the tax is structured as a franchise tax. In addition some states, such as Texas, constitutionally prohibit taxing income but not a franchise. Table 13.1 lists the corporate tax rate on banks as well as state franchise tax rates, and any share tax on banks for 1993 and 2007. Some franchise tax states use corporate income as the base, and when this base is used, the bank corporate tax rate column of table 13.1 is zero. A significant number of states use a different tax base with the franchise tax, however, such as assets, deposits, or gross receipts. These are recognizable by the significantly lower rate than states that use the corporate income base, and an attempt is made to identify the base in table 13.1. Most states appear to have eliminated any tax on shares, with Pennsylvania being the exception.

The corporate tax rate on banks often mirrors the non-bank corporate tax, but not always. The states for which the financial corporate tax rate is above or below the non-bank rate in 2007 are indicated in table 13.1 with asterisks, one if above and two if below. For instance, the non-bank corporate tax in Massachusetts is 9.5 percent while the financial corporate tax is 10.5 percent; the rationale given is that it is supposed to compensate for exemption from personal property and net worth taxes. Besides Massachusetts, states with higher corporate rates on banks for 2007 are California, Hawaii, and Missouri. As with the non-bank corporate tax, and as noted by Tannenwald (2000), states currently use formula apportionment for banks, so the tax is based on the proportion of in-state to total property, payroll, and sales (with weights sometimes differing among states).

Table 13.1
US state bank taxes, 1993 and 2007 or recent

	1993			2007 or recent		
State	Financial corporate income tax rate	Franchise tax rate	Share tax rate	Financial corporate income tax rate	Franchise tax rate	Share tax rate
Alabama	0	6.5	1	0	6.5	0
Alaska	9.4	0	0	9.4	0	0
Arizona	9.3	0	0	6.968	0	0
Arkansas	6.5	0.27	0	6.5	0	0
California*	0	11.1	0	0	10.84	0
Colorado	5.1	0	0	4.63	0	0
Connecticut	0	11.5	0	7.5	0	0
Delaware	0	8.7	0	0	8.7–1.7	0
District of Columbia	0	10.25	0	9.975	0	0
Florida	0	5.5	0.15	5.5	0	0
Georgia[a]	6	0.25	0	6	a	0
Hawaii[*b]	0	11.7	0	7.92	b	0
Idaho	8	0	0	7.6	0	0
Illinois	7.3	0.25	0	7.3	0.25	0
Indiana	0	8.5	0.25	0	8.5	0
Iowa**	0	5	0	0	5	0
Kansas**	0	6.625	0	0	2.25	0
Kentucky**	0	0.001	0.95	0	1.1	0
Louisiana**	0	0	0	8	0.3	0
Maine**	0	1	0.14	0	1+0.08(assets)	0
Maryland	0	7	0	7	0	0
Massachusetts*	0	12.54	0	10.5	0	0
Michigan	0	0	0	4.95	0	0
Minnesota	0	9.8	0	0	9.8	0
Mississippi	5	0.25	0	5	0.25	0
Missouri*	5	7	0.05	7	.03	0
Montana	0	7.329	0	0	6.75	0
Nebraska**	0	0.469	0	0	0.00047(deposits)	0
Nevada	0	0	0	0	0	0
New Hampshire	8	1	0	8.5	0	0

Table 13.1
(Continued)

	1993			2007 or recent		
State	Financial corporate income tax rate	Franchise tax rate	Share tax rate	Financial corporate income tax rate	Franchise tax rate	Share tax rate
New Jersey	0	9.375	0	9	0	0
New Mexico	7.6	0	0	7.6	0	0
New York	0	10.35	0	7.5	or 0.01 (AMT-assets)	0
North Carolina	7.9	0.003	0	6.9	0.0015	0
North Dakota	0	7	0	0	7	0
Ohio**	0	1.5	0	0	1.3(net value of stock)	0
Oklahoma	6	0.125	0	6	0	0
Oregon	0	6.6	0	6.6	0	0
Pennsylvania**	0	0	1.25	0	0	1.25
Rhode Island	0	8	0	9	0.0625(on deposits)	0
South Carolina**	0	4.5	0	0	4.5	0
South Dakota*	0	6	0	0	6	0
Tennessee	6	0.25	0	6.5	0.25	0
Texas	0	0.25	0	0	1	0
Utah	0	5	0	0	5	0
Vermont**	0	0.00004	0	0	0.0096(on deposits)	0
Virginia	0	1	0	0	1(on net worth)	0
Washington	0	0	0	0	0.018(gross receipts)	0
West Virginia	9	0.75	0	8.75	0.55(on capital)	0
Wisconsin	0	8.3345	0	0	7.9	0
Wyoming	0	0	0	0	0	0

Sources: Fox and Black (1994) for 1993; Tax Foundation for 2007 and individual State Bureau of Taxation websites as accessed in November 2012 to categorize franchise and share tax rates. If a search for "franchise tax" on a state's website has no results, the state is categorized as having a 0 rate.

Note: *2007 financial corporate tax rate higher than corporate tax rate; ** 2007 financial corporate tax rate lower than corporate tax rate.

a. Georgia imposes a gross receipts tax known as the "state occupation tax" as well and financial institutions are additionally subject to personal property taxes, real property taxes, corporate net worth taxes, and corporate income taxes.

b. Hawaii considered eliminating its franchise tax in in 2006, but it is unclear whether the corporate tax is currently considered a franchise tax.

13.4   Data

The data that I use combines individual-level data on wages and individual characteristics from IPUMS (Integrated Public Use Microdata Series) for 2003 with state data on tax rates, regulatory environments, and agglomeration effects. The large literature on wage determination in labor economics has established strong connections between earnings and human capital, race, age, and sex. I therefore use these as control variables. I also use IPUMS information on the state of residence and industry. The tax variables I use are the top statutory bank and non-bank corporate rates, taken from the Tax Foundation.

The IPUMS database compiles a consistent record of individuals. It includes individual characteristics as well as employment information. To compute this wage information, I use three variables: usual hours worked per week in the last 12 months, weeks worked in the last 12 months, and annual income in the last 12 months. Multiplying the first two pieces of data gives total hours worked in the last 12 months, and then dividing annual wage and salary income by total hours gives our measure of the wage rate. The annual income measure reports each individual's total before-tax wage and salary income for the past 12 months. Sources of income include wages, salaries, commissions, cash bonuses, tips, and other money income received from an employer. Payments-in-kind or reimbursements for business expenses are not included. The weeks worked variable reports the number of weeks that the individual worked for profit, pay, or as an unpaid family worker during the previous 12 months. The usual hours worked per week reports the number of hours per week that the individual usually worked during the previous 12 months if the person worked. Since the data include unpaid family workers, there are some individuals who would end up with a tiny wage rate in this calculation. To adjust for this, I eliminate individuals with a calculated wage less than five dollars since the minimum wage in 2003 was $5.15.

For industry classification, I use the IPUMS industry variable that mirrors the Census Bureau's 1990 classification system; it tells us the industry in which each individual worked. In some of the regression specifications I aggregate industries while in other specifications I use the full set of three-digit industries. Each observation also has a state of residence indicator as well as race, sex, educational attainment, and age. My sample year is 2003, and I eliminate people who did not work and those who had zero income in addition to those with a calculated wage below five dollars as mentioned above. My final sample size is 522, 934 individual observations.

I supplement this dataset with information on states. These state data include the top marginal tax rates on corporations, banks, individuals, and retail sales. I also construct two state-level dummy variables. One is for states with right-to-work laws to reflect differences in wages due to different laws on union membership; the other is for states that deregulated their banking sector relatively early.

To construct the state dummy with respect to the timing of bank deregulation, I rely on Jayaratne and Strahan (1996, p. 641) and Kroszner and Strahan (1999). A first way that states began to deregulate banking was to permit intrastate branching. Table 13.2 lists three categories of states with respect to the timing of their banking deregulation: those that permitted intrastate banking prior to 1972, those that deregulated in this way after 1972, and those who continue to disallow intrastate branching. Among those that deregulated early are states that are well known for friendly banking environments such as Delaware and South Dakota.

Another important factor is the factor intensity of the banking sector. The literature discussing the Harberger model of incidence notes that generally labor will bear less of the burden of capital taxes, the less labor intense is that sector. Table 13.3 indicates the labor intensity by industry of the US economy in 2002. The figures are computed using the IRS Statistics of Income (SOI) data from tax returns of US companies and divide wages and salaries by total assets. By this measure the finance and insurance sector is less labor intensive (more capital intensive) than the average of the economy. This alone suggests that labor will bear less of the corporate tax in the banking sector, as noted in the literature review.

Finally, to account for any agglomeration effects, wI construct the proportion of a state's GDP that emanates from the banking sector. Table 13.4 lists the finance and insurance share of GDP for each state for 2003. The states with the four highest shares of finance and insurance in 2003 were Delaware, South Dakota, Connecticut, and New York in that order.

Summary statistics for the main variables used in the analysis are presented in table 13.5. The correlation matrix is presented in table 13.6.

Table 13.2
Timing of state deregulation of banking sector (intrastate branching permitted)

Deregulated before 1972	Deregulated after 1972	Did not deregulate
Alaska	Alabama	Iowa
Arizona	Arkansas	
California	Colorado	
Delaware	Connecticut	
District of Columbia	Florida	
Idaho	Georgia	
Maryland	Hawaii	
Nevada	Illinois	
North Carolina	Indiana	
Rhode Island	Kansas	
South Dakota	Kentucky	
Vermont	Louisiana	
	Maine	
	Massachusetts	
	Michigan	
	Minnesota	
	Mississippi	
	Missouri	
	Montana	
	Nebraska	
	New Hampshire	
	New Jersey	
	New Mexico	
	New York	
	North Dakota	
	Ohio	
	Oklahoma	
	Oregon	
	Pennsylvania	
	South Carolina	
	Tennessee	
	Texas	
	Utah	
	Virginia	
	Washington	
	West Virginia	
	Wisconsin	
	Wyoming	

Sources: Jayaratne and Strahan (1996); Kroszner and Strahan (1999)

Table 13.3
US labor intensity by industry, 2002

Industry	L/K ratio
All industries	0.042
Agriculture, forestry, fishing, and hunting	0.081
Mining	0.019
Utilities	0.016
Construction	0.097
Manufacturing	0.042
Wholesale and retail trade	0.151
Transportation and warehousing	0.193
Information	0.048
Finance and insurance	0.012
Real estate and rental and leasing	0.059
Professional, scientific and technical services	0.272
Management of companies (holding companies)	0.010
Administrative and support and waste management and remediation services	0.181
Educational services	0.369
Health care and social assistance	0.540
Arts, entertainment, and recreation	0.162
Accommodation and food services	0.174
Other services	0.196

Source: Author calculation of (wages and salaries/total assets) from SOI returns of active corporations, Form 1120

Table 13.4
Finance and insurance share of GDP by state, 2003

State	Share of GDP
Alabama	5.59
Alaska	4.30
Arizona	8.63
Arkansas	4.60
California	6.84
Colorado	7.13
Connecticut	15.33
Delaware	37.05
District of Columbia	5.48
Florida	6.80
Georgia	6.81

Table 13.4
(Continued)

State	Share of GDP
Hawaii	4.58
Idaho	4.45
Illinois	10.04
Indiana	6.36
Iowa	11.95
Kansas	6.64
Kentucky	5.18
Louisiana	4.12
Maine	6.91
Maryland	6.99
Massachusetts	10.66
Michigan	6.36
Minnesota	9.87
Mississippi	4.81
Missouri	6.50
Montana	5.39
Nebraska	8.81
Nevada	8.87
New Hampshire	8.39
New Jersey	7.77
New Mexico	3.65
New York	14.76
North Carolina	10.58
North Dakota	6.50
Ohio	8.18
Oklahoma	5.31
Oregon	5.70
Pennsylvania	7.75
Rhode Island	12.90
South Carolina	5.07
South Dakota	19.97
Tennessee	6.44
Texas	6.53
United States	8.16
Utah	10.03
Vermont	6.23
Virginia	7.57
Washington	5.86
West Virginia	4.30
Wisconsin	7.31
Wyoming	3.13

Table 13.5
Summary statistics

Variable	Observations	Mean	Standard deviation	Min	Max
Age	522,934	41.38025	13.56772	16	93
Sex	522,934	1.48479	0.499769	1	2
Marital status	522,934	2.703882	2.163499	1	6
Race	522,934	1.586835	1.600735	1	9
Educ attainment	522,934	7.396027	2.265519	0	11
Log wage	522,934	2.763637	0.672703	1.60944	11.3621
Corporate tax rate	522,934	6.630453	3.040776	0	12
Bank tax rate	522,934	5.535408	3.742748	0	10.84
Sales tax rate	522,934	5.25288	1.534957	0	7.25
Individual tax rate	522,934	5.382237	2.931602	0	11
Right-to-work state	522,934	0.398176	0.489523	0	1
Bank deregulation	522,934	0.233836	0.42327	0	1
Banking share of GDP	522,934	8.177581	4.063135	3.12811	37.05357

Source: Author calculations

13.5   The Wage Premium in the Financial Sector

I begin my analysis of the data by examining the wage premium of the financial sector. It is useful to first note that the annual income data includes wages, salaries, commissions, cash bonuses, tips, and other money income received from an employer, but not payments-in-kind or reimbursements for business expenses. There is some top-coding at the high end of the annual income data. For the 2003 American Community Survey, values up to the 99.5th percentile within each state are actual values; higher values are the state means of all values above these cutoffs.

Table 13.7 provides summary statistics on the computed wage, annual income, educational attainment, and age variables by aggregated industry. The average wage in the banking sector is computed as $32.44 for 30,469 observations while the overall average is $22.45 for 522,934 observations. With respect to the computed wage, the raw statistics indicate a wage premium in the banking sector of about 45 percent relative to wages for all industries. This could be partially economic rents but, of course, could also be due to greater human capital or experience in the financial sector. Indeed the average level of educational attainment in the banking sector is greater than for any

Table 13.6
Correlation matrix

	Age	Sex	Marital status	Race	Educ attainment	Wage	Corporate tax rate	Bank tax rate	Sales tax rate	Individual tax rate	Right-to-work state	Bank deregulation	banking share of GDP
Age	1												
Sex	-0.0017	1											
Marital status	-0.3963	0.0353	1										
Race	-0.0908	-0.0039	0.0478	1									
Educ attainment	0.0763	0.043	-0.1107	-0.0851	1								
Wage	0.0308	-0.0176	-0.0194	-0.0043	0.0425	1							
Corporate tax rate	0.0098	0.0048	0.018	-0.0097	0.0226	0.0027	1						
Bank tax rate	-0.0036	0.0024	0.0346	0.1005	0.042	0.0096	0.5587	1					
Sales tax rate	-0.0062	-0.0068	0.0094	0.0706	-0.012	0.0032	-0.0511	0.0002	1				
Individual tax rate	-0.0036	0.0008	0.0153	0.0492	0.0154	0.0036	0.6223	0.5171	-0.0887	1			
Right-to-work state	0.001	-0.0022	-0.0372	-0.0456	-0.058	-0.0065	-0.3591	-0.2583	-0.0012	-0.3226	1		
Bank deregulation	-0.0124	-0.0021	0.0284	0.1014	0.0036	0.0085	0.1414	0.3908	0.1263	0.3075	-0.0592	1	
Banking share of GDP	0.0048	0.0069	0.0144	-0.0344	0.0315	0.005	0.1328	0.1435	-0.288	0.0447	-0.1507	0.154	1

Source: Author calculations

Table 13.7
Calculated wage, annual income, age, and education by industry

Variable	Observations	Mean	Standard deviation	Min	Max
All industries					
Wage	522,934	22.44949	160.7975	5	86,000
Annual income	522,934	37,001.65	40,456.22	10	526,000
Age	522,934	41.38025	13.56772	16	93
Educ attainment	522,934	7.396027	2.265519	0	11
Banking industry					
Wage	30,469	32.44162	512.9819	5	86,000
Annual income	30,469	53,349.38	61,988.27	20	526,000
Age	30,469	40.94125	12.41096	16	92
Educ attainment	30,469	8.07483	1.97368	0	11
Agriculture, forestry, fishing					
Wage	9,140	17.79564	149.9502	5	14,000
Annual income	9,140	25,365.85	29,867.06	20	445,000
Age	9,140	39.60744	15.41938	16	92
Educ attainment	9,140	6.080744	2.560664	0	11
Mining					
Wage	2,798	26.81655	61.04231	5	1,511.111
Annual income	2,798	50,364.28	36,507.66	240	418,000
Age	2,798	43.29664	11.51036	16	81
Educ attainment	2,798	6.61258	2.025052	0	11
Construction					
Wage	34,991	21.69404	87.59745	5	9,000
Annual income	34,991	36,273.82	33,848.46	10	526,000
Age	34,991	39.95596	12.78829	16	92
Educ attainment	34,991	6.232517	1.961564	0	11
Manufacturing					
Wage	76,246	23.20919	93.29181	5	21,250
Annual income	76,246	43,001.21	38,731.44	10	526,000
Age	76,246	42.95668	11.99424	16	93
Educ attainment	76,246	6.962765	2.223635	0	11
Transportation					
Wage	32,996	24.58184	95.06315	5	7,500
Annual income	32,996	42,127.62	35,471.87	50	526,000
Age	32,996	42.95181	12.10735	16	93
Educ attainment	32,996	7.145715	1.932874	0	11

Table 13.7
(Continued)

Variable	Observations	Mean	Standard deviation	Min	Max
Utilities					
Wage	7,139	26.23421	122.7541	5	10,000
Annual income	7,139	48,576.07	33,500.85	10	445,000
Age	7,139	44.13181	11.10299	16	92
Educ attainment	7,139	7.146239	1.944787	0	11
Wholesale and retail trade					
Wage	110,342	17.33023	68.88434	5	10,500
Annual income	110,342	27,675.85	33,405.41	10	526,000
Age	110,342	38.14906	14.94788	16	93
Educ attainment	110,342	6.698546	1.952369	0	11
Real estate					
Wage	7,658	29.76143	142.2038	5	6,166.667
Annual income	7,658	42,621.65	52,980.11	20	526,000
Age	7,658	46.00757	14.27575	16	92
Educ attainment	7,658	7.453121	2.1431	0	11
Arts and entertainment					
Wage	8,331	17.16663	43.20642	5	2,400
Annual income	8,331	23,026.2	30,748.76	20	445,000
Age	8,331	36.14176	15.8286	16	91
Educ attainment	8,331	6.877086	2.081824	0	11
Health care					
Wage	55,647	23.59166	92.89728	5	17,500
Annual income	55,647	39,946.37	47,319.56	10	526,000
Age	55,647	42.65511	12.52318	16	93
Educ attainment	55,647	7.945532	2.114604	0	11
Other					
Wage	147,177	23.03603	137.1407	5	40,000
Annual income	147,177	35,817.19	38,594.13	10	526,000
Age	147,177	42.57716	13.62037	16	93
Educ attainment	147,177	8.262942	2.349176	0	11

Source: Author calculations

other industry. The average level of educational attainment in the banking sector is a bit over two years of college, while it is a bit less than one year of college in manufacturing, for instance. Experience in the banking sector, as measured by age, is slightly below the overall average across all industries.

13.6 Regression Results

In this section I attempt to gauge whether and how much banking regulations and corporate taxes on the banking sector are reflected in wages in that sector. The exact empirical specifications vary, but the general idea is that I regress tax rates, a measure of bank regulation, individual controls, state controls, and industry dummies on the log of wages:

$$
\begin{aligned}
\text{Log wage}_{ij s} = {} & \alpha_0 + \alpha_1 corptax_s + \alpha_2 banktax_s + \alpha_3 bankreg_s \\
& + \alpha_4 bankreg_s * D_{bank} + \alpha_5 banktax_s * D_{bank} \\
& + \sum \beta_m individual\_controls_{mi} \\
& + \sum \varphi_m other\_state\_controls_{ms} + \sum \gamma_m D_{mj} + u_{is},
\end{aligned}
\tag{13.1}
$$

where the individual controls include variables suggested by the labor economics literature: age, age squared, education level, race, and sex. Other state-level controls are the sales tax rate and the top personal income tax rate. US states moreover differ with respect to unionization laws. Some states require all workers to participate in unions once the union has been approved within a company. Other states ("right-to-work" states) do not. Studies of the effect of unions on wages find important differences across these types of states. I thus include a dummy for right-to-work states following Felix and Hines (2009). For my main policy variables, I use the corporate top marginal tax rate and the top marginal tax rate on banks. With respect to bank regulation I use Jayaratne and Strahan's (1996, p. 641) description of states that deregulated before 1972 and after 1972. Given the size of the lag, this measure seems likely to be exogenous.

I am able to control for industry but unable to use state fixed effects for most of the specifications since the policy variables of interest are state-level variables. (I present some state fixed effect regressions and include only interactions of the policy variables.) Since the underlying data are individual-level data, this can lead to a downward bias in standard errors (and hence unwarranted significance in coefficients). I address the downward bias problem by clustering the standard errors, which allows for an arbitrary correlation in the errors of the cluster. I present results clustering by state, thereby allowing for arbitrary correlations of the errors within states.

The main empirical question is the degree to which bank regulations and company-level taxes affect wages. I begin the analysis by looking at the effect of corporate taxes on wages in the manufacturing sector and comparing this to the effect of the financial corporate tax on wages in the banking sector. Columns 1 and 2 of table 13.8 present the results. Column 1 of table 13.8 presents regression results for only the data in the manufacturing sector. There is a clear and significant negative effect of the corporate tax on wages in the manufacturing sector. The estimated elasticity from column 1 is quite low, –0.06, which is even lower than the –0.14 result of Felix (2009). Column 2 of table 13.8 presents the results when the sample is limited to just the banking sector. The results are strikingly different. The tax in the banking sector indicates a significant positive effect on wages in that sector. This is somewhat surprising and in marked contrast to the results with respect to the manufacturing sector.

The control variables of table 13.8 all have the expected signs. Age increases wages, but at a decreasing rate. Females earn less, as do blacks, American Indians, and mixed race individuals. Greater educational attainment is associated with higher wages.

The control variable on right-to-work laws is negative and highly significant. Consistent with the literature on unions, this suggests that union wage premiums are diminished in these states. Another interesting difference between manufacturing and banking is with respect to the individual income tax. A higher individual income tax is found to lower wages in the banking sector but not in the manufacturing sector.

Columns 3 and 4 of table 13.8 add variables representing the timing of bank regulations and agglomeration effects to the column 2 tax specification. To examine banking regulations, I add a dummy that reflects whether a state deregulated its banking sector before or after 1972. States that deregulated early on can be thought of as having banking sectors that are more elastic in supply. This would result in wages in the banking sector being reduced in these states relative to the banking industries in other states that did not deregulate so soon. Agglomeration results from increased productivity due to a lot of similar firms located near each other, which would increase wages

Table 13.8
Effect of taxes on wages by industry (2003, standard errors clustered at state level)

	(1)	(2)	(3)	(4)
Dependent variable: log of wage	Manufacturing sector only	Banking sector only	Banking with agglomeration and deregulation effects	Banking with tax interactions
Corporate tax	−0.00819*			
	(0.00408)			
Bank tax		0.0209***	0.0198***	0.0101
		(0.00393)	(0.00455)	(0.00976)
Age	0.0462***	0.0658***	0.0659***	0.0658***
	(0.00140)	(0.00452)	(0.00450)	(0.00456)
Age squared	−0.000416***	−0.000633***	−0.000634***	−0.000632***
	(1.45e-05)	(5.46e-05)	(5.44e-05)	(5.50e-05)
Female	−0.244***	−0.353***	−0.351***	−0.350***
	(0.00710)	(0.0144)	(0.0146)	(0.0144)
Educ attainment	0.116***	0.115***	0.114***	0.114***
	(0.00384)	(0.00638)	(0.00599)	(0.00597)
Black	−0.100***	−0.120***	−0.122***	−0.127***
	(0.0226)	(0.0172)	(0.0176)	(0.0156)
Am Indian	−0.113***	−0.0752	−0.0546	−0.0577
	(0.0340)	(0.0799)	(0.0858)	(0.0865)
Chinese	0.102***	0.0369	0.0344	0.0323
	(0.0294)	(0.0518)	(0.0496)	(0.0492)
Japanese	0.181***	−0.171	−0.154	−0.149
	(0.0530)	(0.116)	(0.107)	(0.102)
Other Asian	−0.0383	−0.0790**	−0.0736**	−0.0761**
	(0.0252)	(0.0341)	(0.0351)	(0.0344)
Other race	−0.0851***	−0.0910***	−0.0895***	−0.0955***
	(0.0159)	(0.0311)	(0.0304)	(0.0286)
Two major races	−0.0541**	−0.116***	−0.107***	−0.108***
	(0.0258)	(0.0376)	(0.0358)	(0.0355)

Table 13.8
(Continued)

	(1)	(2)	(3)	(4)
Dependent variable: log of wage	Manufacturing sector only	Banking sector only	Banking with agglomeration and deregulation effects	Banking with tax interactions
Three+ major races	−0.00460	−0.0861	−0.0644	−0.0617
	(0.0827)	(0.0997)	(0.0937)	(0.0895)
Right-to-work state	−0.105***	−0.119***	−0.105***	−0.0947***
	(0.0203)	(0.0339)	(0.0314)	(0.0345)
Individual tax	0.00331	−0.0120**	−0.00945	−0.0112*
	(0.00573)	(0.00518)	(0.00565)	(0.00582)
Sales tax	0.00789	0.00925	0.0206***	0.0201**
	(0.00948)	(0.00859)	(0.00750)	(0.00815)
Bank dereg			−0.0212	−0.0727
			(0.0460)	(0.112)
Bank dereg*bank tax				0.00833
				(0.0137)
Bank share of GDP			0.00673*	−0.000523
			(0.00354)	(0.00901)
Bank share*bank tax				0.00105
				(0.00108)
Constant	1.263***	1.059***	0.929***	0.999***
	(0.106)	(0.108)	(0.131)	(0.156)
Observations	76,246	19,724	19,724	19,724
R^2	0.291	0.315	0.317	0.318

Note: Robust standard errors are in parentheses; *** $p < 0.01$, ** $p < 0.05$, * $p < 0.1$.

other things equal. My measure of agglomeration in the banking sector is the share of state GDP that comes from banking.

The results with respect to the timing of bank regulations suggest a negative impact of early deregulation on wages in banking, but the coefficient is insignificant. The coefficient on agglomeration is positive and significant in column 3 of table 13.8, but becomes insignificant in column 4 when interacted with the corporate tax in the banking sector.

Table 13.9 presents results that are similar to column 2 of table 13.8, but uses the entire sample and controls for industry with dummy variables. Column 1 of table 13.9 uses no industry dummies, column 2 adds aggregate industry dummies, column 3 adds interactions of industry dummies and the tax variables, and column 4 uses fixed effects, dropping state-level variables but keeping their industry interactions. The coefficients on the tax terms remain strongly significant across all specifications. The interaction of the bank tax with the banking dummy is significant in the third and fourth columns, while the interaction of the manufacturing dummy and the corporate tax is insignificant. When state fixed effects are include in the final column (and all state variables dropped), the significance of the interactions of the tax and regulatory variables are consistent with the previous columns, giving some confidence that the results in the previous columns are not due to state differences.

The other control variables in table 13.9 maintain their sign and significance. Age and educational attainment increase wages. Females, blacks, and American Indians earn less. And right-to-work laws lower union wage premiums, resulting in lower wages in these states.

Table 13.10 presents results similar to columns 3 and 4 of table 13.8 by adding controls for the timing of deregulation in the banking sector and agglomeration effects of the banking industry. Columns 1 and 2 of table 13.10 present results for the deregulation variable, column 1 using aggregate industry dummies and column 2 disaggregated industry dummies. Columns 3 and 4 do the same with respect to the agglomeration variable, column 3 using aggregate industry dummies and column 4 disaggregated industry dummies. Column 5 of table 13.10 adds fixed effects and uses interactions of tax, agglomeration, and deregulation variables but necessarily drops the non-interaction of these state-level variables.

The interaction of the dummy for early bank deregulation with the banking sector dummy is negative but insignificant in both columns 1 and 2. However, when fixed state effects are added in column 5, the

Table 13.9
Effect of taxes on wages with industry dummies (2003, standard errors clustered at state level)

Dependent variable: log of wage	(1) No industry dummies	(2) Industry dummies	(3) Industry dummies and interaction	(4) State fixed effects
Corporate tax	-0.00739***	-0.00804***	-0.00734***	
	(0.00263)	(0.00262)	(0.00271)	
Bank tax	0.0130***	0.0135***	0.0131***	
	(0.00243)	(0.00246)	(0.00246)	
Age	0.0488***	0.0429***	0.0429***	0.0428***
	(0.00102)	(0.00107)	(0.00108)	(0.00105)
Age squared	-0.000454***	-0.000391***	-0.000392***	-0.000391***
	(1.08e-05)	(1.13e-05)	(1.13e-05)	(1.10e-05)
Female	-0.240***	-0.229***	-0.229***	-0.228***
	(0.00583)	(0.00509)	(0.00507)	(0.00507)
Educ attainment	0.103***	0.103***	0.103***	0.102***
	(0.00189)	(0.00168)	(0.00168)	(0.00179)
Black	-0.0570***	-0.0619***	-0.0623***	-0.0852***
	(0.0116)	(0.0117)	(0.0117)	(0.00989)
Am Indian	-0.0911***	-0.0867***	-0.0867***	-0.0687***
	(0.0232)	(0.0226)	(0.0225)	(0.0174)
Chinese	0.0396***	0.0426***	0.0425***	0.0132*
	(0.0120)	(0.0120)	(0.0120)	(0.00745)
Japanese	0.0118	0.0225	0.0228	0.0267
	(0.0370)	(0.0350)	(0.0349)	(0.0202)
Other Asian	-0.0258*	-0.0283*	-0.0282*	-0.0518***

Table 13.9
(Continued)

Dependent variable: log of wage	(1) No industry dummies	(2) Industry dummies	(3) Industry dummies and interaction	(4) State fixed effects
	(0.0152)	(0.0162)	(0.0161)	(0.0126)
Other race	-0.0582***	-0.0562***	-0.0559***	-0.0828***
	(0.0114)	(0.0117)	(0.0117)	(0.00918)
Two major races	-0.0421***	-0.0389***	-0.0389***	-0.0450***
	(0.00927)	(0.00930)	(0.00926)	(0.00697)
Three+ major races	-0.0374	-0.0324	-0.0320	-0.0305
	(0.0298)	(0.0273)	(0.0273)	(0.0204)
Bank tax*bank			0.00643**	0.00512**
			(0.00266)	(0.00232)
Corp tax*manufacturing			-0.00407	-0.00407
			(0.00334)	(0.00323)
Right-to-work state	-0.0990***	-0.0991***	-0.0985***	
	(0.0159)	(0.0161)	(0.0161)	
Individual tax	-0.00513	-0.00503	-0.00508*	
	(0.00311)	(0.00300)	(0.00301)	
Sales tax	0.00997*	0.00993*	0.00993*	
	(0.00524)	(0.00525)	(0.00524)	
Constant	1.196***	1.262***	1.259***	1.192***
	(0.0530)	(0.0552)	(0.0560)	(0.0360)
Observations	522,934	522,934	522,934	522,934
R^2	0.257	0.274	0.275	0.283

Note: Robust standard errors are in parentheses; *** $p < 0.01$, ** $p < 0.05$, * $p < 0.1$.

interaction is highly significant. The magnitude is significant: a state that deregulated early has wages in the banking sector 8.4 percent lower than states that did not deregulate early. This suggests that deregulation in the banking sector, by making supply more elastic, decreases wages relative to regulated, less elastic states.

Columns 3 and 4 of table 13.10 examine the impact of agglomeration on wages in the banking sector. The interaction of the agglomeration indicator with the banking sector dummy yields a positive but insignificant coefficient in columns 3 and 4. However, as with the deregulation variable, when fixed state effects are added in column five, the interaction is highly significant. This suggests that agglomeration of banks increases wages in the banking sector.

13.7 Conclusion

Banks, regulation of banks, and the financial sector have, in general, come under increased scrutiny since the 2008 financial crisis. The 2010 IMF Report to the G20 (Claessens, Keen, and Pazarbaioglu 2010) evaluates bank taxes as a means to correct for externalities and other issues in light of the financial crisis, and recommends the financial activities tax that combines a tax on bank profits and payments to labor. (As such it is equivalent to a VAT.) The IMF recommendation thus combines two types of taxes that have been discussed, a tax on the profits of banks and a tax on bank wages. As the corporate tax may be borne by labor, a natural question to ask is whether the economic incidence of these two potentially separate taxes differs. Moreover the cost of regulations can also be passed on, a potentially important factor in determining incidence in the banking sector.

The aims of this chapter are empirical and twofold. First, I ask whether there is an earnings premium in the financial sector. Second, I examine the issue of tax and regulatory incidence by estimating the degree to which banking regulations and company taxes on banks influence wages in the banking sector.

To shed light on these issues, I examine data on wages gathered at the individual level from the Integrated Public Use Micro-data Series (IPUMS). These wage data correspond to the American Community Survey for 2003. Using these data I am also able to control for a number of individual- level variables known to affect wages, such as age, sex, education level, and race. I am also able to identify the industry of the worker and the state in which they reside. I combine this information

Table 13.10
Effect of bank regulations and agglomeration on wages (2003, clustered at state level)

Dependent variable: log of wage	(1) Bank deregulation with aggregate industry	(2) Bank deregulation with detailed industry	(3) Bank agglomeration with aggregate industry	(4) Bank Agglomeration with detailed industry	(5) Deregulation and agglomeration—fixed state and industry effects
Corporate tax	-0.00642**	-0.00588**	-0.00749**	-0.00690***	
	(0.00254)	(0.00228)	(0.00282)	(0.00252)	
Bank tax	0.0120***	0.0110***	0.0128***	0.0116***	
	(0.00267)	(0.00240)	(0.00251)	(0.00222)	
Age	0.0429***	0.0392***	0.0430***	0.0392***	0.0428***
	(0.00107)	(0.00102)	(0.00107)	(0.00102)	(0.000321)
Age squared	-0.000391***	-0.000349***	-0.000392***	-0.000349***	-0.000391***
	(1.13e-05)	(1.06e-05)	(1.12e-05)	(1.05e-05)	(3.68e-06)
Female	-0.229***	-0.204***	-0.229***	-0.204***	-0.228***
	(0.00509)	(0.00488)	(0.00510)	(0.00489)	(0.00169)
Educ attainment	0.103***	0.0932***	0.103***	0.0931***	0.102***
	(0.00169)	(0.00132)	(0.00167)	(0.00130)	(0.000381)
Black	-0.0624***	-0.0456***	-0.0626***	-0.0457***	-0.0852***
	(0.0115)	(0.0104)	(0.0116)	(0.0105)	(0.00303)
Am Indian	-0.0899***	-0.0760***	-0.0815***	-0.0678***	-0.0687***
	(0.0207)	(0.0206)	(0.0229)	(0.0228)	(0.00943)
Chinese	0.0400***	0.0164	0.0418***	0.0180*	0.0128
	(0.0112)	(0.0110)	(0.0114)	(0.0106)	(0.00838)
Japanese	0.0253	0.0225	0.0302	0.0276	0.0264**
	(0.0316)	(0.0250)	(0.0313)	(0.0244)	(0.0133)

Table 13.10
(Continued)

Dependent variable: log of wage	(1) Bank deregulation with aggregate industry	(2) Bank deregulation with detailed industry	(3) Bank agglomeration with aggregate industry	(4) Bank Agglomeration with detailed industry	(5) Deregulation and agglomeration—fixed state and industry effects
Other Asian	−0.0299*	−0.0364**	−0.0267	−0.0333**	−0.0518***
	(0.0164)	(0.0162)	(0.0162)	(0.0161)	(0.00483)
Other race	−0.0585***	−0.0489***	−0.0566***	−0.0471***	−0.0830***
	(0.0116)	(0.0111)	(0.0113)	(0.0108)	(0.00444)
Two major races	−0.0394***	−0.0337***	−0.0357***	−0.0300***	−0.0447***
	(0.00855)	(0.00788)	(0.00885)	(0.00820)	(0.00730)
Three+ major races	−0.0290	−0.0178	−0.0246	−0.0132	−0.0303
	(0.0243)	(0.0245)	(0.0253)	(0.0254)	(0.0249)
Bank tax*bank	0.00615	0.00452	−0.00696	−0.00757	0.00464*
	(0.00397)	(0.00336)	(0.00919)	(0.00801)	(0.00238)
Corp tax*manufacturing	−0.00511	−0.00316	−0.00527	−0.00334	−0.00497***
	(0.00329)	(0.00264)	(0.00327)	(0.00266)	(0.000771)
Bank tax*bank*dereg	0.00919	0.00905			0.00652**
	(0.00922)	(0.00856)			(0.00309)
Bank dereg	0.0287	0.0265			
	(0.0235)	(0.0210)			
Bank dereg*bank	−0.104	−0.0898			−0.0840***
	(0.0625)	(0.0587)			(0.0267)
Right-to-work state	−0.0956***	−0.0933***	−0.0908***	−0.0885***	
	(0.0165)	(0.0146)	(0.0167)	(0.0147)	

Table 13.10
(Continued)

Dependent variable: log of wage	(1) Bank deregulation with aggregate industry	(2) Bank deregulation with detailed industry	(3) Bank agglomeration with aggregate industry	(4) Bank Agglomeration with detailed industry	(5) Deregulation and agglomeration—fixed state and industry effects
RTW state*manuf	-0.0241	-0.0156	-0.0243	-0.0159	-0.0223***
	(0.0172)	(0.0137)	(0.0169)	(0.0136)	(0.00480)
Individual tax	-0.00617**	-0.00537**	-0.00441	-0.00365	
	(0.00282)	(0.00261)	(0.00309)	(0.00291)	
Sales tax	0.00871*	0.00793*	0.0126**	0.0118**	
	(0.00467)	(0.00420)	(0.00541)	(0.00499)	
Bank share of GDP			0.00290	0.00297	
			(0.00217)	(0.00202)	
Bank share*bank			-0.00775	-0.00745	0.00638***
			(0.00645)	(0.00575)	(0.00246)
Share*bank*bank tax			0.00157	0.00151	-7.61e-05
			(0.00110)	(0.000956)	(0.000300)
Constant	1.264***	1.262***	1.218***	1.217***	1.195***
	(0.0514)	(0.0483)	(0.0600)	(0.0548)	(0.0103)
Observations	522,934	522,934	522,934	522,934	522,934
R^2	0.275	0.305	0.275	0.305	0.283

Note: Robust standard errors are in parentheses; *** $p < 0.01$, ** $p < 0.05$, * $p < 0.1$.

on individuals and industries with information on US states, such as the state tax rate on banks and the share of a state's GDP that emanates from the banking sector.

I find (1) a raw 45 percent earnings premium in the financial sector, (2) a negative effect of corporate tax on wages in the manufacturing sector but a positive or no effect on wages in the banking sector, (3) lower wages in the banking sector in states that deregulated earlier, and (4) states with concentrations of financial sector activity have higher wages in that industry. The tax incidence result is somewhat surprising though it is consistent with Huizinga, Voget, and Wagner (2011), who find that home country corporate income taxation of foreign-source bank income is almost fully passed through to higher interest margins charged abroad. The result may have to do with specifics of the banking industry such as market power, labor mobility, or inelastic demand and elastic supply of banking services. Differentiating between these possible explanations is an interesting area for further research.

Notes

I would like to thank CES-Ifo for hosting and travel support for the conference "Taxation of the Financial Sector" Venice Summer Institute 2012, and Victor Stango, Gaëtan Nicodème, Olena Havrylchyk, and participants in the Venice conference for helpful and stimulating comments and discussion.

1. A number of general equilibrium papers using an open-economy version of the Harberger model have attempted to measure the burden of the corporate income tax in an open economy environment. Among these are Randolph (2006) and Gravelle and Smetters (2006). Randolph finds that labor bears about 70 percent of the burden, while Gravelle and Smetters find a much lower proportion borne by labor.

References

Arulampalam, Wiji, Michael P. Devereux, and Giorgia Mafinni. 2010. The direct incidence of corporate income tax on wages. Discussion paper 5293. Institute for the Study of Labor (IZA).

Capelle-Blancard, Gunther, and Olena Havrylchyk. 2012. The ability of banks to shift taxes to their customers. Presented at CES-Ifo Venice Conference.

Claessens, Stijn, Michael Keen, and Ceyla Pazarbasioglu, eds. 2010. *Financial Sector Taxation: The IMF's Report to the G-20 and Background Material*. Washington, DC: IMF.

Desai, Mihir, Fritz Foley, and James R. Hines Jr. 2007. Labor and capital share of the corporate tax burden: International evidence. Working paper. Available at: http://www.people.hbs.edu/mdesai/PDFs/Labor%20and%20Capital.pdf.

Egger, Peter, Maximilian von Ehrlich, and Doina Radulescu. 2012. How much it pays to work in the financial sector. *CESifo Economic Studies* 58: 110–39.

Felix, R. Alison. 2007. Passing the burden: Corporate tax incidence in open economies. Working paper WP 07–01. Federal Reserve Bank of Kansas City Regional Research.

Felix, R. Alison. 2009. Do state corporate income taxes reduce wages? *Federal Reserve Bank of Kansas City Economic Review* 94 (1): 5–30.

Felix, R. Alison, and James Hines. 2009. Corporate taxes and union wages in the United States. Working paper 15263. NBER.

Fox, William F., and Harold H. Black. 1994. The influence of state taxation and regulation on selected bank activites. *Public Finance Review* 22: 267–90.

Gentry, William. 2007. A review of the evidence on the incidence of the corporate income tax. *OTA Paper 101*. Washington, DC: US Treasury.

Gordon, Roger H. 1986. Taxation of investment and savings in a world economy. *American Economic Review* 76 (5): 1086–1102.

Gravelle, Jane G., and Kent A. Smetters. 2006. Does the open economy assumption really mean that labor bears the burden of a capital income tax? In *Advances in Economic Analysis and Policy*, vol. 6. Berkeley: Berkeley Electronic Press, 1–44.

Harberger, Arnold C. 1962. The incidence of the corporation income tax. *Journal of Political Economy* 70 (3): 215–40.

Huizinga, Harry P., J. Voget, and W. Wagner. 2011. International taxation and cross-border banking. Discussion paper 8436. CEPR.

Jayaratne, Jith, and Philip E. Strahan. 1996. The finance-growth nexus: Evidence from bank branch deregulation. *Quarterly Journal of Economics* 111 (3): 639–70.

Kroszner, Randall S., and Philip E. Strahan. 1999. What drives deregulation? Economics and politics of the relaxation of bank branching. *Quarterly Journal of Economics* 114 (4): 1437–67.

Liu, Li, and Rosanne Altshuler. 2013. Measuring the burden of the corporate income tax under imperfect competition. *National Tax Journal* 66 (1): 215–38.

McCray, S. B. 1987. Constitutional issues in state income taxes: Financial institutions. *Albany Law Review* 51: 895–933.

Miezskowski, Peter. 1967. On the theory of tax incidence. *Journal of Political Economy* 75: 250–62.

Mieszkowski, Peter, and George R. Zodrow. 1985. The incidence of partial state corporate income tax. *National Tax Journal* 38 (4): 489–96.

Philippon, Thomas, and Ariell Reshef. 2009. Wages and human capital in the U.S. financial industry: 1909–2006. Working paper 14644. NBER.

Price-Waterhouse-Coopers. 2012. Review of current practices for taxation of financial instruments, profits and remuneration of the financial sector. Working paper 31–2012. European Commission on Taxation.

Randolph, William G. 2006. International burdens of the corporate income tax. Working paper 9. Congressional Budget Office.

Razin, Assaf, and Efraim Sadka. 1991. International tax competition and gains from tax harmonization. *Economics Letters* 37: 69–76.

Sylla, Richard, John B. Legler, and John J. Wallis. 1987. Banks and state public finance in the New Republic: The United States, 1790–1860. *Journal of Economic History* 47 (2): 391–403.

Tannenwald, Robert. 2000. The neutrality of Massachusetts' taxation of financial institutions. *New England Economic Review* (May/June): 41–56.

Wilson, John D. 1986. A theory of interregional tax competition. *Journal of Urban Economics* 19 (3): 296–315.

Zodrow, George R., and Peter Mieszkowski. 1986. Pigou, Tiebout, property taxation, and the underprovision of local public goods. *Journal of Urban Economics* 19: 356–70.

14 Impact of the Bank Transactions Tax on Deposits in Argentina

Ricardo Fenochietto, Carola Pessino, and Ernesto Crivelli

14.1 Introduction

This chapter analyses the impact of the bank transactions tax (BTT) on financial intermediation in Argentina. A tax on transactions from savings and checking accounts (CSP) was established in March 2001 due to the economic crisis. The initial tax rate was 0.25 percent on debits and credits (a total of 0.5 percent), but it was increased twice over the course of the year, first to 0.4 percent and finally to 0.6 percent (a total of 1.2 percent). After the crisis passed, the tax was maintained at the 0.6 percent nominal rate, and only partial credits against other taxes (income tax and VAT) were allowed. At present, the nominal tax rate continues at 1.2 percent, and only 34 percent of the tax paid can be credited from the income tax.

Argentina has adopted the BTT twice in the aftermath of economic and financial crises, with slightly different characteristics. The BTT was established on December 29, 1989 (with the name "tax on debits from bank accounts," TDBA), as Argentina faced a serious financial crisis and a hyperinflationary period. During most of the time the tax was in place, taxpayers were allowed to credit the tax (up to 75 percent of the tax) against income tax or VAT. The TDBA was abolished on July 1, 1992. A new BTT was reestablished on March 24, 2001 by Law 25413. Unlike the TDBA, which was paid only on debits from bank accounts, the BTT was imposed on both debits and credits from bank accounts. Exempted from the BTT are mainly bank accounts of government and diplomatic emissaries (under the condition of reciprocity, whereby the accounts are exempt only if the bank accounts of Argentine diplomatic emissaries abroad are also tax exempt), and deposits originated from salaries and pensions. The tax on bank transactions is collected and administered by the federal government, and 70 percent of this revenue

Table 14.1
BTT tax revenue, 2006 to 2011 (in percent of GDP)

	Argentina	Colombia	Dominican Republic	Peru	Bolivia
2006	1.79	0.70	0.30	0.28	0.49
2007	1.85	0.69	0.28	0.31	0.37
2008	1.89	0.67	0.28	0.31	0.37
2009	1.80	0.61	0.23	0.25	0.32
2010	1.86	0.59	0.22	0.22	0.31
2011	1.96	0.82	0.21	0.08	0.27

Source: Ministries of Finance and Tax Administrations

is allocated to the federal government and 30 percent to the provincial governments.

Over the last thirty years a number of countries, mostly in Latin America, have imposed taxes on banking transactions. These taxes are usually levied on withdrawals from bank accounts, including check clearance, cash withdrawals, and payments of loan installments. At least eight Latin American countries (Argentina, Bolivia, Brazil, Colombia, Dominican Republic, Ecuador, Peru, and Venezuela) have turned to a BTT in times of crisis, in order to temporarily collect a sizable sum of money (Coelho et al. 2001; Kirilenko and Summers 2003; Baca-Campodonico et al. 2006). Table 14.1 shows the BTT tax revenues of selected countries.

The most recent experience with the adoption of a BTT is that of Hungary. The Hungarian government established a BTT at a rate of 1 percent in January 2013. The tax is paid on credit transfers, direct debit operations, cash payments into bank accounts, cash withdrawals from bank accounts, cash transfers, checks, and any payment initiated by the beneficiary (including credit card payments). There is a 6,000 HUF cap on the fee (about US$27). There are therefore significant differences in rate and exemptions with the Argentinean BTT.[1]

The widespread adoption of the BTT can be explained by the relatively low collection and administration costs, in addition to the sizable revenue. Collection and administration costs of these taxes are low, since financial institutions can collect the tax on behalf of the government. Basically the government enjoys an immediate and continuous revenue stream because the tax is collected from transactions in real time. Revenue from these taxes in Latin American has varied widely but has typically been in the order of 1 percent of GDP (Honohan and Yoder 2010).[2]

Only a few papers have studied the impact of BTT on financial disintermediation. Koyama and Nakane (2001), using a co-integration model for Brazil, found that the number of checks used in the economy was reduced significantly during the application of the BTT. Kirilenko and Summers (2003) found that for each dollar raised through a bank debit tax, an amount up to 28 cents in Venezuela, up to 41 cents in Colombia, and up to 47 cents in Ecuador was lost in disintermediation. The authors also found that disintermediation effects appear to intensify as the taxes remain in place, as would indicate dynamic effects. More recently Giraldo and Buckles (2011) used an econometric model, controlling for economic crises, to estimate the impact of the BTT on main deposit instruments in Colombia and found a significant negative effect on checking account balances.

This chapter empirically assesses the extent to which the BTT resulted in a decrease in the level of CSP in Argentina between 1996 and 2010. While no study has yet examined this issue for the case of Argentina for so long a period of time (174 months), the main contribution of this chapter to the literature consists in the use of co-integration techniques to estimate the long-run relationship between the level of CSP and the tax rate on bank transactions. To test for robustness, we estimated different empirical models, such as VECM, DOLS, and FMOLS, and included also policy variables that help explain better the behavior of CSP in Argentina during the period of study. The chapter finds significant evidence in favor of the hypothesis that the BTT in Argentina has had a strong negative impact on the level of deposits. The estimated long-run semi-elasticity of CSP with regard to the net banking transactions tax rate is estimated at $-1/3$, which indicates a decrease in the level of deposits by about 3 percent for each increase in the tax rate by 0.1 percentage points.

The rest of the chapter is organized as follows. Section 14.2 describes the economic effects of the BTT. Section 14.3 presents the main hypothesis to be empirically tested, and section 14.4 the data used in the empirical analysis. Section 14.5 describes the empirical findings, and section 14.6 provides a discussion of the policy implications. Section 14.7 summarizes the results and concludes.

14.2 Economic Effects of the BTT

Although the tax on bank transactions has been successful in raising revenue in the short term (Coelho et al. 2001), it generates several distortions to economic activity. The most important distortions being that (1) it is a cascading turnover tax and (2) it generates financial disintermediation. The total tax paid depends on the number of transactions made through the banking system, making it difficult to identify the exact impact of the tax on the cost of production (the tax also cannot be refunded on exports). Neither the issue of final incidence of the tax, nor its potential impact on income distribution has been formally addressed in the literature.

Since the BTT is levied on financial transactions, it is likely to result in disintermediation, thus encouraging informality. As a result more transactions will be conducted in the form of payment by cash, by barter, or accounts not subject to taxes in order to avoid the additional cost associated with the tax. Disintermediation results not only in the reduction of the tax base but also in a possible misallocation of financial resources (Kirilenko and Summers 2003).

More broadly, it has been suggested that financial transaction taxes (FTTs) could increase the tax burden on the financial sector, lessen systemic risks, and reduce the volatility of financial asset prices (including the exchange rate, if applied to international currency transactions), but the results are inconclusive. The price volatility effect of FTTs is ambiguous, and this could be counterproductive in that, unless set at prohibitive rates, FTTs would not prevent major capital outflows during a crisis; FTTs are found to be subject to high risk of tax avoidance in the medium to long term (Brondolo 2011); and FTTs levied on centralized clearing systems could increase systemic risk if they push transactions outside such systems. FTTs are inefficient (taxing intermediate transactions), while the incidence is unclear but likely to be borne by bank account holders if asset values fall as a result (Claessens, Keen, and Pazarbasioglu 2010; Matheson 2010).

14.3 Empirical Specification

The main hypothesis to be tested is that the BTT has a negative impact on the total checking and savings accounts balance in Argentina (CSP). A reduced form of this relationship can be written as

$$CSPt \ (GDP, NTR, NIR, C) = f \ (GDPt, NTRt, NIRt, Ct), \qquad (14.1)$$

where CSPt denotes the log of the sum of checking and savings accounts at constant prices, GDPt is the monthly GDP at 1993 constant prices,

NTRt is BTT rate net from allowed credits, and Ct is a vector of control variables.

The aim of this study is to estimate the impact of the BTT on the CSP by examining the long-run relationship between CSP and its determinants. The analysis starts with the hypothesis that the relationship between the CSP, BTT, and other independent variables is loglinear. The complete testing includes three steps: a group unit root test is performed, followed by a co-integration test, using the Johansen approach for vector autoregressions (VARs) constructed in levels and first differences. Finally, after verifying that the model is co-integrated, short and long-run relationships are estimated using four different models: the fully modified least squares (FMOLS) model (Phillips and Hansen 1990), the canonical co-integration regression (Park 1992), the dynamic least squares (DOLS) (Saikkonen 1992; Stock and Watson 1993), and the vector error correction model (VECM).

FMOLS involves a class of Wald tests modified by semiparametric corrections for serial correlation and for endogeneity. FMOLS employs preliminary estimates of the symmetric and one-sided long-run covariance matrices of the residuals to avoid the problems due to the long-run correlation between the co-integrating equation and stochastic regressor innovations. The canonical co-integrating regression (CCR) employs transformed data with simple adjustments of the integrated processes using stationary components in co-integrating models. The DOLS approach adds not only lags but also leads of the first-differenced regressors to the specification. Finally, the VECM model restricts the long-run behavior of the endogenous variables to converge to their co-integrating relationships and allows for short-run adjustment dynamics. The error correction term corrects the deviation from long-run equilibrium through a series of partial short-run adjustments.

14.4 Data

The dataset includes monthly data for Argentina between January 1996 and June 2010. Data on deposits were collected from the Central Bank of Argentina. The dependent variable (CSP) is constructed using the log of the sum of checking and savings accounts in domestic currency (excluding government and other public sector institutions and term deposits that are not subject to BTT) at 1993 constant prices (using the wholesale price index). Figure 14.1 shows the level of CSP in real terms

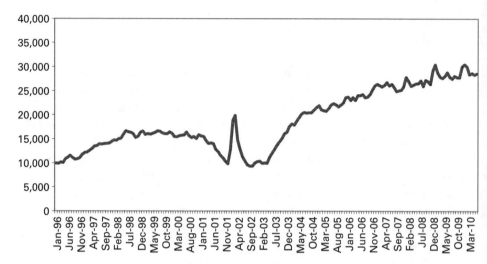

Figure 14.1
Total checking and savings accounts balance (in millions AR$, 1993 constant prices)

along the period under study (see also appendix A for independent variables).

The BTT nominal rate changed several times during the time period of the sample. At the time the tax was introduced in March 24, 2001, the BTT's nominal rate was 0.25 percent. For most of the period under study (107 months), the tax rate was 0.6 percent for debits and 0.6 percent for credits from checking and savings accounts. Therefore, given that the tax is applied to debits and credits, the most common total nominal tax rate was 1.2 percent (in force along 107 months, figure 14.2). In addition the nominal BTT rate was adjusted to account for the possibility of partial deduction against other taxes, such as personal income tax (PIT), corporate income tax (CIT), or VAT. During the period under study the tax was in force 111 months, during which, the most common net rate was the current one of 0.792 percent, in force in 74 periods. During these 74 months 0.34 percent of the BTT paid was allowed to be credited against the income tax. The second most common net rate was 1.2 percent in force 27 months in which no deductibility was allowed (figure 14.2). The main hypothesis to be tested is for the net tax rate to have a negative impact on the total checking and saving accounts balance.

A number of control variables were considered based on institutional arrangements and regulations set forth during the period of the

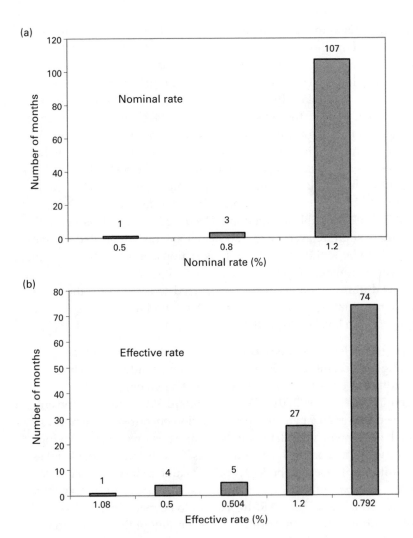

Figure 14.2
Nominal and net BTT tax rate and period of application

economic crisis. In mid-1999, as a response to the loss of confidence generated in the months before the economic crisis of 2001, total deposits in checking and savings accounts decreased considerably. Figure 14.1 shows that total deposits decreased by about 35 percent in constant prices from December 1999 to November 2001. In order to prevent further such deficits, the government adopted a number of regulations aiming at encouraging or simply forcing citizens to maintain their money in the banking system. The severity and force of regulations changed: clearly, the most severe measure was the prohibition of bank account withdrawals in a weekly amount higher than AR$250 (equivalent to US$250) that was set in place between December 1, 2001, and April 7, 2002 (República Argentina, Decree 1570/01).[3] This regulation was then soon relaxed, first, allowing salaries deposited in bank accounts to be withdrawn without restrictions, and finally the regulation was eliminated in November 2002.

Four dummy variables were constructed to account for the following four regulations that a priori may have had a positive short-term impact on the level of deposits:

- *VAT refund for transactions made with debit or credit card (VATref)* Starting on December 20, 2001, all transactions made with debit or credit card benefit from a VAT refund of 5 percent (República Argentina, Decree 1402/01).[4] With a standard VAT rate at 21 percent (reduced rate at 10.5 percent) this regulation encourages consumers to make payments with debit/credit cards, thus presumably having a positive impact on the level of deposits. Our dummy variable takes the value 0 until December 2001, and the value 1 since January 2002.
- *Means of payment (RG 151)* Starting June 25, 1998, all transactions in an amount higher than AR$10,000 had to be made by check or bank account transfer. In April 2001, the amount of the transaction was reduced to AR$1,000.[5] For the purpose of analysis, the dummy variable takes the value 0 from January 1996 to May 1998 and the value 1 since June 1998.
- *Obligation to pay salaries through bank accounts (SAL)* Starting in November 1997, all companies with more than 500 employees were asked to deposit salaries in bank accounts. Starting in August 2001, this regulation was extended to all companies (Ministry of Economy Resolution 360).[6] A dummy variable is built, taking the value of 0 for the period until October 1997 and the value of 1 starting in November 1997.

• *Freezing of deposits and bank accounts (FRE)*   During the period December 2001 to April 7, 2002, there was a prohibition to make bank account withdrawals in a weekly amount higher than AR$250. This regulation was relaxed thereafter, allowing for salaries deposited on bank accounts to be withdrawn without restrictions, and finally eliminated in November 2002. This dummy variable takes the value 0 until November 2001 and the value 1 from December 2001 to April 2002.

Only three of the four dummies described above were included in the model. The variable RG 151 was excluded because it was found highly correlated with SAL (while RG 151 was in force since November 2007, SAL was in force since June 1998). However, the results remain qualitatively unchanged including either of these variables.

Last, the remaining control variables—monthly GDP and nominal interest rate (NIR) —were obtained from the National Institute of Statistics and the Central Bank of Argentina's database, respectively. GDP measured at 1993 constant prices was used in the regression (expressed in natural logarithm). The interest rate variable was constructed using the monthly reference rate for guaranteed deposits from 7 to 59 days. These variables are often considered determinants of the level of deposits in the economy (Barro 1976). Summary descriptive statistics are presented in table 14.2.

14.5   Empirical Findings

Once nonstationarity has been identified in the data,[7] a test for co-integration was performed, using the Johansen method (Johansen 1988, 1991, 1995). Based on the Hannan–Quinn information criterion a lag length of 17 for the analysis of co-integration was chosen (see table B14.1 in the appendix)[8]. For the analysis that proceeds, the following variables are considered as exogenous: the net banking transaction tax rate (NTR), as well as the rest of the dummies accounting for regulations. Table 14.3 shows (see also table B14.2 in the appendix) the results of the Johansen co-integration tests. The trace and maximum-eigenvalue tests reject the null hypothesis of no co-integration relationship at 5 percent significance level and the hypothesis of at most 1 co-integrating equations also at 5 percent. The results thus unanimously indicate one co-integration relationships between the three variables implying a stationary long-run relationship.

Table 14.2
Descriptive statistics

	LNCSP	LNGDP	NIR	NTR	VATREF	SAL	FRE
Mean	9.78	4.83	0.87	0.56	0.59	0.87	0.02
Maximum	10.32	5.23	6.39	1.20	1.00	1.00	1.00
Minimum	9.14	4.47	0.17	0.00	0.00	0.00	0.00
Standard deviation	0.34	0.17	0.92	0.45	0.49	0.33	0.15
Observations	174	174	174	174	174	174	174

Table 14.3
Johansen co-integration tests

Hypothesis	Trace test		Max eigenvalue test	
	Test-statistic	p-Value	Test-statistic	p-Value
$r = 0$	120.24**	0.000	116.89**	0.000
$r \leq 1$	3.35	0.948	3.21	0.932
$r \leq 2$	0.14	0.708	0.14	0.709

Notes: r is the number of co-integrated vectors. *, **, and *** indicate 10, 5, and 1 percent levels of significance, respectively.

Attention here focuses on the effect of the BTT on the level of deposits, for which long-run elasticities of the CSP were estimated using the different time series approaches presented in section 14.3. The results from the different models are presented in table 14.4.

For the preferred model specifications (FMOLS, CCR, and DOLS with a low number of lags and leads) all coefficients are found significant and their signs accord to theory. In terms of the main result for the endogenous variables (GDP and the interest rate), there are no significant differences between any of the models.

FMOLS and CCR provide better estimations than that of DOLS and VECM because they do not use lags and leads. In fact, when DOLS is run with one lag and one lead (table 14.4, column 3) it provides similar estimates to FMOLS and CCR. While the use of DOLS leads to very similar results as FMOLS and CCR when the number of leads and lags is low (lower than 6), the results begin to change when the number of lags and leads increases: the variable FRE becomes statistically insignificant. This is explained by the fact that the information criterion selection of the number of lag and lead orders in DOLS and lags in

Table 14.4
CSP: FMOLS, CCR, DOLS, and VECM coefficient estimates

	Fully modified least squares (FMOLS)	Canonical co-integrating regression (CCR)	Dynamic least squares (DOLS)		VECM lags = 17
			Fixed specification lag = 1; lead = 1	Hannan–Quinn criterion lag = 13; lead = 6	
	(1)	(2)	(3)	(4)	(5)
Intercept	3.622***	3.585***	3.352***	3.361***	3.467
	(0.507)	(0.530)	(0.504)	(0.262)	
			Endogenous variables		
LNGDP	1.226***	1.235***	1.288***	1.337***	1.381***
	(0.107)	(0.112)	(0.106)	(0.055)	(0.043)
NIR	−0.057***	−0.057***	−0.071***	−0.223***	−0.372***
	(0.014)	(0.014)	(0.016)	(0.020)	(0.015)
			Exogenous variables		
NTR	−0.306***	−0.299***	−0.306***	−0.033	0.002
	(0.095)	(0.099)	(0.091)	(0.054)	(0.023)
VATref	0.411***	0.404***	0.421***	0.259***	0.019
	(0.091)	(0.094)	(0.086)	(0.056)	(0.021)
SAL	0.226***	0.225***	0.208***	0.074***	0.007
	(0.042)	(0.042)	(0.039)	(0.023)	(0.020)
FRE	0.151*	0.153*	0.097	−0.090	0.139***
	(0.0.087)	(0.087)	(0.089)	(0.108)	(0.036)
Error correction term					−0.068
R^2	0.872	0.872	0.988	0.988	0.828
Adjusted R^2	0.867	0.867	0.983	0.983	0.731
Standard error of regression	0.124	0.124	0.042	0.042	
Durbin–Watson statistic	0.814	0.813	1.058	1.058	

Notes: Standard errors in parenthesis; *** (**, *) indicate significance at 1(5, 10) percent, respectively.

VECM is chosen arbitrarily. This affects dummy variables; particularly FRE that aims at identifying the impact of a policy measure that was in place during only four months, while the number of optimal lags and leads chosen by these models exceeds this time period. Based on the Hannan–Quinn information criterion, for example, the optimal number of leads and lags (6 and 13) for the model clearly exceeds the time period in which FRE was in place.

14.5.1 Main Results under the FMOLS

FMOLS results for the coefficients of all independent variables are significant at the conventional level and have the expected signs and magnitudes.[9] The coefficient of the NTR has the expected negative sign and is statistically significant. The estimated long-run semi-elasticity of CSP with regard to the NTR (−0.306) indicates that when NTR (the net BTT rate) increases by 0.1 percentage points, the level of CSP decreases by approximately 3 percent in the long run.[10]

This estimated semi-elasticity implies a negative impact on the level of bank deposits in Argentina of between 16.5 percent and 44.4 percent in the period from December 2001 to June 2010, when going from the minimum NTR of 0.5 percent to the maximum NTR of 1.2 percent.[11] This represents a negative impact on the overall level of savings and checking account deposits of about 2 percent of GDP. Currently the BTT impact is lower because of the deductibility of the BTT against other taxes (37.5 percent of the tax paid) and it is equivalent to 27.4 percent of the total CSP balance.

The impact of the control variables on the level of CSP is also as expected. The long-run elasticity of CSP with regard to the GDP of 1.227 indicates that if monthly GDP increases by 1 percent, the CSP increases by approximately 1.2 percent, indicating that deposits increase slightly more than proportional to real income.[12] Also as expected, the interest rate impacts negatively the level of deposits since an increase in the interest rate induces substitution toward interest-bearing financial instruments such as time deposits. The policy variables (SAL, VATref, and FRE) have also a significant impact on CPS in the long run.

14.5.2 Further Results

Dynamic Effects
Attention focuses here on the possibility that over time the negative impact of the tax on the level of deposits becomes larger as economic

agents discover new ways of avoiding the tax. For that purpose a subsample is chosen to run the FMOLS model over the earlier period January 1996 to January 2006. The coefficient of the NTR for this subsample turns to be much lower (−0.20) and statistically significant.[13] Although this result may be influenced by the smaller sample size, it provides some preliminary evidence in favor of the existence of dynamic effects. The impact of the tax on deposit balances over time appears to be larger, even when the tax rate has been reduced.

Tax Credit
A further robustness check has been performed to analyze the relationship between the nominal banking transaction tax rate (NOR) and the portion of this rate that can be deducted against other taxes (CRE) using the FMOLS approach. As expected, the analysis shows that an increase in the rate of deductibility of the BTT significantly reduces the negative impact of the BTT on the level of deposits. The results are presented in table B14.3 in the appendix.

14.6   Policy Implications: Discussion

The main argument brought against the adoption of BTTs is the tax's distortive effect: its negative impact on financial intermediation, which in turn ends up causing a decline in the productivity of the tax over time. As a result of a declining revenue yield, policy makers are left with the option of periodically modifying the tax rate, finding ways to review the constantly eroding base or simply letting the tax expire.

The BTT, by targeting exactly those financial instruments (bank transactions) that are meant to reduce the cost of commercial transactions, operates in a direction that is opposite to the objective of settling transactions quickly and at a low cost, thus hitting at the heart of the financial machinery. No wonder that economic agents over time will gradually develop alternative payment mechanisms to avoid the tax. A trivial such mechanism is to make payments in cash, rather than in checks, which has been confirmed by the evidence, suggesting an increase in the ratio of currency held by the public to bank deposits in several countries in the period right after the adoption of BTTs (Arbelaez et al. 2005). However, financial disintermediation may take other forms, like transferring bank balances abroad or portfolio reallocations.

The results presented in section 14.5 provide empirical evidence supporting the hypothesis that indeed, as in the case of Argentina, the

BTT has caused financial disintermediation by providing incentives to economic agents to draw down on their bank deposits subjected to the tax. This negative effect has been estimated at about 2 percentage points of GDP, depending on time period and, clearly, the tax rate.

An equally relevant issue is how sizeable is the effect, also compared to other financial transaction taxes, and what could explain the size of the impact. Box 14.1 summarizes the impact of alternative financial transaction taxes on their respective tax base for a number of countries. The BTT semi-elasticity in Argentina (0.3 to a tax increase of 1 basis point) appears to be low in comparison. This can be explained by the fact that the BTT base in Argentina has less substitution alternatives than other financial instruments, even more considering that Argentina is not a financially integrated economy. However, as it is mentioned (box 14.1), semi-elasticities tend to be region/instrument specific which makes extrapolation of FTTs to other countries very difficult.

14.7 Concluding Remarks

Like many other LACs, Argentina turned to a BTT during a crisis with the aim of increasing tax collection rapidly and eliminating it once the crisis had finished. The tax was nonetheless maintained at a high rate once the economic crisis was over, in spite of its potential distortions. Although some countries only tax withdrawals, in Argentina the scope of the BTT includes deposits and withdrawals from savings and checking accounts.

The aim of this study was to estimate the impact of the BTT on savings and checking account deposits (CSP) in Argentina. For this purpose the long-run relationship between CSP and its determinants has been examined, using four different models based on co-integration techniques. Overall, the econometric analysis shows a negative impact of the BTT on the level of bank deposits in Argentina that is robust to different model specifications, and the inclusion of alternative policy variables.

The estimated coefficients based on the preferred model specification indicate a long-run semi-elasticity of CSP with regard to the NTR of −0.306, which means that when NTR (the net BTT rate) increases by 0.1 percentage points the level of CSP decreases by approximately 3 percent in the long run. This result is taken as an indication that, as in other countries, the BTT has also caused financial disintermediation in Argentina. The BTT appears to have provided incentives to economic agents

Box 14.1
Semi-elasticity of existing taxes on financial transactions

Previous literature has focused on how individual (selective) financial transactions taxes (broadly defined) negatively affect the volume of transactions. A survey of this literature is presented in a recent paper by Copenhagen Economics (2012).

In addition to the BTT, financial transactions taxes include:

- *Securities transaction tax (STT)*   Levied on the gross transaction volume of equity securities, debt securities, and related derivate products including options, swaps, futures, and forward traded in exchanges and over-the-counter.
- *Currency transaction tax (CTT)*   Levied on the gross transaction volume of foreign exchange transactions in spot markets as well as in future and derivatives markets involving currency transactions.

The most common transaction tax among G20 countries is a tax on transactions in equity and bonds (Australia, Brazil, Chile, France, Italy, Russia, South Africa, Switzerland, Turkey, United Kingdom, etc.). Only a few countries (United Kingdom, India, and Taiwan) impose taxes on derivative transactions such as options and futures. Brazil is a prominent example of a country that levies a tax on foreign exchange transactions and capital inflows. Tax rates on equity transactions are usually between 0.1 and 0.5 percent with some variation across countries.

The size of the semi-elasticity is most likely related to:

- *Substitution alternatives*   If the financial product being taxed has many substitutes, the tax base will be very elastic.
- *Region*   Since elasticity estimates can be very sensitive to the specific region and market analyzed.
- *Time frame*   Long-run elasticities seem larger than short-run elasticities as over time, there will be larger opportunities for financial innovation and trading transfer to off-shore markets.

For the country studies analyzed in previous literature, the size of the semi-elasticities, measured as the response in the volume of traded financial products to a tax increase of 1 basis point (0.01 percent), has been in the range of 0.5 to 4 on equity transactions and 28 to 85 on fixed income securities (the latest value was explained in the literature by a massive shift in Sweden, 1948 to 1991, where the elasticity reached 98 percent, from futures trade on exchanges to over-the-counter forward contracts that were exempt from the tax).

to develop alternative payment mechanisms to avoid the tax, such as relying more on cash to make commercial transactions, and other forms of portfolio reallocation. A somehow more sophisticated form of financial disintermediation implies the transfer of bank balances abroad.

The BTT elasticity in Argentina compared with the response of other financial transactions to FTTs (box 14.1) appears to be low. This can be explained by the fact that the BTT base in Argentina has less substitution alternatives than other financial instruments, even more considering that Argentina is not a financially integrated economy.

While this study is the first to analyze the impact of the BTT on deposits in Argentina, it confirms the results obtained in previous literature for other Latin American countries. While the negative impact of the tax on the level of deposits in Argentina is quantitatively very much in line with those found in other countries such as Venezuela, Colombia, and Ecuador (e.g., see Kirilenko and Summers 2003), this study confirm the results in the literature of a negative impact of the BTT on financial intermediation, thereby undermining savings, investment, and growth, particularly in emerging market economies (Arbelaez et al. 2005; Matheson 2010).

Appendix A: Dependent and Independent Variables

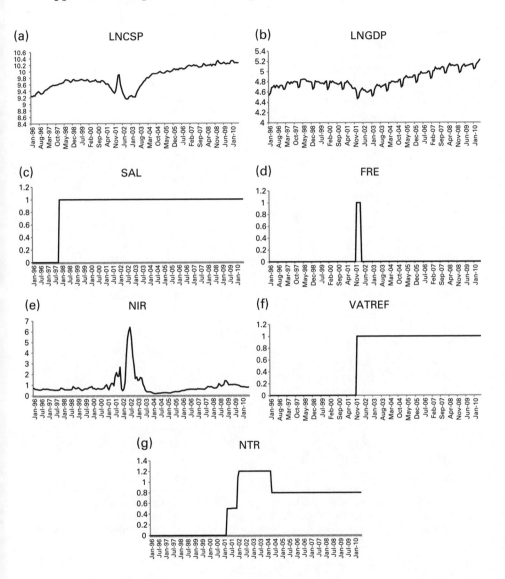

Appendix B: Cointegration Analysis and Further Results

Table B14.1
VAR lag order selection criteria

Endogenous variables: LNCSP LNGDP NIR
Exogenous variables: C NTR FRE SAL VATREF
Sample: 1996M01 2010M06
Included observations: 154

Lag	Log L	LR	FPE	AIC	SC	HQ
0	21.42	NA	0.00	−0.08	0.21	0.04
1	469.50	849.60	0.00	−5.79	−5.31	−5.59
2	495.92	49.08	0.00	−6.01	−5.36	−5.75
3	531.15	64.04	0.00	−6.35	−5.52	−6.02
4	548.96	31.70	0.00	−6.47	−5.46	−6.06
5	572.67	41.26	0.00	−6.66	−5.47	−6.18
6	587.74	25.63	0.00	−6.74	−5.38	−6.18
7	601.61	23.07	0.00	−6.80	−5.26	−6.18
8	610.36	14.19	0.00	−6.80	−5.08	−6.10
9	637.13	42.42	0.00	−7.03	−5.13	−6.26
10	657.29	31.15	0.00	−7.17	−5.10	−6.33
11	763.40	159.85	0.00	−8.43	−6.19	−7.52
12	796.79	49.01	0.00	−8.75	−6.32	−7.77
13	824.81	40.02	0.00	−9.00	−6.39*	−7.94
14	840.12	21.28	0.00	−9.08	−6.30	−7.95
15	853.55	18.14	0.00	−9.14	−6.18	−7.94
16	870.41	22.12	0.00	−9.24	−6.10	−7.97
17	889.31	24.05	0.00	−9.37	−6.05	−8.02
18	904.80	19.12*	0.00	−9.45	−5.96	−8.03*
19	914.89	12.05	0.00	−9.47	−5.80	−7.98
20	929.46	16.85	0.00*	−9.53*	−5.69	−7.98

Note: * indicates lag order selected by the criterion. LR: sequential modified LR test statistic (each test at 5% level). FPE: Final prediction error. AIC: Akaike information criterion. SC: Schwarz information criterion. HQ: Hannan–Quinn information criterion

Table B14.2
Johansen co-integration test summary
Sample: 1996M01 2010M06

Included observations:156
Series: LNCSP LNGDP NIR
Exogenous series: NTR FRE SAL VATREF
Lags interval: 1 to 17

Data trend:	None	None	Linear	Linear	Quadratic
Test type	No Intercept	Intercept	Intercept	Intercept	Intercept
	No trend	No trend	No trend	Trend	Trend
Trace	1	1	1	1	1
Max eigenvalue	1	1	1	1	1

*Critical values based on MacKinnon–Haug–Michelis (1999)

Information criteria by rank and model

Data trend	None	None	Linear	Linear	Quadratic
Rank or	No Intercept	Intercept	Intercept	Intercept	Intercept
number of CEs	No trend	No trend	No trend	Trend	Trend

Loglikelihood by rank (rows) and model (columns)

0	855.27	855.27	856.69	856.69	866.95
1	902.80	913.81	915.13	915.28	917.03
2	905.72	916.74	916.74	920.79	921.79
3	905.72	916.81	916.81	922.39	922.39

Akaike information criteria by rank (rows) and model (columns)

0	−9.00	−9.00	−8.98	−8.98	−9.08
1	−9.54	−9.66*	−9.66	−9.64	−9.64
2	−9.50	−9.61	−9.60	−9.63	−9.63
3	−9.42	−9.52	−9.52	−9.56	−9.56

Schwarz criteria by rank (rows) and model (columns)

0	−6.01	−6.01	−5.93	−5.93	−5.97
1	−6.43	−6.53*	−6.49	−6.46	−6.42
2	−6.27	−6.35	−6.31	−6.30	−6.28
3	−6.08	−6.12	−6.12	−6.10	−6.10

Table B14.3
FMOLS and CCR coefficients estimates (NOR)

	Fully modified least squares		Canonical co-integrating regression	
	Coefficient	Standard error	Coefficient	Standard error
Intercept	3.925***	0.555	3.83***	0.587
Endogenous variables				
LNGDP	1.163***	0.117	1.183***	0.124
NIR	−0.055***	0.014	-0.057***	0.014
Exogenous variables				
NOR	−0.350***	0.095	−0.337***	0.096
CRE	0.348***	0.122	0.327***	0.129
VATref	0.458***	0.091	0.446***	0.091
SAL	0.230***	0.042	0.228***	0.042
FRE	0.151*	0.087	0.158*	0.090
R^2	0.872		0.872	
Adjusted R^2	0.867		0.860	
Standard error of regression	0.124		0.124	
Durbin–Watson statistic	0.814		0.820	

Note: *** (**, *) indicate significance at 1(5, 10) percent, respectively.

Notes

We are grateful to Ruud De Mooij, Gaëtan Nicodème, Marcel Gérard, Herman Kamil, Bernardo Lischinsky, Thornton Matheson, and John Norregaard for their useful comments and suggestions. The views expressed herein are those of the authors and should not be attributed to the IMF, its Executive Board, or its Management. Financial support from CESifo to this study is gratefully acknowledged.

1. The Hungarian BTT presents only very few exemptions, for instance, on the operations carried out by the Central Bank.

2. The highest revenue achieved in relative terms was the 3.4 percent of GDP reached in Ecuador's short-lived Impuesto a la Circulacion de los Capitales ICC (1999–2000), creditable against income tax. Brazil's unpopular CPMF (Contribuição Provisória sobre Movimentação ou Transmissão de Valores e de Créditos e Direitos de Natureza Financeira), dating back to 1993, levied a charge of 0.38 percent (originally 0.25 percent) on all withdrawals from checking accounts. It raised as much as US$10 billion per annum or about 4 percent of total government revenue. This tax expired in December 2007 (though another transactions tax known as the IOF was retained, albeit subject to modifications during 2008). A much higher tax rate of 1.5 percent was imposed by Venezuela in its bank debits tax of 2007, but this was limited to debits on behalf of enterprises. Colombia has a bank debit tax that was made permanent at a rate of 0.3 percent in 2001. Its revenue contribution equals to about 0.8 percent of GDP, or over 5 percent of total tax revenue (Arbelaez et al. 2005). The comparison of the BTT revenue must be used with caution, since some measures and regulations encourage people to use the banking system (means of payments), andthis may also explain the level of BTT revenue.

3. Since January 2002 the amount of bank account weekly withdrawals increased to AR$500.

4. The VAT credit card refund was 3 percent, and it was in force until December 2007. The debit card refund is still in force.

5. Aimed at reducing evasion, it was originally implemented by the federal tax administration (AFIP) by Resolution 151, and replaced in 2003 by AFIP Resolution 1547. In November 2000, a law (República Argentina, Ley 25345/00) ratified the previous AFIP Resolutions. In April 2001, a new law (República Argentina, Ley 25413/01) reinforced the previous legislation by reducing the amount to AR$1,000.

6. This regulation was extended gradually in 1997, 1998, and 2000 adding companies with 250 employees or more, 100 employees or more, and 25 employees or more, respectively, until it was finally extended to all companies.

7. Two unit root tests were performed for each variable (excluding dummies) using Augmented Dickey–Fuller (ADF) and Phillips–Perron (PP) tests. The results indicate the presence of a unit root for the variables measured in levels; however, they do not fail to reject the null hypothesis of a unit root for the variables measured in first differences.

8. We also include linear trend in the data and a constant in the co-integrating equation.

9. This result controls for seasonality by introducing centered (orthogonalized) seasonal-dummy variables (which shift the mean without contributing to the trend of the VAR) for December, June, and July.

10. The elasticity evaluated at the mean of the NTR (when the tax was in force between April 2001 and June 2010) of 0.87 is −0.27; that is, with a 10 percent increase in NTR, deposits decrease in 2.7 percent approximately (this 10 percent increase is somewhat lower than the 0.1 percentage point increase).

11. The highest negative impact occurred between March 2002 and May 2004 when the tax rate reached its maximum of 1.2 percent and no tax credit was allowed.

12. Additionally a control for GDP per capita has been included to capture any general trends in financial intermediation. The result, however, does not differ significantly either qualitatively or quantitatively.

13. All other variables also show the expected signs and are also statistically significant.

References

Arbelaez, M., L. Burman, and S. Zuluaga. 2005. The bank debit tax in Colombia. In R. Bird, J. Poterba, and J. Slemrod, eds., *Fiscal Reform in Colombia: Problems and Prospects*. Cambridge: MIT Press, 225–45.

Baca-Campodonico, J., L. de Mello, and A. Kirilenko. 2006. The rates and revenue of bank transaction taxes. Working paper 494. Economics Department, OECD.

Barro, R. J. 1976. Integral constraints and aggregation in an inventory model of money demand. *Journal of Finance* 31 (1): 77–88.

Brondolo, J. 2011. Taxing financial transactions: An assessment of administrative feasibility. Working paper 11/185. IMF.

Claessens, S., M. Keen, and C. Pazarbasioglu. 2010. *Financial Sector Taxation. The IMF's Report to the G-20 and Background Material.* Washington, DC: IMF.

Coelho, I., L. Ebrill, and V. Summers. 2001. Bank debit taxes in Latin America: An analysis of recent trends. Working paper 01/67. IMF.

Copenhagen Economics. 2012. Elasticities of financial instruments, profits and remuneration. Taxation paper 30-2012.

Giraldo, M., and B. Buckles. 2011. The impact of financial transactions taxes on money demand in Colombia. *Latin American Journal of Economics* 48 (1): 65–88.

Honohan, P., and S. Yoder. 2010. Financial transactions tax: Panacea, threat, or damp squib? *The World Bank Research Observer* 25(2): 138–61. .

Johansen, S. 1988. Statistical analysis of co-integration vectors. *Journal of Economic Dynamics and Control* 12: 231–54.

Johansen, S. 1991. Estimation and hypothesis testing of co-integration vectors in Gaussian vector autoregressive models. *Econometrica* 59: 1551–80.

Johansen, S. 1995. *Likelihood-Based Inference in Co-integrated Vector Autoregressive Models.* New York: Oxford University Press.

Kirilenko, A., and V. Summers. 2003. Bank debit taxes: Yield versus disintermediation. In P. Honohan, ed., *Taxation of Financial Intermediation: Theory and Practice for Emerging Economies.* New York: Oxford University Press, 313–24.

Koyama, S., and M. Nakane. 2001. Os efeitos da CPMF sobre a intermediaão financeira. Trabalhos para discussão 23. Banco Central do Brasil.

MacKinnon, J., A. Haug, and L. Michelis. 1999. Numerical distribution Functions of likelihood ratio tests for cointegration. *Journal of Applied Econometrics* 14: 563–77.

Matheson, T. 2010. Taxing financial transactions: Issues and evidence. Working paper 11/54. IMF.

Park, J. Y. 1992. Canonical co-integrating regressions. *Econometrica* 60 (January): 119–43.

Phillips, P., and B. Hansen. 1990. Statistical inference in instrumental variables regression with (I) processes. *Review of Economic Studies* 57: 99–125.

República Argentina. 2000. Ley 25345/00. Boletin Oficial. November.

República Argentina. 2001. Ley 25413/01. Boletin Oficial. April.

República Argentina. 2001. Decreto 1402/01. Boletin Oficial.November.

República Argentina. 2001. Decreto 1570/01. Boletin Oficial. December.

Saikkonen, P. 1992. Estimation and testing of co-integrated systems by an autoregressive approximation. *Econometric Theory* 8: 1–27.

Stock, J. H., and M. W. Watson. 1993. A simple estimator of co-integrated vectors in higher order integrated systems. *Econometrica* 61 (4): 783–820.

15 The 2011 FDIC Assessment on Banks' Managed Liabilities: Interest Rate and Balance-Sheet Responses

Lawrence L. Kreicher, Robert N. McCauley, and Patrick McGuire

15.1 Introduction

The global financial crisis led to a variety of proposals to levy taxes on the financial sector (Alworth and Arachi 2012; Hemmelgarn and Nicodème 2012; Lloyd 2012). Some proposed *corrective or Pigovian* taxes that would raise the private cost of financial choices that impose broader social costs. By analogy, economists have long proposed to curb air pollution efficiently by imposing taxes that make the polluter pay the social costs of sulfur emissions (Schultze 1977). In addition to regulating banks to limit leverage or dependence on short-term funding, the government could tax borrowing or short-term debt (Masciandaro and Passarelli 2012).

Proposals for corrective taxes on the financial sector have focused either on big *institutions* or on fragile *balance-sheet structures*. Acharya et al. (2009) argued for a systemic risk tax on individual banks with large market equity capitalization losses during big market sell-offs. Shin (2010) urged a tax on non-core liabilities and Weder di Mauro (2010a, b) proposed a hybrid. While the Basel Committee on Banking Supervision (2012) reports post-crisis international cooperation on higher required capital for systemically important banks, new taxes on banks have been national. Some European countries have taxed bonuses (IMF 2010; Alworth and Arachi 2012). Similarly, while not explicitly a tax, Dodd–Frank's widening of the FDIC assessment (in effect, tax) base from domestic deposits to assets less tangible equity affected only US chartered banks and not even all banks in the United States.

This widening of the FDIC base had a rapid effect on prices *and* quantities. The price effect is easily stated: banks passed the cost of the new assessment on to lenders of short-term funds, and lowered the cost of short-term US dollar debt. And linkages between onshore and offshore money market yields weakened. The quantity effects differ because the policy change only affected a subset of banks. It bound banks in the United States holding a US charter, and these banks shifted their funding, repaying wholesale funding from abroad and relying more on domestic deposits. With few exceptions the policy change did not bind foreign bank branches in the United States, and they drew in massive net wholesale funding from abroad.

Viewed as a corrective policy, the policy can be seen as a partial success. US chartered banks now rely more on stable domestic deposits and less on volatile wholesale funds. But, thanks to the massive injection of bank reserves that financed the Federal Reserve's large purchases of bonds, the risk of a unilateral policy, in the sense that it affects one particular category of banks, is already evident.[1] The policy has had the unintended side effect of increasing the share of US banking assets on the books of US branches of foreign-chartered banks.

A world in which banks headquartered outside the United States intermediate a larger share of dollars may not prove more financially stable, despite more stable funding for US chartered banks. Banks *without* a US charter have much of their dollar assets outside the United States, which cannot readily be discounted at the Federal Reserve. Their ongoing reliance on wholesale dollar funding could leave them more vulnerable to runs. To be sure, this concern remains hypothetical as long as foreign banks are flush with reserves at the Fed. However, we interpret foreign banks' disproportionate take-up of Fed reserves as merely the *initial manifestation* of the reconfiguration of global dollar banking to which the new incentives lead.[2]

The rest of this chapter is in four parts. In section 15.2, we describe the change in the FDIC assessment. In section 15.3, we examine its impact on overnight and term interest rates. In section 15.4, we analyze banks' balance-sheet responses using quarterly call reports and flow of funds data. We conclude in section 15.5.

15.2   The FDIC Assessment Change

The Banking Act of 1933 created the Federal Deposit Insurance Corporation (FDIC) as an independent agency of the US government in response to widespread banking failures, depositor losses, and bank runs. The FDIC currently insures deposits at US chartered banks up to a limit of $250,000 per account. In addition it has primary or backup supervisory responsibility for all insured banks and acts as the receiver for failed banks. Assessments paid by insured banks and earnings on its investment portfolio fund the FDIC's Deposit Insurance Fund.

Signed into law on July 21, 2010, Dodd–Frank mandated the FDIC to widen its assessments base (on which charges are levied to build up the FDIC insurance fund) from adjusted domestic deposits to total assets less tangible shareholders' equity (see Hein et al. 2012). The FDIC issued proposals in November 2010 and published final rules and regulations in February 2011 (FDIC 2011).

Before the FDIC published the proposed rules in November, market participants hoped that reserve holdings at the Federal Reserve might be excluded from the asset base (Smedley 2010). Apart from a partial exemption for custodian banks, the FDIC generally included reserve holdings in the FDIC assessment base.

This inclusion would disturb the so-called arbitrage in which banks borrowed overnight from non-banks unable to place at the Fed at its going rate of 25 basis points. If banks were going to have to pay the FDIC to borrow from wholesale lenders, then they would have to offer fewer basis points for overnight funds.[3]

How many fewer basis points would depend on the rate paid to the FDIC on the newly assessed liabilities. This is not easily ascertained from the FDIC schedule, especially for large and highly complex institutions (table 15.1). The rate depends on a bank's riskiness, as summarized by its regulatory (CAMELS) rating, with adjustments for more long-term unsecured debt (downward) and more brokered deposits (upward). Whalen (2011, p. 7), cites an estimate from the specialist *IRA Bank Monitor* for JPMorgan Chase of $1.4 billion on an assessment base of $1.785 trillion, for an estimated 8 basis point rate. Given market estimates of CAMELS, mega-bank Wells Fargo is generally considered to pay a lower rate, and Citigroup a higher rate.

The clear intention of the wider assessment and lower rate on deposits was to shift the burden of FDIC assessments from small to big banks. "Aggregate premiums paid by institutions with less than $10 billion in assets will decline by approximately 30 percent, primarily due to the assessment base change," testified the FDIC's Gruenberg (2011).[4] Whalen (2011) cites estimates of a 33 to 576 percent rise for the top ten banks (table 15.2). "The result will be a sharing of the assessment burden that better reflects each group's share of industry assets" (Bair 2011).

When would one expect banks to begin to respond to the policy change? Until the November 2010 FDIC proposal, bankers had hoped

Table 15.1
FDIC insurance schedule as of April 1, 2011 (basis points)

	Risk category I	Risk category II	Risk category III	Risk category IV	Large and highly complex institutions
Initial base assessment rate	5–9	14	23	35	5–35
Unsecured debt adjustment	–4.5–0	–5–0	–5–0	–5–0	–5–0
Brokered deposit adjustment	....	0–10	0–10	0–10	0–10
Total base assessment rate	2.5–9	9–24	18–33	30–45	2.5–45

Source: FDIC (2011, 10717)
Note: Total base assessment rates exclude the depository institution debt adjustment.
Risk categories range from low (I) to high (IV).

Table 15.2
Estimated change in FDIC assessment base for top ten US banks

	2010 base ($ billions)	2011 base ($ billions)	Percent change
JPMorgan Chase	670	1,785	167
Bank of America	943	1,737	84
Citigroup	336	1,317	291
Wells Fargo	786	1,155	47
US Bancorp	178	308	74
PNC Financial	182	272	50
Capital One Financial	122	199	64
Bank of New York Mellon	76	196	156
SunTrust Banks	122	163	33
State Street Corp	23	156	576

Source: Whalen (2011, 7), citing FDIC(RIS)/*The IRA Bank Monitor*

that holdings of reserves would be excluded the FDIC's definition of the assessment base. By the end of the year 2010, bankers could foresee the new regime that would start in April 2011.

Therefore we interpret the first quarter of 2011 as the beginning of the adjustment period to the new FDIC policy. To the extent that the policy change gave incentives for an altered flow of short-term funds, new channels would require the arrangement of new credit lines and increases in existing lines. Since the assessment for the second quarter would depend on the average balance sheet in that quarter, bankers needed to start rearranging their balance sheets before the end of the first quarter. Thus in what follows, we take calendar 2010 as the *before* period, and April 1, 2011, to March 31, 2012, as the *after* period.

This timing means that the adjustment to the new FDIC policy coincided with the forced increase in bank reserves that resulted from the Federal Reserve's decision in its early November 2010 meeting to increase its holdings of Treasury securities by some $600 billion (the so-called QE2 or second phase of quantitative easing), or 5 percent of bank assets in the United States, over the months through June 2011 (Ennis and Wolman 2011).

The coincidence of the FDIC assessment change and the Fed's injection of assets that only banks in the United States can hold presented challenges to the US chartered banks, including US subsidiaries of foreign-headquartered banks, that dominate US commercial banking. They funded only two-thirds of their assets of $10 trillion at end of September 2010 with deposits, and large banks even less (see below); most of the rest was funded by managed liabilities such as interbank borrowings, repos, and funds borrowed from their overseas affiliates (so-called eurodollars). Since these wholesale funding sources would now be part of their FDIC assessment base, US chartered banks had every reason to drop their bids for such funds and to take on as little of the new claims on the Fed as possible.

For their part, US branches and agencies of foreign banks could hold more reserves at the Fed without paying the FDIC assessment on any wholesale funding. That is because they are not generally covered by deposit insurance.[5]

15.3   Money Market Rates, Onshore and Offshore

This section analyzes the effect the change in the FDIC assessment base on money market rates, the primary channels through which the Fed communicated and implemented its monetary policy. We have two questions in mind. First, what happened to the *level* of money market rates? We find that overnight and term money market rates fell by 5 to 10 basis points, which suggests that banks largely passed on the tax to providers of wholesale funding.[6] Second, what happened to the *linkage* between onshore and offshore rates in the global dollar money market? Falling only on some banks in the United States, the new assessment loosened this linkage, suggesting an unintended consequence of a less immediate monetary transmission. A looser linkage between onshore and offshore rates also provides perspective on the disparate balance-sheet responses examined in the next section.

We analyze not two, but three overnight rates because the financial crisis of 2007 to 2008 disrupted the normal functioning of uncollateralised overnight dollar money markets (see the appendix for a description).[7] As providers of funds became more wary about taking on credit risk in lending to banks, unsecured markets (fed funds, eurodollars) dried up, while transactions in secured markets such as repurchase agreements (repos) held up.[8] While previous analyses of the relationship between onshore and offshore overnight rates have focused on federal funds and eurodollars, we also include overnight repos to reflect the shift in liquidity to that secured market during the crisis. The federal funds market, the eurodollar market, and the Treasury general collateral finance repo market serve as key funding sources for global banks. Numerous large non-bank entities are also active participants in these markets, including securities firms, money market mutual funds, and government agencies (table 15.3).

The source for our price data on overnight eurodollar and Treasury repo transactions is ICAP, one of the premier inter-dealer brokers in the

Table 15.3
Major US dollar money market participants

	Federal funds market (1)	Eurodollar market (2)	Repo market (3)
Borrowers	Depository institutions	Depository institutions	Depository institutions Broker-dealers
Lenders	Depository institutions Broker-dealers Government-sponsored enterprises	Money market funds Financial and nonfinancial lenders	Money market funds Securities lenders Government-sponsored enterprises

Source: Marquez et al (2012)

global marketplace. We make use of their daily effective rates for euro-dollars and Treasury repo, which are based on transactions occurring during the New York City trading day.[9] For consistency, we also use ICAP's measure of the effective fed funds rate.

15.3.1 The Overnight Market for Unsecured Funds in the Post-crisis Period

When the Federal Reserve began paying interest on required and excess bank reserve balances in October 2008, it thought that "[p]aying interest on excess balances should help to establish a lower bound on the federal funds rate."[10] At the outset, however, this expectation turned out to be incorrect as the effective fed funds rate (and its closely aligned sister rate on overnight eurodollars) both traded below the interest-on-excess-reserves rate. In December 2008 the Fed accepted this outcome by setting the interest rate on excess reserves equal to 25 basis points, and establishing a target range for the fed funds rate of 0 to 25 basis points.[11]

Overnight rates trading below the Fed's interest rate on excess reserves leaves an arbitrage opportunity—depository institutions with accounts at the Fed (e.g., US chartered banks and US branches and agencies of foreign banks) could borrow cheap funds in the market and then take delivery of those funds at the Fed, earning a risk-free profit. Why did it persist? Following Bech and Klee (2011), it persisted because banks that could receive the 25 basis points were unwilling to leverage their balance sheets without earning a spread, even though the excess reserves are seen as risk-free. Cash-rich non-banks such as the government-sponsored enterprises (Fannie Mae and Freddie Mac), and money market mutual funds were at the same time *not* able to receive the 25 basis points from the Fed.

This equilibrium in the market for overnight, unsecured funds is illustrated in the right-hand panel of figure 15.1. Total demand for overnight unsecured funds (here we combine the fed funds and euro-dollar markets for ease of exposition) is shown by the downward-sloping solid black line in the right-hand panel. Government-sponsored enterprises, money market funds, and others, supply overnight funds along the upward-sloping solid black line. Their intersection illustrates the market equilibrium with quantity T_0 of funds changing hands at an overnight rate equal to r_0. In the left-hand panel we have decomposed the demand for overnight funds between that of US chartered banks and that of US branches and agencies of foreign banks. These schedules are downward sloping because banks are assumed to require ever larger concessions to the rate received on excess reserves to expand their balance sheets by borrowing. Since branches and agencies have an aggregate balance sheet that is much smaller than that of US chartered banks, their demand for funds is assumed to be less—shifted to the left—at every interest rate, while again for ease of exposition, we assume that the average minimum concession for all banks with access to the Fed's 25 basis points is $[25 - R^0]$. The initial equilibrium uptakes are D_0 for US chartered banks and F_0 for foreign branches and agencies.

The new FDIC balance-sheet assessment raised the all-in cost of funds for US chartered banks performing this arbitrage, leaving them at a disadvantage relative to branches of foreign banks. The size of this disadvantage, that is, the FDIC assessment *rate*, is particular to each US chartered bank, risk-related, and not made public by the FDIC, as described in section 15.2. Clearly, US chartered banks, paying the new assessment on wholesale funding, could not pay 18 basis points for overnight funding and 10 basis points to the FDIC only to receive 25 basis points from the Fed.

An insured bank necessarily must lower its bid for overnight funding, shown as a leftward shift in the demand schedule for US chartered banks to the dashed line in figure 15.1, left-hand panel. A new equilibrium for overnight unsecured funds is predictably found at a smaller quantity T_1 and lower interest rate r_1, in the right-hand panel of figure 15.1, where the size of the changes depend on the interest rate elasticities of the total supply and demand schedules. Notice

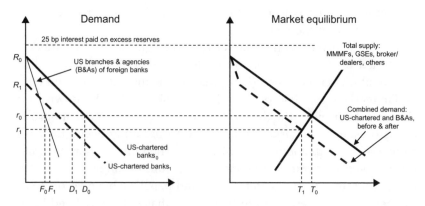

Figure 15.1
Supply of and demand for overnight unsecured funds

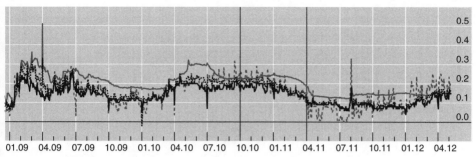

— Effective federal funds rate
— Libor
····· Eurodollar[a]
--- Repo[b]

Figure 15.2
US dollar overnight money market rates. The vertical lines indicate the announcement of the change to the FDIC assessment base and its implementation (April 1, 2011). (a) Uncollateralized, HEDDR; (b) collateralized with Treasury securities, i-repo.
Sources: ICAP, British Bankers' Association, Bloomberg

that the uptake of overnight funds by US chartered banks falls to D_1 from D_0, in the left-hand panel of figure 15.1, but the uptake by now more competitive branches and agencies of foreign banks actually rises from F_0 to F_1.

The price and quantity predictions of this simple model of US dollar overnight rates are readily confirmed. In figure 15.2 the solid black and dotted lines for the effective fed funds and overnight eurodollar both declined in the lead-up to the April 1, 2011, widening of the FDIC assessment base. Unlike the pre-crisis targeting of a single rate for the effective federal funds, the Fed's target of a 25 basis point range allowed new balance-sheet constraints on market participants to change overnight rates without Fed resistance.

The aggregate quantity of fed funds sold also dropped. Call report data indicate that, across all banks in the United States, the amount of "fed funds sold," or Fed reserves lent out by one bank to another (mostly overnight), stood at $255 billion at end-2008 (figure 15.3, upper panel). This stock fell to $89 billion by end-Q1 2010, when the Fed's first round of bond-buying with excess reserves ("quantitative easing") came to a close. As predicted, it fell further, to $54 billion by end-Q4 2011, after the change in the FDIC assessment as well as the Fed's second round of quantitative easing. The lower panel of figure 15.3 shows that non-banks with accounts at the Fed like Fannie and Freddie

(a)

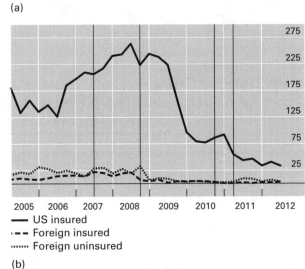

2005   2006   2007   2008   2009   2010   2011   2012
— US insured
·== Foreign insured
······ Foreign uninsured

(b)

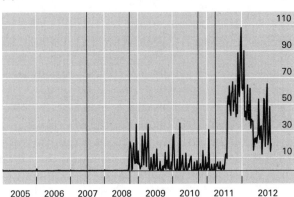

2005   2006   2007   2008   2009   2010   2011   2012

Figure 15.3
Activity and friction in the federal funds market (in billions of US dollars). (a) Federal funds sold; (b) other nonreserve deposits at the Federal Reserve. The vertical lines indicate the start of the financial crisis (end-Q2 2007), the collapse of Lehman Brothers (end-Q3 2008), the announcement of the change to the FDIC assessment base (end-Q3 2010) and its implementation (April 1, 2011).
Sources: Federal Financial Institutions Examination Council, Call Reports (form FFIEC 002); Federal Reserve H.4.1 release

(Wall 2011) often failed to sell their holdings at the Fed, suggesting credit and strategic (Bech and Klee 2011) frictions.

15.3.2 The New FDIC Assessment, Overnight Yields and Who Pays

Insured banks were quick to anticipate the FDIC change. Their balance-sheet adjustments were well under way in the weeks and months leading up to the April 2011 changeover even though many banks did not learn of their new individual FDIC assessment rates until the summer of 2011. Conversations with informed observers indicated that the FDIC change cut overnight rates at the margin by 5 to 10 basis points. The lenders of short-term funds appear to have borne the brunt of this reduction.

Trading on the day of April 1, 2011, was especially turbulent, and some overnight instruments briefly traded with negative yields. One anecdote had FDIC staffers calling money market dealers that day, asking why rates had cratered. Stepping back, a review of average rates during the four quarters before and since the FDIC change tells a clear story.

Table 15.4 confirms that a transition in the level of overnight dollar interest rates occurred around April 1, 2011, with rates falling from already low levels (near 20 basis points on average) to ultra-low levels below 10 basis points. Marginal bank borrowers lowered their bids not

Table 15.4
FDIC assessment change and overnight yields *Average levels of overnight interest rates in percent before and after April 1, 2011*

Quarterly period	Effective federal funds	Eurodollars	Treasury repo	Memo: three-month OIS
1 Jan–31 Mar 2010	0.1321	0.1438	0.1289	*0.1653*
1 Apr–30 Jun 2010	0.1923	0.2168	0.2006	*0.2214*
1 Jul–30 Sep 2010	0.1822	0.2094	0.2296	*0.1852*
1 Oct–31 Dec 2010	0.1852	0.2115	0.2174	*0.1797*
1 Jan–31 Mar 2011	0.1510	0.1676	0.1566	*0.1535*
1 Apr–30 Jun 2011	0.0928	0.0994	0.0630	*0.1123*
1 Jul–30 Sep 2011	0.0883	0.0909	0.0674	*0.0931*
1 Oct–31 Dec 2011	0.0761	0.0818	0.0940	*0.0897*
1 Jan–31 Mar 2012	0.1074	0.1205	0.1537	*0.1109*

Sources: ICAP and author calculations

only in the fed funds market but in the offshore (eurodollar) market and the (secured) repo market. The new FDIC assessment affected every type of bank borrowing so that, as lenders scrambled to place their funds, the entire overnight rate complex was squeezed down toward zero. The evidence in table 15.4 is consistent with the prevailing market wisdom: the FDIC change pushed down already low overnight rates by additional 5 to 10 basis points.

Box 15.1 shows that the lower overnight rate carried over to the key benchmark short-term rate, three-month Libor. As a result a host of payers of floating interest rates, ranging from nonfinancial firms, through households with floating-rate mortgages, benefited from the wider FDIC assessment.

Box 15.1

The key to linking the FDIC assessment to term lending rates like Libor or the now defunct New York funding rate (NYFR) is a third-term rate, the dollar overnight index swap (OIS) rate. This is a fixed rate quoted by brokers that can be swapped against the average value of the effective fed funds rate over a contracted term, say three months (Wheatley 2012, pp. 47–48). Libor is simply the sum of this OIS rate and a bank credit-risk premium. Therefore the impact of the FDIC assessment on Libor operating through its impact on current and expected overnight fed funds rates is reflected in the OIS rate.

As overnight rates dropped in the first quarter of 2011, the three-month overnight index swap rate also began to fall (figure 15.4, dotted line), averaging roughly 15 basis points during this transition quarter, down from 18 basis points during the fourth quarter of 2010 (table 15.4, memo column). That is, market participants treated the declines in overnight rates as lasting ones. The three-month overnight index swap rate continued to track overnight rates lower in the two quarters after April 1, eventually matching the average decline of 9 basis points in the effective federal funds rate. After April 1, both the three-month Libor (dashed line) and the NYFR (solid line) moved lower, substantially restoring their respective pre-FDIC spreads with the OIS rate mid-year. Although European events led to wider credit-risk premia in the summer of 2011 (as well as credit frictions in the overnight market in figure 15.3, right-hand panel), the OIS rate allows us to conclude that the FDIC-induced decline in overnight rates during the first half of 2011 was substantially passed through to three-month Libor, benefiting borrowers and floating-rate payers in derivative contracts.

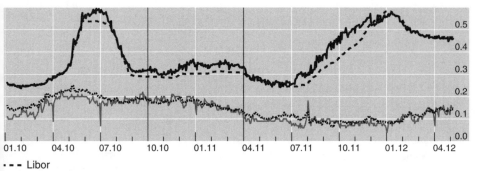

- - - Libor
········ Overnight index swap
——— Overnight effective federal funds rate
——— New York funding rate

Figure 15.4
US dollar three-month money market rates. The vertical lines indicate the announcement of the change to the FDIC assessment base and its implementation (April 1, 2011). The dollar overnight index swap is a rate for three months that can be swapped against the average effective federal funds rate for the same three months. The New York funding rate is a mid-market three-month rate reported by anonymous survey participants in the New York morning. ICAP ceased its publication in August 2012 as bank participation declined.
Sources: British Bankers' Association, ICAP

15.3.3   The FDIC Assessment Change and Money Market Integration

Because the wider FDIC assessment bound US chartered banks but not US branches and agencies of foreign banks, any overnight interest rate makes for different all-in costs for these two groups of potential borrowers. These circumstances could only weaken the linkages between market segments, especially if the composition of participants differs across market segments. In this section we consider various cross-market statistics that show that overnight dollar money markets indeed became less integrated after the FDIC assessment change.

Table 15.5 shows in the simplest terms how the relationships among our three key overnight rates have weakened, both in level terms and in terms of day-to-day changes. The tightness of every market link, as measured by its correlation coefficient, was weaker in the 12-month period after the widening of the FDIC assessment base than before. Links were looser not only for pairs involving eurodollars, which might have been particularly affected by sovereign strains in Europe, but also for the federal funds–repo pair.

Table 15.5
FDIC assessment and correlations among overnight yields and their changes

	Time period	
Rate series or change pair	Pre-FDIC 1 Jan–31 Dec 2010	Post-FDIC 1 Apr–31 Mar 2012
Fed funds vs. eurodollar	0.9259	0.8837
Fed funds vs. repo	0.8341	0.6570
Eurodollar vs. repo	0.8384	0.6854
ΔFed funds vs. Δeurodollar	0.7477	0.5719
ΔFed funds vs. Δrepo	0.6361	0.4838
ΔEurodollar vs. Δrepo	0.5876	0.4990

Sources: ICAP and author calculations

Table 15.6
Pre- and post-FDIC overnight rate convergence
Estimation of $\Delta Spread_{i\text{-}j,t} = \alpha_{i\text{-}j} + \beta_{i\text{-}j} \times Spread_{i\text{-}j,t\text{-}1} + \sum \theta_n \times \Delta Spread_{i\text{-}j,t\text{-}n} + \varepsilon_{i\text{-}j,t}$

	Time period	
Rate series spread	Pre-FDIC assessment change 1 Jan–31 Dec 2010	Post-FDIC assessment change 1 Apr 2011–31 Mar 2012
Eurodollar minus fed funds (lag = 2): beta half-life	−0.2771 2.16	−0.2172 2.83
Repo minus fed funds (lag=1): beta half-life	−0.2597 2.30	−0.2133 2.89
Eurodollar minus repo (lag = 1): beta half-life	−0.3271 1.75	−0.2352 2.59

Sources: ICAP and author calculations

A more precise regression-based analysis that focuses on the interest rate spreads between markets (table 15.6) allows us to measure the speed with which each pair of markets returns to equilibrium following a shock. The half-life of a deviation is measured as $-\ln(2)/\ln(1+\beta)$. This analysis suggests that the FDIC assessment change has slowed arbitrage across dollar overnight money markets. For example, in the key overnight fed funds and eurodollar markets during the pre-FDIC period, we observe that half of any disturbance to their rate spread away from its center of gravity is retraced in roughly two (2.16) days. Following the FDIC assessment change, that half-life lengthens to nearly three (2.83) days, an increase of more than 30 percent. Similarly the half-lives for the fed funds–repo and eurodollar–repo linkages increase by 26 and 48 percent, respectively. Clearly, the results suggest that the wider FDIC assessment loosened the integration of overnight money market segments. When the Federal Reserve again starts to change the federal funds target to signal its policy, it will have to contend with money markets that spread its policy across those markets with less immediacy.

The rate effects discussed in this section are associated with sizable adjustments in the balance sheets of US chartered and foreign-headquartered banks, adjustments made to avoid or to exploit the widening of the FDIC assessment base. In the next section we discuss what we might expect to happen, and what actually happened, in the way of balance-sheet adjustments. It turns out that the weakening of arbitrage between onshore and offshore money markets happened during a period of unwinding of cross-border funding positions.

15.4   Balance-Sheet Response to the FDIC Assessment and QE2

In this section, we analyze how US chartered banks altered their funding mix in response to the change in the FDIC assessment base. We also examine its interaction with the expansion of bank reserves at the Fed (QE2) using both aggregate flows of funds and bank-level data. The Federal Reserve's injection of a large sum of excess reserves acted like time-lapse photography by compressing what might have been longer-term adjustments into several quarters. The Fed forced US commercial banks to add 5 percent to their $12 trillion in assets in seven months in the form of excess reserves yielding 25 basis points.

Such an assessment on *nondeposit* liabilities held by some banks in the United States in an environment of forced asset growth would justify three expectations, which we explore below. First, the affected entities should rely less on the newly assessed liabilities. The data confirm that the funding model of the affected US chartered banks responded strongly to the change in the relative cost of deposits and wholesale funding. In particular, these banks bid for more deposits and at the same time repaid newly assessed liabilities to their foreign affiliates. This behavior was most marked among the biggest banks that relied more on wholesale funding and that must pay a premium for complexity in the FDIC assessment matrix.

Second, unaffected foreign bank branches and agencies could be expected to take up a disproportionate share of the excess reserves at the Fed since the all-in cost of their more elastic source of funds had not risen. The data again confirm this, notwithstanding the deterioration in the credit standing of banks from the euro area, which had some of the largest US branches and agencies.

Third, the non-affected banks would have no reason to avoid funding with the liabilities on which other banks are now paying assessments. Again, the bank-level data confirm this; foreign branches and agencies funded the new claims on the Fed by reducing their net claims on their foreign affiliates.

15.4.1 US Chartered Banks' Change in Funding Model

A tax on the *non-deposit* liabilities of US chartered banks operating in the United States can be expected to set in train important changes on the liability side of these banks' balance sheets. Specifically, the banks should economize on the newly assessed wholesale funds. The only way that they can do that is to raise more equity, which is likely to be expensive, or to gather more deposits. Indeed banks should now favor deposit over nondeposit liabilities because the (relative) regulatory cost of deposits has gone down, owing to a lower assessment on deposits (to leave the measure revenue neutral) and a new assessment on other liabilities. For example, a big bank that before paid a 10 basis point premium to the FDIC on its domestic deposits afterward pays 8 basis points on both deposit and nondeposit liabilities. Before the wider assessment base, the regulatory costs of the two funding sources differed by 10 basis points, and afterward by zero basis points. Particularly in an environment of very low rates, one would expect banks to change their funding habits in the face of such a shift in relative costs.

This is illustrated in figure 15.5, which shows how a representative bank would respond to the all-in cost of deposits falling and the all-in cost of wholesale liabilities rising (i.e., the shift from the solid lines to dashed lines). Here we make the assumption that the marginal cost of deposits is lower than the cost of wholesale funding up to a point (D_0), after which wholesale funding is cheaper. The upward shift in the all-in cost of wholesale funds leads to a higher loan rate, r_1. At the same time, a downward shift in the all-in cost of deposits leads to an increase in deposits from D_0 to D_1, and thus a rise in the ratio of deposits to loans (D_0/L_0 to D_1/L_1).

Bank quality would figure in the response of US chartered banks to the FDIC move, and affect the take-up of the Federal Reserve excess reserves. Higher quality banks with relatively low FDIC assessments

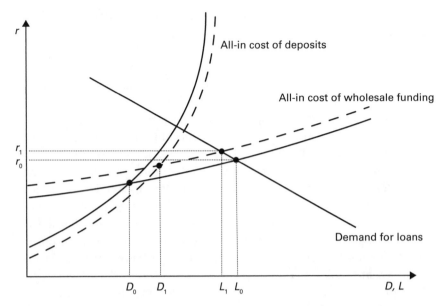

Figure 15.5
Change in the FDIC assessment base and reliance on deposits. The change in the FDIC assessment base affects the all-in cost of deposit and wholesale funding sources (shift from the solid lines to the dashed lines) for FDIC-insured banks. The widening of the assessment base from domestic deposits to total assets less equity increases the relative cost of wholesale funding. The equilibrium level of deposits shifts from D_0 to D_1.

would experience a smaller shift in the regulatory cost of deposit and nondeposit liabilities. In particular, an 8 basis point assessment of a good bank would represent a smaller wedge in the gap between the Federal funds rate and the 25 basis points on excess reserves received from the Federal Reserve, leaving more incentive to do the intermediation.

To some extent the Fed's purchase of Treasury bonds from non-bank investors produced an inflow of domestic deposits. In the first instance, an investor selling a bond to the Fed receives a credit to her bank account equal to the sales proceeds. In fact households reduced their holdings of Treasury securities by $330 billion between September 2010 and June 2011, and increased their holdings of bank deposits by $240 billion. However, institutional investors continued to accumulate Treasury securities and did not much increase their holdings of bank deposits.[12]

On balance, US chartered banks have come to rely much more on deposit funding. They took in almost $500 billion in deposits from households and firms from September 2010 to mid-2011 (table 15.7), more than double their incremental holding of reserves at the Fed. As a result of deposits growing faster than assets, US chartered banks raised their reliance on deposits from 66.7 percent of total assets in September 2010 to 69.9 percent in June 2011 and 72.6 percent by end-2011 (table 15.7).[13]

From a longer term perspective, a 7 percentage point rise in the deposit-to-asset ratio in the seven quarters through mid-2012 has no precedent (figure 15.7, lower left-hand panel). To be sure, the turning point came when dependence on wholesale funding created the greatest vulnerability, namely in the fourth quarter of 2008. However, the subsequent rise owes all to the increase in deposits (table 15.7).

Digging into the cross section, the upper panel of figure 15.6 shows that US chartered banks, whether domestic or foreign owned, raised their reliance on deposits. (In contrast, foreign bank branches in the United States, discussed in the next section, did not.) The lower panel of figure 15.6 shows that the change in the funding structure was most pronounced among large banks. Indeed the top five banks raised their ratio of deposits to assets by almost 20 percentage points. With their prior reliance on wholesale funding, these banks stood to pay up with the new FDIC assessment base (table 15.2). To avoid paying more, they sought to bring their funding model into alignment with that of smaller banks.

The wholesale funding that the big banks let run off comprised not only fed funds (figure 15.3, left-hand panel) but also eurodollar funding sourced from their affiliates offshore (figure 15.7, lower right-hand panel, rising solid line). Liabilities to affiliates abroad declined by about $100 billion during the three quarters of QE2 and by another $300 billion into 2012 (Anderson and Duca, 2014). A strong force was at work to reduce to zero in very short order a stock of liabilities that had taken years to build up.

15.4.2   US Branches of Foreign Banks and Holdings of Reserves at the Fed

Our second prediction shifts the focus from the liabilities of the banks affected by the wider FDIC assessment to the assets of the unaffected US branches of foreign banks. Unconstrained by a rise in the cost of their liabilities, foreign branches took on a disproportionate share of the reserves used by the Fed to pay for Treasury securities in QE2 (figure 15.7, upper left-hand panel, solid lines). In particular, they took

Table 15.7
Reliance on deposits by US chartered banks, in billions of US dollars

	Q3 2010	Q4 2010	Q1 2011	Q2 2011	Q3 2011	Q4 2011	Q1 2012	Q2 2012
Checkable	838	941	978	1,060	1,155	1,261	1,220	1,230
Small time	5,790	5,889	5,980	6,131	6,293	6,426	6,599	6,639
Large time	901	849	824	819	802	814	743	778
Total	7,530	7,679	7,782	8,010	8,250	8,500	8,562	8,646
Memo:								
Total assets	11,293	11,291	11,309	11,453	11,557	11,706	11,656	11,748
Deposits assets (%)	66.67	68.01	68.81	69.94	71.38	72.61	73.45	73.60

Source: Federal Reserve *Flow of Funds Statistics*

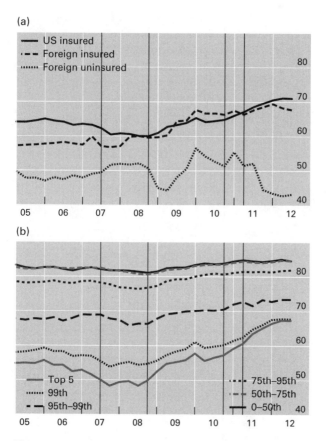

Figure 15.6
FDIC assessment change, quantitative easing, and banks' deposit funding. (a) Deposit/asset ratio; (b) deposit/asset ratio for FDIC insured banks, by percentile. The vertical lines indicate the start of the financial crisis (end-Q2 2007), the collapse of Lehman Brothers (end-Q3 2008), the announcement of the change to the FDIC assessment base (end-Q3 2010) and its implementation (April 1, 2011). Top 5 refers to the top five US chartered banks in terms of total assets in mid-2012.
Sources: Federal Financial Institutions Examination Council, Call Reports.

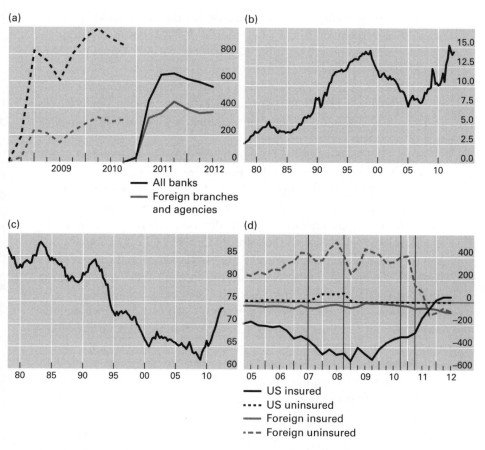

Figure 15.7
Balance-sheet responses to quantitative easing and the FDIC assessment change. (a) Cumulative change in reserves at the Federal Reserve, in billions of US dollars, showing cumulative change in balances due from Federal Reserve banks during the first round of Fed bond-buying (QE1, dashed lines) and the second round (QE2, solid lines); (b) asset share of foreign branches and agencies, in percent, showing total assets of foreign branches and agencies (flow of funds) in total bank assets in the United States (excluding credit unions); (c) deposit-to-asset ratio for US chartered banks, in billions of US dollars; (d) interoffice claims by bank nationality and FDIC status, showing sum across banks of net due from (asset side) and net due to (liabilities side). The vertical lines indicate the start of the financial crisis (end-Q2 2007), the collapse of Lehman Brothers (end-Q3 2008), the announcement of the change to the FDIC assessment base (end-Q3 2010), and the implementation of the change (April 1, 2011).
Sources: Federal Reserve *Flow of Funds Statistics*; Federal Financial Institutions Examination Council, Call Reports

roughly two thirds of the cumulative change in reserves at the Fed from the end of September 2010 to the middle of 2012. Recall that foreign branches and agencies had about $1.5 trillion of assets, while US chartered banks had over $10 trillion.

Not only was the share of foreign branches disproportionate, but it was *more disproportionate* than during QE1 (dashed lines) from late 2008 to early 2010. Then foreign branches claimed a share of only a quarter to a third of the overall increase.

We use regression analysis on bank-level data taken from the US call reports to formally investigate this asymmetric uptake of excess reserves. As in figure 15.7, upper left-hand panel, we exploit the natural experiment represented by the Fed's two episodes of large-scale bond purchases by separately examining the determinants of banks' increases in holdings of reserves at the Fed during QE1 and QE2. Our regressions aim to measure the partial effect of the FDIC change in the assessment base on changes in banks' holdings of reserves after controlling for other bank characteristics that may have affected them as well.

We define three alternative dependent variables, each of which captures individual banks' changes in reserve holdings during the quantitative easing window. The first is ΔFRB_i, which is simply the dollar change in bank i's holdings of reserves from the beginning to the end of the quantitative easing operation. The second is $\Delta FRB_i/TA_i$, where, again, the numerator is the change in bank i's holding of reserves over the quantitative easing period, and the denominator is bank i's total assets measured at the end of the quarter before the operation. The third is $\Delta(FRB_i/TA_i)$, which is the change in the *share of* bank i's reserve holdings in its total assets during the quantitative easing period. While we are agnostic about which of these dependent variables is most appropriate, $\Delta(FRB_i/TA_i)$ interests us most because it indicates a shift in balance-sheet composition toward reserve holdings.

We choose independent variables to isolate the effect of FDIC insurance from other bank characteristics that may have affected the uptake of reserves. These include bank size, measured by total assets (and total assets squared), and the level of reserve holdings prior to the quantitative easing operations. The independent variables of interest are (1) a dummy that takes the value of 1 for FDIC-insured entities (0 otherwise); and (2) bank nationality dummies, which control for home country fixed effects. For instance, when money market funds cut deposits in German banks in 2011, the dummy for German banks would soak up the average effect.[14]

As described above, the change in the FDIC assessment should be evident in two ways. First, we test for whether FDIC insurance exerted a different effect in the two periods of quantitative easing. If indeed the change in the FDIC assessment led to the outsized uptake of reserves during QE2, we should see a negative and statistically significant coefficient on the FDIC dummy during QE2, but not during QE1. Second, this coefficient should remain significant even after the inclusion of our control variables. Specifically, the sample of banks is asymmetric in the sense that (virtually) all US-headquartered banks are insured by the FDIC whereas non-US banking entities are mixed. If it was other factors (e.g., credit risk concerns because of a bank's exposure to troubled European sovereigns) that drove the increase in reserve holdings, we should find a statistically insignificant coefficient on the FDIC dummy since bank nationality dummies should proxy for these other factors.

Table 15.8 shows the result of this analysis of the full sample of banks in the United States with positive reserve holdings at the Federal Reserve just before the quantitative easing operations.[15] The first three columns of table 15.8 show the results of regressions for the QE1 period, while the last three columns show the results of similar regressions for QE2. Note that even these simple regressions account for much of the cross-sectional variation in the change in reserve holdings (the R-squared statistics are quite high). Not surprisingly, bank size is positively related to the change in reserve holdings, regardless of the dependent variable.

The results point to the change in the FDIC assessment base, rather than any country-specific factors, as the explanation of the changes in banks' holdings of reserves. This is demonstrated by the negative and very statistically significant coefficient on the FDIC dummy for the QE2 period regressions. When we use the change in the share of reserves in total assets as a baseline case (last column), we obtain an estimated coefficient that implies that uninsured banks' share of reserves in total assets increased by 5 percentage points more than that of insured banks. Note that this result is robust to the inclusion of a full set of bank nationality dummies. Importantly, in contrast to the QE2 regressions, the coefficient on the FDIC insurance dummy is negative but statistically insignificant in all specifications for the QE1 period.

In ending up with a disproportionate share of QE2 reserves, foreign bank branches gained asset share in US commercial banking (figure 15.7, upper right-hand panel). Their share reached an all-time high, surpassing the levels seen in the mid-1990s. We contend that the new

Table 15.8
Change in reserve holdings during QE1 and QE2 and FDIC insurance at US chartered banks and foreign branches and agencies

Dependent variables[a]	QE1: Q3 2008–Q1 2010			QE2: Q3 2010–Q4 2011		
	ΔFRB_i	$\Delta FRB_i/TA_i$	$\Delta(FRB_i/TA_i)$	ΔFRB_i	$\Delta FRB_i/TA_i$	$\Delta(FRB_i/TA_i)$
FDIC dummy	−0.460	−2.516	−1.979	−2.314	−11.036	−4.98
	(−0.96)	(−1.07)	(−1.35)	(−5.11)	(−2.68)	(−4.17)
Total assets	0.092	0.024	0.012	0.083	0.045	0.037
	(20.87)	(1.10)	(0.87)	(22.34)	(1.33)	(3.77)
Total assets squared	−0.000	−0.000	−0.000	−0.000	−0.000	−0.000
	(−7.10)	(−0.78)	(−0.61)	(−22.36)	(−1.40)	(−3.95)
Due from FRB[b]	−1.066	−0.586	−0.277	0.001	0.07	0.053
	(−24.71)	(−2.77)	(−2.10)	(0.06)	(0.30)	(0.78)
Constant	0.09	284.94	81.821	0.919	478.587	3.082
	(0.03)	(21.19)	(9.76)	(0.49)	(28.03)	(0.62)
Bank nationality dummies[c]	Yes	Yes	Yes	Yes	Yes	Yes
R^2	0.543	0.449	0.328	0.312	0.374	0.221
Observation number	1,780	1,780	1,780	1,957	1,957	19,56

a. The table shows the coefficients from OLS regressions of the change in individual banks' holdings of reserves at the Federal Reserve on a dummy for FDIC insurance and various controls. ΔFRB_i is the change in bank i's absolute reserve holdings from the beginning to the end of the respective period of quantitative easing. $\Delta FRB_i / TA_i$ is the change in bank i's reserves expressed as a share of total assets measured prior to the quantitative easing operations. $\Delta(FRB_i / TA_i)$ is the change in bank i's share of reserve holdings in total assets during the quantitative easing operation. t-Statistics are shown in parentheses under each coefficient.
b. Level of bank i's reserve holdings measured at the beginning of the quantitative easing operations.
c. Dummies for the headquarters country of each bank.

FDIC assessment on wholesale funding, which does not apply to branches and agencies, explains this observation.

Other accounts emphasize European sovereign strains and their effect on the balance sheets of foreign branches in the United States.[16] Indeed, when we break down the assets of foreign branches and agencies by nationality, it is evident that euro area bank assets did behave differently from others in a manner consistent with recurrent credit problems (figure 15.8). Whereas the aggregate of branches and agencies increased their US assets (upper left-hand panel), those from the euro area (lower left-hand panel) shrank their assets since the onset of the global financial crisis and since the worsening of sovereign strains in Europe.

However, the disproportionate uptake of reserves at the Fed was not particular to European banks. Their buildup of reserves at the Fed in QE2 was, if anything, *less* than that by Japanese, Swiss, and UK banks (upper right-hand panel) or other banks, including Canadian, Australian, and Swedish banks, that have retained their strong credit standing in recent years (lower right-hand panel). All foreign branches in the United States might well have ended up with an even higher fraction of the new reserves at the Federal Reserve had it not been for the European sovereign strains.

To investigate more formally, we return to regression analysis, but this time we focus on a restricted sample of non–US-headquartered banks' entities located in the United States. Some of them are subsidiaries insured by the FDIC and others are uninsured branches or agencies (table 15.9). Here we carry over the dependent variables and time periods (QE1 and QE2) from the regressions reported in table 15.8, but we now introduce holding company dummies to control for individual foreign bank parents that own more than one US banking entity. In these cross-sectional regressions, these bank-holding company dummies control for much of the credit risk of individual institutions (e.g., as would be picked up by credit default swap spreads or ratings). This set of regressions thereby most precisely measures the partial role of FDIC insurance independent of these credit-risk factors.[17]

Some simple sample statistics offer a preview of the regression results. Of the 241 foreign banking institutions in the United States that reported positive reserve holdings just prior to the start of QE2, 58 were FDIC insured and 183 were not. Their combined holdings of reserves increased by $414 billion during QE2. FDIC-insured banks increased the share of reserve holdings in total assets by less than 1 percentage

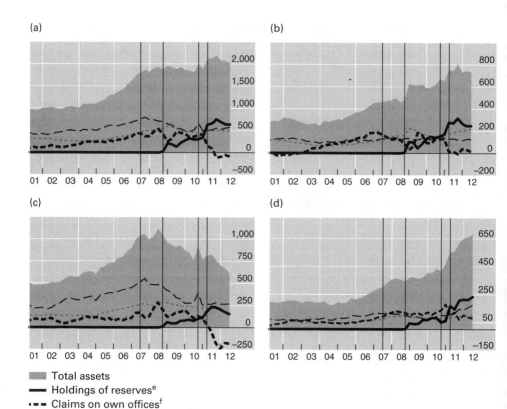

■ Total assets
— Holdings of reserves[e]
▪▪▪ Claims on own offices[f]
---- Loans
--- Other assets

Figure 15.8
Foreign banks' uninsured branches and agencies in the United States, in billions of US dollars. Balance sheets of foreign banks' uninsured branches and agencies are aggregated by bank nationality. (a) All banks; (b) Japanese, Swiss, and UK banks; (c) euro area banks; (d) Other banks; (e) balances due from Federal Reserve; (f) sum of net due from (asset side) and net due to (liability side) related depository institutions. The vertical lines indicate the start of the financial crisis (end-Q2 2007), the collapse of Lehman Brothers (end-Q3 2008), the announcement of the change to the FDIC assessment base (end-Q3 2010) and the implementation of the change (April 1, 2011).
Sources: Federal Financial Institutions Examination Council, Call Reports

Table 15.9
Change in reserve holdings during QE1 and QE2 and FDIC insurance at non–US chartered banks

	QE1: 2008Q3–2010Q1			QE2: 2010Q3–2011Q4		
Dependent variables[a]	ΔFRB_i	$\Delta FRB_i/TA_i$	$\Delta(FRB_i/TA_i)$	ΔFRB_i	$\Delta FRB_i/TA_i$	$\Delta(FRB_i/TA_i)$
FDIC dummy	−0.655	−0.798	−0.049	−4.522	−20.551	−6.525
	(−0.41)	(−0.16)	(−0.01)	(−3.28)	(−1.44)	(−1.83)
Total assets	0.198	0.171	0.161	0.185	0.526	0.304
	(2.88)	(0.79)	(0.91)	(2.91)	(0.73)	(1.83)
Total assets squared	−0.000	−0.001	−0.001	−0.000	−0.003	−0.001
	(−0.56)	(−0.39)	(−0.52)	(−0.88)	(−0.60)	(−1.30)
Due from FRB[b]	−0.890	1.857	−0.188	−0.265	−0.612	0.045
	(−1.70)	(1.14)	(0.14)	(−2.18)	(−0.45)	(0.14)
Constant	−0.011	−0.011	−0.061	8.97	−39.903	−0.047
	(−0.00)	(−0.00)	(−0.00)	(1.36)	(−0.54)	(−0.00)
Bank nationality dummies[c]	Yes	Yes	Yes	Yes	Yes	Yes
Holding company dummies[d]	Yes	Yes	Yes	Yes	Yes	Yes
R^2	0.595	0.744	0.8	0.585	0.325	0.382
Observation number	138	138	116	155	155	154

Note: The sample includes only those foreign-owned banking entities that are part of a larger banking group that has at least two entities operating in the United States.
a. The table shows the coefficients from OLS regressions of the change in individual banks' holdings of reserves at the Federal Reserve on a dummy for FDIC insurance and various controls. ΔFRB_i is the change in bank i's absolute reserve holdings from the beginning to the end of the respective period of quantitative easing. $\Delta FRB_i/TA_i$ is the change in bank i's reserves expressed as a share of total assets measured prior to the quantitative easing operations. $\Delta(FRB_i/TA_i)$ is the change in bank i's share of reserve holdings in total assets during the quantitative easing operation. t-Statistics are shown in parentheses under each coefficient.
b. Level of bank i's reserve holdings measured at the beginning of the quantitative easing operations.
c. Dummies for the headquarters country of each bank.
d. Dummies for individual holding companies of banking entities

point; uninsured banks increased their share by almost 6 percentage points. *Within each banking organization*, asset growth was skewed toward branches able to increase managed liabilities assessment free, and away from subsidiaries.

This result survives the regression analysis that includes controls for the parent group (table 15.9). The coefficients on the FDIC dummy variable during the QE2 operations exceed those during QE1, and are statistically significant in all but the second specification. These findings further confirm that it is non–US banks' advantage in having uninsured branches that explains their asymmetric uptake of Fed reserves, not some other characteristic specific to them.[18]

In summary, aggregate and bank-level analysis both point to the importance of the new FDIC assessment in explaining the distribution of the asset growth forced by the Fed's financing of its bond purchases. In aggregate, foreign branches took up more of QE2 after the FDIC change than they had taken up of QE1 before this change. Precautionary demand for reserves would suggest that euro area banks should have taken more than their fair share of the Fed reserves, but the reverse is the case. Instead, the banks least affected by losses in US housing and Europe took most of the new Fed reserves. And regression analysis confirms the importance of FDIC coverage in explaining the scale of acquisition of Fed reserves, even across subsidiaries and branches of individual foreign banks in the United States.

15.4.3   Foreign Branches and Agencies' Funding

Consistent with our hypothesis, foreign branches in the United States funded their holdings of Fed reserves with the sort of wholesale funds that would have attracted an FDIC assessment if used by US chartered banks. Rather than domestic sources such as federal funds or repo, however, the particular source of funds that the US branches and agencies of foreign banks drew on makes this a global banking story. Specifically, they drew on their own affiliates outside the United States to fund their asset growth. The flow of funds data show that their claims on all banks outside the United States of $359 billion in September 2010 had been worked down to a net liability by June 2011 that had mounted to $166 billion by September 2011, a swing of $525 billion in four quarters. The similar decline in figure 15.7 (lower right-hand panel, dashed line) implies that the sizable change took place against own offices outside the United States.

Indeed, for each nationality group of foreign branches in figure 15.8, a close relationship emerges between the increase in its holdings at the Fed and the drawdown of its claims on its affiliates abroad. The upper left-hand panel juxtaposes net inter-office claims to other assets. In aggregate, as claims on the Fed became the largest category of assets, foreign branches repatriated dollars that they had previously advanced to affiliates abroad. A regression of the change in reserve holdings at the Fed by a sample of 130 branches and agencies on the change in their net claims on own offices abroad (and other controls) indicates a very tight relationship: for every dollar increase in holdings at the Fed, net due to own offices rose by 44 cents.[19] The lower left-hand panel of figure 15.8 shows that this relationship held even for banks in the euro area whose funding was squeezed in mid-2011 by credit concerns. The upper right-hand panel shows that it held as well for the well-established Japanese, Swiss, and UK banks, whose assets leveled off. And the lower right-hand panel shows that it held as well for the Australian, Canadian, Swedish, and other banks of unimpaired creditworthiness, which attracted local deposits as well as reduced claims on foreign affiliates.

These observations suggest that a powerful force was at work. After all, as noted by Shin (2012), foreign banks in the United States had built up their claims on their foreign offices from the turn of the century. Yet the net claims were run down and turned into a liability in a matter of quarters.

They also provide perspective on the finding above that the onshore and offshore money markets have become less tightly linked in the period since April 1, 2011. Previously, foreign banks had sourced dollars onshore in the United States, while US banks had sourced dollars offshore, and these two-way flows had accumulated into offsetting stocks (figure 15.7, lower right-hand panel). The widening of the FDIC assessment base to eurodollar liabilities led US banks to repay them. For their part, foreign banks' US branches drew down their net advances of dollars to their affiliates abroad, which in effect funded their disproportionate share of the new claims on the Federal Reserve. In short, rather than US chartered banks' funding themselves extensively from abroad and foreign branches lending dollars extensively to affiliates abroad, both reduced their intragroup cross-border positions toward zero. This reduced interpenetration of funding was associated with a marked lengthening of the time taken for the onshore and offshore money market rates to converge.

The opposite movement of dollars, with foreign banks repaying funds raised in the United States and US chartered banks repaying funds raised outside the United States, makes no sense when viewed from a macroeconomic perspective. But it makes good sense as a response to the US chartered banks having to pay the FDIC assessment on funds raised outside the United States.

15.5 Conclusions

The widening of the FDIC assessment base for US chartered banks from domestic deposits to total assets less tangible equity in effect imposed a corrective or Pigovian tax on wholesale liabilities such as federal funds, repos, and eurodollars. Such funding comes with an externality, namely a risk to financial stability because of the potential for contagious runs. The observed response in both prices and quantities allows us to draw four conclusions.

First, it appears that US chartered banks shifted the cost of the widened FDIC assessment base onto providers of wholesale funding around April 1, 2011. Moreover arbitrage relationships between US dollar federal funds rates targeted by the Federal Reserve and eurodollars became looser: the estimated half-life of any divergence between them lengthened from two to three days. The decline in the structure of overnight rates seemed to have been transmitted to three month Libor and thereby to the stock of floating-rate dollar liabilities and derivatives.

Second, US chartered banks responded by changing their funding model to rely more on deposits. This is precisely what an environmental engineer imposing a Pigovian tax would wish for: firms avoided paying by cleaning up their act.

Third, unaffected by the wider FDIC assessment, US branches and agencies of foreign-chartered banks ended up with a disproportionate share of the new excess reserves from the Fed's QE2. In a regression of changes in holdings of claims on the Fed in this period, a dummy for FDIC insurance has an economically large and statistically significant negative effect. In contrast, there was no such effect during QE1, before the change in the FDIC assessment. When we narrow the analysis to US subsidiaries (holding a US charter and so subject to the FDIC assessment) and branches of the same foreign-headquartered bank, we find that the branch, not subject to the FDIC assessment, accounts for most of increased holdings of Fed reserves (even after controlling for the creditworthiness of the parent organization). Foreign banks' branches took up the bulk of QE2's reserves notwithstanding the strains in the creditworthiness of European banks in 2011.

Fourth, global dollar funding flowed in a counterintuitive fashion during what is called QE2. Fears that QE2 would flood the global interbank market with dollars proved unfounded. True, US chartered banks lowered the cost of the wider FDIC assessment base by paying back a large stock of eurodollars borrowed abroad. But at the same time, foreign banks repatriated hundreds of billions of dollars back into the United States to finance their disproportionate take-up of the new claims on the Federal Reserve. On balance, dollars flowed into the United States.[20]

Viewed as a Pigovian tax on unstable managed liabilities, this policy has only partially contributed to financial stability. Doubtless the funding structure of US chartered banks shifted away from wholesale funding. If managed liabilities are more prone to runs than deposits, then these banks now fund themselves in a way that is more conducive to financial stability. The benefit is all the greater since it was systemically important big banks that most improved their funding models.

However, US chartered banks compete globally with foreign-chartered banks, including their branches in the United States. Since these were not affected by the wider FDIC assessment, they could take market share from US chartered banks.[21] Thus the effectiveness of a tax on financial pollution produced by institutions chartered in only one jurisdiction can be undermined by competition from those chartered in another. Thanks to the coincidence of the Fed's QE2, amounting to some 4 percent of commercial bank assets in the United States, we have witnessed a fast-forwarding of the effect of the wider FDIC assessment on the market share of foreign-chartered banks. BIS statistics show that banks outside the United States held $2.6 trillion in claims on US non-banks in September 2012. This sum could grow larger as foreign banks put to work their advantage in raising wholesale funds.

This is not simply a case of wholesale funding moving from one set of institutions to another, with no implication for financial stability. US chartered banks book most of their dollar credit in the United States, where it can readily serve as collateral at the Fed's discount window. Foreign-chartered banks, by contrast, book most of their dollar credit outside the United States.[22] The Federal Reserve extended dollar swaps to major central banks in 2008 and 2009 to allow them to fund foreign banks that needed dollars but had no or limited access to its discount window (Committee on the Global Financial System 2010a,b). Ironically, a unilateral levy on bank managed liabilities, by shifting dollar intermediation away from US-owned banks, may make international cooperation in liquidity regulation and provision more important.

Appendix: Three Overnight Dollar Money Markets

Federal Funds

All depository institutions operating in the United States are required to hold reserves against various liabilities on their balance sheets. These reserves are held primarily in the form of deposits at the appropriate regional Federal Reserve Bank.

When a depository institution has a reserve balance in excess of the required level, it may lend ("sell") the excess to another institution with a reserve deficiency. These unsecured loans, usually with an overnight maturity, are referred to as federal funds, and the average interest rate on such loans is called the effective fed funds rate. Importantly, borrowed ("purchased") Fed funds are not subject to reserve requirements.

The Federal Reserve, through its Federal Open Market Committee (FOMC), sets a target level for the fed funds rate, which before the crisis was its primary tool for implementing monetary policy. It pursued this target by controlling the total amount of bank reserves available to the financial system. Fed funds transactions neither increase nor decrease total bank reserves but instead redistribute them. While only depository institutions may borrow in the fed funds market, loans from securities dealers as well as various US government-sponsored enterprises (e.g., Fannie Mae, Freddie Mac, and the Federal Home Loan Banks) are also classified as fed funds.

Eurodollars

Eurodollars are dollar-denominated deposit liabilities of banks operating outside the United States. Banks in the United States can borrow or lend eurodollars indirectly through their non-US offices or through their International Banking Facilities (in-house branches with separate sets of books that operate as if located outside the United States). Unlike the fed funds market where participation is essentially limited to institutions that have accounts at the Federal Reserve, the market for eurodollars is open to a wide variety of US and non-US borrowers and lenders. Of special note are US money market mutual funds, a form of non-bank that have come to play a key role as providers of short-term dollar funding to banks.

The use of eurodollars by US banks as an alternative to fed funds prior to 1990 was limited by a reserve requirement on banks' eurodollar liabilities. Interest rates in the two markets were kept in line by bank arbitrage, but eurodollars remained at a competitive disadvantage. Following the reduction of the reserve requirement to zero in 1990, the eurodollar market emerged as the dominant source of unsecured short-term funding for US banks.

Treasury Repo

Repos, short for "repurchase agreements," are contracts for the sale and future buyback of financial assets, most often Treasury securities. On the repurchase date, the seller buys back the asset at the initial sales price and also pays a rate of interest on the initial cash received called the repo rate. Although legally a sale and repurchase, for all intents and purposes a repo is a short-term collateralized loan. While banks borrow in the fed funds and eurodollar markets for general funding purposes, they usually borrow in the repo market to finance the specific assets pledged as collateral.

The repo market has seen considerable growth in recent years as a result of coincident fiscal and credit developments. The amount of US government debt requiring financing has increased dramatically. More-over credit concerns about financial institutions around the world have crimped unsecured lending to the benefit of the (collateralized) repo market. Finally, as was the case with eurodollars, there are a many potential lenders of repo who are unable to trade in fed funds, in par-ticular the aforementioned US money market funds.

Notes

This chapter was presented to the CESIfo Venice Summer Institute Workshop on Taxation of the Financial Sector, July 20, 2012. The authors are grateful to Matina Negka and Michela Scatigna for research assistance and to Bill Allen, Morten Bech, Steve Cecchetti, Ricardo Correa, Lou Crandall, Ruud de Mooij, Torsten Ehlers, Blaise Gadanecz, Marco Petracco Guidici, Spence Hilton, Richhild Moessner, Enrico Perotti, and Larry Wall for discussion. We extend a special thanks to ICAP for its generous provision of overnight interest rate data. The views expressed in this chapter are those of the authors and do not necessarily reflect those of Dartmouth College or of the BIS.

1. In this case the polluter does not even have to move across the border. Proponents of a such a tax well understood the risks of a narrowly applied measure. Shin (2010) cautioned: "A globally coordinated introduction of a non-core liabilities tax (perhaps through the G20 process) would maximize its effectiveness and minimize the distortions through possible circumvention or shifts in the pattern of capital flows." McDonald and Johnson (2010) noted that "Taxing the domestic financial sector may actually encourage instability by providing more incentive to use [the] external finance sector." See also Perotti and Suarez (2010) and Ostry et al. (2012).

2. Dodd–Frank in some way takes us back to 1990, when reserve requirements provided an incentive for intermediation to occur in foreign banks outside the United States (He and McCauley 2012).

3. Wall (2011) reckons that Fannie Mae and Freddie Mac between them sold $64 billion in Federal funds to banks in the first quarter of 2011 at something like 10 basis points. The banks, including branches of foreign banks, would then have earned a spread of 15 basis points or annualized earnings of $96 million. See also Bech and Klee (2011).

4. Ely (2011) notes that while in the 2007 to 2010 period the FDIC had no losses on banks with assets in excess of $25 billion, these stood to pay 72 percent of assessments in 2011.

5. Total assets at insured branches and agencies stood at $28.7 billion out of a total of $1.5 trillion in September 2010. On the FDIC's list of insured banks with $10 billion or more of assets, there is only one branch of a foreign-chartered institution, namely Bank of China, with $12 billion in assets.

6. Kreicher (1982) and McCauley and Seth (1992) found that Libid tended to trade at the all-in cost of US CDs, paying a premium roughly equal to the cost of the reserve requirement and FDIC insurance on a domestic deposit. Put otherwise, a domestic depositor in effect paid the cost to the bank of reserve requirements and deposit insurance. Reserve requirements on large deposits were reduced to zero in 1990, and FDIC assessments fell effectively to zero in the mid-1990s (FDIC 2011), so the two studies covered most of the relevant data.

7. Stigum and Crescenzi (2007) describe these markets. Before the crisis, Lee (2003) and Demiralp et al. (2006) found small unexploited arbitrage opportunities between federal funds and eurodollars, but they used the Board of Governors' overnight eurodollar rate, which is known to have limitations. Bartolini et al. (2008) found these markets very well integrated pre-crisis.

8. ECB (2011) reports that unsecured transactions remained a third to a half below their 2007 peak in 2010 and 2011, while secured transactions had recovered to 2007 levels. The survey also finds that unsecured transactions were more than ever extended only overnight.

9. These are known, respectively, as HEDDR (eurodollars) and i-Repo (Treasury repo). ICAP's measure of the effective fed funds rate is known as HEFFR. This last series is an important component in the NY Fed's benchmark calculation for the effective fed funds rate and is virtually identical to that benchmark in the post-December 2008 period (details available from authors upon request).

10. Federal Reserve Board of Governors, Press Release, October 6, 2008.

11. Federal Reserve Board of Governors, Press Release, December 16, 2008.

12. US chartered banks slightly reduced their holdings of Treasury securities during QE2, while pension funds, insurance companies, mutual funds and foreign investors increased their holdings.

13. Admittedly, the FDIC assessment on managed liabilities was not the only feature of Dodd–Frank in play. The legislation also extended blanket, unlimited FDIC insurance on non–interest-bearing deposits, which expired on schedule at the end of 2012. In the event, there was surprisingly little response by bank deposits to the expiration of this guarantee.

14. For the long-standing dependence of European banks on US money market funds for US dollar funding, see Baba et al. (2009); for the money market funds' reduction of exposure to European banks, see Fitch Ratings (2011).

15. Of the 7,000 banks in the United States covered by the call reports, only about 2,000 held positive reserves at the Federal Reserve in early 2009. Smaller banks tend to hold reserves in larger banks.

16. Allen and Moessner (2013) hold that European banks exposed to troubled sovereigns hoarded liquidity to reassure investors or to satisfy supervisors. Correa et al. (2012) find that European branches and agencies that lost wholesale US funding reduced their US loans. See Committee on the Global Financial System (2011).

17. Note that this is more restrictive than necessary. Similar regressions that include all non-US institutions but do not include bank holding company dummies also yield similar results in that the FDIC insurance dummy is negative and statistically significant in the QE2 period.

18. Correa et al. (2012, 18) argue that investors focused on the sovereign risk "in a somewhat indiscriminate way," and capture this notion with dummies for the bank country of origin. If so, our inclusion of bank nationality dummies above should ensure that the FDIC result is not an artifact of European sovereign strains, but here we include dummies for bank group as well.

19. The regression described here contains all control variables used in table 15.9, except the FDIC dummy. The R squared from this regression is 0.617, and the t-statistics on the net due to own offices is 9.62.

20. See Martin et al. (2011) for the argument that the Federal Reserve introduced assets into the banking system that compete with other dollar assets in bank portfolios.

21. Korinek (2012) might regard the FDIC assessment as an imperfect instrument. We would suggest that the instrument may be fine but that its uncoordinated application can have perverse results. See Goodhart (2012) on the genesis of Basel I.

22. The contrast between the dollar funding of Canadian as compared to European banks in late 2008 is instructive. Canadian banks, with subsidiaries chartered in the United States, were able to draw on the Federal Reserve's discount window facilities. In contrast, many European banks were only able to obtain sufficient dollar funding by providing collateral to their home central banks, which in turn obtained dollars through swaps with the Federal Reserve.

References

Acharya, V., L. Pedersen, T. Philippon, and M. Richardson. 2009. Regulating systemic risk. In V. Acharya and M. Richardson, eds., *Restoring Financial Stability: How to Repair a Failed System*. Hoboken, NJ: Wiley, 283–304.

Allen, W., and R. Moessner. 2013. The liquidity consequences of the euro area sovereign debt crisis. Working paper 390. BIS.

Alworth, J., and G. Arachi. 2012. Introduction. In J. Alworth and G. Arachi, eds., *Taxation and the Financial Crisis*. Oxford University Press, 1–27.

Anderson, R. G., and J. V. Duca. 2014. Money demand and the liquidity accelerator in an era of financial uncertainty and innovation. Working paper.

Baba, N., R. McCauley, and S. Ramaswamy. 2009. US dollar money market funds and non-US banks. *BIS Quarterly Review* (March): 65–81.

Bair, S. 2011. Testimony at hearing on "State of the FDIC: Deposit insurance, consumer protection, and financial stability," before the Committee on Banking, Housing and Urban Affairs; United States Senate (June 30).

Bartolini, L., S. Hilton, and A. Prati. 2008. Money market integration. *Journal of Money, Credit and Banking* 40 (1): 193–213.

Basel Committee on Banking Supervision. 2012. Report to G20 Finance Ministers and Central Bank Governors on Basel III implementation (October).

Bech, M., and E. Klee. 2011. The mechanics of a graceful exit: interest on reserves and segmentation in the federal funds market. *Journal of Monetary Economics* 58 (5): 415–31.

Board of Governors of the Federal Reserve Board, Press Release, October 6, 2008 and December 16, 2008.

Committee on the Global Financial System. 2010a. *The Functioning and Resilience of Cross-border Funding Markets*. CGFS publication 37. Basel: BIS.

Committee on the Global Financial System. 2010b. *Funding Patterns and Liquidity Management of Internationally Active Banks*. CGFS publication 39. Basel: BIS.

Committee on the Global Financial System. 2011. *The Impact of Sovereign Credit Risk on Bank Funding Conditions*. CGFS publication 43. Basel: BIS.

Correa, R., H. Sapriza, and A. Zlate. 2012. Liquidity shocks, dollar funding costs and the bank lending channel during the European sovereign crisis. International finance discussion paper 1059. Board of Governors of the Federal Reserve System, Washington, DC.

Demiralp, S., B. Preslopsky, and W. Whitesell. 2006. Overnight interbank loan markets. *Journal of Economics and Business* 58: 67–83.

Ely, B. 2011. Re RIN number 3064–AD66; assessments, large bank pricing NPR; assessments, assessment base and rates NPR. Comment letter to FDIC (3 January).

Ennis, H., and A. L. Wolman. 2012. Large excess reserves in the US: a view from the cross-section of banks. Working paper 12–05. Federal Reserve Bank of Richmond.

ECB. 2011. *Euro money market survey* (September).

Federal Deposit Insurance Corporation. 2011. 12 CFR Part 327, RIN 3064–AD66: Assessments, large bank pricing. *Federal register* 76 (38): 10672–733.

Fitch Ratings. 2011. US money funds and European banks: Exposures down, maturities shorter. *Fitch Macro Credit Research* (August 22).

Goodhart, C. 2012. *The Basel Committee on Banking Supervision: A History of the Early Years 1974–1997*. Cambridge, UK: Cambridge University Press.

Gruenberg, M. 2011. Testimony at hearing on "Enhanced oversight after the financial crisis: Wall Street reform at one year," before the Committee on Banking, Housing and Urban Affairs, United States Senate (July 21).

He, D., and R. McCauley. 2012. Eurodollar banking and currency internationalisation, *BIS Quarterly Review* (June): 33-46

Hein, S., T. Koch, and C. Nounamo. 2012. Moving FDIC insurance to an asset-based assessment system: Evidence from the special assessment of 2009. *Journal of Economics and Business* 64 (1):7–23.

Hemmelgarn, T., and G. Nicodeme. 2012. Can tax policy help to prevent financial crisis? In J. Alworth and G. Arachi, eds., *Taxation and the Financial Crisis*. New York: Oxford University Press, 116–47.

International Monetary Fund. 2010. A fair and substantial contribution by the financial sector. Final Report for the G20. IMF.

Korinek, A. 2012. Capital controls and currency wars. Unpublished manuscript. University of Maryland.

Kreicher, L. 1982. Eurodollar arbitrage. *Federal Reserve Bank of New York Quarterly Review* 7 (2): 10–22.

Lee, Y.-S. 2003. The Federal funds market and the overnight eurodollar market. *Journal of Banking and Finance* 27: 749–71.

Lloyd, G. 2012. Moving beyond the crisis: Strengthening understanding of how tax policies affect the soundness of financial markets. In J. Alworth and G. Arachi, eds., *Taxation and the Financial Crisis*. Oxford University Press, 190–213.

Marquez, J., A. Morse, and B. Schlusche. 2012. The Federal Reserve's balance sheet and overnight interest rates and reserve balances: econometric modeling of exit strategies. Finance and economics discussion series 66. Federal Reserve Board.

Martin, A., J. McAndrews, and D. Skeie. 2011. A note on bank lending in times of large bank reserves. Staff report 497. Federal Reserve Bank of New York.

Masciandaro, D., and F. Passarelli. 2012. Regulation and taxation: Economics and politics. In J. Alworth and G. Arachi, eds., *Taxation and the Financial Crisis*. New York: Oxford University Press, 247–69.

McCauley, R., and R. Seth. 1992. Foreign bank credit to US corporations: The implications of offshore loans. *Federal Reserve Bank of New York Quarterly Review* 17 (1): 52–65.

McDonald, J., and S. Johnson. 2010. Tax policies to improve the stability of financial markets. Paper presented at the Bank of Italy workshop, "Fiscal Policy: Lessons from the Crisis," Perugia, May 25–27.

Ostry, J., A. Ghosh, and A. Korinek. 2012. Multilateral aspects of managing the capital account. IMF Staff discussion note SDN/12/10, IMF.

Perotti, E., and J. Suarez. 2011. A Pigovian approach to liquidity regulation. *International Journal of Central Banking* 7 (4): 3–41.

Schultze, C. L. 1977. *The Public Use of Private Interest*. Washington, DC: Brookings Institution Press.

Shin, H. S. 2010. Non-core liabilities tax as a tool for prudential regulation. Mimeo. Princeton University. Available at: http://www.princeton.edu/~hsshin/www/NonCoreLiabilitiesTax.pdf.

Shin, H. S. 2012. Global banking glut and loan risk premium. *IMF Review* 60 (2): 155–92.

Smedley, B. 2010. FDIC proposal should lead to lower rates. *Bank of America Merrill Lynch US Rates Weekly* (November 12): 11–13.

Stigum, M., and A. Crescenzi. 2007. *Stigum's Money Market*, 4th ed. New York: Dow Jones-Irwin.

Wall, L. 2011. Three individually reasonable decisions, one unintended consequence, and a solution. *Notes from the Vault* (May/June). Atlanta: Federal Reserve Bank of Atlanta.

Weder di Mauro, B. 2010a. Taxing systemic risk: Proposal for a systemic risk charge and a systemic risk fund. Mimeo. University of Mainz.

Weder di Mauro, B. 2010b. Quantitative impact of taxing or regulating systemic risk. In S. Claessens, M. Keen, and C. Pazarbasioglu, eds., *Financial Sector Taxation: The IMF's Report to the G-20 and Background Material*. Washington, DC: IMF, 96–105

Whalen, C. 2011. What is a core deposit and why does it matter? Legislative and regulatory actions regarding FDIC-insured bank deposits pursuant to the Dodd–Frank Act. Working paper 14. Network Financial Institute, Indiana University.

Wheatley Review of LIBOR. 2012. *Final Report* (September). London: UK Treasury.

Contributors

Thiess Buettner
University of Erlangen-Nuremberg and CESifo

Jin Cao
Norges Bank

Giuseppina Cannas
Joint Research Centre of the European Commission

Gunther Capelle-Blancard
Université Paris 1 Panthéon-Sorbonne and CEPII

Jessica Cariboni
Joint Research Centre of the European Commission

Brian Coulter
Saïd Business School, University of Oxford

Ernesto Crivelli
International Monetary Fund

Ruud de Mooij
International Monetary Fund and CESifo

Michael P. Devereux
Oxford University Centre for Business Taxation,
Saïd Business School and European Tax Policy Forum

Katharina Erbe
University of Erlangen-Nuremberg

Ricardo Fenochietto
International Monetary Fund

Marco Petracco Giudici
Joint Research Centre of the European Commission

Timothy J. Goodspeed
Hunter College, CUNY Graduate Center, and CESifo

Reint Gropp
Goethe University Frankfurt, SAFE, and CFS

Olena Havrylchyk
Paris West University Nanterre La Défense and CEPII

Michael Keen
International Monetary Fund

Lawrence L. Kreicher
Dartmouth College

Julia Lendvai
European Commission

Ben Lockwood
University of Warwick, CBT, and CEPR

Massimo Marchesi
European Commission

Donato Masciandaro
Department of Economics and Baffi Centre, Bocconi University

Colin Mayer
Saïd Business School, University of Oxford, CEPR, and ECGI

Robert N. McCauley
BIS

Patrick McGuire
BIS

Gaëtan Nicodème
European Commission, ULB, CEPR, and CESifo

Masanori Orihara
University of Illinois at Urbana-Champaign and Ministry of Finance, Japan

Francesco Passarelli
Università di Teramo and Bocconi University

Carola Pessino
Universidad del CEMA

Rafal Raciborski
European Commission

John Vickers
All Souls College, University of Oxford

Lukas Vogel
European Commission

Stefano Zedda
Joint Research Centre of the European Commission, University of Cagliari

Index

Accountability, 6
Acharya, V., 70, 115, 117, 138, 204
Admati, Anat R., 32, 63, 73
Adrian, T., 60–61, 70, 204
Adverse selection, 2
Akritidis, L., 135
Albertazzi, U., 254, 257, 277n1
Alesina, A., 116
Allen, F., 99, 101
Allowance for corporate equity (ACE), 37–38, 72–73, 244–46, 250n16
Altshuler, Rosanne, 283
Alworth, J., 10, 333
American Community Survey, 279, 292, 307
American International Group, 1
Angelini, P., 255
Arachi, G., 10, 333
Arbelaez, M., 323, 326
Arbitrage, 20
  eurodollars and, 365, 366n7
  Federal Deposit Insurance Corporation (FDIC) and, 335, 339–40, 346–47, 362
  macroprudential regulation and, 106
  stability and, 57
Arellano, Manuel, 237, 250n7, 262, 267
Argentina
  bank transactions tax (BTT) and, 11, 18–19, 311–30
  Central Bank of, 315
  diplomatic emissaries and, 311
  Law 25413 and, 311
Arm's-length funding, 62
Arrelano-Bover estimator, 266t, 267, 269t, 272t–73t
Arulampalam, Wiji, 283
Asymmetric information
  crisis and, 2
  Federal Deposit Insurance Corporation (FDIC) and, 354–55, 360

macroprudential regulation and, 13, 90, 106
new bank taxes and, 32
stability and, 62
systemic risk and, 72
Atkinson, A., 143, 151
Auerbach, A., 135, 137, 141, 157, 255
Augmented Dickey–Fuller (ADF) tests, 331n7
Australia, 325b, 357, 361
Austria, 28b, 250n12, 253, 256

Baca-Campodonico, J., 312
Bailouts
  conditional, 100–101
  corporate income tax (CIT) and, 17, 263, 274
  externality and, 41
  financial transaction tax (FTT) and, 177
  liquidity gap and, 13–14
  macroeconomic issues and, 177
  macroprudential regulation and, 90, 100–101, 103–104, 106, 114n4
  new bank taxes and, 35–36, 41
  stability and, 57–59, 63
  systemic risk and, 68–69, 75, 78–79, 83–84, 117
  TARP and, 4, 35, 58
  too-big-to-fail subsidies and, 6–7, 12, 29–31, 59, 74, 177, 233, 263
Balance sheets
  cash-flow taxation and, 174n1
  corporate income tax (CIT) and, 255–56, 261
  crisis and, 231, 234, 247–48
  Federal Deposit Insurance Corporation (FDIC) and, 333–34, 337, 339–41, 347–62, 364